West's Law School Advisory Board

Documents Supplement to

International Commercial Arbitration

A Transnational Perspective

Fourth Edition

■ ■ ■

By

Tibor Várady

Professor of Law, Central European University, Budapest, and Emory University School of Law

John J. Barceló III

William Nelson Cromwell Professor of International and Comparative Law, Cornell Law School

Arthur T. von Mehren

Late Story Professor of Law, Emeritus, Harvard Law School

AMERICAN CASEBOOK SERIES®

WEST®

A Thomson Reuters business

Mat #40760674

610 Opperman Drive
St. Paul, MN 55123
1–800–313–9378

Printed in the United States of America

ISBN: 978–0–314–19543–2

TEXT IS PRINTED ON 10% POST
CONSUMER RECYCLED PAPER

Table of Contents

DOCUMENTS SUPPLEMENT TO

INTERNATIONAL COMMERCIAL ARBITRATION

A TRANSNATIONAL PERSPECTIVE

Fourth Edition

*

I. INTERNATIONAL CONVENTIONS ON ARBITRATION

■ ■ ■

A. UNITED NATIONS CONVENTION ON THE RECOGNITION AND ENFORCEMENT OF FOREIGN ARBITRAL AWARDS (NEW YORK CONVENTION OF 1958)*

(Done at New York, June 10, 1958.)

Article I

1. This Convention shall apply to the recognition and enforcement of arbitral awards made in the territory of a State other than the State where the recognition and enforcement of such awards are sought, and arising out of differences between persons, whether physical or legal. It shall also apply to arbitral awards not considered as domestic awards in the State where their recognition and enforcement are sought.

2. The term "arbitral awards" shall include not only awards made by arbitrators appointed for each case but also those made by permanent arbitral bodies to which the parties have submitted.

3. When signing, ratifying or acceding to this Convention, or notifying extension under article X hereof, any State may on the basis of reciprocity declare that it will apply the Convention to the recognition and enforcement of awards made only in the territory of another Contracting State. It may also declare that it will apply the Convention only to differences arising out of legal relationships, whether contractual or not, which are considered as commercial under the national law of the State making such declaration.

Article II

1. Each Contracting State shall recognize an agreement in writing under which the parties undertake to submit to arbitration all or any differences which have arisen or which may arise between them in respect of a defined legal relationship, whether contractual or not, concerning a subject matter capable of settlement by arbitration.

---

* The Convention can be found at the UNCITRAL Website at http://www.uncitral.org/pdf/english/texts/arbitration/NY-conv/XXII_1_e.pdf

2. The term "agreement in writing" shall include an arbitral clause in a contract or an arbitration agreement, signed by the parties or contained in an exchange of letters or telegrams.

3. The court of a Contracting State, when seized of an action in a matter in respect of which the parties have made an agreement within the meaning of this article, shall, at the request of one of the parties, refer the parties to arbitration, unless it finds that the said agreement is null and void, inoperative or incapable of being performed.

Article III

Each Contracting State shall recognize arbitral awards as binding and enforce them in accordance with the rules of procedure of the territory where the award is relied upon, under the conditions laid down in the following articles. There shall not be imposed substantially more onerous conditions or higher fees or charges on the recognition or enforcement of arbitral awards to which this Convention applies than are imposed on the recognition or enforcement of domestic arbitral awards.

Article IV

1. To obtain the recognition and enforcement mentioned in the preceding article, the party applying for recognition and enforcement shall, at the time of the application, supply:

(a) The duly authenticated original award or a duly certified copy thereof;

(b) The original agreement referred to in article II or a duly certified copy thereof.

2. If the said award or agreement is not made in an official language of the country in which the award is relied upon, the party applying for recognition and enforcement of the award shall produce a translation of these documents into such language. The translation shall be certified by an official or sworn translator or by a diplomatic or consular agent.

Article V

1. Recognition and enforcement of the award may be refused, at the request of the party against whom it is invoked, only if that party furnishes to the competent authority where the recognition and enforcement is sought, proof that:

(a) The parties to the agreement referred to in article II were, under the law applicable to them, under some incapacity, or the said agreement is not valid under the law to which the parties have subjected it or, failing any indication thereon, under the law of the country where the award was made; or

(b) The party against whom the award is invoked was not given proper notice of the appointment of the arbitrator or of the arbitration proceedings or was otherwise unable to present his case; or

(c) The award deals with a difference not contemplated by or not falling within the terms of the submission to arbitration, or it contains decisions on matters beyond the scope of the submission to arbitration, provided that, if the decisions on matters submitted to arbitration can be separated from those not so submitted, that part of the award which contains decisions on matters submitted to arbitration may be recognized and enforced; or

(d) The composition of the arbitral authority or the arbitral procedure was not in accordance with the agreement of the parties, or, failing such agreement, was not in accordance with the law of the country where the arbitration took place; or

(e) The award has not yet become binding on the parties, or has been set aside or suspended by a competent authority of the country in which, or under the law of which, that award was made.

2. Recognition and enforcement of an arbitral award may also be refused if the competent authority in the country where recognition and enforcement is sought finds that:

(a) The subject matter of the difference is not capable of settlement by arbitration under the law of that country; or

(b) The recognition or enforcement of the award would be contrary to the public policy of that country.

Article VI

If an application for the setting aside or suspension of the award has been made to a competent authority referred to in article V(1)(e), the authority before which the award is sought to be relied upon may, if it considers it proper, adjourn the decision on the enforcement of the award and may also, on the application of the party claiming enforcement of the award, order the other party to give suitable security.

Article VII

1. The provisions of the present Convention shall not affect the validity of multilateral or bilateral agreements concerning the recognition and enforcement of arbitral awards entered into by the Contracting States nor deprive any interested party of any right he may have to avail himself of an arbitral award in the manner and to the extent allowed by the law or the treaties of the country where such award is sought to be relied upon.

2. The Geneva Protocol on Arbitration Clauses of 1923 and the Geneva Convention on the Execution of Foreign Arbitral Awards of 1927 shall cease to have effect between Contracting States on their becoming bound and to the extent that they become bound, by this Convention.

Article VIII

1. This Convention shall be open until 31 December 1958 for signature on behalf of any Member of the United Nations and also on behalf of

any other State which is or hereafter becomes a member of any specialized agency of the United Nations, or which is or hereafter becomes a party to the Statute of the International Court of Justice, or any other State to which an invitation has been addressed by the General Assembly of the United Nations.

2. This Convention shall be ratified and the instrument of ratification shall be deposited with the Secretary–General of the United Nations.

Article IX

1. This Convention shall be open for accession to all States referred to in article VIII.

2. Accession shall be effected by the deposit of an instrument of accession with the Secretary–General of the United Nations.

Article X

1. Any State may, at the time of signature, ratification or accession, declare that this Convention shall extend to all or any of the territories for the international relations of which it is responsible. Such a declaration shall take effect when the Convention enters into force for the State concerned.

2. At any time thereafter any such extension shall be made by notification addressed to the Secretary–General of the United Nations and shall take effect as from the ninetieth day after the day of receipt by the Secretary–General of the United Nations of this notification, or as from the date of entry into force of the Convention for the State concerned, whichever is the later.

3. With respect to those territories to which this Convention is not extended at the time of signature, ratification or accession, each State concerned shall consider the possibility of taking the necessary steps in order to extend the application of this Convention to such territories, subject, where necessary for constitutional reasons, to the consent of the Governments of such territories.

Article XI

In the case of a federal or non-unitary State the following provisions shall apply:

(a) With respect to those articles of this Convention that come within the legislative jurisdiction of the federal authority, the obligations of the federal Government shall to this extent be the same as those of Contracting States which are not federal States;

(b) With respect to those articles of this Convention that come within the legislative jurisdiction of constituent states or provinces which are not, under the constitutional system of the federation, bound to take legislative action, the federal Government shall bring such articles with a favorable recommendation to the notice of the appropriate authorities of constituent states or provinces at the earliest possible moment;

(c) A federal State Party to this Convention shall, at the request of any other Contracting State transmitted through the Secretary–General of the United Nations, supply a statement of the law and practice of the federation and its constituent units in regard to any particular provision of this Convention, showing the extent to which effect has been given to that provision by legislative or other action.

Article XII

1. This Convention shall come into force on the ninetieth day following the date of deposit of the third instrument of ratification or accession.

2. For each State ratifying or acceding to this Convention after the deposit of the third instrument of ratification or accession, this Convention shall enter into force on the ninetieth day after deposit by such State of its instrument of ratification or accession.

Article XIII

1. Any Contracting State may denounce this Convention by a written notification to the Secretary–General of the United Nations. Denunciation shall take effect one year after the date of receipt of the notification by the Secretary–General.

2. Any State which has made a declaration or notification under article X may, at any time thereafter, by notification to the Secretary–General of the United Nations, declare that this Convention shall cease to extend to the territory concerned one year after the date of the receipt of the notification by the Secretary–General.

3. This Convention shall continue to be applicable to arbitral awards in respect of which recognition or enforcement proceedings have been instituted before the denunciation takes effect.

Article XIV

A Contracting State shall not be entitled to avail itself of the present Convention against other Contracting States except to the extent that it is itself bound to apply the Convention.

Article XV

The Secretary–General of the United Nations shall notify the States contemplated in article VIII of the following:

(a) Signatures and ratifications in accordance with article VIII;

(b) Accessions in accordance with article IX;

(c) Declarations and notifications under articles I, X and XI;

(d) The date upon which this Convention enters into force in accordance with article XII;

(e) Denunciations and notifications in accordance with article XIII.

Article XVI

1. This Convention, of which the Chinese, English, French, Russian and Spanish texts shall be equally authentic, shall be deposited in the archives of the United Nations.

2. The Secretary–General of the United Nations shall transmit a certified copy of this Convention to the States contemplated in article VIII.

LIST OF PARTIES TO THE NEW YORK CONVENTION AS OF FEBRUARY 2009*[1]

STATUS: Parties: 144.

State	Signature	Ratification, Accession (a), Succession (d)	Entry into force
Afghanistan	-	30 November 2004	28 February 2005
Albania	-	27 June 2001	25 September 2001
Algeria	-	7 February 1989	8 May 1989

* List can be found at the UN Website at http://treaties.un.org/Pages/ViewDetails.aspx?src=TREATY&id=465&chapter=22&lang=en.

1. a) The following States, having adopted the "reciprocity declaration," will restrict application of the Convention to recognition and enforcement of awards made in the territory of another Contracting State: Afghanistan, Algeria, Antigua and Barbuda, Argentina, Armenia, Bahrain, Barbados, Belgium, Bosnia and Herzegovina, Botswana, Brunei Darussalam, Central African Republic, China, Cook Islands, Croatia, Cyprus, Denmark, Ecuador, France, Greece, Guatemala, Holy See, Hungary, India, Indonesia, Iran (Islamic Republic of), Ireland, Jamaica, Japan, Kenya, Kuwait, Lebanon, Luxembourg, Madagascar, Malaysia, Malta, Mauritius, Monaco, Mongolia, Montenegro, Morocco, Mozambique, Nepal, Netherlands, New Zealand, Nigeria, Norway, Pakistan, Philippines, Poland, Portugal, Republic of Korea, Republic of Moldova, Saint Vincent and the Grenadines, Saudi Arabia, Serbia, Singapore, The former Yugoslav Republic of Macedonia, Trinidad and Tobago, Tunisia, Turkey, Uganda, United Kingdom of Great Britain and Northern Ireland, United Republic of Tanzania, United States of America, Venezuela (Bolivarian Republic of).

Four other States (Belarus, Lithuania, the Russian Federation and Ukraine) have stated that they will apply the Convention with respect to non-contracting States as well, but on the condition of reciprocal treatment.

Four States (Bulgaria, Cuba, Romania and Vietnam) have declared that they will only apply the Convention with regard to awards made in a Contracting State, but have added that they will nevertheless apply the Convention with regard to awards rendered in non-contracting States on the condition of reciprocal treatment.

b) The following States have adopted the "commercial declaration": Afghanistan, Algeria, Antigua and Barbuda, Argentina, Armenia, Bahrain, Barbados, Bosnia and Herzegovina, Botswana, Canada (except for Quebec), Central African Republic, China, Cuba, Cyprus, Denmark, Ecuador, Greece, Guatemala, Holy See, Hungary, India, Indonesia, Iran (Islamic Republic of), Jamaica, Madagascar, Malaysia, Monaco, Mongolia, Nepal, Nigeria, Philippines, Poland, Republic of Korea, Romania, Saint Vincent and the Grenadines, Serbia and Montenegro, Slovenia, Trinidad and Tobago, Tunisia, Turkey, United States of America, Venezuela (Bolivarian Republic of), Vietnam. These States will apply the Convention only with regard to differences arising out of a legal relationship which is considered commercial under the municipal law of the State making the declaration.

State	Signature	Ratification, Accession (a), Succession (d)	Entry into force
Antigua and Barbuda	-	2 February 1989	3 May 1989
Argentina	26 August 1958	14 March 1989	12 June 1989
Armenia	-	29 December 1997	29 March 1998
Australia	-	26 March 1975	24 June 1975
Austria	-	2 May 1961	31 July 1961
Azerbaijan	-	29 February 2000	29 May 2000
Bahamas	-	20 December 2006	20 March 2007
Bahrain	-	6 April 1988	5 July 1988
Bangladesh	-	6 May 1992	4 August 1992
Barbados	-	16 March 1993	14 June 1993
Belarus	29 December 1958	15 November 1960	13 February 1961
Belgium	15 June 1958	18 August 1975	16 November 1975
Benin	-	16 May 1974	14 August 1974
Bolivia	-	28 April 1995	27 July 1995
Bosnia and Herzegovina	-	1 September 1993	6 March 1992
Botswana	-	20 December 1971	19 March 1972
Brazil	-	7 June 2002	5 September 2002
Brunei Darussalam	-	25 July 1996	23 October 1996
Bulgaria	17 December 1958	10 October 1961	8 January 1962
Burkina Faso	-	23 March 1987	21 June 1987
Cambodia	-	5 January 1960	4 April 1960
Cameroon	-	19 February 1988	19 May 1988
Canada	-	12 May 1986	10 August 1986
Central African Republic	-	15 October 1962	13 January 1963
Chile	-	4 September 1975	3 December 1975
China	-	22 January 1987	22 April 1987
Colombia	-	25 September 1979	24 December 1979
Cook Islands	-	12 January 2009	12 April 2009
Costa Rica	10 June 1958	26 October 1987	24 January 1988

State	Signature	Ratification, Accession (a), Succession (d)	Entry into force
Côte d'Ivoire	-	1 February 1991	2 May 1991
Croatia	-	26 July 1993	8 October 1991
Cuba	-	30 December 1974	30 March 1975
Cyprus	-	29 December 1980	29 March 1981
Czech Republic	-	30 September 1993	1 January 1993
Denmark	-	22 December 1972	22 March 1973
Djibouti	-	14 June 1993	27 June 1977
Dominica	-	28 October 1988	26 January 1989
Dominican Republic	-	11 April 2002	10 July 2002
Ecuador	17 December 1958	3 January 1962	3 April 1962
Egypt	-	9 March 1959	7 June 1959
El Salvador	10 June 1958	26 February 1998	27 May 1998
Estonia	-	30 August 1993	28 November 1993
Finland	29 December 1958	19 January 1962	19 April 1962
France	25 November 1958	26 June 1959	24 September 1959
Gabon	-	15 December 2006	15 March 2007
Georgia	-	2 June 1994	31 August 1994
Germany	10 June 1958	30 June 1961	28 September 1961
Ghana	-	9 April 1968	8 July 1968
Greece	-	16 July 1962	14 October 1962
Guatemala	-	21 March 1984	19 June 1984
Guinea	-	23 January 1991	23 April 1991
Haiti	-	5 December 1983	4 March 1984
Holy See	-	1 May 1975	12 August 1975
Honduras	-	3 October 2000	1 January 2001
Hungary	-	5 March 1962	3 June 1962
Iceland	-	24 January 2002	24 April 2002
India	10 June 1958	13 July 1960	1 October 1960
Indonesia	-	7 October 1981	5 January 1982

State	Signature	Ratification, Accession (a), Succession (d)	Entry into force
Iran (Islamic Rep. of)	-	15 October 2001	13 January 2002
Ireland	-	12 May 1981	10 August 1981
Israel	10 June 1958	5 January 1959	7 June 1959
Italy	-	31 January 1969	1 May 1969
Jamaica	-	20 July 2002	8 October 2002
Japan	-	20 June 1961	18 September 1961
Jordan	10 June 1958	15 November 1979	13 February
Kazakhstan	-	20 November 1995	18 February 1996
Kenya	-	10 February 1989	11 May 1989
Kuwait	-	28 April 1978	27 July 1978
Kyrgyztan	-	18 December 1996	16 March 1997
Lao People's Democratic Republic	-	17 June 1998	15 September 1998
Latvia	-	14 April 1992	13 July 1992
Lebanon	-	11 August 1998	9 November 1998
Lesotho	-	13 June 1989	11 September 1989
Liberia	-	16 September 2005	15 December 2005
Lithuania	-	14 March 1995	12 June 1995
Luxembourg	11 November 1958	9 September 1983	8 December 1983
Madagascar	-	16 July 1962	14 October 1962
Malaysia	-	5 November 1985	3 February 1986
Mali	-	8 September 1994	7 December 1994
Malta	-	22 June 2000	20 September 2000
Marshall Islands	-	21 December 2006	21 March 2007
Mauritania	-	30 January 1997	30 April 1997
Mauritius	-	19 June 1996	17 September 1996
Mexico	-	14 April 1971	13 July 1971
Monaco	31 December 1958	2 June 1982	31 August 1982

State	Signature	Ratification, Accession (a), Succession (d)	Entry into force
Mongolia	-	24 October 1994	22 January 1995
Montenegro	-	23 October 2006	3 June 2006
Morocco	-	12 February 1959	7 June 1959
Mozambique	-	11 June 1998	9 September 1998
Nepal	-	4 March 1998	2 June 1998
Netherlands	10 June 1958	24 April 1964	23 July 1964
New Zealand	-	6 January 1983	6 April 1983
Nicaragua	-	24 September 2003	23 December 2003
Niger	-	14 October 1964	12 January 1965
Nigeria	-	17 March 1970	15 June 1970
Norway	-	14 March 1961	12 June 1961
Oman	-	25 February 1999	26 May 1999 1980
Pakistan	30 December 1958	-	-
Panama	-	10 October 1984	8 January 1985
Paraguay	-	8 October 1997	6 January 1998
Peru	-	7 July 1988	5 October 1988
Philippines	10 June 1958	6 July 1967	4 October 1967
Poland	10 June 1958	3 October 1961	1 January 1962
Portugal	-	18 October 1994	16 January 1995
Qatar	-	30 December 2002	30 March 2003
Republic of Korea	-	8 February 1973	9 May 1973
Republic of Moldova	-	18 September 1998	17 December 1998
Romania	-	13 September 1961	12 December 1961
Russian Federation	29 December 1958	24 August 1960	22 November 1960
Rwanda	-	31 October 2008	29 January 2009
Saint Vincent and the Grenadines	-	12 September 2000	11 December 2000
San Marino	-	17 May 1979	15 August 1979
Saudi Arabia	-	19 April 1994	18 July 1994
Senegal	-	17 October 1994	15 January 1995

State	Signature	Ratification, Accession (a), Succession (d)	Entry into force
Serbia	-	12 March 2001	27 April 1992
Singapore	-	21 August 1986	19 November 1986
Slovakia	-	28 May 1993	1 January 1993
Slovenia	-	6 July 1992	25 June 1991
South Africa	-	3 May 1976	1 August 1976
Spain	-	12 May 1977	10 August 1977
Sri Lanka	30 December 1958	9 April 1962	8 July 1962
Sweden	23 December 1958	28 January 1972	27 April 1972
Switzerland	29 December 1958	1 June 1965	30 August 1965
Syrian Arab Republic	-	9 March 1959	7 June 1959
Thailand	-	21 December 1959	20 March 1960
The Former Yugoslav Republic of Macedonia	-	10 March 1994	17 September 1994
Trinidad and Tobago	-	1 February 1966	15 May 1966
Tunisia	-	17 July 1967	15 October 1967
Turkey	-	2 July 1992	30 September 1992
Uganda	-	12 February 1992	12 May 1992
Ukraine	29 December 1958	10 October 1960	8 January 1961
United Arab Emirates	-	21 August 2006	19 November 2006
United Kingdom of Great Britain and Northern Ireland	-	24 September 1975	23 December 1975
United Republic of Tanzania	-	13 October 1964	12 January 1965
United States of America	-	30 September 1970	29 December 1970
Uruguay	-	30 March 1983	28 June 1983
Uzbekistan	-	7 February 1996	7 May 1996
Venezuela	-	8 February 1995	9 May 1995
Vietnam	-	12 September 1995	11 December 1995
Zambia	-	14 March 2002	12 June 2002

State	Signature	Ratification, Accession (a), Succession (d)	Entry into force
Zimbabwe	-	29 September 1994	28 December 1994

B. EUROPEAN (GENEVA) CONVENTION ON INTERNATIONAL COMMERCIAL ARBITRATION OF 1961*

[Done at Geneva, 21 April 1961. Entered into force, 7 January 1964. United Nations Treaty Series, vol. 484, p. 364 No. 7041 (1963–1964)]

Article I. Scope of the Convention

1. This Convention shall apply:

(a) to arbitration agreements concluded for the purpose of settling disputes arising from international trade between physical or legal persons having, when concluding the agreement, their habitual place of residence or their seat in different Contracting States;

(b) to arbitral procedures and awards based on agreements referred to in paragraph 1(a) above.

2. For the purpose of this Convention,

(a) the term "arbitration agreement" shall mean either an arbitral clause in a contract or an arbitration agreement being signed by the parties, or contained in an exchange of letters, telegrams, or in a communication by teleprinter and, in relations between States whose laws do not require that an arbitration agreement be made in writing, any arbitration agreement concluded in the form authorized by these laws;

(b) the term "arbitration" shall mean not only settlement by arbitrators appointed for each case (ad hoc arbitration) but also by permanent arbitral institutions;

(c) the term "seat" shall mean the place of the situation of the establishment that has made the arbitration agreement.

Article II. Right of legal persons of public law to resort to arbitration

1. In the cases referred to in Article I, paragraph 1, of this Convention, legal persons considered by the law which is applicable to them as "legal persons of public law" have the right to conclude valid arbitration agreements.

* The Convention can be found at http://www.jurisint.org/doc/html/ins/en/2002/2002jiinsen6.html or at http://www.law.berkeley.edu/faculty/ddcaron/Documents/RPIDĎocuments/rp04011.html

2. On signing, ratifying or acceding to this Convention any State shall be entitled to declare that it limits the above faculty to such conditions as may be stated in its declaration.

Article III. Right of foreign nationals to be designated as arbitrators

In arbitration covered by this Convention, foreign nationals may be designated as arbitrators.

Article IV. Organization of the arbitration

1. The parties to an arbitration agreement shall be free to submit their disputes:

- (a) to a permanent arbitral institution; in this case, the arbitration proceedings shall be held in conformity with the rules of the said institution;
- (b) to an ad hoc arbitral procedure; in this case, they shall be free inter alia
  - (i) to appoint arbitrators or to establish means for their appointment in the event of an actual dispute;
  - (ii) to determine the place of arbitration; and
  - (iii) to lay down the procedure to be followed by the arbitrators.

2. Where the parties have agreed to submit any disputes to an ad hoc arbitration, and where within thirty days of the notification of the request for arbitration to the respondent one of the parties fails to appoint his arbitrator, the latter shall, unless otherwise provided, be appointed at the request of the other party by the President of the competent Chamber of Commerce of the country of the defaulting party's habitual place of residence or seat at the time of the introduction of the request for arbitration. This paragraph shall also apply to the replacement of the arbitrator(s) appointed by one of the parties or by the President of the Chamber of Commerce above referred to.

3. Where the parties have agreed to submit any disputes to an ad hoc arbitration by one or more arbitrators and the arbitration agreement contains no indication regarding the organization of the arbitration, as mentioned in paragraph 1 of this article, the necessary steps shall be taken by the arbitrator(s) already appointed, unless the parties are able to agree thereon and without prejudice to the case referred to in paragraph 2 above. Where the parties cannot agree on the appointment of the sole arbitrator or where the arbitrators appointed cannot agree on the measures to be taken, the claimant shall apply for the necessary action, where the place of arbitration has been agreed upon by the parties, at his option to the President of the Chamber of Commerce of the place of arbitration agreed upon or to the President of the competent Chamber of Commerce of the respondent's habitual place of residence or seat at the time of the

introduction of the request for arbitration. Where such a place has not been agreed upon, the claimant shall be entitled at his option to apply for the necessary action either to the President of the competent Chamber of Commerce of the country of the respondent's habitual place of residence or seat at the time of the introduction of the request for arbitration, or to the Special Committee whose composition and procedure are specified in the Annex to this Convention. Where the claimant fails to exercise the rights given to him under this paragraph the respondent or the arbitrator(s) shall be entitled to do so.

4. When seized of a request the President or the Special Committee shall be entitled as need be:

(a) to appoint the sole arbitrator, presiding arbitrator, umpire, or referee;

(b) to replace the arbitrator(s) appointed under any procedure other than that referred to in paragraph 2 above;

(c) to determine the place of arbitration, provided that the arbitrator(s) may fix another place of arbitration;

(d) to establish directly or by reference to the rules and statutes of a permanent arbitral institution the rules of procedure to be followed by the arbitrator(s), provided that the arbitrators have not established these rules themselves in the absence of any agreement thereon between the parties.

5. Where the parties have agreed to submit their disputes to a permanent arbitral institution without determining the institution in question and cannot agree thereon, the claimant may request the determination of such institution in conformity with the procedure referred to in paragraph 3 above.

6. Where the arbitration agreement does not specify the mode of arbitration (arbitration by a permanent arbitral institution or an ad hoc arbitration) to which the parties have agreed to submit their dispute, and where the parties cannot agree thereon, the claimant shall be entitled to have recourse in this case to the procedure referred to in paragraph 3 above to determine the question. The President of the competent Chamber of Commerce or the Special Committee, shall be entitled either to refer the parties to a permanent arbitral institution or to request the parties to appoint their arbitrators within such time-limits as the President of the competent Chamber of Commerce or the Special Committee may have fixed and to agree within such time-limits on the necessary measures for the functioning of the arbitration. In the latter case, the provisions of paragraphs 2, 3 and 4 of this Article shall apply.

7. Where within a period of sixty days from the moment when he was requested to fulfil one of the functions set out in paragraphs 2, 3, 4, 5 and 6 of this Article, the President of the Chamber of Commerce designated by virtue of these paragraphs has not fulfilled one of these functions,

the party requesting shall be entitled to ask the Special Committee to do so.

Article V. Plea as to arbitral jurisdiction

1. The party which intends to raise a plea as to the arbitrator's jurisdiction based on the fact that the arbitration agreement was either non-existent or null and void or had lapsed shall do so during the arbitration proceedings, not later than the delivery of its statement of claim or defense relating to the substance of the dispute; those based on the fact that an arbitrator has exceeded his terms of reference shall be raised during the arbitration proceedings as soon as the question on which the arbitrator is alleged to have no jurisdiction is raised during the arbitral procedure. Where the delay in raising the plea is due to a cause which the arbitrator deems justified, the arbitrator shall declare the plea admissible.

2. Pleas to the jurisdiction referred to in paragraph 1 above that have not been raised during the time-limits there referred to, may not be entered either during a subsequent stage of the arbitral proceedings where they are pleas left to the sole discretion of the parties under the law applicable by the arbitrator, or during subsequent court proceedings concerning the substance or the enforcement of the award where such pleas are left to the discretion of the parties under the rule of conflict of the court seized of the substance of the dispute or the enforcement of the award. The arbitrator's decision on the delay in raising the plea, will, however, be subject to judicial control.

3. Subject to any subsequent judicial control provided for under the lex fori, the arbitrator whose jurisdiction is called in question shall be entitled to proceed with the arbitration, to rule on his own jurisdiction and to decide upon the existence or the validity of the arbitration agreement or of the contract of which the agreement forms part.

Article VI. Jurisdiction of courts of law

1. A plea as to the jurisdiction of the court made before the court seized by either party to the arbitration agreement, on the basis of the fact that an arbitration agreement exists shall, under penalty of estoppel, be presented by the respondent before or at the same time as the presentation of his substantial defense, depending upon whether the law of the court seized regards this plea as one of procedure or of substance.

2. In taking a decision concerning the existence or the validity of an arbitration agreement, courts of Contracting States shall examine the validity of such agreement with reference to the capacity of the parties, under the law applicable to them, and with reference to other questions

(a) under the law to which the parties have subjected their arbitration agreement;

(b) failing any indication thereon, under the law of the country in which the award is to be made;

(c) failing any indication as to the law to which the parties have subjected the agreement, and where at the time when the question is raised in court the country in which the award is to be made cannot be determined, under the competent law by virtue of the rules of conflict of the court seized of the dispute. The courts may also refuse recognition of the arbitration agreement if under the law of their country the dispute is not capable of settlement by arbitration.

3. Where either party to an arbitration agreement has initiated arbitration proceedings before any resort is had to a court, courts of Contracting States subsequently asked to deal with the same subject-matter between the same parties or with the question whether the arbitration agreement was non-existent or null and void or had lapsed, shall stay their ruling on the arbitrator's jurisdiction until the arbitral award is made, unless they have good and substantial reasons to the contrary.

4. A request for interim measures or measures of conservation addressed to a judicial authority shall not be deemed incompatible with the arbitration agreement, or regarded as a submission of the substance of the case to the court.

Article VII. Applicable law

1. The parties shall be free to determine, by agreement, the law to be applied by the arbitrators to the substance of the dispute. Failing any indication by the parties as to the applicable law, the arbitrators shall apply the proper law under the rule of conflict that the arbitrators deem applicable. In both cases the arbitrators shall take account of the terms of the contract and trade usages.

2. The arbitrators shall act as amiables compositeurs if the parties so decide and if they may do so under the law applicable to the arbitration.

Article VIII. Reasons for the award

The parties shall be presumed to have agreed that reasons shall be given for the award unless they

(a) either expressly declare that reasons shall not be given; or

(b) have assented to an arbitral procedure under which it is not customary to give reasons for awards, provided that in this case neither party requests before the end of the hearing, or if there has not been a hearing then before the making of the award, that reasons be given.

Article IX. Setting aside of the arbitral award

1. The setting aside in a Contracting State of an arbitral award covered by this Convention shall only constitute a ground for the refusal of recognition or enforcement in another Contracting State where such

setting aside took place in a State in which, or under the law of which, the award has been made and for one of the following reasons:

(a) the parties to the arbitration agreement were under the law applicable to them, under some incapacity or the said agreement is not valid under the law to which the parties have subjected it or, failing any indication thereon, under the law of the country where the award was made; or

(b) the party requesting the setting aside of the award was not given proper notice of the appointment of the arbitrator or of the arbitration proceedings or was otherwise unable to present his case; or

(c) the award deals with a difference not contemplated by or not falling within the terms of the submission to arbitration, or it contains decisions on matters beyond the scope of the submission to arbitration, provided that, if the decisions on matters submitted to arbitration can be separated from those not so submitted, that part of the award which contains decisions on matters submitted to arbitration need not be set aside;

(d) the composition of the arbitral authority or the arbitral procedure was not in accordance with the agreement of the parties, or failing such agreement, with the provisions of Article IV of this Convention.

2. In relations between Contracting States that are also parties to the New York Convention on the Recognition and Enforcement of Foreign Arbitral Awards of 10th June 1958, paragraph 1 of this Article limits the application of Article V(1)(e) of the New York Convention solely to the cases of setting aside set out under paragraph 1 above.

Article X. Final clauses

1. This Convention is open for signature or accession by countries members of the Economic Commission for Europe and countries admitted to the Commission in a consultative capacity under paragraph 8 of the Commission's terms of reference.

2. Such countries as may participate in certain activities of the Economic Commission for Europe in accordance with paragraph 11 of the Commission's terms of reference may become Contracting Parties to this Convention by acceding thereto after its entry into force.

3. The Convention shall be open for signature until 31 December 1961 inclusive. Thereafter, it shall be open for accession.

4. This Convention shall be ratified.

5. Ratification or accession shall be effected by the deposit of an instrument with the Secretary–General of the United Nations.

6. When signing, ratifying or acceding to this Convention, the Contracting Parties shall communicate to the Secretary–General of the United Nations a list of the Chambers of Commerce or other institutions in their country who will exercise the functions conferred by virtue of Article IV of this Convention on Presidents of the competent Chambers of Commerce.

7. The provisions of the present Convention shall not affect the validity of multilateral or bilateral agreements concerning arbitration entered into by Contracting States.

8. This Convention shall come into force on the ninetieth day after five of the countries referred to in paragraph 1 above have deposited their instruments of ratification or accession. For any country ratifying or acceding to it later this Convention shall enter into force on the ninetieth day after the said country has deposited its instrument of ratification or accession.

9. Any Contracting Party may denounce this Convention by so notifying the Secretary–General of the United Nations. Denunciation shall take effect twelve months after the date of receipt by the Secretary–General of the notification of denunciation.

10. If, after the entry into force of this Convention, the number of Contracting Parties is reduced, as a result of denunciations, to less than five, the Convention shall cease to be in force from the date on which the last of such denunciations takes effect.

11. The Secretary–General of the United Nations shall notify the countries referred to in paragraph 1, and the countries which have become Contracting Parties under paragraph 2 above, of

(a) declarations made under Article II, paragraph 2;

(b) ratifications and accessions under paragraphs 1 and 2 above;

(c) communications received in pursuance of paragraph 6 above;

(d) the dates of entry into force of this Convention in accordance with paragraph 8 above;

(e) denunciations under paragraph 9 above;

(f) the termination of this Convention in accordance with paragraph 10 above.

12. After 31 December 1961, the original of this Convention shall be deposited with the Secretary–General of the United Nations, who shall transmit certified true copies to each of the countries mentioned in paragraphs 1 and 2 above.

IN WITNESS WHEREOF the undersigned, being duly authorized thereto, have signed this Convention.

DONE at Geneva, this twenty-first day of April, one thousand nine hundred and sixty-one, in a single copy in the English, French and Russian languages, each text being equally authentic.

LIST OF PARTIES TO THE 1961 GENEVA CONVENTION ON INTERNATIONAL COMMERCIAL ARBITRATION AS OF FEBRUARY 2009*

STATUS: Signatories: 16. Parties: 31.

State	Signature	Ratification, Accession, Succession
Albania		27 June 2001
Austria	21 April 1961	6 March 1964
Azerbaijan		17 January 2005
Belarus	21 April 1961	14 October 1963
Belgium (2)	21 April 1961	9 October 1975
Bosnia and Herzegovina		1 September 1993
Bulgaria	21 April 1961	13 May 1964
Burkina Faso		26 January 1965
Croatia		26 July 1993
Cuba		1 September 1965
Czech Republic		30 September 1993
Denmark	21 April 1961	22 December 1972
Finland		21 December 1961
France	21 April 1961	16 December 1966
Germany	21 April 1961	27 October 1964
Hungary	21 April 1961	9 October 1963
Italy	21 April 1961	3 August 1970
Kazakhstan		20 November 1995
Latvia		20 March 2003
Luxembourg		26 March 1982
Montenegro		23 October 2006
Poland	21 April 1961	15 September 1964
Republic of Moldova		5 March 1998
Romania	21 April 1961	16 August 1963
Russian Federation	21 April 1961	27 June 1962
Serbia		12 March 2001
Slovakia		28 May 1993
Slovenia		6 July 1992
Spain	14 December 1961	12 May 1975
The former Yugoslav Republic of Macedonia		10 March 1994
Turkey	21 April 1961	24 January 1992
Ukraine (8)	21 April 1961	18 March 1963

* The list of participants can be found at the website of the UN http://treaties.un.org/Pages/ViewDetails.aspx?src=TREATY&id=466&chapter=22&lang=en

C. INTER–AMERICAN CONVENTION ON INTERNATIONAL COMMERCIAL ARBITRATION*

[Done at Panama City, 30 January, 1975; entered into force January 16, 1976; *reprinted in* 14 I.L.M. 336 (1975)]

The Governments of the Member States of the Organization of American States, desirous of concluding a convention on international commercial arbitration, have agreed as follows:

Article 1

An agreement in which the parties undertake to submit to arbitral decision any differences that may arise or have arisen between them with respect to a commercial transaction is valid. The agreement shall be set forth in an instrument signed by the parties, or in the form of an exchange of letters, telegrams, or telex communications.

Article 2

Arbitrators shall be appointed in the manner agreed upon by the parties. Their appointment may be delegated to a third party, whether a natural or juridical person.

Arbitrators may be nationals or foreigners.

Article 3

In the absence of an express agreement between the parties, the arbitration shall be conducted in accordance with the rules of procedure of the Inter–American Commercial Arbitration Commission.

Article 4

An arbitral decision or award that is not appealable under the applicable law or procedural rules shall have the force of a final judicial judgement. Its execution or recognition may be ordered in the same manner as that of decisions handed down by national or foreign ordinary courts, in accordance with the procedural laws of the country where it is to be executed and the provisions of international treaties.

Article 5

1. The recognition and execution of the decision may be refused, at the request of the party against which it is made, only if such party is able to prove to the competent authority of the State in which recognition and execution are requested:

---

* Reproduced with kind permission from March 1975 issue of International Legal Materials, © The American Society of International Law. The Convention can be found at the Website of the Organization of American States at http://www.oas.org/juridico/english/treaties/b–35.html

a. That the parties to the agreement were subject to some incapacity under the applicable law or that the agreement is not valid under the law to which the parties have submitted it, or, if such law is not specified, under the law of the State in which the decision was made; or

b. That the party against which the arbitral decision has been made was not duly notified of the appointment of the arbitrator or of the arbitration procedure to be followed, or was unable, for any other reason, to present his defense; or

c. That the decision concerns a dispute not envisaged in the agreement between the parties to submit to arbitration; nevertheless, if the provisions of the decision that refer to issues submitted to arbitration can be separated from those not submitted to arbitration, the former may be recognized and executed; or

d. That the constitution of the arbitral tribunal or the arbitration procedure has not been carried out in accordance with the terms of the agreement signed by the parties or, in the absence of such agreement, that the constitution of the arbitral tribunal or the arbitration procedure has not been carried out in accordance with the law of the State where the arbitration took place; or

e. That the decision is not yet binding on the parties or has been annulled or suspended by a competent authority of the State in which, or according to the law of which, the decision has been made.

2. The recognition and execution of an arbitral decision may also be refused if the competent authority of the State in which the recognition and execution is requested finds:

a. That the subject of the dispute cannot be settled by arbitration under the law of that State; or

b. That the recognition or execution of the decision would be contrary to the public policy ("ordre public") of that State.

Article 6

If the competent authority mentioned in Article 5. 1. e has been requested to annual or suspend the arbitral decision, the authority before which such decision is invoked may, if it deems it appropriate, postpone a decision on the execution of the arbitral decision and, at the request of the party requesting execution, may also instruct the other party to provide appropriate guaranties.

Article 7

This Convention shall be open for signature by the Member States of the Organization of American States.

Article 8

This Convention is subject to ratification. The instruments of ratification shall be deposited with the General Secretariat of the Organization of American States.

Article 9

This Convention shall remain open for accession by any other State. The instruments of accession shall be deposited with the General Secretariat of the Organization of American States.

Article 10

This Convention shall enter into force on the thirtieth day following the date of deposit of the second instrument of ratification.

For each State ratifying or acceding to the Convention after the deposit of the second instrument of ratification, the Convention shall enter into force on the thirtieth day after deposit by such State of its instrument of ratification or accession.

Article 11

If a State Party has two or more territorial units in which different systems of law apply in relation to the matters dealt with in this Convention, it may, at the time of signature, ratification or accession, declare that this Convention shall extend to all its territorial units or only to one or more of them.

Such declaration may be modified by subsequent declarations, which shall expressly indicate the territorial unit or units to which the Convention applies. Such subsequent declarations shall be transmitted to the General Secretariat of the Organization of American States, and shall become effective thirty days after the date of their receipt.

Article 12

This Convention shall remain in force indefinitely, but any of the States Parties may denounce it. The instrument of denunciation shall be deposited with the General Secretariat of the Organization of American States. After one year from the date of deposit of the instrument of denunciation, the Convention shall no longer be in effect for the denouncing State, but shall remain in effect for the other States Parties.

Article 13

The original instrument of this Convention, the English, French, Portuguese and Spanish texts of which are equally authentic, shall be deposited with the General Secretariat of the Organization of American States. The Secretariat shall notify the Member States of the Organization of American States and the States that have acceded to the Convention of the signatures, deposits of instruments of ratification, accession, and denunciation as well as of reservations, if any. It shall also transmit the declarations referred to in Article 11 of this Convention.

LIST OF PARTIES TO THE INTER-AMERICAN CONVENTION ON INTERNATIONAL COMMERCIAL ARBITRATION AS OF FEBRUARY 2009*

Signatory Countries	Signature	Ratification	Deposit of Instrument
Argentina	03/15/91	11/03/94	01/05/95
Bolivia	08/02/83	10/08/98	04/29/99
Brazil	01/30/75	08/31/95	11/27/95
Chile	01/30/75	04/08/76	05/17/76
Colombia	01/30/75	11/18/86	12/29/86
Costa Rica	01/30/75	01/02/78	01/20/78
Dominican Republic	04/18/77	02/11/08	07/07/08
Ecuador	01/30/75	08/06/91	10/23/91
El Salvador	01/30/75	06/27/80	08/11/80
Guatemala	01/30/75	07/07/86	08/20/86
Honduras	01/30/75	01/08/79	03/22/79
Mexico	10/27/77	02/15/78	03/27/78
Nicaragua	01/30/75	07/15/03	10/02/03
Panama	01/30/75	11/11/75	12/17/75
Paraguay	08/26/75	12/02/76	12/15/76
Peru	04/21/88	05/02/89	05/22/89
United States	06/09/78	11/10/86	09/27/90
Uruguay	01/30/75	03/29/77	04/25/77
Venezuela	01/30/75	03/22/85	05/16/85

* List can be found at the website of the Organization of American States http://www.oas.org/juridico/english/sigs/b–35.html

II. UNCITRAL (UN Commission on International Trade Law) Enactments and Other Model Norms

■ ■ ■

A. UNCITRAL MODEL LAW ON INTERNATIONAL COMMERCIAL ARBITRATION [A PROPOSAL FOR NATIONAL LEGISLATION]

A.1. THE 1985 TEXT OF THE UNCITRAL MODEL LAW ON INTERNATIONAL COMMERCIAL ARBITRATION

Chapter I

General Provisions

Article 1

***Scope of application*[1]**

(1) This Law applies to international commercial[2] arbitration, subject to any agreement in force between this State and any other State or States.

(2) The provisions of this Law, except articles 8, 9, 35 and 36, apply only if the place of arbitration is in the territory of this State.

(3) An arbitration is international if:

(a) the parties to an arbitration agreement have, at the time of the conclusion of that agreement, their places of business in different States; or

---

1. Article headings are for reference purposes only and are not to be used for purposes of interpretation.

2. The term "commercial" should be given a wide interpretation so as to cover matters arising from all relationships of a commercial nature, whether contractual or not. Relationships of a commercial nature include, but are not limited to, the following transactions: any trade transaction for the supply or exchange of goods or services; distribution agreement; commercial representation or agency; factoring; leasing; construction of works; consulting; engineering; licensing; investment; financing; banking; insurance; exploitation agreement or concession; joint venture and other forms of industrial or business co-operation; carriage of goods or passengers by air, sea, rail or road.

(b) one of the following places is situated outside the State in which the parties have their places of business:

(i) the place of arbitration if determined in, or pursuant to, the arbitration agreement;

(ii) any place where a substantial part of the obligations of the commercial relationship is to be performed or the place with which the subject-matter of the dispute is most closely connected; or

(c) the parties have expressly agreed that the subject-matter of the arbitration agreement relates to more than one country.

(4) For the purposes of paragraph (3) of this article:

(a) if a party has more than one place of business, the place of business is that which has the closest relationship to the arbitration agreement;

(b) if a party does not have a place of business, reference is to be made to his habitual residence.

(5) This Law shall not affect any other law of this State by virtue of which certain disputes may not be submitted to arbitration or may be submitted to arbitration only according to provisions other than those of this Law.

Article 2

Definitions and rules of interpretation

For the purposes of this Law:

(a) "arbitration" means any arbitration whether or not administered by a permanent arbitral institution;

(b) "arbitral tribunal" means a sole arbitrator or a panel of arbitrators;

(c) "court" means a body or organ of the judicial system of a State;

(d) where a provision of this Law, except article 28, leaves the parties free to determine a certain issue, such freedom includes the right of the parties to authorize a third party, including an institution, to make that determination;

(e) where a provision of this Law refers to the fact that the parties have agreed or that they may agree or in any other way refers to an agreement of the parties, such agreement includes any arbitration rules referred to in that agreement;

(f) where a provision of this Law, other than in articles 25 (a) and 32 (2) (a), refers to a claim, it also applies to a counter-claim, and where it refers to a defense, it also applies to a defense to such counter-claim.

Article 3

Receipt of written communications

(1) Unless otherwise agreed by the parties:

(a) any written communication is deemed to have been received if it is delivered to the addressee personally or if it is delivered at his place of business, habitual residence or mailing address; if none of these can be found after making a reasonable inquiry, a written communication is deemed to have been received if it is sent to the addressee's last-known place of business, habitual residence or mailing address by registered letter or any other means which provides a record of the attempt to deliver it;

(b) the communication is deemed to have been received on the day it is so delivered.

(2) The provisions of this article do not apply to communications in court proceedings.

Article 4

Waiver of right to object

A party who knows that any provision of this Law from which the parties may derogate or any requirement under the arbitration agreement has not been complied with and yet proceeds with the arbitration without stating his objection to such non-compliance without undue delay or, if a time-limit is provided therefore, within such period of time, shall be deemed to have waived his right to object.

Article 5

Extent of court intervention

In matters governed by this Law, no court shall intervene except where so provided in this Law.

Article 6

Court or other authority for certain functions of arbitration assistance and supervision

The functions referred to in articles 11(3), 11(4), 13(3), 14, 16(3) and 34(2) shall be performed by ... [Each State enacting this model law specifies the court, courts or, where referred to therein, other authority competent to perform these functions.]

Chapter II

Arbitration Agreement

Article 7

Definition and form of arbitration agreement

(1) "Arbitration agreement" is an agreement by the parties to submit to arbitration all or certain disputes which have arisen or which may arise between them in respect of a defined legal relationship, whether contractual or not. An arbitration agreement may be in the form of an arbitration clause in a contract or in the form of a separate agreement.

(2) The arbitration agreement shall be in writing. An agreement is in writing if it is contained in a document signed by the parties or in an exchange of letters, telex, telegrams or other means of telecommunication which provide a record of the agreement, or in an exchange of statements of claim and defense in which the existence of an agreement is alleged by one party and not denied by another. The reference in a contract to a document containing an arbitration clause constitutes an arbitration agreement provided that the contract is in writing and the reference is such as to make that clause part of the contract.

Article 8

Arbitration agreement and substantive claim before court

(1) A court before which an action is brought in a matter which is the subject of an arbitration agreement shall, if a party so requests not later than when submitting his first statement on the substance of the dispute, refer the parties to arbitration unless it finds that the agreement is null and void, inoperative or incapable of being performed.

(2) Where an action referred to in paragraph (1) of this article has been brought, arbitral proceedings may nevertheless be commenced or continued, and an award may be made, while the issue is pending before the court.

Article 9

Arbitration agreement and interim court measures

It is not incompatible with an arbitration agreement for a party to request, before or during arbitral proceedings, from a court an interim measure of protection and for a court to grant such measure.

Chapter III

Composition of Arbitral Tribunal

Article 10

Number of arbitrators

(1) The parties are free to determine the number of arbitrators.

(2) Failing such determination, the number of arbitrators shall be three.

Article 11

Appointment of arbitrators

(1) No person shall be precluded by reason of his nationality from acting as an arbitrator, unless otherwise agreed by the parties.

(2) The parties are free to agree on a procedure of appointing the arbitrator or arbitrators, subject to the provisions of paragraphs (4) and (5) of this article.

(3) Failing such agreement,

(a) in an arbitration with three arbitrators, each party shall appoint one arbitrator, and the two arbitrators thus appointed shall appoint the third arbitrator; if a party fails to appoint the arbitrator within thirty days of receipt of a request to do so from the other party, or if the two arbitrators fail to agree on the third arbitrator within thirty days of their appointment, the appointment shall be made, upon request of a party, by the court or other authority specified in article 6;

(b) in an arbitration with a sole arbitrator, if the parties are unable to agree on the arbitrator, he shall be appointed, upon request of a party, by the court or other authority specified in article 6.

(4) Where, under an appointment procedure agreed upon by the parties,

(a) a party fails to act as required under such procedure, or

(b) the parties, or two arbitrators, are unable to reach an agreement expected of them under such procedure, or

(c) a third party, including an institution, fails to perform any function entrusted to it under such procedure, any party may request the court or other authority specified in article 6 to take the necessary measure, unless the agreement on the appointment procedure provides other means for securing the appointment.

(5) A decision on a matter entrusted by paragraph (3) or (4) of this article to the court or other authority specified in article 6 shall be subject to no appeal. The court or other authority, in appointing an arbitrator, shall have due regard to any qualifications required of the arbitrator by the agreement of the parties and to such considerations as are likely to secure the appointment of an independent and impartial arbitrator and, in the case of a sole or third arbitrator, shall take into account as well the advisability of appointing an arbitrator of a nationality other than those of the parties.

Article 12

Grounds for challenge

(1) When a person is approached in connection with his possible appointment as an arbitrator, he shall disclose any circumstances likely to give rise to justifiable doubts as to his impartiality or independence. An arbitrator, from the time of his appointment and throughout the arbitral proceedings, shall without delay disclose any such circumstances to the parties unless they have already been informed of them by him.

(2) An arbitrator may be challenged only if circumstances exist that give rise to justifiable doubts as to his impartiality or independence, or if he does not possess qualifications agreed to by the parties. A party may challenge an arbitrator appointed by him, or in whose appointment he has

participated, only for reasons of which he becomes aware after the appointment has been made.

Article 13

Challenge procedure

(1) The parties are free to agree on a procedure for challenging an arbitrator, subject to the provisions of paragraph (3) of this article.

(2) Failing such agreement, a party who intends to challenge an arbitrator shall, within fifteen days after becoming aware of the constitution of the arbitral tribunal or after becoming aware of any circumstance referred to in article 12(2), send a written statement of the reasons for the challenge to the arbitral tribunal. Unless the challenged arbitrator withdraws from his office or the other party agrees to the challenge, the arbitral tribunal shall decide on the challenge.

(3) If a challenge under any procedure agreed upon by the parties or under the procedure of paragraph (2) of this article is not successful, the challenging party may request, within thirty days after having received notice of the decision rejecting the challenge, the court or other authority specified in article 6 to decide on the challenge, which decision shall be subject to no appeal; while such a request is pending, the arbitral tribunal, including the challenged arbitrator, may continue the arbitral proceedings and make an award.

Article 14

Failure or impossibility to act

(1) If an arbitrator becomes de jure or de facto unable to perform his functions or for other reasons fails to act without undue delay, his mandate terminates if he withdraws from his office or if the parties agree on the termination. Otherwise, if a controversy remains concerning any of these grounds, any party may request the court or other authority specified in article 6 to decide on the termination of the mandate, which decision shall be subject to no appeal.

(2) If, under this article or article 13 (2), an arbitrator withdraws from his office or a party agrees to the termination of the mandate of an arbitrator, this does not imply acceptance of the validity of any ground referred to in this article or article 12 (2).

Article 15

Appointment of substitute arbitrator

Where the mandate of an arbitrator terminates under article 13 or 14 or because of his withdrawal from office for any other reason or because of the revocation of his mandate by agreement of the parties or in any other case of termination of his mandate, a substitute arbitrator shall be appointed according to the rules that were applicable to the appointment of the arbitrator being replaced.

Chapter IV

Jurisdiction of Arbitral Tribunal

Article 16

Competence of arbitral tribunal to rule on its jurisdiction

(1) The arbitral tribunal may rule on its own jurisdiction, including any objections with respect to the existence or validity of the arbitration agreement. For that purpose, an arbitration clause which forms part of a contract shall be treated as an agreement independent of the other terms of the contract. A decision by the arbitral tribunal that the contract is null and void shall not entail ipso jure the invalidity of the arbitration clause.

(2) A plea that the arbitral tribunal does not have jurisdiction shall be raised not later than the submission of the statement of defense. A party is not precluded from raising such a plea by the fact that he has appointed, or participated in the appointment of, an arbitrator. A plea that the arbitral tribunal is exceeding the scope of its authority shall be raised as soon as the matter alleged to be beyond the scope of its authority is raised during the arbitral proceedings. The arbitral tribunal may, in either case, admit a later plea if it considers the delay justified.

(3) The arbitral tribunal may rule on a plea referred to in paragraph (2) of this article either as a preliminary question or in an award on the merits. If the arbitral tribunal rules as a preliminary question that it has jurisdiction, any party may request, within thirty days after having received notice of that ruling, the court specified in article 6 to decide the matter, which decision shall be subject to no appeal; while such a request is pending, the arbitral tribunal may continue the arbitral proceedings and make an award.

Article 17

Power of arbitral tribunal to order interim measures

Unless otherwise agreed by the parties, the arbitral tribunal may, at the request of a party, order any party to take such interim measure of protection as the arbitral tribunal may consider necessary in respect of the subject-matter of the dispute. The arbitral tribunal may require any party to provide appropriate security in connection with such measure.

Chapter V

Conduct of Arbitral Proceedings

Article 18

Equal treatment of parties

The parties shall be treated with equality and each party shall be given a full opportunity of presenting his case.

Article 19

Determination of rules of procedure

(1) Subject to the provisions of this Law, the parties are free to agree on the procedure to be followed by the arbitral tribunal in conducting the proceedings.

(2) Failing such agreement, the arbitral tribunal may, subject to the provisions of this Law, conduct the arbitration in such manner as it considers appropriate. The power conferred upon the arbitral tribunal includes the power to determine the admissibility, relevance, materiality and weight of any evidence.

Article 20

Place of arbitration

(1) The parties are free to agree on the place of arbitration. Failing such agreement, the place of arbitration shall be determined by the arbitral tribunal having regard to the circumstances of the case, including the convenience of the parties.

(2) Notwithstanding the provisions of paragraph (1) of this article, the arbitral tribunal may, unless otherwise agreed by the parties, meet at any place it considers appropriate for consultation among its members, for hearing witnesses, experts or the parties, or for inspection of goods, other property or documents.

Article 21

Commencement of arbitral proceedings

Unless otherwise agreed by the parties, the arbitral proceedings in respect of a particular dispute commence on the date on which a request for that dispute to be referred to arbitration is received by the respondent.

Article 22

Language

(1) The parties are free to agree on the language or languages to be used in the arbitral proceedings. Failing such agreement, the arbitral tribunal shall determine the language or languages to be used in the proceedings. This agreement or determination, unless otherwise specified therein, shall apply to any written statement by a party, any hearing and any award, decision or other communication by the arbitral tribunal.

(2) The arbitral tribunal may order that any documentary evidence shall be accompanied by a translation into the language or languages agreed upon by the parties or determined by the arbitral tribunal.

Article 23

Statements of claim and defense

(1) Within the period of time agreed by the parties or determined by the arbitral tribunal, the claimant shall state the facts supporting his

claim, the points at issue and the relief or remedy sought, and the respondent shall state his defense in respect of these particulars, unless the parties have otherwise agreed as to the required elements of such statements. The parties may submit with their statements all documents they consider to be relevant or may add a reference to the documents or other evidence they will submit.

(2) Unless otherwise agreed by the parties, either party may amend or supplement his claim or defense during the course of the arbitral proceedings, unless the arbitral tribunal considers it inappropriate to allow such amendment having regard to the delay in making it.

Article 24

Hearings and written proceedings

(1) Subject to any contrary agreement by the parties, the arbitral tribunal shall decide whether to hold oral hearings for the presentation of evidence or for oral argument, or whether the proceedings shall be conducted on the basis of documents and other materials. However, unless the parties have agreed that no hearings shall be held, the arbitral tribunal shall hold such hearings at an appropriate stage of the proceedings, if so requested by a party.

(2) The parties shall be given sufficient advance notice of any hearing and of any meeting of the arbitral tribunal for the purposes of inspection of goods, other property or documents.

(3) All statements, documents or other information supplied to the arbitral tribunal by one party shall be communicated to the other party. Also any expert report or evidentiary document on which the arbitral tribunal may rely in making its decision shall be communicated to the parties.

Article 25

Default of a party

Unless otherwise agreed by the parties, if, without showing sufficient cause,

(a) the claimant fails to communicate his statement of claim in accordance with article 23(1), the arbitral tribunal shall terminate the proceedings;

(b) the respondent fails to communicate his statement of defense in accordance with article 23(1), the arbitral tribunal shall continue the proceedings without treating such failure in itself as an admission of the claimant's allegations;

(c) any party fails to appear at a hearing or to produce documentary evidence, the arbitral tribunal may continue the proceedings and make the award on the evidence before it.

Article 26

Expert appointed by arbitral tribunal

(1) Unless otherwise agreed by the parties, the arbitral tribunal

(a) may appoint one or more experts to report to it on specific issues to be determined by the arbitral tribunal;

(b) may require a party to give the expert any relevant information or to produce, or to provide access to, any relevant documents, goods or other property for his inspection.

(2) Unless otherwise agreed by the parties, if a party so requests or if the arbitral tribunal considers it necessary, the expert shall, after delivery of his written or oral report, participate in a hearing where the parties have the opportunity to put questions to him and to present expert witnesses in order to testify on the points at issue.

Article 27

Court assistance in taking evidence

The arbitral tribunal or a party with the approval of the arbitral tribunal may request from a competent court of this State assistance in taking evidence. The court may execute the request within its competence and according to its rules on taking evidence.

Chapter VI

Making of Award and Termination of Proceedings

Article 28

Rules applicable to substance of dispute

(1) The arbitral tribunal shall decide the dispute in accordance with such rules of law as are chosen by the parties as applicable to the substance of the dispute. Any designation of the law or legal system of a given State shall be construed, unless otherwise expressed, as directly referring to the substantive law of that State and not to its conflict of laws rules.

(2) Failing any designation by the parties, the arbitral tribunal shall apply the law determined by the conflict of laws rules which it considers applicable.

(3) The arbitral tribunal shall decide ex aequo et bono or as amiable compositeur only if the parties have expressly authorized it to do so.

(4) In all cases, the arbitral tribunal shall decide in accordance with the terms of the contract and shall take into account the usages of the trade applicable to the transaction.

Article 29

Decision-making by panel of arbitrators

In arbitral proceedings with more than one arbitrator, any decision of the arbitral tribunal shall be made, unless otherwise agreed by the parties, by a majority of all its members. However, questions of procedure may be decided by a presiding arbitrator, if so authorized by the parties or all members of the arbitral tribunal.

Article 30

Settlement

(1) If, during arbitral proceedings, the parties settle the dispute, the arbitral tribunal shall terminate the proceedings and, if requested by the parties and not objected to by the arbitral tribunal, record the settlement in the form of an arbitral award on agreed terms.

(2) An award on agreed terms shall be made in accordance with the provisions of article 31 and shall state that it is an award. Such an award has the same status and effect as any other award on the merits of the case.

Article 31

Form and contents of award

(1) The award shall be made in writing and shall be signed by the arbitrator or arbitrators. In arbitral proceedings with more than one arbitrator, the signatures of the majority of all members of the arbitral tribunal shall suffice, provided that the reason for any omitted signature is stated.

(2) The award shall state the reasons upon which it is based, unless the parties have agreed that no reasons are to be given or the award is an award on agreed terms under article 30.

(3) The award shall state its date and the place of arbitration as determined in accordance with article 20(1). The award shall be deemed to have been made at that place.

(4) After the award is made, a copy signed by the arbitrators in accordance with paragraph (1) of this article shall be delivered to each party.

Article 32

Termination of proceedings

(1) The arbitral proceedings are terminated by the final award or by an order of the arbitral tribunal in accordance with paragraph (2) of this article.

(2) The arbitral tribunal shall issue an order for the termination of the arbitral proceedings when:

(a) the claimant withdraws his claim, unless the respondent objects thereto and the arbitral tribunal recognizes a legitimate interest on his part in obtaining a final settlement of the dispute;

(b) the parties agree on the termination of the proceedings;

(c) the arbitral tribunal finds that the continuation of the proceedings has for any other reason become unnecessary or impossible.

(3) The mandate of the arbitral tribunal terminates with the termination of the arbitral proceedings, subject to the provisions of articles 33 and 34(4).

Article 33

Correction and interpretation of award; additional award

(1) Within thirty days of receipt of the award, unless another period of time has been agreed upon by the parties:

(a) a party, with notice to the other party, may request the arbitral tribunal to correct in the award any errors in computation, any clerical or typographical errors or any errors of similar nature;

(b) if so agreed by the parties, a party, with notice to the other party, may request the arbitral tribunal to give an interpretation of a specific point or part of the award.

If the arbitral tribunal considers the request to be justified, it shall make the correction or give the interpretation within thirty days of receipt of the request. The interpretation shall form part of the award.

(2) The arbitral tribunal may correct any error of the type referred to in paragraph (1)(a) of this article on its own initiative within thirty days of the date of the award.

(3) Unless otherwise agreed by the parties, a party, with notice to the other party, may request, within thirty days of receipt of the award, the arbitral tribunal to make an additional award as to claims presented in the arbitral proceedings but omitted from the award. If the arbitral tribunal considers the request to be justified, it shall make the additional award within sixty days.

(4) The arbitral tribunal may extend, if necessary, the period of time within which it shall make a correction, interpretation or an additional award under paragraph (1) or (3) of this article.

(5) The provisions of article 31 shall apply to a correction or interpretation of the award or to an additional award.

Chapter VII

Recourse Against Award

Article 34

Application for setting aside as exclusive recourse against arbitral award

(1) Recourse to a court against an arbitral award may be made only by an application for setting aside in accordance with paragraphs (2) and (3) of this article.

(2) An arbitral award may be set aside by the court specified in article 6 only if:

(a) the party making the application furnishes proof that:

(i) a party to the arbitration agreement referred to in article 7 was under some incapacity; or the said agreement is not valid under the law to which the parties have subjected it or, failing any indication thereon, under the law of this State; or

(ii) the party making the application was not given proper notice of the appointment of an arbitrator or of the arbitral proceedings or was otherwise unable to present his case; or

(iii) the award deals with a dispute not contemplated by or not falling within the terms of the submission to arbitration, or contains decisions on matters beyond the scope of the submission to arbitration, provided that, if the decisions on matters submitted to arbitration can be separated from those not so submitted, only that part of the award which contains decisions on matters not submitted to arbitration may be set aside; or

(iv) the composition of the arbitral tribunal or the arbitral procedure was not in accordance with the agreement of the parties, unless such agreement was in conflict with a provision of this Law from which the parties cannot derogate, or, failing such agreement, was not in accordance with this Law; or

(b) the court finds that:

(i) the subject-matter of the dispute is not capable of settlement by arbitration under the law of this State; or

(ii) the award is in conflict with the public policy of this State.

(3) An application for setting aside may not be made after three months have elapsed from the date on which the party making that application had received the award or, if a request had been made under article 33, from the date on which that request had been disposed of by the arbitral tribunal.

(4) The court, when asked to set aside an award, may, where appropriate and so requested by a party, suspend the setting aside proceedings for a period of time determined by it in order to give the arbitral tribunal an opportunity to resume the arbitral proceedings or to take such other action as in the arbitral tribunal's opinion will eliminate the grounds for setting aside.

Chapter VIII

Recognition and Enforcement of Awards

Article 35

Recognition and enforcement

(1) An arbitral award, irrespective of the country in which it was made, shall be recognized as binding and, upon application in writing to the competent court, shall be enforced subject to the provisions of this article and of article 36.

(2) The party relying on an award or applying for its enforcement shall supply the duly authenticated original award or a duly certified copy thereof, and the original arbitration agreement referred to in article 7 or a duly certified copy thereof. If the award or agreement is not made in an official language of this State, the party shall supply a duly certified translation thereof into such language.[3]

Article 36

Grounds for refusing recognition or enforcement

(1) Recognition or enforcement of an arbitral award, irrespective of the country in which it was made, may be refused only:

(a) at the request of the party against whom it is invoked, if that party furnishes to the competent court where recognition or enforcement is sought proof that:

(i) a party to the arbitration agreement referred to in article 7 was under some incapacity; or the said agreement is not valid under the law to which the parties have subjected it or, failing any indication thereon, under the law of the country where the award was made; or

(ii) the party against whom the award is invoked was not given proper notice of the appointment of an arbitrator or of the arbitral proceedings or was otherwise unable to present his case; or

(iii) the award deals with a dispute not contemplated by or not falling within the terms of the submission to arbitration, or it contains decisions on matters beyond the scope of the submission to arbitration, provided that, if the decisions on matters submitted to arbitration can be separated from those not so submitted, that part of the award which contains decisions on matters submitted to arbitration may be recognized and enforced; or

(iv) the composition of the arbitral tribunal or the arbitral procedure was not in accordance with the agreement of the parties or, failing such agreement, was not in accor-

3. The conditions set forth in this paragraph are intended to set maximum standards. It would, thus, not be contrary to the harmonization to be achieved by the model law if a State retained even less onerous conditions.

dance with the law of the country where the arbitration took place; or

(v) the award has not yet become binding on the parties or has been set aside or suspended by a court of the country in which, or under the law of which, that award was made; or

(b) if the court finds that:

(i) the subject-matter of the dispute is not capable of settlement by arbitration under the law of this State; or

(ii) the recognition or enforcement of the award would be contrary to the public policy of this State.

(2) If an application for setting aside or suspension of an award has been made to a court referred to in paragraph (1)(a)(v) of this article, the court where recognition or enforcement is sought may, if it considers it proper, adjourn its decision and may also, on the application of the party claiming recognition or enforcement of the award, order the other party to provide appropriate security.

A.2. THE 2006 AMENDMENTS TO THE UNCITRAL MODEL LAW ON INTERNATIONAL COMMERCIAL ARBITRATION*

Article 1

Scope of application

* * *

(2) The provisions of this Law, except articles 8, 9, 17 H, 17 I, 17 J, 35 and 36, apply only if the place of arbitration is in the territory of this State.

* * *

Article 2 A.

International origin and general principles

(1) In the interpretation of this Law, regard is to be had to its international origin and to the need to promote uniformity in its application and the observance of good faith.

(2) Questions concerning matters governed by this Law which are not expressly settled in it are to be settled in conformity with the general principles on which this Law is based.

* * *

* The consolidated text of the amended Model Law can be found at the UNCITRAL Website at http://www.uncitral.org/pdf/english/texts/arbitration/ml-arb/07-86998_Ebook.pdf

CHAPTER II

Arbitration Agreement

Option I

Article 7.

Definition and form of arbitration agreement

(1) "Arbitration agreement" is an agreement by the parties to submit to arbitration all or certain disputes which have arisen or which may arise between them in respect of a defined legal relationship, whether contractual or not. An arbitration agreement may be in the form of an arbitration clause in a contract or in the form of a separate agreement.

(2) The arbitration agreement shall be in writing.

(3) An arbitration agreement is in writing if its content is recorded in any form, whether or not the arbitration agreement or contract has been concluded orally, by conduct, or by other means.

(4) The requirement that an arbitration agreement be in writing is met by an electronic communication if the information contained therein is accessible so as to be useable for subsequent reference; "electronic communication" means any communication that the parties make by means of data messages; "data message" means information generated, sent, received or stored by electronic, magnetic, optical or similar means, including, but not limited to, electronic data interchange (EDI), electronic mail, telegram, telex or telecopy.

(5) Furthermore, an arbitration agreement is in writing if it is contained in an exchange of statements of claim and defence in which the existence of an agreement is alleged by one party and not denied by the other.

(6) The reference in a contract to any document containing an arbitration clause constitutes an arbitration agreement in writing, provided that the reference is such as to make that clause part of the contract.

Option II

Article 7.

Definition of arbitration agreement

"Arbitration agreement" is an agreement by the parties to submit to arbitration all or certain disputes which have arisen or which may arise between them in respect of a defined legal relationship, whether contractual or not.

* * *

CHAPTER IV A

Interim measures and preliminary orders

Section 1. Interim measures

Article 17.

Power of arbitral tribunal to order interim measures

1) Unless otherwise agreed by the parties, the arbitral tribunal may, at the request of a party, grant interim measures.

2) An interim measure is any temporary measure, whether in the form of an award or in another form, by which, at any time prior to the issuance of the award by which the dispute is finally decided, the arbitral tribunal orders a party to:

(a) Maintain or restore the status quo pending determination of the dispute;

(b) Take action that would prevent, or refrain from taking action that is likely to cause, current or imminent harm or prejudice to the arbitral process itself;

(c) Provide a means of preserving assets out of which a subsequent award may be satisfied; or

(d) Preserve evidence that may be relevant and material to the resolution of the dispute.

Article 17 A.

Conditions for granting interim measures

(1) The party requesting an interim measure under article 17(2)*(a)*, *(b)* and *(c)* shall satisfy the arbitral tribunal that:

(a) Harm not adequately reparable by an award of damages is likely to result if the measure is not ordered, and such harm substantially outweighs the harm that is likely to result to the party against whom the measure is directed if the measure is granted; and

(b) There is a reasonable possibility that the requesting party will succeed on the merits of the claim. The determination on this possibility shall not affect the discretion of the arbitral tribunal in making any subsequent determination.

(2) With regard to a request for an interim measure under article 17(2)*(d)*, the requirements in paragraphs (1)*(a)* and *(b)* of this article shall apply only to the extent the arbitral tribunal considers appropriate.

Section 2. Preliminary orders

Article 17 B.

Applications for preliminary orders and conditions for granting preliminary orders

(1) Unless otherwise agreed by the parties, a party may, without notice to any other party, make a request for an interim measure together

with an application for a preliminary order directing a party not to frustrate the purpose of the interim measure requested.

(2) The arbitral tribunal may grant a preliminary order provided it considers that prior disclosure of the request for the interim measure to the party against whom it is directed risks frustrating the purpose of the measure.

(3) The conditions defined under article 17A apply to any preliminary order, provided that the harm to be assessed under article 17A(1)*(a)*, is the harm likely to result from the order being granted or not.

Article 17 C.

Specific regime for preliminary orders

(1) Immediately after the arbitral tribunal has made a determination in respect of an application for a preliminary order, the arbitral tribunal shall give notice to all parties of the request for the interim measure, the application for the preliminary order, the preliminary order, if any, and all other communications, including by indicating the content of any oral communication, between any party and the arbitral tribunal in relation thereto.

(2) At the same time, the arbitral tribunal shall give an opportunity to any party against whom a preliminary order is directed to present its case at the earliest practicable time.

(3) The arbitral tribunal shall decide promptly on any objection to the preliminary order.

(4) A preliminary order shall expire after twenty days from the date on which it was issued by the arbitral tribunal. However, the arbitral tribunal may issue an interim measure adopting or modifying the preliminary order, after the party against whom the preliminary order is directed has been given notice and an opportunity to present its case.

(5) A preliminary order shall be binding on the parties but shall not be subject to enforcement by a court. Such a preliminary order does not constitute an award.

Section 3. Provisions applicable to interim measures and preliminary orders

Article 17 D.

Modification, suspension, termination

The arbitral tribunal may modify, suspend or terminate an interim measure or a preliminary order it has granted, upon application of any party or, in exceptional circumstances and upon prior notice to the parties, on the arbitral tribunal own initiative.

Article 17 E.

Provision of security

(1) The arbitral tribunal may require the party requesting an interim measure to provide appropriate security in connection with the measure.

(2) The arbitral tribunal shall require the party applying for a preliminary order to provide security in connection with the order unless the arbitral tribunal considers it inappropriate or unnecessary to do so.

Article 17 F.

Disclosure

(1) The arbitral tribunal may require any party promptly to disclose any material change in the circumstances on the basis of which the measure was requested or granted.

(2) The party applying for a preliminary order shall disclose to the arbitral tribunal all circumstances that are likely to be relevant to the arbitral tribunal determination whether to grant or maintain the order, and such obligation shall continue until the party against whom the order has been requested has had an opportunity to present its case. Thereafter, paragraph (1) of this article shall apply.

Article 17 G.

Costs and damages

The party requesting an interim measure or applying for a preliminary order shall be liable for any costs and damages caused by the measure or the order to any party if the arbitral tribunal later determines that, in the circumstances, the measure or the order should not have been granted. The arbitral tribunal may award such costs and damages at any point during the proceedings.

Section 4. Recognition and enforcement of interim measures

Article 17 H.

Recognition and enforcement

(1) An interim measure issued by an arbitral tribunal shall be recognized as binding and, unless otherwise provided by the arbitral tribunal, enforced upon application to the competent court, irrespective of the country in which it was issued, subject to the provisions of article 17 I.

(2) The party who is seeking or has obtained recognition or enforcement of an interim measure shall promptly inform the court of any termination, suspension or modification of that interim measure.

(3) The court of the State where recognition or enforcement is sought may, if it considers it proper, order the requesting party to provide appropriate security if the arbitral tribunal has not already made a

determination with respect to security or where such a decision is necessary to protect the rights of third parties.

Article 17 I.

Grounds for refusing recognition or enforcement[†]

(1) Recognition or enforcement of an interim measure may be refused only:

(a) At the request of the party against whom it is invoked if the court is satisfied that:
- (i) Such refusal is warranted on the grounds set forth in article 36(1)*(a)*(i), (ii), (iii) or (iv); or
- (ii) The arbitral tribunal decision with respect to the provision of security in connection with the interim measure issued by the arbitral tribunal has not been complied with; or
- (iii) The interim measure has been terminated or suspended by the arbitral tribunal or, where so empowered, by the court of the State in which the arbitration takes place or under the law of which that interim measure was granted; or

(b) If the court finds that:
- (i) The interim measure is incompatible with the powers conferred upon the court unless the court decides to reformulate the interim measure to the extent necessary to adapt it to its own powers and procedures for the purposes of enforcing that interim measure and without modifying its substance; or
- (ii) Any of the grounds set forth in article 36(1)*(b)*(i) or (ii), apply to the recognition and enforcement of the interim measure.

(2) Any determination made by the court on any ground in paragraph (1) of this article shall be effective only for the purposes of the application to recognize and enforce the interim measure. The court where recognition or enforcement is sought shall not, in making that determination, undertake a review of the substance of the interim measure.

Section 5. Court-ordered interim measures

Article 17 J.

Court-ordered interim measures

A court shall have the same power of issuing an interim measure in relation to arbitration proceedings, irrespective of whether their place is in the territory of this State, as it has in relation to proceedings in courts.

† The conditions set forth in article 17 I are intended to limit the number of circumstances in which the court may refuse to enforce an interim measure. It would not be contrary to the level of harmonization sought to be achieved by these model provisions if a State were to adopt fewer circumstances in which enforcement may be refused.

The court shall exercise such power in accordance with its own procedures in consideration of the specific features of international arbitration.

* * *

Article 35

Recognition and enforcement

* * *

(2) The party relying on an award or applying for its enforcement shall supply the original award or a copy thereof. If the award is not made in an official language of this State, the court may request the party to supply translation thereof into such language.‡

B. UNCITRAL ARBITRATION RULES, 1976*

Section I

Introductory rules

Scope of Application

Article 1

1. Where the parties to a contract have agreed in writing that disputes in relation to that contract shall be referred to arbitration under the UNCITRAL Arbitration Rules, then such disputes shall be settled in accordance with these Rules subject to such modification as the parties may agree in writing.

2. These Rules shall govern the arbitration except that where any of these Rules is in conflict with a provision of the law applicable to the arbitration from which the parties cannot derogate, that provision shall prevail.

Notice, Calculation of Periods of Time

Article 2

1. For the purposes of these Rules, any notice, including a notification, communication or proposal is deemed to have been received if it is physically delivered to the addressee or if it is delivered at his habitual residence, place of business or mailing address, or, if none of these can be found after making reasonable inquiry, then at the addressee's last known residence or place of business. Notice shall be deemed to have been received on the day it is so delivered.

‡ The conditions set forth in this paragraph are intended to set maximum standards. It would, thus, not be contrary to the harmonization to be achieved by the model law if a State retained even less onerous conditions.

* Document can be found at the UNCITRAL website at http://www.uncitral.org/pdf/english/texts/arbitration/arb-rules/arb-rules.pdf

2. For the purposes of calculating a period of time under these Rules, such period shall begin to run on the day following the day when a notice, notification communication or proposal is received. If the last day of such period is an official holiday or a non-business day at the residence or place of business of the addressee, the period is extended until the first business day which follows. Official holidays or non-business days occurring during the running of the period of time are included in calculating the period.

Notice of Arbitration

Article 3

1. The party initiating recourse to arbitration (hereinafter called the "claimant") shall give to the other party (hereinafter called the "respondent") a notice of arbitration.

2. Arbitral proceedings shall be deemed to commence on the date on which the notification of arbitration is received by the respondent.

3. The notice of arbitration shall include the following:

(a) A demand that the dispute be referred to arbitration;

(b) The names and addresses of the parties;

(c) A reference to the arbitration clause or agreement that is invoked;

(d) A reference to the contract out of or in relation to which the dispute arises;

(e) The general nature of the claim and an indication of the amount involved, if any;

(f) The relief or remedy sought;

(g) A proposal as to the number of arbitrators (i.e. one or three), if parties have not previously agreed thereon.

4. The notice of arbitration may also include:

(a) The proposals for the appointments of a sole arbitrator and an appointing authority referred to in article 6, paragraph 1;

(b) The notification of the appointment of an arbitrator referred to in article 7;

(c) The statement of claim referred to in article 18.

Representation and Assistance

Article 4

The parties may be represented or assisted by persons of their choice. The names and addresses of such persons must be communicated in writing to the other party; such communication must specify whether the appointment is being made for purposes of representation or assistance.

Section II

Composition of the arbitral tribunal

Number of Arbitrators

Article 5

If the parties have not previously agreed on the number of arbitrators (i.e. one or three), and if within 15 days after the receipt by the respondent of the notice of arbitration the parties have not agreed that there shall be only one arbitrator, three arbitrators shall be appointed.

Appointment of Arbitrators (Articles 6 to 8)

Article 6

1. If a sole arbitrator is to be appointed, either party may propose to the other:

(a) The names of one or more persons, one of whom would serve as the sole arbitrator; and

(b) If no appointing authority has been agreed upon by the parties, the name or names of one or more institutions or persons, one of whom would serve as appointing authority.

2. If within 30 days after receipt by a party of a proposal made in accordance with paragraph 1 the parties have not reached agreement on the choice of a sole arbitrator, the sole arbitrator shall be appointed by the appointing authority agreed upon by the parties. If no appointing authority has been agreed upon by the parties, or if the appointing authority agreed upon refuses to act or fails to appoint the arbitrator within 60 days of the receipt of a party's request therefore, either party may request the Secretary–General of the Permanent Court of Arbitration at The Hague to designate an appointing authority.

3. The appointing authority shall, at the request of one of the parties, appoint the sole arbitrator as promptly as possible. In making the appointment the appointing authority shall use the following list-procedure, unless both parties agree that the list-procedure should not be used or unless the appointing authority determines in its discretion that the use of the list-procedure is not appropriate for the case:

(a) At the request of one of the parties the appointing authority shall communicate to both parties an identical list containing at least three names;

(b) Within 15 days after the receipt of this list, each party may return the list to the appointing authority after having deleted the name or names to which he objects and numbered the remaining names on the list in the order of his preference;

(c) After the expiration of the above period of time the appointing authority shall appoint the sole arbitrator from among the names approved on the lists returned to it and in accordance with the order of preference indicated by the parties;

(d) If for any reason the appointment cannot be made according to this procedure, the appointing authority may exercise its discretion in appointing the sole arbitrator.

4. In making the appointment, the appointing authority shall have regard to such considerations as are likely to secure the appointment of an independent and impartial arbitrator and shall take into account as well the advisability of appointing an arbitrator of a nationality other than the nationalities of the parties.

Article 7

1. If three arbitrators are to be appointed, each party shall appoint one arbitrator. The two arbitrators thus appointed shall choose the third arbitrator who will act as the presiding arbitrator of the tribunal.

2. If within 30 days after the receipt of a party's notification of the appointment of an arbitrator the other party has not notified the first party of the arbitrator it has appointed:

(a) The first party may request the appointing authority previously designated by the parties to appoint the second arbitrator; or

(b) If no such authority has been previously designated by the parties, or if the appointing authority previously designated refuses to act or fails to appoint the arbitrator within 30 days after receipt of a party's request therefore, the first party may request the Secretary–General of the Permanent Court of Arbitration at The Hague to designate the appointing authority. The first party may then request the appointing authority so designated to appoint the second arbitrator. In either case, the appointing authority may exercise its discretion in appointing the arbitrator.

3. If within 30 days after the appointment of the second arbitrator the two arbitrators have not agreed on the choice of the presiding arbitrator, the presiding arbitrator shall be appointed by an appointing authority in the same way as a sole arbitrator would be appointed under article 6.

Article 8

1. When an appointing authority is requested to appoint an arbitrator pursuant to article 6 or article 7, the party which makes the request shall send to the appointing authority a copy of the notice of arbitration, a copy of the contract out of or in relation to which the dispute has arisen and a copy of the arbitration agreement if it is not contained in the contract. The appointing authority may require from either party such information as it deems necessary to fulfil its function.

2. Where the names of one or more persons are proposed for appointment as arbitrators, their full names, addresses and nationalities shall be indicated, together with a description of their qualifications.

Challenge of Arbitrators (Articles 9 to 12)

Article 9

A prospective arbitrator shall disclose to those who approach him in connection with his possible appointment any circumstances likely to give rise to justifiable doubts as to his impartiality or independence. An arbitrator, once appointed or chosen, shall disclose such circumstances to the parties unless they have already been informed by him of these circumstances.

Article 10

1. Any arbitrator may be challenged if circumstances exist that give rise to justifiable doubts as to the arbitrator's impartiality or independence.

2. A party may challenge the arbitrator appointed by him only for reasons of which he becomes aware after the appointment has been made.

Article 11

1. A party who intends to challenge an arbitrator shall send notice of his challenge within 15 days after the appointment of the challenged arbitrator has been notified to the challenging party or within 15 days after the circumstances mentioned in articles 9 and 10 became known to that party.

2. The challenge shall be notified to the other party, to the arbitrator who is challenged and to the other members of the arbitral tribunal. The notification shall be in writing and shall state the reasons for the challenge.

3. When an arbitrator has been challenged by one party, the other party may agree to the challenge. The arbitrator may also, after the challenge, withdraw from his office. In neither case does this imply acceptance of the validity of the grounds for the challenge. In both cases the procedure provided in article 6 or 7 shall be used in full for the appointment of the substitute arbitrator, even if during the process of appointing the challenged arbitrator a party had failed to exercise his right to appoint or to participate in the appointment.

Article 12

1. If the other party does not agree to the challenge and the challenged arbitrator does not withdraw, the decision on the challenge will be made:

(a) When the initial appointment was made by an appointing authority, by that authority;

(b) When the initial appointment was not made by an appointing authority, but an appointing authority has been previously designated, by that authority;

(c) In all other cases, by the appointing authority to be designated in accordance with the procedure for designating an appointing authority as provided for in article 6.

2. If the appointing authority sustains the challenge, a substitute arbitrator shall be appointed or chosen pursuant to the procedure applicable to the appointment or choice of an arbitrator as provided in articles 6 to 9 except that, when this procedure would call for the designation of an appointing authority, the appointment of the arbitrator shall be made by the appointing authority which decided on the challenge.

Replacement of an Arbitrator

Article 13

1. In the event of the death or resignation of an arbitrator during the course of the arbitral proceedings, a substitute arbitrator shall be appointed or chosen pursuant to the procedure provided for in articles 6 to 9 that was applicable to the appointment or choice of the arbitrator being replaced.

2. In the event that an arbitrator fails to act or in the event of the *de jure* or *de facto* impossibility of his performing his functions, the procedure in respect of the challenge and replacement of an arbitrator as provided in the preceding articles shall apply.

Repetition of Hearings in the Event of the Replacement of an Arbitrator

Article 14

If under articles 11 to 13 the sole or presiding arbitrator is replaced, any hearings held previously shall be repeated; if any other arbitrator is replaced, such prior hearings may be repeated at the discretion of the arbitral tribunal.

Section III

Arbitral proceedings

General Provisions

Article 15

1. Subject to these Rules, the arbitral tribunal may conduct the arbitration in such manner as it considers appropriate, provided that the parties are treated with equality and that at any stage of the proceedings each party is given a full opportunity of presenting its case.

2. If either party so requests at any stage of the proceedings, the arbitral tribunal shall hold hearings for the presentation of evidence by witnesses, including expert witnesses or for oral argument. In the absence

of such a request, the arbitral tribunal shall decide whether to hold such hearings or whether the proceedings shall be conducted on the basis of documents and other materials.

3. All documents or information supplied to the arbitral tribunal by one party shall at the same time be communicated by that party to the other party.

Place of Arbitration

Article 16

1. Unless the parties have agreed upon the place where the arbitration is to be held, such place shall be determined by the arbitral tribunal, having regard to the circumstances of the arbitration.

2. The arbitral tribunal may determine the locale of the arbitration within the country agreed upon by the parties. It may hear witnesses and hold meetings for consultation among its members at any place it deems appropriate, having regard to the circumstances of the arbitration.

3. The arbitral tribunal may meet at any place it deems appropriate for the inspection of goods, other property or documents. The parties shall be given sufficient notice to enable them to be present at such inspection.

4. The award shall be made at the place of arbitration.

Language

Article 17

1. Subject to an agreement by the parties, the arbitral tribunal shall, promptly after its appointment, determine the language or languages to be used in the proceedings. This determination shall apply to the statement of claim, the statement of defense, and any further written statements and, if oral hearings take place, to the language or languages to be used in such hearings.

2. The arbitral tribunal may order that any documents annexed to the statement of claim or statement of defense, and any supplementary documents or exhibits submitted in the course of the proceedings, delivered in their original language, shall be accompanied by a translation into the language or languages agreed upon by the parties or determined by the arbitral tribunal.

Statement of Claim

Article 18

1. Unless the statement of claim was contained in the notice of arbitration, within a period of time to be determined by the arbitral tribunal, the claimant shall communicate his statement of claim in writing to the respondent and to each of the arbitrators. A copy of the contract, and of the arbitration agreement if not contained in the contract, shall be annexed thereto.

2. The statement of claim shall include the following particulars:

(a) The names and addresses of the parties;

(b) A statement of the facts supporting the claim;

(c) The points at issue;

(d) The relief or remedy sought.

The claimant may annex to his statement of claim all documents he deems relevant or may add a reference to the documents or other evidence he will submit.

Statement of Defense

Article 19

1. Within a period of time to be determined by the arbitral tribunal, the respondent shall communicate his statement of defense in writing to the claimant and to each of the arbitrators.

2. The statement of defense shall reply to the particulars (b), (c) and (d) of the statement of claim (article 18, para. 2). The respondent may annex to his statement the documents on which he relies for his defense or may add a reference to the documents or other evidence he will submit.

3. In his statement of defense, or at a later stage in the arbitral proceedings if the arbitral tribunal decides that the delay was justified under the circumstances, the respondent may make a counter-claim arising out of the same contract or rely on a claim arising out of the same contract for the purpose of a set-off.

4. The provisions of article 18, paragraph 2 shall apply to a counter-claim and a claim relied on for the purpose of a set-off.

Amendments to the Claim or Defense

Article 20

During the course of arbitral proceedings either party may amend or supplement his claim or defense unless the arbitral tribunal considers it inappropriate to allow such amendment having regard to the delay in making it or prejudice to the other party or any other circumstances. However, a claim may not be amended in such a manner that the amended claim falls outside the scope of the arbitration clause or separate arbitration agreement.

Pleas as to Arbitrator's Jurisdiction

Article 21

1. The arbitral tribunal shall have the power to rule on objections that it has no jurisdiction, including any objections with respect to the existence or validity of the arbitration clause or of the separate arbitration agreement.

2. The arbitral tribunal shall have the power to determine the existence or the validity of the contract of which an arbitration clause forms a part. For the purposes of article 21, an arbitration clause which forms part of a contract and which provides for arbitration under these Rules shall be treated as an agreement independent of the other terms of the contract. A decision by the arbitral tribunal that the contract is null and void shall not entail *ipso jure* the invalidity of the arbitration clause.

3. A plea that the arbitral tribunal does not have jurisdiction shall be raised not later than in the statement of defense or, with respect to a counter-claim, in the reply to the counter-claim.

4. In general, the arbitral tribunal should rule on a plea concerning its jurisdiction as a preliminary question. However, the arbitral tribunal may proceed with the arbitration and rule on such a plea in their final award.

Further Written Statements

Article 22

The arbitral tribunal shall decide which further written statements, in addition to the statement of claim and the statement of defense, shall be required from the parties or may be presented by them, and shall fix the periods of time for communicating such statements.

Periods of Time

Article 23

The periods of time fixed by the arbitral tribunal for the communication of written statements (including the statement of claim and statement of defense) should not exceed 45 days. However, the arbitral tribunal may extend the time-limits if it concludes that an extension is justified.

Evidence and Hearings (Articles 24 and 25)

Article 24

1. Each party shall have the burden of proving the facts relied on to support his claim or defense.

2. The arbitral tribunal may, if it considers it appropriate, require a party to deliver to each of the arbitrators and to the other party, within such a period of time as the arbitral tribunal shall decide, a summary of the documents and other evidence which that party intends to present in support of the facts in issue set out in his statement of claim or statement of defense.

3. At any time during the arbitral proceedings the arbitral tribunal may require the parties to produce documents, exhibits or other evidence within such a period of time as the tribunal shall determine.

Article 25

1. In the event of an oral hearing, the arbitral tribunal shall give the parties adequate advance notice of the date, time and place thereof.

2. If witnesses are to be heard, at least 15 days before the hearing each party shall communicate to the arbitral tribunal and to the other party the names and addresses of the witnesses he intends to present, the subject upon and the languages in which such witnesses will give their testimony.

3. The arbitral tribunal shall make arrangements for the translation of oral statements made at a hearing and for a record of the hearing if either is deemed necessary by the tribunal under the circumstances of the case, or if the parties have agreed thereto and have communicated such agreement to the tribunal at least 15 days before the hearing.

4. Hearings shall be held in camera unless the parties agree otherwise. The arbitral tribunal may require the retirement of any witness or witnesses during the testimony of other witnesses. The arbitral tribunal is free to determine the manner in which witnesses are examined.

5. Evidence of witnesses may also be presented in the form of written statements signed by them.

6. The arbitral tribunal shall determine the admissibility, relevance, materiality and weight of the evidence offered.

Interim Measures of Protection

Article 26

1. At the request of either party, the arbitral tribunal may take any interim measures it deems necessary in respect of the subject-matter of the dispute, including measures for the conservation of the goods forming the subject-matter in dispute, such as ordering their deposit with a third person or the sale of perishable goods.

2. Such interim measures may be established in the form of an interim award. The arbitral tribunal shall be entitled to require security for the costs of such measures.

3. A request for interim measures addressed by any party to a judicial authority shall not be deemed incompatible with the agreement to arbitrate, or as a waiver of that agreement.

Experts

Article 27

1. The arbitral tribunal may appoint one or more experts to report to it, in writing, on specific issues to be determined by the tribunal. A copy of the expert's terms of reference, established by the arbitrators, shall be communicated to the parties.

2. The parties shall give the expert any relevant information or produce for his inspection any relevant documents or goods that he may

require of them. Any dispute between a party and such expert as to the relevance of the required information or production shall be referred to the arbitral tribunal for decision.

3. Upon receipt of the expert's report, the arbitral tribunal shall communicate a copy of the report to the parties who shall be given the opportunity to express, in writing, their opinion on the report. A party shall be entitled to examine any document on which the expert has relied in his report.

4. At the request of either party the expert, after delivery of the report, may be heard at a hearing where the parties shall have the opportunity to be present and to interrogate the expert. At this hearing either party may present expert witnesses in order to testify on the points at issue. The provisions of article 25 shall be applicable to such proceedings.

Default

Article 28

1. If, within the period of time fixed by the arbitral tribunal, the claimant has failed to communicate his claim, without showing sufficient cause for such failure, the arbitral tribunal shall issue an order for the termination of the arbitral proceedings. If, within the period of time fixed by the arbitral tribunal, the respondent has failed to communicate his statement of defense without showing sufficient cause for such failure, the arbitral tribunal shall order that the proceedings continue.

2. If one of the parties, duly notified under these Rules, fails to appear at a hearing, without showing sufficient cause for such failure, the arbitral tribunal may proceed with the arbitration.

3. If one of the parties, duly invited to produce documentary evidence, fails to do so within the established period of time, without showing sufficient cause for such failure, the arbitral tribunal may make the award on the evidence before it.

Closure of Hearings

Article 29

1. The arbitral tribunal may inquire of the parties if they have any further proofs to offer or witnesses to be heard or submissions to make and, if there are none, it may declare the hearing closed.

2. The arbitral tribunal may, if it considers it necessary owing to exceptional circumstances, decide, on its own motion or upon application of a party, to reopen the hearings at any time before the award is made.

Waiver of Rules

Article 30

A party who knows that any provision of, or requirement under, these Rules has not been complied with and yet proceeds with the arbitration without promptly stating his objection to such non-compliance, shall be deemed to have waived his right to object.

Section IV

The award

Decisions

Article 31

1. When there are three arbitrators, any award or other decision of the arbitral tribunal shall be made by a majority of the arbitrators.

2. In the case of questions of procedure, when there is no majority or when the arbitral tribunal so authorizes, the presiding arbitrator may decide on his own, subject to revision, if any, by the arbitral tribunal.

Form and Effect of the Award

Article 32

1. In addition to making a final award, the arbitral tribunal shall be entitled to make interim, interlocutory, or partial awards.

2. The award shall be made in writing and shall be final and binding on the parties. The parties undertake to carry out the award without delay.

3. The arbitral tribunal shall state the reasons upon which the award is based, unless the parties have agreed that no reasons are to be given.

4. An award shall be signed by the arbitrators and it shall contain the date on which and the place where the award was made. Where there are three arbitrators and one of them fails to sign, the award shall state the reason for the absence of the signature.

5. The award may be made public only with the consent of both parties.

6. Copies of the award signed by the arbitrators shall be communicated to the parties by the arbitral tribunal.

7. If the arbitration law of the country where the award is made requires that the award be filed or registered by the arbitral tribunal, the tribunal shall comply with this requirement within the period of time required by law.

Applicable Law, Amiable Compositeur

Article 33

1. The arbitral tribunal shall apply the law designated by the parties as applicable to the substance of the dispute. Failing such designation by the parties, the arbitral tribunal shall apply the law determined by the conflict of laws rules which it considers applicable.

2. The arbitral tribunal shall decide as *amiable compositeur* or *ex aequo et bono* only if the parties have expressly authorized the arbitral tribunal to do so and if the law applicable to the arbitral procedure permits such arbitration.

3. In all cases, the arbitral tribunal shall decide in accordance with the terms of the contract and shall take into account the usages of the trade applicable to the transaction.

Settlement or Other Grounds for Termination

Article 34

1. If, before the award is made, the parties agree on a settlement of the dispute, the arbitral tribunal shall either issue an order for the termination of the arbitral proceedings or, if requested by both parties and accepted by the tribunal, record the settlement in the form of an arbitral award on agreed terms. The arbitral tribunal is not obliged to give reasons for such an award.

2. If, before the award is made, the continuation of the arbitral proceedings becomes unnecessary or impossible for any reason not mentioned in paragraph 1, the arbitral tribunal shall inform the parties of its intention to issue an order for the termination of the proceedings. The arbitral tribunal shall have the power to issue such an order unless a party raises justifiable grounds for objection.

3. Copies of the order for termination of the arbitral proceedings or of the arbitral award on agreed terms, signed by the arbitrators, shall be communicated by the arbitral tribunal to the parties. Where an arbitral award on agreed terms is made, the provisions of article 32, paragraphs 2 and 4 to 7, shall apply.

Interpretation of the Award

Article 35

1. Within 30 days after the receipt of the award, either party, with notice to the other party, may request that the arbitral tribunal give an interpretation of the award.

2. The interpretation shall be given in writing within 45 days after the receipt of the request. The interpretation shall form part of the award and the provisions of article 32, paragraphs 2 to 7 shall apply.

Correction of the Award

Article 36

1. Within 30 days after the receipt of the award, either party, with notice to the other party, may request the arbitral tribunal to correct in the award any errors in computation, any clerical or typographical errors, or any errors of similar nature. The arbitral tribunal may within 30 days after the communication of the award make such corrections on its own initiative.

2. Such corrections shall be in writing, and the provisions of article 32, paragraphs 2 to 7, shall apply.

Additional Award

Article 37

1. Within 30 days after the receipt of the award, either party, with notice to the other party, may request the arbitral tribunal to make an additional award as to claims presented in the arbitral proceedings but omitted from the award.

2. If the arbitral tribunal considers the request for an additional award to be justified and considers that the omission can be rectified without any further hearing or evidence, it shall complete its award within 60 days after the receipt of the request.

3. When an additional award is made, the provisions of article 32, paragraphs 2 to 7, shall apply.

Costs (Articles 38 to 40)

Article 38

The arbitral tribunal shall fix the costs of arbitration in its award. The term "costs" includes only:

(a) The fees of the arbitral tribunal to be stated separately as to each arbitrator and to be fixed by the tribunal itself in accordance with article 39;

(b) The travel and other expenses incurred by the arbitrators;

(c) The costs of expert advice and of other assistance required by the arbitrators;

(d) The travel and other expenses of witnesses to the extent such expenses are approved by the arbitral tribunal;

(e) The costs for legal representation and assistance of the successful party if such costs were claimed during the arbitral proceedings, and only to the extent that the arbitral tribunal determines that the amount of such costs is reasonable;

(f) Any fees and expenses of the appointing authority as well as the expenses of the Secretary–General of the Permanent Court of Arbitration at The Hague.

Article 39

1. The fees of the arbitral tribunal shall be reasonable in amount, taking into account the amount in dispute, the complexity of the subject-matter, the time spent by the arbitrators and any other relevant circumstances of the case.

2. If an appointing authority has been agreed upon by the parties or designated by the Secretary–General of the Permanent Court of Arbitration at The Hague, and if that authority has issued a schedule of fees for

arbitrators in international cases which it administers, the arbitral tribunal in fixing its fees shall take that schedule of fees into account to the extent that it considers appropriate in the circumstances of the case.

3. If such appointing authority has not issued a schedule of fees for arbitrators in international cases, any party may at any time request the appointing authority to furnish a statement setting forth the basis for establishing fees which is customarily followed in international cases in which the authority appoints arbitrators. If the appointing authority consents to provide such a statement, the arbitral tribunal in fixing its fees shall take such information into account to the extent that it considers appropriate in the circumstances of the case.

4. In cases referred to in paragraphs 2 and 3, when a party so requests and the appointing authority consents to perform the function, the arbitral tribunal shall fix its fees only after consultations with the appointing authority which may make any comment it deems appropriate to the arbitrators concerning the fees.

Article 40

1. Except as provided in paragraph 2, the costs of arbitration shall in principle be borne by the unsuccessful party. However, the arbitral tribunal may apportion each of such costs between the parties if it determines that apportionment is reasonable, taking into account the circumstances of the case.

2. With respect to the costs of legal representation and assistance referred to in article 38, paragraph (e), the arbitral tribunal, taking into account the circumstances of the case, shall be free to determine which party shall bear such costs or may apportion such costs between the parties if it determines that apportionment is reasonable.

3. When the arbitral tribunal issues an order for the termination of the arbitral proceedings or makes an award on agreed terms, it shall fix the costs of arbitration referred to in article 38 and article 39, paragraph 1 in the text of that order or award.

4. No additional fees may be charged by an arbitral tribunal for interpretation or correction or completion of its award under articles 35 to 37.

Deposit of Costs

Article 41

1. The arbitral tribunal, on its establishment, may request each party to deposit an equal amount as an advance for the costs referred to in article 38, paragraphs (a), (b) and (c).

2. During the course of the arbitral proceedings the arbitral tribunal may request supplementary deposits from the parties.

3. If an appointing authority has been agreed upon by the parties or designated by the Secretary–General of the Permanent Court of Arbitra-

tion at The Hague, and when a party so requests and the appointing authority consents to perform the function, the arbitral tribunal shall fix the amounts of any deposits or supplementary deposits only after consultation with the appointing authority which may make any comments to the arbitral tribunal which it deems appropriate concerning the amount of such deposits and supplementary deposits.

4. If the required deposits are not paid in full within 30 days after the receipt of the request, the arbitral tribunal shall so inform the parties in order that one or another of them may make the required payment. If such payment is not made, the arbitral tribunal may order the suspension or termination of the arbitral proceedings.

5. After the award has been made, the arbitral tribunal shall render an accounting to the parties of the deposits received and return any unexpended balance to the parties.

C. UNCITRAL NOTES ON ORGANIZING ARBITRAL PROCEEDINGS, 1996*

INTRODUCTION

Purpose of the Notes

1. The purpose of the Notes is to assist arbitration practitioners by listing and briefly describing questions on which appropriately timed decisions on organizing arbitral proceedings may be useful. The text, prepared with a particular view to international arbitrations, may be used whether or not the arbitration is administered by an arbitral institution.

Non-binding character of the Notes

2. No legal requirement binding on the arbitrators or the parties is imposed by the Notes. The arbitral tribunal remains free to use the Notes as it sees fit and is not required to give reasons for disregarding them.

3. The Notes are not suitable to be used as arbitration rules, since they do not establish any obligation of the arbitral tribunal or the parties to act in a particular way. Accordingly, the use of the Notes cannot imply any modification of the arbitration rules that the parties may have agreed upon.

Discretion in conduct of proceedings and usefulness of timely decisions organizing proceedings

4. Laws governing the arbitral procedure and arbitration rules that parties may agree upon typically allow the arbitral tribunal broad discretion and flexibility in the conduct of arbitral proceedings. This is useful in that it enables the arbitral tribunal to take decisions on the organization of proceedings that take into account the circumstances of the case, the

* The Notes can be found at the UNCITRAL Website at http://www.uncitral.org/pdf/english/texts/arbitration/arb-notes/arb-notes-e.pdf

expectations of the parties and of the members of the arbitral tribunal, and the need for a just and cost-efficient resolution of the dispute.

5. Such discretion may make it desirable for the arbitral tribunal to give the parties a timely indication as to the organization of the proceedings and the manner in which the tribunal intends to proceed. This is particularly desirable in international arbitrations, where the participants may be accustomed to differing styles of conducting arbitrations. Without such guidance, a party may find aspects of the proceedings unpredictable and difficult to prepare for. That may lead to misunderstandings, delays and increased costs.

Multi-party arbitration

6. These Notes are intended for use not only in arbitrations with two parties but also in arbitrations with three or more parties. Use of the Notes in multi-party arbitration is referred to below in paragraphs 86–88 (item 18).

Process of making decisions on organizing arbitral proceedings

7. Decisions by the arbitral tribunal on organizing arbitral proceedings may be taken with or without previous consultations with the parties. The method chosen depends on whether, in view of the type of the question to be decided, the arbitral tribunal considers that consultations are not necessary or that hearing the views of the parties would be beneficial for increasing the predictability of the proceedings or improving the procedural atmosphere.

8. The consultations, whether they involve only the arbitrators or also the parties, can be held in one or more meetings, or can be carried out by correspondence or telecommunications such as telefax or conference telephone calls or other electronic means. Meetings may be held at the venue of arbitration or at some other appropriate location.

9. In some arbitrations a special meeting may be devoted exclusively to such procedural consultations; alternatively, the consultations may be held in conjunction with a hearing on the substance of the dispute. Practices differ as to whether such special meetings should be held and how they should be organized. Special procedural meetings of the arbitrators and the parties separate from hearings are in practice referred to by expressions such as "preliminary meeting", "pre-hearing conference", "preparatory conference", "pre-hearing review", or terms of similar meaning. The terms used partly depend on the stage of the proceedings at which the meeting is taking place.

List of matters for possible consideration in organizing arbitral proceedings

10. The Notes provide a list, followed by annotations, of matters on which the arbitral tribunal may wish to formulate decisions on organizing arbitral proceedings.

11. Given that procedural styles and practices in arbitration vary widely, that the purpose of the Notes is not to promote any practice as best practice, and that the Notes are designed for universal use, it is not attempted in the Notes to describe in detail different arbitral practices or express a preference for any of them.

12. The list, while not exhaustive, covers a broad range of situations that may arise in an arbitration. In many arbitrations, however, only a limited number of the matters mentioned in the list need to be considered. It also depends on the circumstances of the case at which stage or stages of the proceedings it would be useful to consider matters concerning the organization of the proceedings. Generally, in order not to create opportunities for unnecessary discussions and delay, it is advisable not to raise a matter prematurely, i.e. before it is clear that a decision is needed.

13. When the Notes are used, it should be borne in mind that the discretion of the arbitral tribunal in organizing the proceedings may be limited by arbitration rules, by other provisions agreed to by the parties and by the law applicable to the arbitral procedure. When an arbitration is administered by an arbitral institution, various matters discussed in the Notes may be covered by the rules and practices of that institution.

ANNOTATIONS

1. Set of arbitration rules

If the parties have not agreed on a set of arbitration rules, would they wish to do so

14. Sometimes parties who have not included in their arbitration agreement a stipulation that a set of arbitration rules will govern their arbitral proceedings might wish to do so after the arbitration has begun. If that occurs, the UNCITRAL Arbitration Rules may be used either without modification or with such modifications as the parties might wish to agree upon. In the alternative, the parties might wish to adopt the rules of an arbitral institution; in that case, it may be necessary to secure the agreement of that institution and to stipulate the terms under which the arbitration could be carried out in accordance with the rules of that institution.

15. However, caution is advised as consideration of a set of arbitration rules might delay the proceedings or give rise to unnecessary controversy.

16. It should be noted that agreement on arbitration rules is not a necessity and that, if the parties do not agree on a set of arbitration rules, the arbitral tribunal has the power to continue the proceedings and determine how the case will be conducted.

2. Language of proceedings

17. Many rules and laws on arbitral procedure empower the arbitral tribunal to determine the language or languages to be used in the proceedings, if the parties have not reached an agreement thereon.

(a) Possible need for translation of documents, in full or in part

18. Some documents annexed to the statements of claim and defense or submitted later may not be in the language of the proceedings. Bearing in mind the needs of the proceedings and economy, it may be considered whether the arbitral tribunal should order that any of those documents or parts thereof should be accompanied by a translation into the language of the proceedings.

(b) Possible need for interpretation of oral presentations

19. If interpretation will be necessary during oral hearings, it is advisable to consider whether the interpretation will be simultaneous or consecutive and whether the arrangements should be the responsibility of a party or the arbitral tribunal. In an arbitration administered by an institution, interpretation as well as translation services are often arranged by the arbitral institution.

(c) Cost of translation and interpretation

20. In taking decisions about translation or interpretation, it is advisable to decide whether any or all of the costs are to be paid directly by a party or whether they will be paid out of the deposits and apportioned between the parties along with the other arbitration costs.

3. Place of arbitration

(a) Determination of the place of arbitration, if not already agreed upon by the parties

21. Arbitration rules usually allow the parties to agree on the place of arbitration, subject to the requirement of some arbitral institutions that arbitrations under their rules be conducted at a particular place, usually the location of the institution. If the place has not been so agreed upon, the rules governing the arbitration typically provide that it is in the power of the arbitral tribunal or the institution administering the arbitration to determine the place. If the arbitral tribunal is to make that determination, it may wish to hear the views of the parties before doing so.

22. Various factual and legal factors influence the choice of the place of arbitration, and their relative importance varies from case to case. Among the more prominent factors are: (a) suitability of the law on arbitral procedure of the place of arbitration; (b) whether there is a multilateral or bilateral treaty on enforcement of arbitral awards between the State where the arbitration takes place and the State or States where the award may have to be enforced; (c) convenience of the parties and the arbitrators, including the travel distances; (d) availability and cost of support services needed; and (e) location of the subject-matter in dispute and proximity of evidence.

(b) Possibility of meetings outside the place of arbitration

23. Many sets of arbitration rules and laws on arbitral procedure expressly allow the arbitral tribunal to hold meetings elsewhere than at the place of arbitration. For example, under the UNCITRAL Model Law

on International Commercial Arbitration "the arbitral tribunal may, unless otherwise agreed by the parties, meet at any place it considers appropriate for consultation among its members, for hearing witnesses, experts or the parties, or for inspection of goods, other property or documents" (article 20(2)). The purpose of this discretion is to permit arbitral proceedings to be carried out in a manner that is most efficient and economical.

4. Administrative services that may be needed for the arbitral tribunal to carry out its functions

24. Various administrative services (e.g. hearing rooms or secretarial services) may need to be procured for the arbitral tribunal to be able to carry out its functions. When the arbitration is administered by an arbitral institution, the institution will usually provide all or a good part of the required administrative support to the arbitral tribunal. When an arbitration administered by an arbitral institution takes place away from the seat of the institution, the institution may be able to arrange for administrative services to be obtained from another source, often an arbitral institution; some arbitral institutions have entered into cooperation agreements with a view to providing mutual assistance in servicing arbitral proceedings.

25. When the case is not administered by an institution, or the involvement of the institution does not include providing administrative support, usually the administrative arrangements for the proceedings will be made by the arbitral tribunal or the presiding arbitrator; it may also be acceptable to leave some of the arrangements to the parties, or to one of the parties subject to agreement of the other party or parties. Even in such cases, a convenient source of administrative support might be found in arbitral institutions, which often offer their facilities to arbitrations not governed by the rules of the institution. Otherwise, some services could be procured from entities such as chambers of commerce, hotels or specialized firms providing secretarial or other support services.

26. Administrative services might be secured by engaging a secretary of the arbitral tribunal (also referred to as registrar, clerk, administrator or rapporteur), who carries out the tasks under the direction of the arbitral tribunal. Some arbitral institutions routinely assign such persons to the cases administered by them. In arbitrations not administered by an institution or where the arbitral institution does not appoint a secretary, some arbitrators frequently engage such persons, at least in certain types of cases, whereas many others normally conduct the proceedings without them.

27. To the extent the tasks of the secretary are purely organizational (e.g. obtaining meeting rooms and providing or coordinating secretarial services), this is usually not controversial. Differences in views, however, may arise if the tasks include legal research and other professional assistance to the arbitral tribunal (e.g. collecting case law or published commentaries on legal issues defined by the arbitral tribunal, preparing

summaries from case law and publications, and sometimes also preparing drafts of procedural decisions or drafts of certain parts of the award, in particular those concerning the facts of the case). Views or expectations may differ especially where a task of the secretary is similar to professional functions of the arbitrators. Such a role of the secretary is in the view of some commentators inappropriate or is appropriate only under certain conditions, such as that the parties agree thereto. However, it is typically recognized that it is important to ensure that the secretary does not perform any decision-making function of the arbitral tribunal.

5. Deposits in respect of costs

(a) Amount to be deposited

28. In an arbitration administered by an institution, the institution often sets, on the basis of an estimate of the costs of the proceedings, the amount to be deposited as an advance for the costs of the arbitration. In other cases it is customary for the arbitral tribunal to make such an estimate and request a deposit. The estimate typically includes travel and other expenses by the arbitrators, expenditures for administrative assistance required by the arbitral tribunal, costs of any expert advice required by the arbitral tribunal, and the fees for the arbitrators. Many arbitration rules have provisions on this matter, including on whether the deposit should be made by the two parties (or all parties in a multi-party case) or only by the claimant.

(b) Management of deposits

29. When the arbitration is administered by an institution, the institution's services may include managing and accounting for the deposited money. Where that is not the case, it might be useful to clarify matters such as the type and location of the account in which the money will be kept and how the deposits will be managed.

(c) Supplementary deposits

30. If during the course of proceedings it emerges that the costs will be higher than anticipated, supplementary deposits may be required (e.g. because the arbitral tribunal decides pursuant to the arbitration rules to appoint an expert).

6. Confidentiality of information relating to the arbitration; possible agreement thereon

31. It is widely viewed that confidentiality is one of the advantageous and helpful features of arbitration. Nevertheless, there is no uniform answer in national laws as to the extent to which the participants in an arbitration are under the duty to observe the confidentiality of information relating to the case. Moreover, parties that have agreed on arbitration rules or other provisions that do not expressly address the issue of confidentiality cannot assume that all jurisdictions would recognize an implied commitment to confidentiality. Furthermore, the participants in an arbitration might not have the same understanding as regards

the extent of confidentiality that is expected. Therefore, the arbitral tribunal might wish to discuss that with the parties and, if considered appropriate, record any agreed principles on the duty of confidentiality.

32. An agreement on confidentiality might cover, for example, one or more of the following matters: the material or information that is to be kept confidential (e.g. pieces of evidence, written and oral arguments, the fact that the arbitration is taking place, identity of the arbitrators, content of the award); measures for maintaining confidentiality of such information and hearings; whether any special procedures should be employed for maintaining the confidentiality of information transmitted by electronic means (e.g. because communication equipment is shared by several users, or because electronic mail over public networks is considered not sufficiently protected against unauthorized access); circumstances in which confidential information may be disclosed in part or in whole (e.g. in the context of disclosures of information in the public domain, or if required by law or a regulatory body).

7. Routing of written communications among the parties and the arbitrators

33. To the extent the question how documents and other written communications should be routed among the parties and the arbitrators is not settled by the agreed rules, or, if an institution administers the case, by the practices of the institution, it is useful for the arbitral tribunal to clarify the question suitably early so as to avoid misunderstandings and delays.

34. Among various possible patterns of routing, one example is that a party transmits the appropriate number of copies to the arbitral tribunal, or to the arbitral institution, if one is involved, which then forwards them as appropriate. Another example is that a party is to send copies simultaneously to the arbitrators and the other party or parties. Documents and other written communications directed by the arbitral tribunal or the presiding arbitrator to one or more parties may also follow a determined pattern, such as through the arbitral institution or by direct transmission. For some communications, in particular those on organizational matters (e.g. dates for hearings), more direct routes of communication may be agreed, even if, for example, the arbitral institution acts as an intermediary for documents such as the statements of claim and defense, evidence or written arguments.

8. Telefax and other electronic means of sending documents

(a) Telefax

35. Telefax, which offers many advantages over traditional means of communication, is widely used in arbitral proceedings. Nevertheless, should it be thought that, because of the characteristics of the equipment used, it would be preferable not to rely only on a telefacsimile of a document, special arrangements may be considered, such as that a partic-

ular piece of written evidence should be mailed or otherwise physically delivered, or that certain telefax messages should be confirmed by mailing or otherwise delivering documents whose facsimile were transmitted by electronic means. When a document should not be sent by telefax, it may, however, be appropriate, in order to avoid an unnecessarily rigid procedure, for the arbitral tribunal to retain discretion to accept an advance copy of a document by telefax for the purposes of meeting a deadline, provided that the document itself is received within a reasonable time thereafter.

(b) Other electronic means (e.g. electronic mail and magnetic or optical disk)

36. It might be agreed that documents, or some of them, will be exchanged not only in paper-based form, but in addition also in an electronic form other than telefax (e.g. as electronic mail, or on a magnetic or optical disk), or only in electronic form. Since the use of electronic means depends on the aptitude of the persons involved and the availability of equipment and computer programs, agreement is necessary for such means to be used. If both paper-based and electronic means are to be used, it is advisable to decide which one is controlling and, if there is a time-limit for submitting a document, which act constitutes submission.

37. When the exchange of documents in electronic form is planned, it is useful, in order to avoid technical difficulties, to agree on matters such as: data carriers (e.g. electronic mail or computer disks) and their technical characteristics; computer programs to be used in preparing the electronic records; instructions for transforming the electronic records into human-readable form; keeping of logs and back-up records of communications sent and received; information in human-readable form that should accompany the disks (e.g. the names of the originator and recipient, computer program, titles of the electronic files and the back-up methods used); procedures when a message is lost or the communication system otherwise fails; and identification of persons who can be contacted if a problem occurs.

9. Arrangements for the exchange of written submissions

38. After the parties have initially stated their claims and defenses, they may wish, or the arbitral tribunal might request them, to present further written submissions so as to prepare for the hearings or to provide the basis for a decision without hearings. In such submissions, the parties, for example, present or comment on allegations and evidence, cite or explain law, or make or react to proposals. In practice such submissions are referred to variously as, for example, statement, memorial, counter-memorial, brief, counter-brief, reply, réplique, duplique, rebuttal or rejoinder; the terminology is a matter of linguistic usage and the scope or sequence of the submission.

(a) Scheduling of written submissions

39. It is advisable that the arbitral tribunal set time-limits for written submissions. In enforcing the time-limits, the arbitral tribunal may wish, on the one hand, to make sure that the case is not unduly protracted and, on the other hand, to reserve a degree of discretion and allow late submissions if appropriate under the circumstances. In some cases the arbitral tribunal might prefer not to plan the written submissions in advance, thus leaving such matters, including time-limits, to be decided in light of the developments in the proceedings. In other cases, the arbitral tribunal may wish to determine, when scheduling the first written submissions, the number of subsequent submissions.

40. Practices differ as to whether, after the hearings have been held, written submissions are still acceptable. While some arbitral tribunals consider post-hearing submissions unacceptable, others might request or allow them on a particular issue. Some arbitral tribunals follow the procedure according to which the parties are not requested to present written evidence and legal arguments to the arbitral tribunal before the hearings; in such a case, the arbitral tribunal may regard it as appropriate that written submissions be made after the hearings.

(b) Consecutive or simultaneous submissions

41. Written submissions on an issue may be made consecutively, i.e. the party who receives a submission is given a period of time to react with its counter-submission. Another possibility is to request each party to make the submission within the same time period to the arbitral tribunal or the institution administering the case; the received submissions are then forwarded simultaneously to the respective other party or parties. The approach used may depend on the type of issues to be commented upon and the time in which the views should be clarified. With consecutive submissions, it may take longer than with simultaneous ones to obtain views of the parties on a given issue. Consecutive submissions, however, allow the reacting party to comment on all points raised by the other party or parties, which simultaneous submissions do not; thus, simultaneous submissions might possibly necessitate further submissions.

10. Practical details concerning written submissions and evidence (e.g. method of submission, copies, numbering, references)

42. Depending on the volume and kind of documents to be handled, it might be considered whether practical arrangements on details such as the following would be helpful:

- Whether the submissions will be made as paper documents or by electronic means, or both (see paragraphs 35–37);
- The number of copies in which each document is to be submitted;
- A system for numbering documents and items of evidence, and a method for marking them, including by tabs;

- The form of references to documents (e.g. by the heading and the number assigned to the document or its date);
- Paragraph numbering in written submissions, in order to facilitate precise references to parts of a text;
- When translations are to be submitted as paper documents, whether the translations are to be contained in the same volume as the original texts or included in separate volumes.

11. Defining points at issue; order of deciding issues; defining relief or remedy sought

(a) Should a list of points at issue be prepared

43. In considering the parties' allegations and arguments, the arbitral tribunal may come to the conclusion that it would be useful for it or for the parties to prepare, for analytical purposes and for ease of discussion, a list of the points at issue, as opposed to those that are undisputed. If the arbitral tribunal determines that the advantages of working on the basis of such a list outweigh the disadvantages, it chooses the appropriate stage of the proceedings for preparing a list, bearing in mind also that subsequent developments in the proceedings may require a revision of the points at issue. Such an identification of points at issue might help to concentrate on the essential matters, to reduce the number of points at issue by agreement of the parties, and to select the best and most economical process for resolving the dispute. However, possible disadvantages of preparing such a list include delay, adverse effect on the flexibility of the proceedings, or unnecessary disagreements about whether the arbitral tribunal has decided all issues submitted to it or whether the award contains decisions on matters beyond the scope of the submission to arbitration. The terms of reference required under some arbitration rules, or in agreements of parties, may serve the same purpose as the above-described list of points at issue.

(b) In which order should the points at issue be decided

44. While it is often appropriate to deal with all the points at issue collectively, the arbitral tribunal might decide to take them up during the proceedings in a particular order. The order may be due to a point being preliminary relative to another (e.g. a decision on the jurisdiction of the arbitral tribunal is preliminary to consideration of substantive issues, or the issue of responsibility for a breach of contract is preliminary to the issue of the resulting damages). A particular order may be decided also when the breach of various contracts is in dispute or when damages arising from various events are claimed.

45. If the arbitral tribunal has adopted a particular order of deciding points at issue, it might consider it appropriate to issue a decision on one of the points earlier than on the other ones. This might be done, for example, when a discrete part of a claim is ready for decision while the other parts still require extensive consideration, or when it is expected that after deciding certain issues the parties might be more inclined to

settle the remaining ones. Such earlier decisions are referred to by expressions such as "partial", "interlocutory" or "interim" awards or decisions, depending on the type of issue dealt with and on whether the decision is final with respect to the issue it resolves. Questions that might be the subject of such decisions are, for example, jurisdiction of the arbitral tribunal, interim measures of protection, or the liability of a party.

(c) Is there a need to define more precisely the relief or remedy sought

46. If the arbitral tribunal considers that the relief or remedy sought is insufficiently definite, it may wish to explain to the parties the degree of definiteness with which their claims should be formulated. Such an explanation may be useful since criteria are not uniform as to how specific the claimant must be in formulating a relief or remedy.

12. Possible settlement negotiations and their effect on scheduling proceedings

47. Attitudes differ as to whether it is appropriate for the arbitral tribunal to bring up the possibility of settlement. Given the divergence of practices in this regard, the arbitral tribunal should only suggest settlement negotiations with caution. However, it may be opportune for the arbitral tribunal to schedule the proceedings in a way that might facilitate the continuation or initiation of settlement negotiations.

13. Documentary evidence

(a) Time-limits for submission of documentary evidence intended to be submitted by the parties; consequences of late submission

48. Often the written submissions of the parties contain sufficient information for the arbitral tribunal to fix the time-limit for submitting evidence. Otherwise, in order to set realistic time periods, the arbitral tribunal may wish to consult with the parties about the time that they would reasonably need.

49. The arbitral tribunal may wish to clarify that evidence submitted late will as a rule not be accepted. It may wish not to preclude itself from accepting a late submission of evidence if the party shows sufficient cause for the delay.

(b) Whether the arbitral tribunal intends to require a party to produce documentary evidence

50. Procedures and practices differ widely as to the conditions under which the arbitral tribunal may require a party to produce documents. Therefore, the arbitral tribunal might consider it useful, when the agreed arbitration rules do not provide specific conditions, to clarify to the parties the manner in which it intends to proceed.

51. The arbitral tribunal may wish to establish time-limits for the production of documents. The parties might be reminded that, if the requested party duly invited to produce documentary evidence fails to do

so within the established period of time, without showing sufficient cause for such failure, the arbitral tribunal is free to draw its conclusions from the failure and may make the award on the evidence before it.

(c) Should assertions about the origin and receipt of documents and about the correctness of photocopies be assumed as accurate

52. It may be helpful for the arbitral tribunal to inform the parties that it intends to conduct the proceedings on the basis that, unless a party raises an objection to any of the following conclusions within a specified period of time: (a) a document is accepted as having originated from the source indicated in the document; (b) a copy of a dispatched communication (e.g. letter, telex, telefax or other electronic message) is accepted without further proof as having been received by the addressee; and (c) a copy is accepted as correct. A statement by the arbitral tribunal to that effect can simplify the introduction of documentary evidence and discourage unfounded and dilatory objections, at a late stage of the proceedings, to the probative value of documents. It is advisable to provide that the time-limit for objections will not be enforced if the arbitral tribunal considers the delay justified.

(d) Are the parties willing to submit jointly a single set of documentary evidence

53. The parties may consider submitting jointly a single set of documentary evidence whose authenticity is not disputed. The purpose would be to avoid duplicate submissions and unnecessary discussions concerning the authenticity of documents, without prejudicing the position of the parties concerning the content of the documents. Additional documents may be inserted later if the parties agree. When a single set of documents would be too voluminous to be easily manageable, it might be practical to select a number of frequently used documents and establish a set of "working" documents. A convenient arrangement of documents in the set may be according to chronological order or subject-matter. It is useful to keep a table of contents of the documents, for example, by their short headings and dates, and to provide that the parties will refer to documents by those headings and dates.

(e) Should voluminous and complicated documentary evidence be presented through summaries, tabulations, charts, extracts or samples

54. When documentary evidence is voluminous and complicated, it may save time and costs if such evidence is presented by a report of a person competent in the relevant field (e.g. public accountant or consulting engineer). The report may present the information in the form of summaries, tabulations, charts, extracts or samples. Such presentation of evidence should be combined with arrangements that give the interested party the opportunity to review the underlying data and the methodology of preparing the report.

14. Physical evidence other than documents

55. In some arbitrations the arbitral tribunal is called upon to assess physical evidence other than documents, for example, by inspecting sam-

ples of goods, viewing a video recording or observing the functioning of a machine.

(a) What arrangements should be made if physical evidence will be submitted

56. If physical evidence will be submitted, the arbitral tribunal may wish to fix the time schedule for presenting the evidence, make arrangements for the other party or parties to have a suitable opportunity to prepare itself for the presentation of the evidence, and possibly take measures for safekeeping the items of evidence.

(b) What arrangements should be made if an on-site inspection is necessary

57. If an on-site inspection of property or goods will take place, the arbitral tribunal may consider matters such as timing, meeting places, other arrangements to provide the opportunity for all parties to be present, and the need to avoid communications between arbitrators and a party about points at issue without the presence of the other party or parties.

58. The site to be inspected is often under the control of one of the parties, which typically means that employees or representatives of that party will be present to give guidance and explanations. It should be borne in mind that statements of those representatives or employees made during an on-site inspection, as contrasted with statements those persons might make as witnesses in a hearing, should not be treated as evidence in the proceedings.

15. Witnesses

59. While laws and rules on arbitral procedure typically leave broad freedom concerning the manner of taking evidence of witnesses, practices on procedural points are varied. In order to facilitate the preparations of the parties for the hearings, the arbitral tribunal may consider it appropriate to clarify, in advance of the hearings, some or all of the following issues.

(a) Advance notice about a witness whom a party intends to present; written witnesses' statements

60. To the extent the applicable arbitration rules do not deal with the matter, the arbitral tribunal may wish to require that each party give advance notice to the arbitral tribunal and the other party or parties of any witness it intends to present. As to the content of the notice, the following is an example of what might be required, in addition to the names and addresses of the witnesses: (a) the subject upon which the witnesses will testify; (b) the language in which the witnesses will testify; and (c) the nature of the relationship with any of the parties, qualifications and experience of the witnesses if and to the extent these are relevant to the dispute or the testimony, and how the witnesses learned about the facts on which they will testify. However, it may not be

necessary to require such a notice, in particular if the thrust of the testimony can be clearly ascertained from the party's allegations.

61. Some practitioners favour the procedure according to which the party presenting witness evidence submits a signed witness's statement containing testimony itself. It should be noted, however, that such practice, which implies interviewing the witness by the party presenting the testimony, is not known in all parts of the world and, moreover, that some practitioners disapprove of it on the ground that such contacts between the party and the witness may compromise the credibility of the testimony and are therefore improper (see paragraph 67). Notwithstanding these reservations, signed witness's testimony has advantages in that it may expedite the proceedings by making it easier for the other party or parties to prepare for the hearings or for the parties to identify uncontested matters. However, those advantages might be outweighed by the time and expense involved in obtaining the written testimony.

62. If a signed witness's statement should be made under oath or similar affirmation of truthfulness, it may be necessary to clarify by whom the oath or affirmation should be administered and whether any formal authentication will be required by the arbitral tribunal.

(b) Manner of taking oral evidence of witnesses

(i) Order in which questions will be asked and the manner in which the hearing of witnesses will be conducted

63. To the extent that the applicable rules do not provide an answer, it may be useful for the arbitral tribunal to clarify how witnesses will be heard. One of the various possibilities is that a witness is first questioned by the arbitral tribunal, whereupon questions are asked by the parties, first by the party who called the witness. Another possibility is for the witness to be questioned by the party presenting the witness and then by the other party or parties, while the arbitral tribunal might pose questions during the questioning or after the parties on points that in the tribunal's view have not been sufficiently clarified. Differences exist also as to the degree of control the arbitral tribunal exercises over the hearing of witnesses. For example, some arbitrators prefer to permit the parties to pose questions freely and directly to the witness, but may disallow a question if a party objects; other arbitrators tend to exercise more control and may disallow a question on their initiative or even require that questions from the parties be asked through the arbitral tribunal.

(ii) Whether oral testimony will be given under oath or affirmation and, if so, in what form an oath or affirmation should be made

64. Practices and laws differ as to whether or not oral testimony is to be given under oath or affirmation. In some legal systems, the arbitrators are empowered to put witnesses on oath, but it is usually in their discretion whether they want to do so. In other systems, oral testimony under oath is either unknown or may even be considered improper as only

an official such as a judge or notary may have the authority to administer oaths.

(iii) May witnesses be in the hearing room when they are not testifying

65. Some arbitrators favour the procedure that, except if the circumstances suggest otherwise, the presence of a witness in the hearing room is limited to the time the witness is testifying; the purpose is to prevent the witness from being influenced by what is said in the hearing room, or to prevent that the presence of the witness would influence another witness. Other arbitrators consider that the presence of a witness during the testimony of other witnesses may be beneficial in that possible contradictions may be readily clarified or that their presence may act as a deterrent against untrue statements. Other possible approaches may be that witnesses are not present in the hearing room before their testimony, but stay in the room after they have testified, or that the arbitral tribunal decides the question for each witness individually depending on what the arbitral tribunal considers most appropriate. The arbitral tribunal may leave the procedure to be decided during the hearings, or may give guidance on the question in advance of the hearings.

(c) The order in which the witnesses will be called

66. When several witnesses are to be heard and longer testimony is expected, it is likely to reduce costs if the order in which they will be called is known in advance and their presence can be scheduled accordingly. Each party might be invited to suggest the order in which it intends to present the witnesses, while it would be up to the arbitral tribunal to approve the scheduling and to make departures from it.

(d) Interviewing witnesses prior to their appearance at a hearing

67. In some legal systems, parties or their representatives are permitted to interview witnesses, prior to their appearance at the hearing, as to such matters as their recollection of the relevant events, their experience, qualifications or relation with a participant in the proceedings. In those legal systems such contacts are usually not permitted once the witness's oral testimony has begun. In other systems such contacts with witnesses are considered improper. In order to avoid misunderstandings, the arbitral tribunal may consider it useful to clarify what kind of contacts a party is permitted to have with a witness in the preparations for the hearings.

(e) Hearing representatives of a party

68. According to some legal systems, certain persons affiliated with a party may only be heard as representatives of the party but not as witnesses. In such a case, it may be necessary to consider ground rules for determining which persons may not testify as witnesses (e.g. certain executives, employees or agents) and for hearing statements of those persons and for questioning them.

16. Experts and expert witnesses

69. Many arbitration rules and laws on arbitral procedure address the participation of experts in arbitral proceedings. A frequent solution is that the arbitral tribunal has the power to appoint an expert to report on issues determined by the tribunal; in addition, the parties may be permitted to present expert witnesses on points at issue. In other cases, it is for the parties to present expert testimony, and it is not expected that the arbitral tribunal will appoint an expert.

(a) Expert appointed by the arbitral tribunal

70. If the arbitral tribunal is empowered to appoint an expert, one possible approach is for the tribunal to proceed directly to selecting the expert. Another possibility is to consult the parties as to who should be the expert; this may be done, for example, without mentioning a candidate, by presenting to the parties a list of candidates, soliciting proposals from the parties, or by discussing with the parties the "profile" of the expert the arbitral tribunal intends to appoint, i.e. the qualifications, experience and abilities of the expert.

(i) The expert's terms of reference

71. The purpose of the expert's terms of reference is to indicate the questions on which the expert is to provide clarification, to avoid opinions on points that are not for the expert to assess and to commit the expert to a time schedule. While the discretion to appoint an expert normally includes the determination of the expert's terms of reference, the arbitral tribunal may decide to consult the parties before finalizing the terms. It might also be useful to determine details about how the expert will receive from the parties any relevant information or have access to any relevant documents, goods or other property, so as to enable the expert to prepare the report. In order to facilitate the evaluation of the expert's report, it is advisable to require the expert to include in the report information on the method used in arriving at the conclusions and the evidence and information used in preparing the report.

(ii) The opportunity of the parties to comment on the expert's report, including by presenting expert testimony

72. Arbitration rules that contain provisions on experts usually also have provisions on the right of a party to comment on the report of the expert appointed by the arbitral tribunal. If no such provisions apply or more specific procedures than those prescribed are deemed necessary, the arbitral tribunal may, in light of those provisions, consider it opportune to determine, for example, the time period for presenting written comments of the parties, or, if hearings are to be held for the purpose of hearing the expert, the procedures for interrogating the expert by the parties or for the participation of any expert witnesses presented by the parties.

(b) Expert opinion presented by a party (expert witness)

73. If a party presents an expert opinion, the arbitral tribunal might consider requiring, for example, that the opinion be in writing, that the

expert should be available to answer questions at hearings, and that, if a party will present an expert witness at a hearing, advance notice must be given or that the written opinion must be presented in advance, as in the case of other witnesses (see paragraphs 60–62).

17. Hearings

(a) Decision whether to hold hearings

74. Laws on arbitral procedure and arbitration rules often have provisions as to the cases in which oral hearings must be held and as to when the arbitral tribunal has discretion to decide whether to hold hearings.

75. If it is up to the arbitral tribunal to decide whether to hold hearings, the decision is likely to be influenced by factors such as, on the one hand, that it is usually quicker and easier to clarify points at issue pursuant to a direct confrontation of arguments than on the basis of correspondence and, on the other hand, the travel and other cost of holding hearings, and that the need of finding acceptable dates for the hearings might delay the proceedings. The arbitral tribunal may wish to consult the parties on this matter.

(b) Whether one period of hearings should be held or separate periods of hearings

76. Attitudes vary as to whether hearings should be held in a single period of hearings or in separate periods, especially when more than a few days are needed to complete the hearings. According to some arbitrators, the entire hearings should normally be held in a single period, even if the hearings are to last for more than a week. Other arbitrators in such cases tend to schedule separate periods of hearings. In some cases issues to be decided are separated, and separate hearings set for those issues, with the aim that oral presentation on those issues will be completed within the allotted time. Among the advantages of one period of hearings are that it involves less travel costs, memory will not fade, and it is unlikely that people representing a party will change. On the other hand, the longer the hearings, the more difficult it may be to find early dates acceptable to all participants. Furthermore, separate periods of hearings may be easier to schedule, the subsequent hearings may be tailored to the development of the case, and the period between the hearings leaves time for analyzing the records and negotiations between the parties aimed at narrowing the points at issue by agreement.

(c) Setting dates for hearings

77. Typically, firm dates will be fixed for hearings. Exceptionally, the arbitral tribunal may initially wish to set only "target dates" as opposed to definitive dates. This may be done at a stage of the proceedings when not all information necessary to schedule hearings is yet available, with the understanding that the target dates will either be confirmed or rescheduled within a reasonably short period. Such provisional planning

can be useful to participants who are generally not available on short notice.

(d) Whether there should be a limit on the aggregate amount of time each party will have for oral arguments and questioning witnesses

78. Some arbitrators consider it useful to limit the aggregate amount of time each party has for any of the following: (a) making oral statements; (b) questioning its witnesses; and (c) questioning the witnesses of the other party or parties. In general, the same aggregate amount of time is considered appropriate for each party, unless the arbitral tribunal considers that a different allocation is justified. Before deciding, the arbitral tribunal may wish to consult the parties as to how much time they think they will need.

79. Such planning of time, provided it is realistic, fair and subject to judiciously firm control by the arbitral tribunal, will make it easier for the parties to plan the presentation of the various items of evidence and arguments, reduce the likelihood of running out of time towards the end of the hearings and avoid that one party would unfairly use up a disproportionate amount of time.

(e) The order in which the parties will present their arguments and evidence

80. Arbitration rules typically give broad latitude to the arbitral tribunal to determine the order of presentations at the hearings. Within that latitude, practices differ, for example, as to whether opening or closing statements are heard and their level of detail; the sequence in which the claimant and the respondent present their opening statements, arguments, witnesses and other evidence; and whether the respondent or the claimant has the last word. In view of such differences, or when no arbitration rules apply, it may foster efficiency of the proceedings if the arbitral tribunal clarifies to the parties, in advance of the hearings, the manner in which it will conduct the hearings, at least in broad lines.

(f) Length of hearings

81. The length of a hearing primarily depends on the complexity of the issues to be argued and the amount of witness evidence to be presented. The length also depends on the procedural style used in the arbitration. Some practitioners prefer to have written evidence and written arguments presented before the hearings, which thus can focus on the issues that have not been sufficiently clarified. Those practitioners generally tend to plan shorter hearings than those practitioners who prefer that most if not all evidence and arguments are presented to the arbitral tribunal orally and in full detail. In order to facilitate the parties' preparations and avoid misunderstandings, the arbitral tribunal may wish to clarify to the parties, in advance of the hearings, the intended use of time and style of work at the hearings.

(g) Arrangements for a record of the hearings

82. The arbitral tribunal should decide, possibly after consulting with the parties, on the method of preparing a record of oral statements and testimony during hearings. Among different possibilities, one method is that the members of the arbitral tribunal take personal notes. Another is that the presiding arbitrator during the hearing dictates to a typist a summary of oral statements and testimony. A further method, possible when a secretary of the arbitral tribunal has been appointed, may be to leave to that person the preparation of a summary record. A useful, though costly, method is for professional stenographers to prepare verbatim transcripts, often within the next day or a similarly short time period. A written record may be combined with tape-recording, so as to enable reference to the tape in case of a disagreement over the written record.

83. If transcripts are to be produced, it may be considered how the persons who made the statements will be given an opportunity to check the transcripts. For example, it may be determined that the changes to the record would be approved by the parties or, failing their agreement, would be referred for decision to the arbitral tribunal.

(h) Whether and when the parties are permitted to submit notes summarizing their oral arguments

84. Some legal counsel are accustomed to giving notes summarizing their oral arguments to the arbitral tribunal and to the other party or parties. If such notes are presented, this is usually done during the hearings or shortly thereafter; in some cases, the notes are sent before the hearing. In order to avoid surprise, foster equal treatment of the parties and facilitate preparations for the hearings, advance clarification is advisable as to whether submitting such notes is acceptable and the time for doing so.

85. In closing the hearings, the arbitral tribunal will normally assume that no further proof is to be offered or submission to be made. Therefore, if notes are to be presented to be read after the closure of the hearings, the arbitral tribunal may find it worthwhile to stress that the notes should be limited to summarizing what was said orally and in particular should not refer to new evidence or new argument.

18. Multi-party arbitration

86. When a single arbitration involves more than two parties (multi-party arbitration), considerations regarding the need to organize arbitral proceedings, and matters that may be considered in that connection, are generally not different from two-party arbitrations. A possible difference may be that, because of the need to deal with more than two parties, multi-party proceedings can be more complicated to manage than bilateral proceedings. The Notes, notwithstanding a possible greater complexity of multi-party arbitration, can be used in multi-party as well as in two-party proceedings.

87. The areas of possibly increased complexity in multi-party arbitration are, for example, the flow of communications among the parties

and the arbitral tribunal (see paragraphs 33, 34 and 38–41); if points at issue are to be decided at different points in time, the order of deciding them (paragraphs 44–45); the manner in which the parties will participate in hearing witnesses (paragraph 63); the appointment of experts and the participation of the parties in considering their reports (paragraphs 70–72); the scheduling of hearings (paragraph 76); the order in which the parties will present their arguments and evidence at hearings (paragraph 80).

88. The Notes, which are limited to pointing out matters that may be considered in organizing arbitral proceedings in general, do not cover the drafting of the arbitration agreement or the constitution of the arbitral tribunal, both issues that give rise to special questions in multiparty arbitration as compared to two-party arbitration.

19. Possible requirements concerning filing or delivering the award

89. Some national laws require that arbitral awards be filed or registered with a court or similar authority, or that they be delivered in a particular manner or through a particular authority. Those laws differ with respect to, for example, the type of award to which the requirement applies (e.g. to all awards or only to awards not rendered under the auspices of an arbitral institution); time periods for filing, registering or delivering the award (in some cases those time periods may be rather short); or consequences for failing to comply with the requirement (which might be, for example, invalidity of the award or inability to enforce it in a particular manner).

Who should take steps to fulfil any requirement

90. If such a requirement exists, it is useful, some time before the award is to be issued, to plan who should take the necessary steps to meet the requirement and how the costs are to be borne.

D. IBA RULES ON THE TAKING OF EVIDENCE IN INTERNATIONAL COMMERCIAL ARBITRATION*

(Adopted by a resolution of the International Bar Association Council, 1 June 1999)

Preamble

1. These IBA Rules on the Taking of Evidence in International Commercial Arbitration (the "IBA Rules of Evidence") are intended to govern in an efficient and economical manner the taking of evidence in international

* Document can be found on the International Bar Association website at http://www.ibanet.org/images/downloads/pubs/IBA–Rules-on-Taking-of-Evidence.pdf

commercial arbitrations, particularly those between Parties from different legal traditions. They are designed to supplement the legal provisions and the institutional or *ad hoc* rules according to which the Parties are conducting their arbitration.

2. Parties and Arbitral Tribunals may adopt the IBA Rules of Evidence, in whole or in part, to govern arbitration proceedings, or they may vary them or use them as guidelines in developing their own procedures. The Rules are not intended to limit the flexibility that is inherent in, and an advantage of, international arbitration, and Parties and Arbitral Tribunals are free to adapt them to the particular circumstances of each arbitration.

3. Each Arbitral Tribunal is encouraged to identify to the Parties, as soon as it considers it to be appropriate, the issues that it may regard as relevant and material to the outcome of the case, including issues where a preliminary determination may be appropriate.

4. The taking of evidence shall be conducted on the principle that each Party shall be entitled to know, reasonably in advance of any evidentiary Hearing, the evidence on which the other Parties rely.

Article 1

Definitions

In the IBA Rules of Evidence:

"*Arbitral Tribunal*" means a sole arbitrator or a panel of arbitrators validly deciding by majority or otherwise;

"*Claimant*" means the Party or Parties who commenced the arbitration and any Party who, through joinder or otherwise, becomes aligned with such Party or Parties;

"*Document*" means a writing of any kind, whether recorded on paper, electronic means, audio or visual recordings or any other mechanical or electronic means of storing or recording information;

"*Evidentiary Hearing*" means any hearing, whether or not held on consecutive days, at which the Arbitral Tribunal receives oral evidence;

"*Expert Report*" means a written statement by a Tribunal-Appointed Expert or a Party–Appointed Expert submitted pursuant to the IBA Rules of Evidence;

"*General Rules*" mean the institutional or *ad hoc* rules according to which the Parties are conducting their arbitration;

"*Party*" means a party to the arbitration;

"*Party-Appointed Expert*" means an expert witness presented by a Party;

"*Request to Produce*" means a request by a Party for a procedural order by which the Arbitral Tribunal would direct another Party to produce documents;

"*Respondent*" means the Party or Parties against whom the Claimant made its claim, and any Party who, through joinder or otherwise, becomes aligned with such Party or Parties, and includes a Respondent making a counter-claim;

"*Tribunal-Appointed Expert*" means a person or organization appointed by the Arbitral Tribunal in order to report to it on specific issues determined by the Arbitral Tribunal.

Article 2

Scope of Application

1. Whenever the Parties have agreed or the Arbitral Tribunal has determined to apply the IBA Rules of Evidence, the Rules shall govern the taking of evidence, except to the extent that any specific provision of them may be found to be in conflict with any mandatory provision of law determined to be applicable to the case by the Parties or by the Arbitral Tribunal.

2. In case of conflict between any provisions of the IBA Rules of Evidence and the General Rules, the Arbitral Tribunal shall apply the IBA Rules of Evidence in the manner that it determines best in order to accomplish the purposes of both the General Rules and the IBA Rules of Evidence, unless the Parties agree to the contrary.

3. In the event of any dispute regarding the meaning of the IBA Rules of Evidence, the Arbitral Tribunal shall interpret them according to their purpose and in the manner most appropriate for the particular arbitration.

4. Insofar as the IBA Rules of Evidence and the General Rules are silent on any matter concerning the taking of evidence and the Parties have not agreed otherwise, the Arbitral Tribunal may conduct the taking of evidence as it deems appropriate, in accordance with the general principles of the IBA Rules of Evidence.

Article 3

Documents

1. Within the time ordered by the Arbitral Tribunal, each Party shall submit to the Arbitral Tribunal and to the other Parties all documents available to it on which it relies, including public documents and those in the public domain, except for any documents that have already been submitted by another Party.

2. Within the time ordered by the Arbitral Tribunal, any Party may submit to the Arbitral Tribunal a Request to Produce.

3. A Request to Produce shall contain:

(a) (*i*) a description of a requested document sufficient to identify it, or

(*ii*) a description in sufficient detail (including subject matter) of a narrow and specific requested category of documents that are reasonably believed to exist;

(b) a description of how the documents requested are relevant and material to the outcome of the case; and

(c) a statement that the documents requested are not in the possession, custody or control of the requesting Party, and of the reason why that Party assumes the documents requested to be in the possession, custody or control of the other Party.

4. Within the time ordered by the Arbitral Tribunal, the Party to whom the Request to Produce is addressed shall produce to the Arbitral Tribunal and to the other Parties all the documents requested in its possession, custody or control as to which no objection is made.

5. If the Party to whom the Request to Produce is addressed has objections to some or all of the documents requested, it shall state them in writing to the Arbitral Tribunal within the time ordered by the Arbitral Tribunal. The reasons for such objections shall be any of those set forth in Article 9.2.

6. The Arbitral Tribunal shall, in consultation with the Parties and in timely fashion, consider the Request to Produce and the objections. The Arbitral Tribunal may order the Party to whom such Request is addressed to produce to the Arbitral Tribunal and to the other Parties those requested documents in its possession, custody or control as to which the Arbitral Tribunal determines that (*i*) the issues that the requesting Party wishes to prove are relevant and material to the outcome of the case, and (*ii*) none of the reasons for objection set forth in Article 9.2 apply.

7. In exceptional circumstances, if the propriety of an objection can only be determined by review of the document, the Arbitral Tribunal may determine that it should not review the document. In that event, the Arbitral Tribunal may, after consultation with the Parties, appoint an independent and impartial expert, bound to confidentiality, to review any such document and to report on the objection. To the extent that the objection is upheld by the Arbitral Tribunal, the expert shall not disclose to the Arbitral Tribunal and to the other Parties the contents of the document reviewed.

8. If a Party wishes to obtain the production of documents from a person or organization who is not a Party to the arbitration and from whom the Party cannot obtain the documents on its own, the Party may, within the time ordered by the Arbitral Tribunal, ask it to take whatever steps are legally available to obtain the requested documents. The Party shall identify the documents in sufficient detail and state why such documents are relevant and material to the outcome of the case. The Arbitral Tribunal shall decide on this request and shall take the necessary steps if in its discretion it determines that the documents would be relevant and material.

9. The Arbitral Tribunal, at any time before the arbitration is concluded, may request a Party to produce to the Arbitral Tribunal and to the other Parties any documents that it believes to be relevant and material to the outcome of the case. A Party may object to such a request based on any of

the reasons set forth in Article 9.2. If a Party raises such an objection, the Arbitral Tribunal shall decide whether to order the production of such documents based upon the considerations set forth in Article 3.6 and, if the Arbitral Tribunal considers it appropriate, through the use of the procedures set forth in Article 3.7.

10. Within the time ordered by the Arbitral Tribunal, the Parties may submit to the Arbitral Tribunal and to the other Parties any additional documents which they believe have become relevant and material as a consequence of the issues raised in documents, Witness Statements or Expert Reports submitted or produced by another Party or in other submissions of the Parties.

11. If copies are submitted or produced, they must conform fully to the originals. At the request of the Arbitral Tribunal, any original must be presented for inspection.

12. All documents produced by a Party pursuant to the IBA Rules of Evidence (or by a non-Party pursuant to Article 3.8) shall be kept confidential by the Arbitral Tribunal and by the other Parties, and they shall be used only in connection with the arbitration. The Arbitral Tribunal may issue orders to set forth the terms of this confidentiality. This requirement is without prejudice to all other obligations of confidentiality in arbitration.

Article 4

Witnesses of Fact

1. Within the time ordered by the Arbitral Tribunal, each Party shall identify the witnesses on whose testimony it relies and the subject matter of that testimony.

2. Any person may present evidence as a witness, including a Party or a Party officer, employee or other representative.

3. It shall not be improper for a Party, its officers, employees, legal advisors or other representatives to interview its witnesses or potential witnesses.

4. The Arbitral Tribunal may order each Party to submit within a specified time to the Arbitral Tribunal and to the other Parties a written statement by each witness on whose testimony it relies, except for those witnesses whose testimony is sought pursuant to Article 4.10 (the "Witness Statement"). If Evidentiary Hearings are organized on separate issues (such as liability and damages), the Arbitral Tribunal or the Parties by agreement may schedule the submission of Witness Statements separately for each Evidentiary Hearing.

5. Each Witness Statement shall contain:

a) the full name and address of the witness, his or her present and past relationship (if any) with any of the Parties, and a description of his or her background, qualifications, training and experience, if such a description may be relevant and material to the dispute or to the contents of the statement;

b) a full and detailed description of the facts, and the source of the witness information as to those facts, sufficient to serve as that witness evidence in the matter in dispute;

(c) an affirmation of the truth of the statement; and

(d) the signature of the witness and its date and place.

6. If Witness Statements are submitted, any Party may, within the time ordered by the Arbitral Tribunal, submit to the Arbitral Tribunal and to the other Parties revised or additional Witness Statements, including statements from persons not previously named as witnesses, so long as any such revisions or additions only respond to matters contained in another Party Witness Statement or Expert Report and such matters have not been previously presented in the arbitration.

7. Each witness who has submitted a Witness Statement shall appear for testimony at an Evidentiary Hearing, unless the Parties agree otherwise.

8. If a witness who has submitted a Witness Statement does not appear without a valid reason for testimony at an Evidentiary Hearing, except by agreement of the Parties, the Arbitral Tribunal shall disregard that Witness Statement unless, in exceptional circumstances, the Arbitral Tribunal determines otherwise.

9. If the Parties agree that a witness who has submitted a Witness Statement does not need to appear for testimony at an Evidentiary Hearing, such an agreement shall not be considered to reflect an agreement as to the correctness of the content of the Witness Statement.

10. If a Party wishes to present evidence from a person who will not appear voluntarily at its request, the Party may, within the time ordered by the Arbitral Tribunal, ask it to take whatever steps are legally available to obtain the testimony of that person. The Party shall identify the intended witness, shall describe the subjects on which the witness testimony is sought and shall state why such subjects are relevant and material to the outcome of the case. The Arbitral Tribunal shall decide on this request and shall take the necessary steps if in its discretion it determines that the testimony of that witness would be relevant and material.

11. The Arbitral Tribunal may, at any time before the arbitration is concluded, order any Party to provide, or to use its best efforts to provide, the appearance for testimony at an Evidentiary Hearing of any person, including one whose testimony has not yet been offered.

Article 5

Party-Appointed Experts

1. A Party may rely on a Party–Appointed Expert as a means of evidence on specific issues. Within the time ordered by the Arbitral Tribunal, a Party-Appointed Expert shall submit an Expert Report.

2. The Expert Report shall contain:

(a) the full name and address of the Party-Appointed Expert, his or her present and past relationship (if any) with any of the Parties, and a description of his or her background, qualifications, training and experience;

(b) a statement of the facts on which he or she is basing his or her expert opinions and conclusions;

(c) his or her expert opinions and conclusions, including a description of the method, evidence and information used in arriving at the conclusions;

(d) an affirmation of the truth of the Expert Report; and

(e) the signature of the Party-Appointed Expert and its date and place.

3. The Arbitral Tribunal in its discretion may order that any Party–Appointed Experts who have submitted Expert Reports on the same or related issues meet and confer on such issues. At such meeting, the Party–Appointed Experts shall attempt to reach agreement on those issues as to which they had differences of opinion in their Expert Reports, and they shall record in writing any such issues on which they reach agreement.

4. Each Party–Appointed Expert shall appear for testimony at an Evidentiary Hearing, unless the Parties agree otherwise and the Arbitral Tribunal accepts this agreement.

5. If a Party–Appointed Expert does not appear without a valid reason for testimony at an Evidentiary Hearing, except by agreement of the Parties accepted by the Arbitral Tribunal, the Arbitral Tribunal shall disregard his or her Expert Report unless, in exceptional circumstances, the Arbitral Tribunal determines otherwise.

6. If the Parties agree that a Party–Appointed Expert does not need to appear for testimony at an Evidentiary Hearing, such an agreement shall not be considered to reflect an agreement as to the correctness of the content of the Expert Report.

Article 6

Tribunal-Appointed Experts

1. The Arbitral Tribunal, after having consulted with the Parties, may appoint one or more independent Tribunal–Appointed Experts to report to it on specific issues designated by the Arbitral Tribunal. The Arbitral Tribunal shall establish the terms of reference for any Tribunal–Appointed Expert report after having consulted with the Parties. A copy of the final terms of reference shall be sent by the Arbitral Tribunal to the Parties.

2. The Tribunal–Appointed Expert shall, before accepting appointment, submit to the Arbitral Tribunal and to the Parties a statement of his or her independence from the Parties and the Arbitral Tribunal. Within the time ordered by the Arbitral Tribunal, the Parties shall inform the

Arbitral Tribunal whether they have any objections to the Tribunal–Appointed Expert independence. The Arbitral Tribunal shall decide promptly whether to accept any such objection.

3. Subject to the provisions of Article 9.2, the Tribunal–Appointed Expert may request a Party to provide any relevant and material information or to provide access to any relevant documents, goods, samples, property or site for inspection. The authority of a Tribunal–Appointed Expert to request such information or access shall be the same as the authority of the Arbitral Tribunal. The Parties and their representatives shall have the right to receive any such information and to attend any such inspection. Any disagreement between a Tribunal-Appointed Expert and a Party as to the relevance, materiality or appropriateness of such a request shall be decided by the Arbitral Tribunal, in the manner provided in Articles 3.5 through 3.7. The Tribunal-Appointed Expert shall record in the report any non-compliance by a Party with an appropriate request or decision by the Arbitral Tribunal and shall describe its effects on the determination of the specific issue.

4. The Tribunal–Appointed Expert shall report in writing to the Arbitral Tribunal. The Tribunal-Appointed Expert shall describe in the report the method, evidence and information used in arriving at the conclusions.

5. The Arbitral Tribunal shall send a copy of such Expert Report to the Parties. The Parties may examine any document that the Tribunal-Appointed Expert has examined and any correspondence between the Arbitral Tribunal and the Tribunal–Appointed Expert. Within the time ordered by the Arbitral Tribunal, any Party shall have the opportunity to respond to the report in a submission by the Party or through an Expert Report by a Party–Appointed Expert. The Arbitral Tribunal shall send the submission or Expert Report to the Tribunal–Appointed Expert and to the other Parties.

6. At the request of a Party or of the Arbitral Tribunal, the Tribunal–Appointed Expert shall be present at an Evidentiary Hearing. The Arbitral Tribunal may question the Tribunal–Appointed Expert, and he or she may be questioned by the Parties or by any Party-Appointed Expert on issues raised in the Parties submissions or in the Expert Reports made by the Party–Appointed Experts pursuant to Article 6.5.

7. Any Expert Report made by a Tribunal–Appointed Expert and its conclusions shall be assessed by the Arbitral Tribunal with due regard to all circumstances of the case.

8. The fees and expenses of a Tribunal–Appointed Expert, to be funded in a manner determined by the Arbitral Tribunal, shall form part of the costs of the arbitration.

Article 7

On Site Inspection

Subject to the provisions of Article 9.2, the Arbitral Tribunal may, at the request of a Party or on its own motion, inspect or require the inspection by a Tribunal-Appointed Expert of any site, property, machinery or any other goods or process, or documents, as it deems appropriate. The Arbitral Tribunal shall, in consultation with the Parties, determine the timing and arrangement for the inspection. The Parties and their representatives shall have the right to attend any such inspection.

Article 8

Evidentiary Hearing

1. The Arbitral Tribunal shall at all times have complete control over the Evidentiary Hearing. The Arbitral Tribunal may limit or exclude any question to, answer by or appearance of a witness (which term includes, for the purposes of this Article, witnesses of fact and any Experts), if it considers such question, answer or appearance to be irrelevant, immaterial, burdensome, duplicative or covered by a reason for objection set forth in Article 9.2. Questions to a witness during direct and redirect testimony may not be unreasonably leading.

2. The Claimant shall ordinarily first present the testimony of its witnesses, followed by the Respondent presenting testimony of its witnesses, and then by the presentation by Claimant of rebuttal witnesses, if any. Following direct testimony, any other Party may question such witness, in an order to be determined by the Arbitral Tribunal. The Party who initially presented the witness shall subsequently have the opportunity to ask additional questions on the matters raised in the other Parties questioning. The Arbitral Tribunal, upon request of a Party or on its own motion, may vary this order of proceeding, including the arrangement of testimony by particular issues or in such a manner that witnesses presented by different Parties be questioned at the same time and in confrontation with each other. The Arbitral Tribunal may ask questions to a witness at any time.

3. Any witness providing testimony shall first affirm, in a manner determined appropriate by the Arbitral Tribunal, that he or she is telling the truth. If the witness has submitted a Witness Statement or an Expert Report, the witness shall confirm it. The Parties may agree or the Arbitral Tribunal may order that the Witness Statement or Expert Report shall serve as that witness direct testimony.

4. Subject to the provisions of Article 9.2, the Arbitral Tribunal may request any person to give oral or written evidence on any issue that the Arbitral Tribunal considers to be relevant and material. Any witness called and questioned by the Arbitral Tribunal may also be questioned by the Parties.

Article 9

Admissibility and Assessment of Evidence

1. The Arbitral Tribunal shall determine the admissibility, relevance, materiality and weight of evidence.

2. The Arbitral Tribunal shall, at the request of a Party or on its own motion, exclude from evidence or production any document, statement, oral testimony or inspection for any of the following reasons:

(a) lack of sufficient relevance or materiality;

(b) legal impediment or privilege under the legal or ethical rules determined by the Arbitral Tribunal to be applicable;

(c) unreasonable burden to produce the requested evidence;

(d) loss or destruction of the document that has been reasonably shown to have occurred;

(e) grounds of commercial or technical confidentiality that the Arbitral Tribunal determines to be compelling;

(f) grounds of special political or institutional sensitivity (including evidence that has been classified as secret by a government or a public international institution) that the Arbitral Tribunal determines to be compelling; or

(g) considerations of fairness or equality of the Parties that the Arbitral Tribunal determines to be compelling.

3. The Arbitral Tribunal may, where appropriate, make necessary arrangements to permit evidence to be considered subject to suitable confidentiality protection.

4. If a Party fails without satisfactory explanation to produce any document requested in a Request to Produce to which it has not objected in due time or fails to produce any document ordered to be produced by the Arbitral Tribunal, the Arbitral Tribunal may infer that such document would be adverse to the interests of that Party.

5. If a Party fails without satisfactory explanation to make available any other relevant evidence, including testimony, sought by one Party to which the Party to whom the request was addressed has not objected in due time or fails to make available any evidence, including testimony, ordered by the Arbitral Tribunal to be produced, the Arbitral Tribunal may infer that such evidence would be adverse to the interests of that Party.

E. UNCITRAL MODEL LAW ON INTERNATIONAL COMMERCIAL CONCILIATION (2002)*

Resolution adopted by the General Assembly

[on the report of the Sixth Committee (A/57/562 and Corr.1)]

57/18 *Model Law on International Commercial Conciliation of the United Nations Commission on International Trade Law*

The General Assembly,

Recognizing the value for international trade of methods for settling commercial disputes in which the parties in dispute request a third person or persons to assist them in their attempt to settle the dispute amicably,

Noting that such dispute settlement methods, referred to by expressions such as conciliation and mediation and expressions of similar import, are increasingly used in international and domestic commercial practice as an alternative to litigation,

Considering that the use of such dispute settlement methods results in significant benefits, such as reducing the instances where a dispute leads to the termination of a commercial relationship, facilitating the administration of international transactions by commercial parties and producing savings in the administration of justice by States,

Convinced that the establishment of model legislation on these methods that is acceptable to States with different legal, social and economic systems would contribute to the development of harmonious international economic relations,

Noting with satisfaction the completion and adoption by the United Nations Commission on International Trade Law of the Model Law on International Commercial Conciliation,*

Believing that the Model Law will significantly assist States in enhancing their legislation governing the use of modern conciliation or mediation techniques and in formulating such legislation where none currently exists,

Noting that the preparation of the Model Law was the subject of due deliberation and extensive consultations with Governments and interested circles,

Convinced that the Model Law, together with the Conciliation Rules recommended by the General Assembly in its resolution 35/52 of 4 December 1980,contributes significantly to the establishment of a har-

* Text can be found at UNCITRAL website http://uncitral.org/pdf/english/texts/arbitration/ml-conc/ml-conc-e.pdf

* Official Records of the General Assembly, Fifty-seventh Session, Supplement No. 17 (A/57/17), annex I.

monized legal framework for the fair and efficient settlement of disputes arising in international commercial relations,

1. *Expresses its appreciation* to the United Nations Commission on International Trade Law for completing and adopting the Model Law on International Commercial Conciliation, the text of which is contained in the annex to the present resolution, and for preparing the Guide to Enactment and Use of the Model Law;

2. *Requests* the Secretary–General to make all efforts to ensure that the Model Law, together with its Guide to Enactment, becomes generally known and available;

3. *Recommends* that all States give due consideration to the enactment of the Model Law, in view of the desirability of uniformity of the law of dispute settlement procedures and the specific needs of international commercial conciliation practice.

UNCITRAL Model Law on International Commercial Conciliation (2002)

Article 1. Scope of application and definitions

1. This Law applies to international[1] commercial[2] conciliation.

2. For the purposes of this Law, "conciliator" means a sole conciliator or two or more conciliators, as the case may be.

3. For the purposes of this Law, "conciliation" means a process, whether referred to by the expression conciliation, mediation or an expression of similar import, whereby parties request a third person or persons ("the conciliator") to assist them in their attempt to reach an amicable settlement of their dispute arising out of or relating to a contractual or other legal relationship. The conciliator does not have the authority to impose upon the parties a solution to the dispute.

4. A conciliation is international if:

(*a*) The parties to an agreement to conciliate have, at the time of the conclusion of that agreement, their places of business in different States; or

(*b*) The State in which the parties have their places of business is different from either:

---

1. States wishing to enact this Model Law to apply to domestic as well as international conciliation may wish to consider the following changes to the text:

—Delete the word "international" in paragraph 1 of article 1; and

—Delete paragraphs 4, 5 and 6 of article 1.

2. The term "commercial" should be given a wide interpretation so as to cover matters arising from all relationships of a commercial nature, whether contractual or not. Relationships of a commercial nature include, but are not limited to, the following transactions: any trade transaction for the supply or exchange of goods or services; distribution agreement; commercial representation or agency; factoring; leasing; construction of works; consulting; engineering; licensing; investment; financing; banking; insurance; exploitation agreement or concession; joint venture and other forms of industrial or business cooperation; carriage of goods or passengers by air, sea, rail or road.

(i) The State in which a substantial part of the obligations of the commercial relationship is to be performed; or

(ii) The State with which the subject matter of the dispute is most closely connected.

5. For the purposes of this article:

(a) If a party has more than one place of business, the place of business is that which has the closest relationship to the agreement to conciliate;

(b) If a party does not have a place of business, reference is to be made to the party's habitual residence.

6. This Law also applies to a commercial conciliation when the parties agree that the conciliation is international or agree to the applicability of this Law.

7. The parties are free to agree to exclude the applicability of this Law.

8. Subject to the provisions of paragraph 9 of this article, this Law applies irrespective of the basis upon which the conciliation is carried out, including agreement between the parties whether reached before or after a dispute has arisen, an obligation established by law, or a direction or suggestion of a court, arbitral tribunal or competent governmental entity.

9. This Law does not apply to:

(a) Cases where a judge or an arbitrator, in the course of judicial or arbitral proceedings, attempts to facilitate a settlement; and

(b) [. . .]

Article 2. Interpretation

1. In the interpretation of this Law, regard is to be had to its international origin and to the need to promote uniformity in its application and the observance of good faith.

2. Questions concerning matters governed by this Law which are not expressly settled in it are to be settled in conformity with the general principles on which this Law is based.

Article 3. Variation by agreement

Except for the provisions of article 2 and article 6, paragraph 3, the parties may agree to exclude or vary any of the provisions of this Law.

Article 4. Commencement of conciliation proceedings[3]

1. Conciliation proceedings in respect of a dispute that has arisen commence on the day on which the parties to that dispute agree to engage in conciliation proceedings.

---

3. The following text is suggested for States that might wish to adopt a provision on the suspension of the limitation period:

Article X. Suspension of limitation period:

2. If a party that invited another party to conciliate does not receive an acceptance of the invitation within thirty days from the day on which the invitation was sent, or within such other period of time as specified in the invitation, the party may elect to treat this as a rejection of the invitation to conciliate.

Article 5. Number and appointment of conciliators

1. There shall be one conciliator, unless the parties agree that there shall be two or more conciliators.

2. The parties shall endeavor to reach agreement on a conciliator or conciliators, unless a different procedure for their appointment has been agreed upon.

3. Parties may seek the assistance of an institution or person in connection with the appointment of conciliators. In particular:

(a) A party may request such an institution or person to recommend suitable persons to act as conciliator; or

(b) The parties may agree that the appointment of one or more conciliators be made directly by such an institution or person.

4. In recommending or appointing individuals to act as conciliator, the institution or person shall have regard to such considerations as are likely to secure the appointment of an independent and impartial conciliator and, where appropriate, shall take into account the advisability of appointing a conciliator of a nationality other than the nationalities of the parties.

5. When a person is approached in connection with his or her possible appointment as conciliator, he or she shall disclose any circumstances likely to give rise to justifiable doubts as to his or her impartiality or independence. A conciliator, from the time of his or her appointment and throughout the conciliation proceedings, shall without delay disclose any such circumstances to the parties unless they have already been informed of them by him or her.

Article 6. Conduct of conciliation

1. The parties are free to agree, by reference to a set of rules or otherwise, on the manner in which the conciliation is to be conducted.

2. Failing agreement on the manner in which the conciliation is to be conducted, the conciliator may conduct the conciliation proceedings in such a manner as the conciliator considers appropriate, taking into account the circumstances of the case, any wishes that the parties may express and the need for a speedy settlement of the dispute.

---

1. When the conciliation proceedings commence, the running of the limitation period regarding the claim that is the subject matter of the conciliation is suspended.

2. Where the conciliation proceedings have terminated without a settlement agreement, the limitation period resumes running from the time the conciliation ended without a settlement agreement.

3. In any case, in conducting the proceedings, the conciliator shall seek to maintain fair treatment of the parties and, in so doing, shall take into account the circumstances of the case.

4. The conciliator may, at any stage of the conciliation proceedings, make proposals for a settlement of the dispute.

Article 7. Communication between conciliator and parties

The conciliator may meet or communicate with the parties together or with each of them separately.

Article 8. Disclosure of information

When the conciliator receives information concerning the dispute from a party, the conciliator may disclose the substance of that information to any other party to the conciliation. However, when a party gives any information to the conciliator, subject to a specific condition that it be kept confidential, that information shall not be disclosed to any other party to the conciliation.

Article 9. Confidentiality

Unless otherwise agreed by the parties, all information relating to the conciliation proceedings shall be kept confidential, except where disclosure is required under the law or for the purposes of implementation or enforcement of a settlement agreement.

Article 10. Admissibility of evidence in other proceedings

1. A party to the conciliation proceedings, the conciliator and any third person, including those involved in the administration of the conciliation proceedings, shall not in arbitral, judicial or similar proceedings rely on, introduce as evidence or give testimony or evidence regarding any of the following:

(a) An invitation by a party to engage in conciliation proceedings or the fact that a party was willing to participate in conciliation proceedings;

(b) Views expressed or suggestions made by a party in the conciliation in respect of a possible settlement of the dispute;

(c) Statements or admissions made by a party in the course of the conciliation proceedings;

(d) Proposals made by the conciliator;

(e) The fact that a party had indicated its willingness to accept a proposal for settlement made by the conciliator;

(f) A document prepared solely for purposes of the conciliation proceedings.

2. Paragraph 1 of this article applies irrespective of the form of the information or evidence referred to therein.

3. The disclosure of the information referred to in paragraph 1 of this article shall not be ordered by an arbitral tribunal, court or other competent governmental authority and, if such information is offered as evidence in contravention of paragraph 1 of this article, that evidence shall be treated as inadmissible. Nevertheless, such information may be disclosed or admitted in evidence to the extent required under the law or for the purposes of implementation or enforcement of a settlement agreement.

4. The provisions of paragraphs 1, 2 and 3 of this article apply whether or not the arbitral, judicial or similar proceedings relate to the dispute that is or was the subject matter of the conciliation proceedings.

5. Subject to the limitations of paragraph 1 of this article, evidence that is otherwise admissible in arbitral or judicial or similar proceedings does not become inadmissible as a consequence of having been used in a conciliation.

Article 11. Termination of conciliation proceedings

The conciliation proceedings are terminated:

(a) By the conclusion of a settlement agreement by the parties, on the date of the agreement;

(b) By a declaration of the conciliator, after consultation with the parties, to the effect that further efforts at conciliation are no longer justified, on the date of the declaration;

(c) By a declaration of the parties addressed to the conciliator to the effect that the conciliation proceedings are terminated, on the date of the declaration; or

(d) By a declaration of a party to the other party or parties and the conciliator, if appointed, to the effect that the conciliation proceedings are terminated, on the date of the declaration.

Article 12. Conciliator acting as arbitrator

Unless otherwise agreed by the parties, the conciliator shall not act as an arbitrator in respect of a dispute that was or is the subject of the conciliation proceedings or in respect of another dispute that has arisen from the same contract or legal relationship or any related contract or legal relationship.

Article 13. Resort to arbitral or judicial proceedings

Where the parties have agreed to conciliate and have expressly undertaken not to initiate during a specified period of time or until a specified event has occurred arbitral or judicial proceedings with respect to an existing or future dispute, such an undertaking shall be given effect by the arbitral tribunal or the court until the terms of the undertaking have been complied with, except to the extent necessary for a party, in its opinion, to preserve its rights. Initiation of such proceedings is not of itself to be regarded as a waiver of the agreement to conciliate or as a termination of the conciliation proceedings.

Article 14. Enforceability of settlement agreement[4]

If the parties conclude an agreement settling a dispute, that settlement agreement is binding and enforceable ... [*the enacting State may insert a description of the method of enforcing settlement agreements or refer to provisions governing such enforcement*].

4. When implementing the procedure for enforcement of settlement agreements, an enacting State may consider the possibility of such a procedure being mandatory.

III. National Legislation on Arbitration

■ ■ ■

A. UNITED STATES FEDERAL ARBITRATION ACT OF 1925

(as last amended in 2002)

FEDERAL ARBITRATION ACT

United States Code

TITLE 9. ARBITRATION

CHAPTER 1.

GENERAL PROVISIONS

§ 1. "Maritime transactions" and "commerce" defined; exceptions to operation of title

"Maritime transactions", as herein defined, means charter parties, bills of lading of water carriers, agreements relating to wharfage, supplies furnished vessels or repairs to vessels, collisions, or any other matters in foreign commerce which, if the subject of controversy, would be embraced within admiralty jurisdiction; "commerce", as herein defined, means commerce among the several States or with foreign nations, or in any Territory of the United States or in the District of Columbia, or between any such Territory and another, or between any such Territory and any State or foreign nation, or between the District of Columbia and any State or Territory or foreign nation, but nothing herein contained shall apply to contracts of employment of seamen, railroad employees, or any other class of workers engaged in foreign or interstate commerce.

§ 2. Validity, irrevocability and enforcement of agreements to arbitrate

A written provision in any maritime transaction or a contract evidencing a transaction involving commerce to settle by arbitration a controversy thereafter arising out of such contract or transaction, or the refusal to perform the whole or any part thereof, or an agreement in writing to submit to arbitration an existing controversy arising out of such a contract, transaction, or refusal, shall be valid, irrevocable, and enforceable, save upon such grounds as exist at law or in equity for the revocation of any contract.

§ 3. Stay of proceedings where issue therein referable to arbitration

If any suit or proceeding be brought in any of the courts of the United States upon any issue referable to arbitration under an agreement in writing for such arbitration, the court in which such suit is pending, upon being satisfied that the issue involved in such suit or proceeding is referable to arbitration under such an agreement, shall on application of one of the parties stay the trial of the action until such arbitration has been had in accordance with the terms of the agreement, providing the applicant for the stay is not in default in proceeding with such arbitration.

§ 4. Failure to arbitrate under agreement; petition to United States court having jurisdiction for order to compel arbitration; notice and service thereof; hearing and determination

A party aggrieved by the alleged failure, neglect, or refusal of another to arbitrate under a written agreement for arbitration may petition any United States district court which, save for such agreement, would have jurisdiction under Title 28 [28 U.S.C. §§ 1 et seq.], in a civil action or in admiralty of the subject matter of a suit arising out of the controversy between the parties, for an order directing that such arbitration proceed in the manner provided for in such agreement. Five days' notice in writing of such application shall be served upon the party in default. Service thereof shall be made in the manner provided by the Federal Rules of Civil Procedure. The court shall hear the parties, and upon being satisfied that the making of the agreement for arbitration or the failure to comply therewith is not in issue, the court shall make an order directing the parties to proceed to arbitration in accordance with the terms of the agreement. The hearing and proceedings, under such agreement, shall be within the district in which the petition for an order directing such arbitration is filed. If the making of the arbitration agreement or the failure, neglect, or refusal to perform the same be in issue, the court shall proceed summarily to the trial thereof. If no jury trial be demanded by the party alleged to be in default, or if the matter in dispute is within admiralty jurisdiction, the court shall hear and determine such issue. Where such an issue is raised, the party alleged to be in default may, except in cases of admiralty, on or before the return day of the notice of application, demand a jury trial of such issue, and upon such demand the court shall make an order referring the issue or issues to a jury in the manner provided by the Federal Rules of Civil Procedure, or may specially call a jury for that purpose. If the jury find that no agreement in writing for arbitration was made or that there is no default in proceeding thereunder, the proceeding shall be dismissed. If the jury find that an agreement for arbitration was made in writing and that there is a default in proceeding thereunder, the court shall make an order summarily directing the parties to proceed with the arbitration in accordance with the terms thereof.

§ 5. Appointment of arbitrators or umpire

If in the agreement provision be made for a method of naming or appointing an arbitrator or arbitrators or an umpire, such method shall be followed; but if no method be provided therein, or if a method be provided and any party thereto shall fail to avail himself of such method, or if for any other reason there shall be a lapse in the naming of an arbitrator or arbitrators or umpire, or in filling a vacancy, then upon the application of either party to the controversy the court shall designate and appoint an arbitrator or arbitrators or umpire, as the case may require, who shall act under the said agreement with the same force and effect as if he or they had been specifically named therein; and unless otherwise provided in the agreement the arbitration shall be by a single arbitrator.

§ 6. Application heard as motion

Any application to the court hereunder shall be made and heard in the manner provided by law for the making and hearing of motions, except as otherwise herein expressly provided.

§ 7. Witnesses before arbitrators; fees; compelling attendance

The arbitrators selected either as prescribed in this title [9 U.S.C. §§ 1 et seq.] or otherwise, or a majority of them, may summon in writing any person to attend before them or any of them as a witness and in a proper case to bring with him or them any book, record, document, or paper which may be deemed material as evidence in the case. The fees for such attendance shall be the same as the fees of witnesses before masters of the United States courts. Said summons shall issue in the name of the arbitrator or arbitrators, or a majority of them, and shall be signed by the arbitrators, or a majority of them, and shall be directed to the said person and shall be served in the same manner as subpoenas to appear and testify before the court; if any person or persons so summoned to testify shall refuse or neglect to obey said summons, upon petition the United States district court for the district in which such arbitrators, or a majority of them, are sitting may compel the attendance of such person or persons before said arbitrator or arbitrators, or punish said person or persons for contempt in the same manner provided by law for securing the attendance of witnesses or their punishment for neglect or refusal to attend in the courts of the United States.

§ 8. Proceedings begun by libel in admiralty and seizure of vessel or property

If the basis of jurisdiction be a cause of action otherwise justiciable in admiralty, then, notwithstanding anything herein to the contrary, the party claiming to be aggrieved may begin his proceeding hereunder by libel and seizure of the vessel or other property of the other party according to the usual course of admiralty proceedings, and the court shall then have jurisdiction to direct the parties to proceed with the arbitration and shall retain jurisdiction to enter its decree upon the award.

§ 9. Award of arbitrators; confirmation; jurisdiction; procedure

If the parties in their agreement have agreed that a judgment of the court shall be entered upon the award made pursuant to the arbitration, and shall specify the court, then at any time within one year after the award is made any party to the arbitration may apply to the court so specified for an order confirming the award, and thereupon the court must grant such an order unless the award is vacated, modified, or corrected as prescribed in sections 10 and 11 of this title [9 U.S.C. §§ 10, 11]. If no court is specified in the agreement of the parties, then such application may be made to the United States court in and for the district within which such award was made. Notice of the application shall be served upon the adverse party, and thereupon the court shall have jurisdiction of such party as though he had appeared generally in the proceeding. If the adverse party is a resident of the district within which the award was made, such service shall be made upon the adverse party or his attorney as prescribed by law for service of notice of motion in an action in the same court. If the adverse party shall be a nonresident, then the notice of the application shall be served by the marshal of any district within which the adverse party may be found in like manner as other process of the court.

§ 10. Same; vacation; grounds; rehearing

(a) In any of the following cases the United States court in and for the district wherein the award was made may make an order vacating the award upon the application of any party to the arbitration—

(1) Where the award was procured by corruption, fraud, or undue means.

(2) Where there was evident partiality or corruption in the arbitrators, or either of them.

(3) Where the arbitrators were guilty of misconduct in refusing to postpone the hearing, upon sufficient cause shown, or in refusing to hear evidence pertinent and material to the controversy; or of any other misbehavior by which the rights of any party have been prejudiced, or

(4) Where the arbitrators exceeded their powers, or so imperfectly executed them that a mutual, final, and definite award upon the subject matter submitted was not made.

(b) if an award is vacated and the time within which the agreement required the award to be made has not expired, the court may, in its discretion, direct a rehearing by the arbitrators.

(c) The United States district court for the district wherein an award was made that was issued pursuant to section 580 of title 5 may make an order vacating the award upon the application of a person, other than a party to the arbitration, who is adversely affected or aggrieved by the award, if the use of arbitration or the award is clearly inconsistent with the factors set forth in section 572 of title 5.

§ 11. Same; modification or correction; grounds; order

In either of the following cases the United States court in and for the district wherein the award was made may make an order modifying or correcting the award upon the application of any party to the arbitration—

(a) Where there was an evident material miscalculation of figures or an evident material mistake in the description of any person, thing, or property referred to in the award.

(b) Where the arbitrators have awarded upon a matter not submitted to them, unless it is a matter not affecting the merits of the decision upon the matter submitted.

(c) Where the award is imperfect in matter of form not affecting the merits of the controversy.

The order may modify and correct the award, so as to effect the intent thereof and promote justice between the parties.

§ 12. Notice of motions to vacate or modify; service; stay of proceedings

Notice of a motion to vacate, modify, or correct an award must be served upon the adverse party or his attorney within three months after the award is filed or delivered. If the adverse party is a resident of the district within which the award was made, such service shall be made upon the adverse party or his attorney as prescribed by law for service of notice of motion in an action in the same court. If the adverse party shall be a nonresident then the notice of the application shall be served by the marshal of any district within which the adverse party may be found in like manner as other process of the court. For the purposes of the motion any judge who might make an order to stay the proceedings in an action brought in the same court may make an order, to be served with the notice of motion, staying the proceedings of the adverse party to enforce the award.

§ 13. Papers filed with order on motions; judgment; docketing; force and effect; enforcement

The party moving for an order confirming, modifying, or correcting an award shall, at the time such order is filed with the clerk for the entry of judgment thereon, also file the following papers with the clerk:

(a) The agreement; the selection or appointment, if any, of an additional arbitrator or umpire; and each written extension of the time, if any, within which to make the award.

(b) The award.

(c) Each notice, affidavit, or other paper used upon an application to confirm, modify, or correct the award, and a copy of each order of the court upon such an application.

The judgment shall be docketed as if it was rendered in an action.

The judgment so entered shall have the same force and effect, in all respects, as, and be subject to all the provisions of law relating to, a judgment in an action; and it may be enforced as if it had been rendered in an action in the court in which it is entered.

§ 14. Contracts not affected

This title [9 U.S.C. §§ 1 et seq.] shall not apply to contracts made prior to January 1, 1926.

§ 15. Inapplicability of the Act of State doctrine

Enforcement of arbitral agreements, confirmation of arbitral awards, and execution upon judgments based on orders confirming such awards shall not be refused on the basis of the Act of State doctrine.

§ 16. Appeals

(a) An appeal may be taken from—

(1) an order—

(A) refusing a stay of any action under section 3 of this title,

(B) denying a petition under section 4 of this title to order arbitration to proceed,

(C) denying an application under section 206 of this title to compel arbitration,

(D) confirming or denying confirmation of an award or partial award, or

(E) modifying, correcting, or vacating an award;

(2) an interlocutory order granting, continuing, or modifying an injunction against an arbitration that is subject to this title; or

(3) a final decision with respect to an arbitration that is subject to this title.

(b) Except as otherwise provided in section 1292(b) of title 28, an appeal may not be taken from an interlocutory order—

(1) granting a stay of any action under section 3 of this title;

(2) directing arbitration to proceed under section 4 of this title;

(3) compelling arbitration under section 206 of this title; or

(4) refusing to enjoin an arbitration that is subject to this title.

CHAPTER 2.

CONVENTION ON THE RECOGNITION AND ENFORCEMENT OF FOREIGN ARBITRAL AWARDS

§ 201. Enforcement of Convention

The Convention on the Recognition and Enforcement of Foreign Arbitral Awards of June 10, 1958, shall be enforced in United States courts in accordance with this chapter [9 U.S.C. §§ 201 et seq.].

§ 202. Agreement or award falling under the Convention

An arbitration agreement or arbitral award arising out of a legal relationship, whether contractual or not, which is considered as commercial, including a transaction, contract, or agreement described in section 2 of this title [9 U.S.C. § 2], falls under the Convention. An agreement or award arising out of such a relationship which is entirely between citizens of the United States shall be deemed not to fall under the Convention unless that relationship involves property located abroad, envisages performance or enforcement abroad, or has some other reasonable relation with one or more foreign states. For the purpose of this section a corporation is a citizen of the United States if it is incorporated or has its principal place of business in the United States.

§ 203. Jurisdiction; amount in controversy

An action or proceeding falling under the Convention shall be deemed to arise under the laws and treaties of the United States. The district courts of the United States (including the courts enumerated in section 460 of title 28 [28 U.S.C. § 460]) shall have original jurisdiction over such an action or proceeding, regardless of the amount in controversy.

§ 204. Venue

An action or proceeding over which the district courts have jurisdiction pursuant to section 203 of this title [9 U.S.C. § 203] may be brought in any such court in which save for the arbitration agreement an action or proceeding with respect to the controversy between the parties could be brought, or in such court for the district and division which embraces the place designated in the agreement as the place of arbitration if such place is within the United States.

§ 205. Removal of cases from State courts

Where the subject matter of an action or proceeding pending in a State court relates to an arbitration agreement or award falling under the Convention, the defendant or the defendants may, at any time before the trial thereof, remove such action or proceeding to the district court of the United States for the district and division embracing the place where the action or proceeding is pending. The procedure for removal of causes otherwise provided by law shall apply, except that the ground for removal provided in this section need not appear on the face of the complaint but may be shown in the petition for removal. For the purposes of Chapter 1 of this title [9 U.S.C. §§ 1 et seq.] any action or proceeding removed under this section shall be deemed to have been brought in the district court to which it is removed.

§ 206. Order to compel arbitration; appointment of arbitrators

A court having jurisdiction under this chapter [9 U.S.C. §§ 201 et seq.] may direct that arbitration be held in accordance with the agreement at any place therein provided for, whether that place is within or without the United States. Such court may also appoint arbitrators in accordance with the provisions of the agreement.

§ 207. Award of arbitrators; confirmation; jurisdiction; proceeding

Within three years after an arbitral award falling under the Convention is made, any party to the arbitration may apply to any court having jurisdiction under this chapter [9 U.S.C. §§ 201 et seq.] for an order confirming the award as against any other party to the arbitration. The court shall confirm the award unless it finds one of the grounds for refusal or deferral of recognition or enforcement of the award specified in the said Convention.

§ 208. Chapter 1 [9 U.S.C. §§ 1 et seq.]; residual application

Chapter 1 [9 U.S.C. §§ 1 et seq.] applies to actions and proceedings brought under this chapter [9 U.S.C. §§ 201 et seq.] to the extent that chapter is not in conflict with this chapter [9 U.S.C. §§ 201 et seq.] or the Convention as ratified by the United States.

CHAPTER 3.

INTER-AMERICAN CONVENTION ON INTERNATIONAL COMMERCIAL ARBITRATION

§ 301. Enforcement of Convention

The Inter-American Convention on International Commercial Arbitration of January 30, 1975, shall be enforced in United States courts in accordance with this chapter [9 U.S.C. §§ 301 et seq.].

§ 302. Incorporation by reference

Sections 202, 203, 204, 205, and 207 of this title shall apply to this chapter [9 U.S.C. §§ 301 et seq.] as if specifically set forth herein, except that for the purposes of this chapter [9 U.S.C. §§ 301 et seq.] "the Convention" shall mean the Inter-American Convention.

§ 303. Order to compel arbitration; appointment of arbitrators; locale

(a) A court having jurisdiction under this chapter [9 U.S.C. §§ 301 et seq.] may direct that arbitration be held in accordance with the agreement at any place therein provided for, whether that place is within or without the United States. The court may also appoint arbitrators in accordance with the provisions of the agreement.

(b) In the event the agreement does not make provision for the place of arbitration or the appointment of arbitrators, the court shall direct that the arbitration shall be held and the arbitrators be appointed in accordance with Article 3 of the Inter–American Convention.

§ 304. Recognition and enforcement of foreign arbitral decisions and awards; reciprocity

Arbitral decisions or awards made in the territory of a foreign State shall, on the basis of reciprocity, be recognized and enforced under this chapter [9 U.S.C. §§ 301 et seq.] only if that State has ratified or acceded to the Inter–American Convention.

§ 305. Relationship between the Inter–American Convention and the Convention on the Recognition and Enforcement of Foreign Arbitral Awards of June 10, 1958

When the requirements for application of both the Inter–American Convention and the Convention on the Recognition and Enforcement of Foreign Arbitral Awards of June 10, 1958, are met, determination as to which Convention applies shall, unless otherwise expressly agreed, be made as follows:

(1) If a majority of the parties to the arbitration agreement are citizens of a State or States that have ratified or acceded to the Inter–American Convention and are member States of the Organization of American States, the Inter–American Convention shall apply.

(2) In all other cases the Convention on the Recognition and Enforcement of Foreign Arbitral Awards of June 10, 1958, shall apply.

§ 306. Applicable rules of Inter–American Commercial Arbitration Commission

(a) For the purposes of this chapter [9 U.S.C. §§ 301 et seq.] the rules of procedure of the Inter–American Commercial Arbitration Commission referred to in Article 3 of the Inter–American Convention shall, subject to subsection (b) of this section, be those rules as promulgated by the Commission on July 1, 1988.

(b) In the event the rules of procedure of the Inter–American Commercial Arbitration Commission are modified or amended in accordance with the procedures for amendment of the rules of that Commission, the Secretary of State, by regulation in accordance with section 553 of title 5, consistent with the aims and purposes of this Convention, may prescribe that such modifications or amendments shall be effective for purposes of this chapter [9 U.S.C. §§ 301 et seq.].

§ 307. Chapter 1; residual application

Chapter 1 [9 U.S.C. §§ 1 et seq.] applies to actions and proceedings brought under this chapter [9 U.S.C. §§ 301 et seq.] to the extent chapter 1 [9 U.S.C. §§ 1 et seq.] is not in conflict with this chapter [9 U.S.C.

§§ 301 et seq.] or the Inter-American Convention as ratified by the United States.

B. FRENCH CODE OF CIVIL PROCEDURE, BOOK FOUR (ARBITRATION LEGISLATION OF 1981)*

(as amended, latest amendment in 2005)

TITLE I

ARBITRATION AGREEMENTS

CHAPTER I

ARBITRATION CLAUSE

Article 1442

An arbitration clause is an agreement whereby the parties to a contract commit themselves to refer to arbitration the disputes that their contract may give rise to.

Article 1443

An arbitration clause must, under penalty of nullity, be stipulated in writing in the main agreement or in a document to which the latter refers.

Under the same sanction, the arbitration clause must, either designate the arbitrator or arbitrators, or provide for the terms and conditions of their designation.

Article 1444

If, once a dispute has arisen, the constitution of the arbitration tribunal encounters a difficulty coming from one of the parties or the implementation of the terms and conditions of designation, the president of the High Court designates the arbitrator or arbitrators.

However, the president of the Commercial Court carries out said designation if the agreement has explicitly stipulated it.

Where the arbitration clause is either, on the face of it, null or insufficient to allow for the constitution of an arbitration tribunal, the president will record the same and declare that there is no need for designation (of arbitrators).

Article 1445

Disputes may be referred to an arbitration tribunal either jointly by the parties or by the first mover.

Article 1446

Where it is null, the arbitration clause will be deemed unwritten.

* English text available on the official French legislation site at http://www.legifrance.gouv.fr/

CHAPTER II

COMPROMISE

Article 1447

A compromise is an agreement whereby the parties to a dispute submit to arbitration composed of one or more persons.

Article 1448

The compromise must, under penalty of nullity, determine the subject-matter of the dispute.

Under the same sanction, it must designate the arbitrator or arbitrators, or provide for the terms and conditions for their appointment.

The compromise will become void where an arbitrator that it designates declines the assignment entrusted upon him.

Article 1449

The compromise is recorded in writing. It may be incorporated in the minutes signed by the arbitrator or the parties.

Article 1450

The parties have the right to refer their dispute to an out-of-court settlement even where they are engaged in an already instituted proceeding before another court.

CHAPTER III

COMMON RULES

Article 1451

The assignment of the arbitrator may only be entrusted upon a natural person; the latter must enjoy the full exercise of his civil rights.

If the arbitration agreement appoints a corporate entity, the latter may exercise the powers only of organizing the arbitration.

Article 1452

The constitution of the arbitration tribunal will be completed only if the arbitrator or arbitrators accept the assignment entrusted upon them.

The arbitrator, who is aware of a ground for his recusal, must inform the parties. In that case, he may accept his assignment only upon the approval of the parties.

Article 1453

The arbitration tribunal consists of one or more arbitrators in odd numbers.

Article 1454

Where the parties designate arbitrators in even numbers, the arbitration tribunal will be completed by an additional arbitrator chosen either in accordance with the expectations of the parties, or in the absence of such expectations, by the appointed arbitrators, or in default of an agreement between the latter, by the president of the High Court.

Article 1455

Where a natural person or corporate entity is entrusted to organise the arbitration, the task of arbitration will be entrusted to one or more arbitrators approved by all parties.

In default of agreement, the person or entity entrusted to organise the arbitration will invite each party to designate an arbitrator and will designate, if necessary, the arbitrator necessary to complete the arbitration tribunal. The person will be appointed where the parties fail to designate an arbitrator, the latter or entity entrusted to organise the arbitration.

The arbitration tribunal may also directly be constituted in accordance with the terms and conditions provided for under the preceding sub-article.

The person or entity entrusted to organise the arbitration may stipulate that the arbitration tribunal will pronounce only a draft award and that if one party contests said draft; the matter will be submitted to a second arbitration tribunal. In the latter event, the person or entity entrusted to organise the arbitration will designate the members of the second (arbitration) tribunal. Each party has the right to get one of the appointed arbitrators replaced.

Article 1456

If the arbitration agreement does not specify the time-limit, the assignment of the arbitrators will last only for a period of six months to be reckoned as of the date on which the last of them accepted the said assignment.

The legal or contractual time-limit may be extended either by virtue of the agreement of the parties, or, at the request of one of them or of the arbitration tribunal, by the president of the High Court, or in the case referred to under Article 1444, sub-article 2, by the president of the Commercial Court.

Article 1457

In the case referred to under Articles 1444, 1454, 1456 and 1463, the president of the court, to whom the case is referred, as in a matter of summary interlocutory procedure, by a party or by the arbitration tribunal, will rule upon it by way of an order not open to any review action.

However, this order may be subject to appeal where the president declares against the appointment of arbitrators in view of the grounds referred to under Article 1444 (sub-article 3). The appeal is brought, managed and determined as in an appellate plea against jurisdiction.

The competent president is that of the court designated in the arbitration agreement or, in default thereof, the one in whose jurisdiction the agreement has located the arbitration proceeding. Where the agreement is silent upon the same, the competent president will be that of the court of the place where one or more respondents to the interlocutory action live(s), or where the respondent does not live in France, the court of the place where the plaintiff dwells.

Article 1458

Where a dispute, referred to an arbitration tribunal pursuant to an arbitration agreement, is brought before a court of law of the State, the latter must decline jurisdiction.

Where the case has not yet been brought before arbitration tribunal, the court must also decline jurisdiction save where the arbitration agreement is manifestly null.

In both cases, the court may not raise sua sponte its lack of jurisdiction.

Article 1459

Any provision or agreement contrary to the rules herein laid down is deemed unwritten.

TITLE II

ARBITRATION PROCEEDING

Article 1460

The arbitrators settle the arbitration proceeding without being bound by the rules governing courts, save where the parties have decided otherwise as stipulated in the arbitration agreement.

However, the governing principles of proceedings provided for under Articles 4 to 10, 11 (sub-article 1) and 13 to 21 (of this code) apply always to arbitration proceeding.

Where a party has in his possession some evidence, the arbitrator may enjoin him to produce the same.

Article 1461

Case management processes and minutes will be executed by all the arbitrators if the compromise does not give them powers to commission one of them.

Third parties are heard without an oath being administered.

Article 1462

An arbitrator must undertake his assignment until its completion.

An arbitrator may not be revoked save on a unanimous consent of the parties.

Article 1463

An arbitrator may not withdraw himself nor be recused save for a ground of recusal that has become apparent or has occurred after his designation.

Difficulties relating to the implementation of this Article are brought before the president of the competent court.

Article 1464

The arbitration proceeding is interrupted, subject to a specific agreement between the parties:

1° by the revocation, death or impediment of an arbitrator as well as his loss of the full exercise of his civil rights;

2° by the withdrawal or recusal of an arbitrator;

3° by the lapsing of the time-limit for arbitration.

Article 1465

The discontinuance of an arbitration proceeding is governed by the provisions of Articles 369 to 376.

Article 1466

If, before an arbitrator, one of the parties has challenged the principle or scope of the powers of the arbitrator, the latter must rule upon the validity and limits of his nomination.

Article 1467

Unless otherwise agreed, an arbitrator has the power to determine the subsidiary interlocutory issues in relation to the verification of writings or of forgery in accordance with the provisions of Articles 287 to 294 and of Article 299.

Where there is a plea of forgery, Article 313 will apply before the arbitrator. The time-limit for arbitration runs from the day on which the subsidiary interlocutory plea has been determined.

Article 1468

The arbitrator determines the date on which the matter will be deliberated.

After that date, no claim may be brought or no ground may be raised. No observation may be submitted nor any document be produced, save at the request of the arbitrator.

TITLE III
ARBITRAL AWARD

Article 1469

The deliberation of arbitrators takes place in camera.

Article 1470

The arbitral award is pronounced by way of majority voting.

Article 1471

The arbitral award must recite summarily the respective claims of the parties and their grounds.

The ruling must be well-reasoned.

Article 1472

The arbitral award contains the following particulars:

— the name of arbitrators who pronounced it;

— the date;

— the venue where it was given;

— the surname, first names and denomination of parties, as well as their domicile or head office;

— if necessary, the name of advocates or any person who represented or assisted the parties.

Article 1473

All the arbitrators must sign the arbitral award.

However, if a minority among them has refused to sign it, the others will refer to that and the award will bear the same value as if all the arbitrators have signed it.

Article 1474

An arbitrator determines a dispute in accordance with the rules of law, save where, in the arbitration agreement, the parties assigned him as an amicable compounder.

Article 1475

An award removes the contention, which it has determined, from the arbitrator.

The arbitrator has nevertheless the power to interpret the award, to correct clerical errors and omissions that affect it and to complete it where he has omitted a ruling on an issue raised. Articles 461 to 463 apply. If an arbitration tribunal may not meet again, such power will appertain to the court that would have otherwise been competent in default of arbitration.

Article 1476

The arbitral award, from the moment that it has been given, will become res judicata with respect to the dispute that it has determined.

Article 1477

The arbitral award may not be subjected to a compulsory enforcement save by virtue of an exequatur pronounced by the High Court in whose jurisdiction the award was given.

To this end, the minutes of the award, together with a copy of the arbitration agreement, will be lodged by one of the arbitrators or by the party who brings the action first to the clerk's office of the court.

Article 1478

The exequatur will be appended on the minutes of the arbitral award.

The judgment disallowing the exequatur must be reasoned.

Article 1479

Rules governing interim enforcement of judgments apply to arbitral awards.

On appeal or review action to vacate, the first president (of the court of appeal) or the judge having the management of the matter as soon as the matter is referred to him, may grant the exequatur to the arbitral award supported with a certificate of interim enforcement. He may also order the interim enforcement in the manner prescribed under Articles 525 and 526; his decision amounts to exequatur.

Article 1480

The provisions of Articles 1471 (sub-article 2), 1472 with respect to the names of arbitrators and the date of the award, and 1473 are laid down under penalty of nullity.

TITLE IV

MEANS OF REVIEW

Article 1481

The arbitral award will not be subject to a motion to set aside and an appeal in cassation.

It may be impugned by a third party motion to set aside before the court that would otherwise have been competent in default of arbitration, subject to the provisions of Article 588 (sub-article 1).

Article 1482

The arbitral award is subject to appeal save where the parties have renounced to an appeal in the arbitration agreement. However, it is not subject to appeal where the arbitrator is assigned to decide as amicable compounder, save where the parties have expressly set aside this right in the arbitration agreement.

Article 1483

Where, following the distinction drawn under Article 1482, the parties have not abandoned the right to appeal or they have expressly conserved for themselves this right in the arbitration agreement, only an appeal will lie, whether it intends to reverse or vacate the arbitral award. The appeal judge will determine the matter as an amicable compounder where the arbitrator has this assignment.

Article 1484

Where, following the distinctions drawn under Article 1482, the parties have abandoned their right to appeal, or where they have not expressly conserved for themselves this right in the arbitration agreement, a review action to vacate the deed termed arbitral award may nevertheless be brought albeit contrary stipulations to the same.

This action is available only in the following cases:

1° if the arbitrator has ruled upon the matter without an arbitration agreement or upon a void lapsed agreement;

2° if the arbitration tribunal has been unlawfully constituted or a sole arbitrator unlawfully designated;

3° if the arbitrator has ruled upon the matter contrary to the assignment given to him;

4° if the adversarial principle has not been respected;

5° in all cases of nullity referred to under Article 1480;

6° if the arbitrator has infringed a rule of public interest.

Article 1485

Where a court to which the review action to vacate is brought vacates an arbitral award, it will rule upon the merits of the case within the confines of the assignment of the arbitrator, save where a contrary intention of all the parties concerned.

Article 1486

The appeal and the review action to vacate will be brought before the court of appeal in whose jurisdiction the arbitral award was given.

These review actions are admissible as soon as the award has been given; they will cease to be so if they have not been brought within the month of the service of the award bearing the exequatur order.

The time-limit to bring these review actions suspends the enforcement of the arbitral award. Likewise, the review action brought within the time-limit suspends (the enforcement of the arbitral award).

Article 1487

The appeal and the review action to vacate are brought, managed and determined according to rules governing the procedure of contentious matters before the court of appeal.

N.B. Decree 2004–1420, 2004–12–23, Article 4: These provisions apply to review actions directed against decisions pronounced as of the 1 January 2005.

Article 1488

The judgment granting the exequatur order is not subject to any review action.

However, an appeal or review action to vacate an award amounts as of right, within the confines of the cognizance of the court of appeal, a review action against the order of the judge who has given the exequatur order or removal of the case from this judge.

Article 1489

The judgment disallowing exequatur may be impugned by appeal action until the end of a one-month time-limit to be reckoned from its service. In the latter event, the court of appeal examines, at the request of the parties, the grounds that the latter would have otherwise raised against the arbitral award, by way of appeal or review action to vacate as the case may be.

Article 1490

The dismissal of the appeal or the review action to vacate will give exequatur to the clauses that are affected by the revision of the court (of appeal).

Article 1491

A review action is available against the arbitral award in the cases and under the conditions provided for with respect to judgments.

It (the review action) is brought before the court of appeal that would have otherwise been competent to examine the other review actions against the award.

TITLE V*

INTERNATIONAL ARBITRATION

Article 1492

An international arbitration is the one that concerns interests of international trade.

* These provisions apply only to arbitration agreements entered into as of the 14th May of 1981, D. n°81–500, 12 May 1981, Article 55.

Article 1493

Directly or by way of reference to a resolution by arbitration, the arbitration agreement may designate the arbitrator (s) or provide for the terms and conditions of their appointment.

If, for arbitration proceedings held in France or those to which the parties have chosen to apply the French law of procedure, the convening of the arbitration tribunal encounters difficulties, the first mover may, unless otherwise agreed, bring his case to the president of the High Court of Paris according to the terms and conditions laid down under Article 1457.

Article 1494

The arbitration agreement may, directly or by way of reference to a resolution by arbitration, lay down the procedure to be followed in the course of the arbitration proceeding; it may also bring the latter under the law applicable to procedural matters that it determines.

Where the agreement is silent, the arbitrator will settle the procedure, to the extent that the same is necessary, either directly or by way of reference to a law or to a regulation of arbitration.

Article 1495

Where an international arbitration is submitted to French law, the provisions of titles I, II and III of this Book will apply only in default of specific agreements and subject to Articles 1493 and 1494.

Article 1496

The arbitrator determines the dispute according to rules of law that the parties have chosen; in default of such a choice, in accordance with rules he deems appropriate.

He takes into account all customs in commercial activities.

Article 1497

The arbitrator will decide as an amicable compounder if the agreement between the parties gives him this assignment.

TITLE VI*

RECOGNITION, COMPULSORY ENFORCEMENT AND MEANS OF REVIEW IN RELATION TO ARBITRAL AWARDS GIVEN ABROAD OR IN MATTERS OF INTERNATIONAL ARBITRATION

CHAPTER I

RECOGNITION AND COMPULSORY ENFORCEMENT IN RELATION TO ARBITRAL AWARDS GIVEN ABROAD OR IN MATTERS OF INTERNATIONAL ARBITRATION

Article 1498

Arbitral awards are recognized in France where the party who relies upon it has established their existence and if this recognition is not manifestly contrary to public international order.

Under the same conditions, they are declared enforceable in France by the judge for enforcement (of court decisions).

Article 1499

The existence of an arbitral award is established by the production of the original with the arbitration agreement or copies of the same that satisfy the conditions required for their authenticity.

If those documents are not drawn up in the French language, a party will produce a certified translation by a translator registered on the list of experts.

Article 1500

The provisions of Articles 1476 to 1479 will apply.

CHAPTER II

MEANS OF REVIEW IN RELATION TO ARBITRAL AWARDS GIVEN ABROAD OR IN MATTERS OF INTERNATIONAL ARBITRATION

Article 1501

The decision disallowing the recognition or enforcement of an award is subject to appeal.

Article 1502

An appeal against the decision, which grants recognition or enforcement, will be available only in the following cases:

* These provisions apply only to arbitration agreements entered into as of the 14th May of 1981, D. n°81–500, 12 May 1981, Article 56.

1° if the arbitrator has ruled upon the matter without an arbitration agreement or based on a void and lapsed agreement;

2° if the arbitration tribunal has been unlawfully constituted or the sole arbitrator has been unlawfully designated;

3° if the arbitrator has ruled upon the matter contrary to the assignment given to him;

4° if the adversarial principle has not been respected;

5° if the recognition or enforcement is contrary to public international order.

Article 1503

The appeal referred to under Articles 1501 and 1502 is brought before the court of appeal to which the judge who ruled upon the matter belongs. It may be brought until the end of a one-month of the time-limit to be reckoned from the service of the decision of the judge.

Article 1504

The arbitral award given in France in matters of international arbitration may be the subject-matter of a review action to vacate in the case provided for under Article 1502.

The judgment allowing the enforcement of this award is subject to a review action. However, the review action to vacate amounts as of right, within the confines of the action brought to the court of appeal, a review action against the judgment of the judge allowing execution or removal of the case from this judge.

Article 1505

The review action to vacate referred to under Article 1504 is brought before the court of appeal in whose jurisdiction the award was given. This action is admissible as soon as the award has been given; it will cease to be admissible if this right has not been exercised within the month of the service of the award declared enforceable.

Article 1506

The time-limit to bring a review action as referred to under Articles 1501, 1502 and 1504 suspends the execution of the arbitral award. Likewise, the review action brought within this time-limit suspends (also the execution of the award).

Article 1507

The provisions of Title IV of this Book, save those of sub-article 1 of Article 1487 and of Article 1490, will not apply to means of review.

C. SWISS PRIVATE INTERNATIONAL LAW ACT OF 1987, CHAPTER 12, INTERNATIONAL ARBITRATION

(as amended in 2007)

Art. 176

1. The provisions of this chapter shall apply to all arbitrations if the seat of the arbitral tribunal is in Switzerland and if, at the time of the conclusion of the arbitration agreement, at least one of the parties had neither its domicile nor its habitual residence in Switzerland.

2. The provisions of this chapter shall not apply where the parties have agreed in writing that the provisions of this chapter are excluded and that the cantonal provisions on arbitration should apply exclusively.

3. The parties, or the arbitral institution designated by them, or if they both fail to do so, the arbitrators, shall determine the seat of the arbitral tribunal.

Art. 177

1. Any dispute involving an economic interest may be the subject matter of arbitration.

2. A state, an enterprise owned, or an organization controlled by, a state which is a party to the arbitration agreement cannot rely on its own law in order to contest its capacity to be a party to an arbitration or the arbitrability of a dispute covered by the arbitration agreement.

Art. 178

1. Concerning form, an arbitration agreement is valid if it is made in writing, by telegram, telex, telecopier or any other means of communication that permits it to be evidenced by a text.

2. Concerning substance [material validity], an arbitration agreement is valid if it conforms either to the law chosen by the parties, or to the law governing the subject matter of the dispute, in particular the principal contract, or to Swiss law.

3. The validity of an arbitration agreement cannot be contested on the ground that the principal contract is not valid or that the arbitration agreement concerns a dispute that has not yet arisen.

Art. 179

1. The arbitrators shall be appointed, removed or replaced in accordance with the agreement of the parties.

2. In the absence of such an agreement, the judge where the tribunal has its seat may be seized with the issue, in which case, he shall apply, by

analogy, the provisions of cantonal law on appointment, removal or replacement of arbitrators.

3. When a judge has been designated as the authority for appointing an arbitrator, he shall make the appointment unless a summary examination shows that no arbitration agreement exists between the parties.

Art. 180

1. An arbitrator may be challenged:

(a) if he does not meet the qualifications agreed upon by the parties;

(b) if a ground for challenge exists under the rules of arbitration agreed upon by the parties;

(c) if circumstances exist that give rise to justifiable doubts as to his independence.

2. No party may challenge an arbitrator nominated by it, or whom it was instrumental in appointing, except on a ground that came to that party's knowledge after such appointment. The arbitral tribunal and the other party must be notified of the ground for challenge without delay.

3. To the extent that the parties have not provided for the challenge procedure, the judge at the seat of the arbitral tribunal shall make the final decision.

Art. 181

The arbitral proceedings shall be pending from the time when one of the parties seizes with a claim the arbitrator or arbitrators designated in the arbitration agreement or, in the absence of such a designation in the arbitration agreement, from the time when one of the parties initiates the procedure for the appointment of the arbitral tribunal.

Art. 182

1. The parties may, directly or by reference to rules of arbitration, determine the arbitral procedure; they may also submit the arbitral procedure to a procedural law of their choice.

2. If the parties have not determined the procedure, the arbitral tribunal shall determine it to the extent necessary, either directly or by reference to a statute or to rules of arbitration.

3. Regardless of the procedure chosen, the arbitral tribunal shall guarantee equal treatment of the parties and the right of both parties to be heard in adversarial proceedings.

Art. 183

1. Unless the parties have otherwise agreed, the arbitral tribunal may, on motion of one party, order provisional or conservatory measures.

2. If the party concerned does not voluntarily comply with these measures, the arbitral tribunal may request the assistance of the competent judge [one having jurisdiction]; the judge shall apply his own law.

3. The arbitral tribunal or the judge may condition the provisional or conservatory measures on the provision of appropriate security.

Art. 184

1. The arbitral tribunal shall itself conduct the taking of evidence.

2. If the assistance of the state judicial authorities is necessary for the taking of evidence, the arbitral tribunal, or one party by agreement with the arbitral tribunal, may request the assistance of the judge at the seat of the arbitral tribunal; the judge shall apply his own law.

Art. 185

For any further judicial assistance the judge at the seat of the arbitral tribunal shall have jurisdiction.

Art. 186

1. The arbitral tribunal shall itself decide on its jurisdiction.

1 bis. It shall decide on its jurisdiction notwithstanding an action on the same matter between the same parties already pending before a State Court or another arbitral tribunal, unless there are serious reasons to stay the proceedings.

2. A plea of lack of jurisdiction must be raised prior to any defense on the merits.

3. The Arbitral Tribunal shall, as a rule, decide on its jurisdiction by preliminary award.

Art. 187

1. The arbitral tribunal shall decide the case according to the rules of law agreed upon by the parties or, in the absence of such a choice, by applying the rules of law with which the dispute has the closest connection.

2. The parties may authorize the arbitral tribunal to decide the case ex aequo et bono.

Art. 188

Unless the parties have agreed otherwise, the arbitral tribunal may render partial awards.

Art. 189

1. The arbitral award shall be rendered in conformity with the rules of procedure and in the form agreed upon by the parties.

2. In the absence of such an agreement, the arbitral award shall be made by a majority, or, in default of a majority, by the presiding arbitrator

alone. The award shall be in writing, supported by reasons, dated and signed. The signature of the presiding arbitrator is sufficient.

Art. 190

1. The award is final once it has been communicated.

2. The award may only be challenged:

(a) When the sole arbitrator was not properly appointed or when the arbitral tribunal was not properly constituted;

(b) When the arbitral tribunal wrongly accepted or declined jurisdiction;

(c) When the arbitral tribunal's decision went beyond the questions submitted to it, or failed to decide one of the items in the claim submitted to it;

(d) When the principle of equality of the parties or the right of the parties to be heard in adversarial proceedings was breached;

(e) When the award is contrary to public policy.

3. Where the tribunal decided on its constitution or on its jurisdiction in a preliminary award, challenge is possible only on the basis of the above subsections 2(a) and 2(b); the time limit runs from the notification of the preliminary award.

Art. 191

1. The action for annulment may only be brought before the Federal Supreme Court. The procedure applicable to the annulment is governed by the provisions of the Federal Statute on the Organization of the Federal Judiciary regarding public law claims.

2. The parties may agree that the judge at the seat of the arbitral tribunal shall make the final decision in lieu of the Federal Supreme Court. For this purpose the cantons designate a sole cantonal authority.

Art. 192

1. If neither of two parties has a domicile, a habitual residence, or a business establishment in Switzerland, the parties may, by an express statement in the arbitration agreement or by a subsequent written agreement, waive completely the action for annulment or they may limit it to one or more of the grounds listed in Art. 190, subsection 2.

2. If the parties have waived completely the action for annulment and if the award is to be enforced in Switzerland, the New York Convention of June 10, 1958 on the Recognition and Enforcement of Foreign Arbitral Awards applies by analogy.

Art. 193

1. Each party may at its own expense deposit a copy of the award with the Swiss court at the seat of the arbitral tribunal.

2. On request of a party, the court shall certify that the award is executable.

3. On request of a party, the arbitral tribunal shall certify that the award was rendered pursuant to the provisions of this Statute; such certificate has the same effect as the deposit of the award.

Art. 194

The recognition and enforcement of a foreign arbitral award is governed by the New York Convention of June 10, 1958 on the Recognition and Enforcement of Foreign Arbitral Awards.

D. ENGLAND: ARBITRATION ACT OF 1996*

PART I

ARBITRATION PURSUANT TO AN ARBITRATION AGREEMENT

Introductory

1. The provisions of this Part are founded on the following principles, and shall be construed accordingly—
   (a) the object of arbitration is to obtain the fair resolution of disputes by an impartial tribunal without unnecessary delay or expense;
   (b) the parties should be free to agree how their disputes are resolved, subject only to such safeguards as are necessary in the public interest;
   (c) in matters governed by this Part the court should not intervene except as provided by this Part.

2. —(1) The provisions of this Part apply where the seat of the arbitration is in England and Wales or Northern Ireland.
   —(2) The following sections apply even if the seat of the arbitration is outside England and Wales or Northern Ireland or no seat has been designated or determined—
   (a) sections 9 to 11 (stay of legal proceedings, & c.), and
   (b) section 66 (enforcement of arbitral awards).

PART I

   —(3) The powers conferred by the following sections apply even if the seat of the arbitration is outside England and Wales or Northern Ireland or no seat has been designated or determined—
   (a) section 43 (securing the attendance of witnesses), and
   (b) section 44 (court powers exercisable in support of arbitral proceedings);
   but the court may refuse to exercise any such power if, in the opinion of the court, the fact that the seat of the arbitration is outside England and Wales or Northern

---

* Reproduced with the kind permission of the Controller of Her Majesty's Stationery Office. Applicable in England, Northern Ireland, and Wales.

Ireland, or that when designated or determined the seat is likely to be outside England and Wales or Northern Ireland, makes it inappropriate to do so.

—(4) The court may exercise a power conferred by any provision of this Part not mentioned in subsection (2) or (3) for the purpose of supporting the arbitral process where—

(a) no seat of the arbitration has been designated or determined, and

(b) by reason of a connection with England and Wales or Northern Ireland the court is satisfied that it is appropriate to do so.

—(5) Section 7 (separability of arbitration agreement) and section 8 (death of a party) apply where the law applicable to the arbitration agreement is the law of England and Wales or Northern Ireland even if the seat of the arbitration is outside England and Wales or Northern Ireland or has not been designated or determined.

3. In this Part "the seat of the arbitration" means the juridical seat of the arbitration designated—

(a) by the parties to the arbitration agreement, or

(b) by any arbitral or other institution or person vested by the parties with powers in that regard, or

(c) by the arbitral tribunal if so authorized by the parties, or determined, in the absence of any such designation, having regard to the parties' agreement and all the relevant circumstances.

4. —(1) The mandatory provisions of this Part are listed in Schedule 1 and have effect notwithstanding any agreement to the contrary.

—(2) The other provisions of this Part (the "non-mandatory provisions") allow the parties to make their own arrangements by agreement but provide rules which apply in the absence of such agreement.

—(3) The parties may make such arrangements by agreeing to the application of institutional rules or providing any other means by which a matter may be decided.

—(4) It is immaterial whether or not the law applicable to the parties' agreement is the law of England and Wales or, as the case may be, Northern Ireland.

—(5) The choice of a law other than the law of England and Wales or Northern Ireland as the applicable law in respect of a matter provided for by a non-mandatory provision of this Part is equivalent to an agreement making provision about that matter.

For this purpose an applicable law determined in accordance with the parties' agreement, or which is objectively determined in the absence of any express or implied choice, shall be treated as chosen by the parties.

5. —(1) The provisions of this Part apply only where the arbitration agreement is in writing, and any other agreement between the parties as to any matter is effective for the purposes of this Part only if in writing. The expressions

"agreement", "agree" and "agreed" shall be construed accordingly.

—(2) There is an agreement in writing—

(a) if the agreement is made in writing (whether or not it is signed by the parties),

(b) if the agreement is made by exchange of communications in writing, or

(c) if the agreement is evidenced in writing.

—(3) Where parties agree otherwise than in writing by reference to terms which are in writing, they make an agreement in writing.

—(4) An agreement is evidenced in writing if an agreement made otherwise than in writing is recorded by one of the parties, or by a third party, with the authority of the parties to the agreement.

—(5) An exchange of written submissions in arbitral or legal proceedings in which the existence of an agreement otherwise than in writing is alleged by one party against another party and not denied by the other party in his response constitutes as between those parties an agreement in writing to the effect alleged.

—(6) References in this Part to anything being written or in writing include its being recorded by any means.

6. —(1) In this Part an "arbitration agreement" means an agreement to submit to arbitration present or future disputes (whether they are contractual or not).

—(2) The reference in an agreement to a written form of arbitration clause or to a document containing an arbitration clause constitutes an arbitration agreement if the reference is such as to make that clause part of the agreement.

7. Unless otherwise agreed by the parties, an arbitration agreement which forms or was intended to form part of another agreement (whether or not in writing) shall not be regarded as invalid, non-existent or ineffective because that other agreement is invalid, or did not come into existence or has become ineffective, and it shall for that purpose be treated as a distinct agreement.

8. —(1) Unless otherwise agreed by the parties, an arbitration agreement is not discharged by the death of a party and may be enforced by or against the personal representatives of that party.

—(2) Subsection (1) does not affect the operation of any enactment or rule of law by virtue of which a substantive right or obligation is extinguished by death.

Stay of Legal Proceedings

9. —(1) A party to an arbitration agreement against whom legal proceedings are brought (whether by way of claim or counterclaim) in respect of a matter which under the agreement is to be referred to arbitration may (upon notice to the other parties to the proceedings) apply to the court in which the proceedings have been brought to stay the proceedings so far as they concern that matter.

—(2) An application may be made notwithstanding that the matter is to be referred to arbitration only after the exhaustion of other dispute resolution procedures.

—(3) An application may not be made by a person before taking the appropriate procedural step (if any) to acknowledge the legal proceedings against him or after he has taken any step in those proceedings to answer the substantive claim.

—(4) On an application under this section the court shall grant a stay unless satisfied that the arbitration agreement is null and void, inoperative, or incapable of being performed.

—(5) If the court refuses to stay the legal proceedings, any provision that an award is a condition precedent to the bringing of legal proceedings in respect of any matter is of no effect in relation to those proceedings.

10. —(1) Where in legal proceedings relief by way of interpleader is granted and any issue between the claimants is one in respect of which there is an arbitration agreement between them, the court granting the relief shall direct that the issue be determined in accordance with the agreement unless the circumstances are such that proceedings brought by a claimant in respect of the matter would not be stayed.

—(2) Where subsection (1) applies but the court does not direct that the issue be determined in accordance with the arbitration agreement, any provision that an award is a condition precedent to the bringing of legal proceedings in respect of any matter shall not affect the determination of that issue by the court.

11. —(1) Where Admiralty proceedings are stayed on the ground that the dispute in question should be submitted to arbitration, the court granting the stay may, if in those proceedings property has been arrested or bail or other security has been given to prevent or obtain release from arrest—

(a) order that the property arrested be retained as security for the satisfaction of any award given in the arbitration in respect of that dispute, or

(b) order that the stay of those proceedings be conditional on the provision of equivalent security for the satisfaction of any such award.

—(2) Subject to any provision made by rules of court and to any necessary modifications, the same law and practice shall apply in relation to property retained in pursuance of an order as would apply if it were held for the purposes of proceedings in the court making the order.

Commencement of Arbitral Proceedings

12. —(1) Where an arbitration agreement to refer future disputes to arbitration provides that a claim shall be barred, or the claimant's right extinguished, unless the claimant takes within a time fixed by the agreement some step—

(a) to begin arbitral proceedings, or
(b) to begin other dispute resolution procedures which must be exhausted before arbitral proceedings can be begun, the court may by order extend the time for taking that step.

—(2) Any party to the arbitration agreement may apply for such an order (upon notice to the other parties), but only after a claim has arisen and after exhausting any available arbitral process for obtaining an extension of time.

—(3) The court shall make an order only if satisfied—
(a) that the circumstances are such as were outside the reasonable contemplation of the parties when they agreed the provision in question, and that it would be just to extend the time, or
(b) that the conduct of one party makes it unjust to hold the other party to the strict terms of the provision in question.

—(4) The court may extend the time for such period and on such terms as it thinks fit, and may do so whether or not the time previously fixed (by agreement or by a previous order) has expired.

—(5) An order under this section does not affect the operation of the Limitation Acts (see section 13).

—(6) The leave of the court is required for any appeal from a decision of the court under this section.

13. —(1) The Limitation Acts apply to arbitral proceedings as they apply to legal proceedings.

—(2) The court may order that in computing the time prescribed by the Limitation Acts for the commencement of proceedings (including arbitral proceedings) in respect of a dispute which was the subject matter—
(a) of an award which the court orders to be set aside or declares to be of no effect, or
(b) of the affected part of an award which the court orders to be set aside in part, or declares to be in part of no effect, the period between the commencement of the arbitration and the date of the order referred to in paragraph (a) or (b) shall be excluded.

—(3) In determining for the purposes of the Limitation Acts when a cause of action accrued, any provision that an award is a condition precedent to the bringing of legal proceedings in respect of a matter to which an arbitration agreement applies shall be disregarded.

—(4) In this Part "the Limitation Acts" means—
(a) in England and Wales, the Limitation Act 1980, the Foreign Limitation Periods Act 1984 and any other enactment (whenever passed) relating to the limitation of actions;
(b) in Northern Ireland, the Limitation (Northern Ireland) Order 1989, the Foreign Limitation Periods (Northern Ireland) Order 1985 and any other enactment (whenever passed) relating to the limitation of actions.

14. —(1) The parties are free to agree when arbitral proceedings are to be regarded as commenced for the purposes of this Part and for the purposes of the Limitation Acts.

—(2) If there is no such agreement the following provisions apply.

—(3) Where the arbitrator is named or designated in the arbitration agreement, arbitral proceedings are commenced in respect of a matter when one party serves on the other party or parties a notice in writing requiring him or them to submit that matter to the person so named or designated.

—(4) Where the arbitrator or arbitrators are to be appointed by the parties, arbitral proceedings are commenced in respect of a matter when one party serves on the other party or parties notice in writing requiring him or them to appoint an arbitrator or to agree to the appointment of an arbitrator in respect of that matter.

—(5) Where the arbitrator or arbitrators are to be appointed by a person other than a party to the proceedings, arbitral proceedings are commenced in respect of a matter when one party gives notice in writing to that person requesting him to make the appointment in respect of that matter.

The arbitral tribunal

15. —(1) The parties are free to agree on the number of arbitrators to form the tribunal and whether there is to be a chairman or umpire.

—(2) Unless otherwise agreed by the parties, an agreement that the number of arbitrators shall be two or any other even number shall be understood as requiring the appointment of an additional arbitrator as chairman of the tribunal.

—(3) If there is no agreement as to the number of arbitrators, the tribunal shall consist of a sole arbitrator.

16. —(1) The parties are free to agree on the procedure for appointing the arbitrator or arbitrators, including the procedure for appointing any chairman or umpire.

—(2) If or to the extent that there is no such agreement, the following provisions apply.

—(3) If the tribunal is to consist of a sole arbitrator, the parties shall jointly appoint the arbitrator not later than 28 days after service of a request in writing by either party to do so.

—(4) If the tribunal is to consist of two arbitrators, each party shall appoint one arbitrator not later than 14 days after service of a request in writing by either party to do so.

—(5) If the tribunal is to consist of three arbitrators—

(a) each party shall appoint one arbitrator not later than 14 days after service of a request in writing by either party to do so, and

(b) the two so appointed shall forthwith appoint a third arbitrator as the chairman of the tribunal.

—(6) If the tribunal is to consist of two arbitrators and an umpire—

(a) each party shall appoint one arbitrator not later than 14 days after service of a request in writing by either party to do so, and

(b) the two so appointed may appoint an umpire at any time after they themselves are appointed and shall do so before any substantive hearing or forthwith if they cannot agree on a matter relating to the arbitration.

—(7) In any other case (in particular, if there are more than two parties) section 18 applies as in the case of a failure of the agreed appointment procedure.

17. —(1) Unless the parties otherwise agree, where each of two parties to an arbitration agreement is to appoint an arbitrator and one party ("the party in default") refuses to do so, or fails to do so within the time specified, the other party, having duly appointed his arbitrator, may give notice in writing to the party in default that he proposes to appoint his arbitrator to act as sole arbitrator.

—(2) If the party in default does not within 7 clear days of that notice being given—

(a) make the required appointment, and

(b) notify the other party that he has done so, the other party may appoint his arbitrator as sole arbitrator whose award shall be binding on both parties as if he had been so appointed by agreement.

—(3) Where a sole arbitrator has been appointed under subsection (2), the party in default may (upon notice to the appointing party) apply to the court which may set aside the appointment.

—(4) The leave of the court is required for any appeal from a decision of the court under this section.

18. —(1) The parties are free to agree what is to happen in the event of a failure of the procedure for the appointment of the arbitral tribunal. There is no failure if an appointment is duly made under section 17 (power in case of default to appoint sole arbitrator), unless that appointment is set aside.

—(2) If or to the extent that there is no such agreement any party to the arbitration agreement may (upon notice to the other parties) apply to the court to exercise its powers under this section.

—(3) Those powers are—

(a) to give directions as to the making of any necessary appointments;

(b) to direct that the tribunal shall be constituted by such appointments (or any one or more of them) as have been made;

(c) to revoke any appointments already made;

(d) to make any necessary appointments itself.

—(4) An appointment made by the court under this section has effect as if made with the agreement of the parties.

—(5) The leave of the court is required for any appeal from a decision of the court under this section.

19. In deciding whether to exercise, and in considering how to exercise, any of its powers under section 16 (procedure for appointment of arbitrators) or section 18 (failure of appointment procedure), the court shall have due regard to any agreement of the parties as to the qualifications required of the arbitrators.

20. —(1) Where the parties have agreed that there is to be a chairman, they are free to agree what the functions of the chairman are to be in relation to the making of decisions, orders and awards.

—(2) If or to the extent that there is no such agreement, the following provisions apply.

—(3) Decisions, orders and awards shall be made by all or a majority of the arbitrators (including the chairman).

—(4) The view of the chairman shall prevail in relation to a decision, order or award in respect of which there is neither unanimity nor a majority under subsection (3).

21. —(1) Where the parties have agreed that there is to be an umpire, they are free to agree what the functions of the umpire are to be, and in particular—

(a) whether he is to attend the proceedings, and

(b) when he is to replace the other arbitrators as the tribunal with power to make decisions, orders and awards.

—(2) If or to the extent that there is no such agreement, the following provisions apply.

—(3) The umpire shall attend the proceedings and be supplied with the same documents and other materials as are supplied to the other arbitrators.

—(4) Decisions, orders and awards shall be made by the other arbitrators unless and until they cannot agree on a matter relating to the arbitration. In that event they shall forthwith give notice in writing to the parties and the umpire, whereupon the umpire shall replace them as the tribunal with power to make decisions, orders and awards as if he were sole arbitrator.

—(5) If the arbitrators cannot agree but fail to give notice of that fact, or if any of them fails to join in the giving of notice, any party to the arbitral proceedings may (upon notice to the other parties and to the tribunal) apply to the court which may order that the umpire shall replace the other arbitrators as the tribunal with power to make decisions, orders and awards as if he were sole arbitrator.

—(6) The leave of the court is required for any appeal from a decision of the court under this section.

22. —(1) Where the parties agree that there shall be two or more arbitrators with no chairman or umpire, the parties are free to agree how the tribunal is to make decisions, orders and awards.

—(2) If there is no such agreement, decisions, orders and awards shall be made by all or a majority of the arbitrators.

23. —(1) The parties are free to agree in what circumstances the authority of an arbitrator may be revoked.

—(2) If or to the extent that there is no such agreement the following provisions apply.

—(3) The authority of an arbitrator may not be revoked except—

(a) by the parties acting jointly, or

(b) by an arbitral or other institution or person vested by the parties with powers in that regard.

—(4) Revocation of the authority of an arbitrator by the parties acting jointly must be agreed in writing unless the parties also agree (whether or not in writing) to terminate the arbitration agreement.

—(5) Nothing in this section affects the power of the court—

(a) to revoke an appointment under section 18 (powers exercisable in case of failure of appointment procedure), or

(b) to remove an arbitrator on the grounds specified in section 24.

24. —(1) A party to arbitral proceedings may (upon notice to the other parties, to the arbitrator concerned and to any other arbitrator) apply to the court to remove an arbitrator on any of the following grounds—

(a) that circumstances exist that give rise to justifiable doubts as to his impartiality;

(b) that he does not possess the qualifications required by the arbitration agreement;

(c) that he is physically or mentally incapable of conducting the proceedings or there are justifiable doubts as to his capacity to do so;

(d) that he has refused or failed—

(i) properly to conduct the proceedings, or

(ii) to use all reasonable despatch in conducting the proceedings or making an award, and that substantial injustice has been or will be caused to the applicant.

—(2) If there is an arbitral or other institution or person vested by the parties with power to remove an arbitrator, the court shall not exercise its power of removal unless satisfied that the applicant has first exhausted any available recourse to that institution or person.

—(3) The arbitral tribunal may continue the arbitral proceedings and make an award while an application to the court under this section is pending.

—(4) Where the court removes an arbitrator, it may make such order as it thinks fit with respect to his entitlement (if any) to fees or expenses, or the repayment of any fees or expenses already paid.

—(5) The arbitrator concerned is entitled to appear and be heard by the court before it makes any order under this section.

—(6) The leave of the court is required for any appeal from a decision of the court under this section.

25. —(1) The parties are free to agree with an arbitrator as to the consequences of his resignation as regards—
(a) his entitlement (if any) to fees or expenses, and
(b) any liability thereby incurred by him.
—(2) If or to the extent that there is no such agreement the following provisions apply.
—(3) An arbitrator who resigns his appointment may (upon notice to the parties) apply to the court—
(a) to grant him relief from any liability thereby incurred by him, and
(b) to make such order as it thinks fit with respect to his entitlement (if any) to fees or expenses or the repayment of any fees or expenses already paid.
—(4) If the court is satisfied that in all the circumstances it was reasonable for the arbitrator to resign, it may grant such relief as is mentioned in subsection (3)(a) on such terms as it thinks fit.
—(5) The leave of the court is required for any appeal from a decision of the court under this section.

26. —(1) The authority of an arbitrator is personal and ceases on his death.
—(2) Unless otherwise agreed by the parties, the death of the person by whom an arbitrator was appointed does not revoke the arbitrator's authority.

27. —(1) Where an arbitrator ceases to hold office, the parties are free to agree—
(a) whether and if so how the vacancy is to be filled,
(b) whether and if so to what extent the previous proceedings should stand, and
(c) what effect (if any) his ceasing to hold office has on any appointment made by him (alone or jointly).
—(2) If or to the extent that there is no such agreement, the following provisions apply.
—(3) The provisions of sections 16 (procedure for appointment of arbitrators) and 18 (failure of appointment procedure) apply in relation to the filling of the vacancy as in relation to an original appointment.
—(4) The tribunal (when reconstituted) shall determine whether and if so to what extent the previous proceedings should stand. This does not affect any right of a party to challenge those proceedings on any ground which had arisen before the arbitrator ceased to hold office.
—(5) His ceasing to hold office does not affect any appointment by him (alone or jointly) of another arbitrator, in particular any appointment of a chairman or umpire.

28. —(1) The parties are jointly and severally liable to pay to the arbitrators such reasonable fees and expenses (if any) as are appropriate in the circumstances.
—(2) Any party may apply to the court (upon notice to the other parties and to the arbitrators) which may order that the amount of the arbitrators' fees and expenses shall be considered and adjusted by such means and upon such terms as it may direct.

—(3) If the application is made after any amount has been paid to the arbitrators by way of fees or expenses, the court may order the repayment of such amount (if any) as is shown to be excessive, but shall not do so unless it is shown that it is reasonable in the circumstances to order repayment.

—(4) The above provisions have effect subject to any order of the court under section 24(4) or 25(3)(b) (order as to entitlement to fees or expenses in case of removal or resignation of arbitrator).

—(5) Nothing in this section affects any liability of a party to any other party to pay all or any of the costs of the arbitration (see sections 59 to 65) or any contractual right of an arbitrator to payment of his fees and expenses.

—(6) In this section references to arbitrators include an arbitrator who has ceased to act and an umpire who has not replaced the other arbitrators.

29. —(1) An arbitrator is not liable for anything done or omitted in the discharge or purported discharge of his functions as arbitrator unless the act or omission is shown to have been in bad faith.

—(2) Subsection (1) applies to an employee or agent of an arbitrator as it applies to the arbitrator himself.

—(3) This section does not affect any liability incurred by an arbitrator by reason of his resigning (but see section 25).

Jurisdiction of the arbitral tribunal

30. —(1) Unless otherwise agreed by the parties, the arbitral tribunal may rule on its own substantive jurisdiction, that is, as to—

(a) whether there is a valid arbitration agreement,
(b) whether the tribunal is properly constituted, and
(c) what matters have been submitted to arbitration in accordance with the arbitration agreement.

—(2) Any such ruling may be challenged by any available arbitral process of appeal or review or in accordance with the provisions of this Part.

31. —(1) An objection that the arbitral tribunal lacks substantive jurisdiction at the outset of the proceedings must be raised by a party not later than the time he takes the first step in the proceedings to contest the merits of any matter in relation to which he challenges the tribunal's jurisdiction. A party is not precluded from raising such an objection by the fact that he has appointed or participated in the appointment of an arbitrator.

—(2) Any objection during the course of the arbitral proceedings that the arbitral tribunal is exceeding its substantive jurisdiction must be made as soon as possible after the matter alleged to be beyond its jurisdiction is raised.

—(3) The arbitral tribunal may admit an objection later than the time specified in subsection (1) or (2) if it considers the delay justified.

—(4) Where an objection is duly taken to the tribunal's substantive jurisdiction and the tribunal has power to rule on its own jurisdiction, it may—

(a) rule on the matter in an award as to jurisdiction, or

(b) deal with the objection in its award on the merits. If the parties agree which of these courses the tribunal should take, the tribunal shall proceed accordingly.

—(5) The tribunal may in any case, and shall if the parties so agree, stay proceedings whilst an application is made to the court under section 32 (determination of preliminary point of jurisdiction).

32. —(1) The court may, on the application of a party to arbitral proceedings (upon notice to the other parties), determine any question as to the substantive jurisdiction of the tribunal. A party may lose the right to object (see section 73).

—(2) An application under this section shall not be considered unless—

(a) it is made with the agreement in writing of all the other parties to the proceedings, or

(b) it is made with the permission of the tribunal and the court is satisfied—

(i) that the determination of the question is likely to produce substantial savings in costs,

(ii) that the application was made without delay, and

(iii) that there is good reason why the matter should be decided by the court.

—(3) An application under this section, unless made with the agreement of all the other parties to the proceedings, shall state the grounds on which it is said that the matter should be decided by the court.

—(4) Unless otherwise agreed by the parties, the arbitral tribunal may continue the arbitral proceedings and make an award while an application to the court under this section is pending.

—(5) Unless the court gives leave, no appeal lies from a decision of the court whether the conditions specified in subsection (2) are met.

—(6) The decision of the court on the question of jurisdiction shall be treated as a judgment of the court for the purposes of an appeal. But no appeal lies without the leave of the court which shall not be given unless the court considers that the question involves a point of law which is one of general importance or is one which for some other special reason should be considered by the Court of Appeal.

The arbitral proceedings

33. —(1) The tribunal shall—

(a) act fairly and impartially as between the parties, giving each party a reasonable opportunity of putting his case and dealing with that of his opponent, and

(b) adopt procedures suitable to the circumstances of the particular case, avoiding unnecessary delay or expense, so as to provide a fair means for the resolution of the matters falling to be determined.

—(2) The tribunal shall comply with that general duty in conducting the arbitral proceedings, in its decisions on matters of procedure and evidence and in the exercise of all other powers conferred on it.

34. —(1) It shall be for the tribunal to decide all procedural and evidential matters, subject to the right of the parties to agree any matter.

—(2) Procedural and evidential matters include—

(a) when and where any part of the proceedings is to be held;

(b) the language or languages to be used in the proceedings and whether translations of any relevant documents are to be supplied;

(c) whether any and if so what form of written statements of claim and defense are to be used, when these should be supplied and the extent to which such statements can be later amended;

(d) whether any and if so which documents or classes of documents should be disclosed between and produced by the parties and at what stage;

(e) whether any and if so what questions should be put to and answered by the respective parties and when and in what form this should be done;

(f) whether to apply strict rules of evidence (or any other rules) as to the admissibility, relevance or weight of any material (oral, written or other) sought to be tendered on any matters of fact or opinion, and the time, manner and form in which such material should be exchanged and presented;

(g) whether and to what extent the tribunal should itself take the initiative in ascertaining the facts and the law;

(h) whether and to what extent there should be oral or written evidence or submissions.

—(3) The tribunal may fix the time within which any directions given by it are to be complied with, and may if it thinks fit extend the time so fixed (whether or not it has expired).

35. —(1) The parties are free to agree—

(a) that the arbitral proceedings shall be consolidated with other arbitral proceedings, or

(b) that concurrent hearings shall be held, on such terms as may be agreed.

—(2) Unless the parties agree to confer such power on the tribunal, the tribunal has no power to order consolidation of proceedings or concurrent hearings.

36. Unless otherwise agreed by the parties, a party to arbitral proceedings may be represented in the proceedings by a lawyer or other person chosen by him.

37. —(1) Unless otherwise agreed by the parties—

(a) the tribunal may—
(i) appoint experts or legal advisers to report to it and the parties, or
(ii) appoint assessors to assist it on technical matters, and may allow any such expert, legal adviser or assessor to attend the proceedings; and
(b) the parties shall be given a reasonable opportunity to comment on any information, opinion or advice offered by any such person.

—(2) The fees and expenses of an expert, legal adviser or assessor appointed by the tribunal for which the arbitrators are liable are expenses of the arbitrators for the purposes of this Part.

38. —(1) The parties are free to agree on the powers exercisable by the arbitral tribunal for the purposes of and in relation to the proceedings.

—(2) Unless otherwise agreed by the parties the tribunal has the following powers.

—(3) The tribunal may order a claimant to provide security for the costs of the arbitration. This power shall not be exercised on the ground that the claimant is—
(a) an individual ordinarily resident outside the United Kingdom, or
(b) a corporation or association incorporated or formed under the law of a country outside the United Kingdom, or whose central management and control is exercised outside the United Kingdom.

—(4) The tribunal may give directions in relation to any property which is the subject of the proceedings or as to which any question arises in the proceedings, and which is owned by or is in the possession of a party to the proceedings—
(a) for the inspection, photographing, preservation, custody or detention of the property by the tribunal, an expert or a party, or
(b) ordering that samples be taken from, or any observation be made of or experiment conducted upon, the property.

—(5) The tribunal may direct that a party or witness shall be examined on oath or affirmation, and may for that purpose administer any necessary oath or take any necessary affirmation.

—(6) The tribunal may give directions to a party for the preservation for the purposes of the proceedings of any evidence in his custody or control.

39. —(1) The parties are free to agree that the tribunal shall have power to order on a provisional basis any relief which it would have power to grant in a final award.

—(2) This includes, for instance, making—
(a) a provisional order for the payment of money or the disposition of property as between the parties, or
(b) an order to make an interim payment on account of the costs of the arbitration.

—(3) Any such order shall be subject to the tribunal's final adjudication; and the tribunal's final award, on the merits or as to costs, shall take account of any such order.

—(4) Unless the parties agree to confer such power on the tribunal, the tribunal has no such power. This does not affect its powers under section 47 (awards on different issues, & c.).

40. —(1) The parties shall do all things necessary for the proper and expeditious conduct of the arbitral proceedings.

—(2) This includes—

(a) complying without delay with any determination of the tribunal as to procedural or evidential matters, or with any order or directions of the tribunal, and

(b) where appropriate, taking without delay any necessary steps to obtain a decision of the court on a preliminary question of jurisdiction or law (see sections 32 and 45).

41. —(1) The parties are free to agree on the powers of the tribunal in case of a party's failure to do something necessary for the proper and expeditious conduct of the arbitration.

—(2) Unless otherwise agreed by the parties, the following provisions apply.

—(3) If the tribunal is satisfied that there has been inordinate and inexcusable delay on the part of the claimant in pursuing his claim and that the delay—

(a) gives rise, or is likely to give rise, to a substantial risk that it is not possible to have a fair resolution of the issues in that claim, or

(b) has caused, or is likely to cause, serious prejudice to the respondent the tribunal may make an award dismissing the claim.

—(4) If without showing sufficient cause a party—

(a) fails to attend or be represented at an oral hearing of which due notice was given, or

(b) where matters are to be dealt with in writing, fails after due notice to submit written evidence or make written submissions, the tribunal may continue the proceedings in the absence of that party or, as the case may be, without any written evidence or submissions on his behalf, and may make an award on the basis of the evidence before it.

—(5) If without showing sufficient cause a party fails to comply with any order or directions of the tribunal, the tribunal may make a peremptory order to the same effect, prescribing such time for compliance with it as the tribunal considers appropriate.

—(6) If a claimant fails to comply with a peremptory order of the tribunal to provide security for costs, the tribunal may make an award dismissing his claim.

—(7) If a party fails to comply with any other kind of peremptory order, then, without prejudice to section 42 (enforcement by court of tribunal's peremptory orders), the tribunal may do any of the following—

(a) direct that the party in default shall not be entitled to rely upon any allegation or material which was the subject matter of the order;
(b) draw such adverse inferences from the act of non-compliance as the circumstances justify;
(c) proceed to an award on the basis of such materials as have been properly provided to it;
(d) make such order as it thinks fit as to the payment of costs of the arbitration incurred in consequence of the non-compliance.

Powers of court in relation to arbitral proceedings

42. —(1) Unless otherwise agreed by the parties, the court may make an order requiring a party to comply with a peremptory order made by the tribunal.

—(2) An application for an order under this section may be made—
(a) by the tribunal (upon notice to the parties),
(b) by a party to the arbitral proceedings with the permission of the tribunal (and upon notice to the other parties), or
(c) where the parties have agreed that the powers of the court under this section shall be available.

—(3) The court shall not act unless it is satisfied that the applicant has exhausted any available arbitral process in respect of failure to comply with the tribunal's order.

—(4) No order shall be made under this section unless the court is satisfied that the person to whom the tribunal's order was directed has failed to comply with it within the time prescribed in the order or, if no time was prescribed, within a reasonable time.

—(5) The leave of the court is required for any appeal from a decision of the court under this section.

43. —(1) A party to arbitral proceedings may use the same court procedures as are available in relation to legal proceedings to secure the attendance before the tribunal of a witness in order to give oral testimony or to produce documents or other material evidence.

—(2) This may only be done with the permission of the tribunal or the agreement of the other parties.

—(3) The court procedures may only be used if—
(a) the witness is in the United Kingdom, and
(b) the arbitral proceedings are being conducted in England and Wales or, as the case may be, Northern Ireland.

—(4) A person shall not be compelled by virtue of this section to produce any document or other material evidence which he could not be compelled to produce in legal proceedings.

44. —(1) Unless otherwise agreed by the parties, the court has for the purposes of and in relation to arbitral proceedings the same power of making orders about the matters

listed below as it has for the purposes of and in relation to legal proceedings.

—(2) Those matters are—

(a) the taking of the evidence of witnesses;

(b) the preservation of evidence;

(c) making orders relating to property which is the subject of the proceedings or as to which any question arises in the proceedings—

(i) for the inspection, photographing, preservation, custody or detention of the property, or

(ii) ordering that samples be taken from, or any observation be made of or experiment conducted upon, the property; and for that purpose authorizing any person to enter any premises in the possession or control of a party to the arbitration;

(d) the sale of any goods the subject of the proceedings;

(e) the granting of an interim injunction or the appointment of a receiver.

—(3) If the case is one of urgency, the court may, on the application of a party or proposed party to the arbitral proceedings, make such orders as it thinks necessary for the purpose of preserving evidence or assets.

—(4) If the case is not one of urgency, the court shall act only on the application of a party to the arbitral proceedings (upon notice to the other parties and to the tribunal) made with the permission of the tribunal or the agreement in writing of the other parties.

—(5) In any case the court shall act only if or to the extent that the arbitral tribunal, and any arbitral or other institution or person vested by the parties with power in that regard, has no power or is unable for the time being to act effectively.

—(6) If the court so orders, an order made by it under this section shall cease to have effect in whole or in part on the order of the tribunal or of any such arbitral or other institution or person having power to act in relation to the subject-matter of the order.

—(7) The leave of the court is required for any appeal from a decision of the court under this section.

45. —(1) Unless otherwise agreed by the parties, the court may on the application of a party to arbitral proceedings (upon notice to the other parties) determine any question of law arising in the course of the proceedings which the court is satisfied substantially affects the rights of one or more of the parties. An agreement to dispense with reasons for the tribunal's award shall be considered an agreement to exclude the court's jurisdiction under this section.

—(2) An application under this section shall not be considered unless—

(a) it is made with the agreement of all the other parties to the proceedings, or

(b) it is made with the permission of the tribunal and the court is satisfied—
    (i) that the determination of the question is likely to produce substantial savings in costs, and
    (ii) that the application was made without delay.

—(3) The application shall identify the question of law to be determined and, unless made with the agreement of all the other parties to the proceedings, shall state the grounds on which it is said that the question should be decided by the court.

—(4) Unless otherwise agreed by the parties, the arbitral tribunal may continue the arbitral proceedings and make an award while an application to the court under this section is pending.

—(5) Unless the court gives leave, no appeal lies from a decision of the court whether the conditions specified in subsection (2) are met.

—(6) The decision of the court on the question of law shall be treated as a judgment of the court for the purposes of an appeal. But no appeal lies without the leave of the court which shall not be given unless the court considers that the question is one of general importance, or is one which for some other special reason should be considered by the Court of Appeal.

The award

46. —(1) The arbitral tribunal shall decide the dispute—
    (a) in accordance with the law chosen by the parties as applicable to the substance of the dispute, or
    (b) if the parties so agree, in accordance with such other considerations as are agreed by them or determined by the tribunal.

—(2) For this purpose the choice of the laws of a country shall be understood to refer to the substantive laws of that country and not its conflict of laws rules.

—(3) If or to the extent that there is no such choice or agreement, the tribunal shall apply the law determined by the conflict of laws rules which it considers applicable.

47. —(1) Unless otherwise agreed by the parties, the tribunal may make more than one award at different times on different aspects of the matters to be determined.

—(2) The tribunal may, in particular, make an award relating—
    (a) to an issue affecting the whole claim, or
    (b) to a part only of the claims or cross-claims submitted to it for decision.

—(3) If the tribunal does so, it shall specify in its award the issue, or the claim or part of a claim, which is the subject matter of the award.

48. —(1) The parties are free to agree on the powers exercisable by the arbitral tribunal as regards remedies.

—(2) Unless otherwise agreed by the parties, the tribunal has the following powers.

—(3) The tribunal may make a declaration as to any matter to be determined in the proceedings.

—(4) The tribunal may order the payment of a sum of money, in any currency.

—(5) The tribunal has the same powers as the court—

(a) to order a party to do or refrain from doing anything;

(b) to order specific performance of a contract (other than a contract relating to land);

(c) to order the rectification, setting aside or cancellation of a deed or other document.

49. —(1) The parties are free to agree on the powers of the tribunal as regards the award of interest.

—(2) Unless otherwise agreed by the parties the following provisions apply.

—(3) The tribunal may award simple or compound interest from such dates, at such rates and with such rests as it considers meets the justice of the case—

(a) on the whole or part of any amount awarded by the tribunal, in respect of any period up to the date of the award;

(b) on the whole or part of any amount claimed in the arbitration and outstanding at the commencement of the arbitral proceedings but paid before the award was made, in respect of any period up to the date of payment.

—(4) The tribunal may award simple or compound interest from the date of the award (or any later date) until payment, at such rates and with such rests as it considers meets the justice of the case, on the outstanding amount of any award (including any award of interest under subsection (3) and any award as to costs).

—(5) References in this section to an amount awarded by the tribunal include an amount payable in consequence of a declaratory award by the tribunal.

—(6) The above provisions do not affect any other power of the tribunal to award interest.

50. —(1) Where the time for making an award is limited by or in pursuance of the arbitration agreement, then, unless otherwise agreed by the parties, the court may in accordance with the following provisions by order extend that time.

—(2) An application for an order under this section may be made—

(a) by the tribunal (upon notice to the parties), or

(b) by any party to the proceedings (upon notice to the tribunal and the other parties), but only after exhausting any available arbitral process for obtaining an extension of time.

—(3) The court shall only make an order if satisfied that a substantial injustice would otherwise be done.

—(4) The court may extend the time for such period and on such terms as it thinks fit, and may do so whether or not the time previously fixed (by or under the agreement or by a previous order) has expired.

—(5) The leave of the court is required for any appeal from a decision of the court under this section.

51. —(1) If during arbitral proceedings the parties settle the dispute, the following provisions apply unless otherwise agreed by the parties.

—(2) The tribunal shall terminate the substantive proceedings and, if so requested by the parties and not objected to by the tribunal, shall record the settlement in the form of an agreed award.

—(3) An agreed award shall state that it is an award of the tribunal and shall have the same status and effect as any other award on the merits of the case.

—(4) The following provisions of this Part relating to awards (sections 52 to 58) apply to an agreed award.

—(5) Unless the parties have also settled the matter of the payment of the costs of the arbitration, the provisions of this Part relating to costs (sections 59 to 65) continue to apply.

52. —(1) The parties are free to agree on the form of an award.

—(2) If or to the extent that there is no such agreement, the following provisions apply.

—(3) The award shall be in writing signed by all the arbitrators or all those assenting to the award.

—(4) The award shall contain the reasons for the award unless it is an agreed award or the parties have agreed to dispense with reasons.

—(5) The award shall state the seat of the arbitration and the date when the award is made.

53. Unless otherwise agreed by the parties, where the seat of the arbitration is in England and Wales or Northern Ireland, any award in the proceedings shall be treated as made there, regardless of where it was signed, despatched or delivered to any of the parties.

54. —(1) Unless otherwise agreed by the parties, the tribunal may decide what is to be taken to be the date on which the award was made.

—(2) In the absence of any such decision, the date of the award shall be taken to be the date on which it is signed by the arbitrator or, where more than one arbitrator signs the award, by the last of them.

55. —(1) The parties are free to agree on the requirements as to notification of the award to the parties.

—(2) If there is no such agreement, the award shall be notified to the parties by service on them of copies of the award, which shall be done without delay after the award is made.

—(3) Nothing in this section affects section 56 (power to withhold award in case of non-payment).

56. —(1) The tribunal may refuse to deliver an award to the parties except upon full payment of the fees and expenses of the arbitrators.

—(2) If the tribunal refuses on that ground to deliver an award, a party to the arbitral proceedings may (upon notice to the other parties and the tribunal) apply to the court, which may order that—

(a) the tribunal shall deliver the award on the payment into court by the applicant of the fees and expenses demanded, or such lesser amount as the court may specify,

(b) the amount of the fees and expenses properly payable shall be determined by such means and upon such terms as the court may direct, and

(c) out of the money paid into court there shall be paid out such fees and expenses as may be found to be properly payable and the balance of the money (if any) shall be paid out to the applicant.

—(3) For this purpose the amount of fees and expenses properly payable is the amount the applicant is liable to pay under section 28 or any agreement relating to the payment of the arbitrators.

—(4) No application to the court may be made where there is any available arbitral process for appeal or review of the amount of the fees or expenses demanded.

—(5) References in this section to arbitrators include an arbitrator who has ceased to act and an umpire who has not replaced the other arbitrators.

—(6) The above provisions of this section also apply in relation to any arbitral or other institution or person vested by the parties with powers in relation to the delivery of the tribunal's award. As they so apply, the references to the fees and expenses of the arbitrators shall be construed as including the fees and expenses of that institution or person.

—(7) The leave of the court is required for any appeal from a decision of the court under this section.

—(8) Nothing in this section shall be construed as excluding an application under section 28 where payment has been made to the arbitrators in order to obtain the award.

57. —(1) The parties are free to agree on the powers of the tribunal to correct an award or make an additional award.

—(2) If or to the extent there is no such agreement, the following provisions apply.

—(3) The tribunal may on its own initiative or on the application of a party—

(a) correct an award so as to remove any clerical mistake or error arising from an accidental slip or omission or clarify or remove any ambiguity in the award, or

(b) make an additional award in respect of any claim (including a claim for interest or costs) which was presented to the tribunal but was not dealt with in the award. These powers shall not be exercised without first affording the other parties a reasonable opportunity to make representations to the tribunal.

—(4) Any application for the exercise of those powers must be made within 28 days of the date of the award or such longer period as the parties may agree.

—(5) Any correction of an award shall be made within 28 days of the date the application was received by the tribunal or, where the correction is made by the tribunal on its own initiative, within 28 days of the date of the award or, in either case, such longer period as the parties may agree.

—(6) Any additional award shall be made within 56 days of the date of the original award or such longer period as the parties may agree.

—(7) Any correction of an award shall form part of the award.

58. —(1) Unless otherwise agreed by the parties, an award made by the tribunal pursuant to an arbitration agreement is final and binding both on the parties and on any persons claiming through or under them.

—(2) This does not affect the right of a person to challenge the award by any available arbitral process of appeal or review or in accordance with the provisions of this Part.

Costs of the arbitration

59. —(1) References in this Part to the costs of the arbitration are to—

(a) the arbitrators' fees and expenses,

(b) the fees and expenses of any arbitral institution concerned, and

(c) the legal or other costs of the parties.

—(2) Any such reference includes the costs of or incidental to any proceedings to determine the amount of the recoverable costs of the arbitration (see section 63).

60. An agreement which has the effect that a party is to pay the whole or part of the costs of the arbitration in any event is only valid if made after the dispute in question has arisen.

61. —(1) The tribunal may make an award allocating the costs of the arbitration as between the parties, subject to any agreement of the parties.

—(2) Unless the parties otherwise agree, the tribunal shall award costs on the general principle that costs should follow the event except where it appears to the tribunal that in the circumstances this is not appropriate in relation to the whole or part of the costs.

62. Unless the parties otherwise agree, any obligation under an agreement between them as to how the costs of the arbitration are to be borne, or under an award allocating the costs of the arbitration, extends only to such costs as are recoverable.

63. —(1) The parties are free to agree what costs of the arbitration are recoverable.

—(2) If or to the extent there is no such agreement, the following provisions apply.

—(3) The tribunal may determine by award the recoverable costs of the arbitration on such basis as it thinks fit. If it does so, it shall specify—

(a) the basis on which it has acted, and
(b) the items of recoverable costs and the amount referable to each.

—(4) If the tribunal does not determine the recoverable costs of the arbitration, any party to the arbitral proceedings may apply to the court (upon notice to the other parties) which may—
(a) determine the recoverable costs of the arbitration on such basis as it thinks fit, or
(b) order that they shall be determined by such means and upon such terms as it may specify.

—(5) unless the tribunal or the court determines otherwise—
(a) the recoverable costs of the arbitration shall be determined on the basis that there shall be allowed a reasonable amount in respect of all costs reasonably incurred, and
(b) any doubt as to whether costs were reasonably incurred or were reasonable in amount shall be resolved in favour of the paying party.

—(6) The above provisions have effect subject to section 64 (recoverable fees and expenses of arbitrators).

—(7) Nothing in this section affects any right of the arbitrators, any expert, legal adviser or assessor appointed by the tribunal, or any arbitral institution, to payment of their fees and expenses.

64. —(1) Unless otherwise agreed by the parties, the recoverable costs of the arbitration shall include in respect of the fees and expenses of the arbitrators only such reasonable fees and expenses as are appropriate in the circumstances.

—(2) If there is any question as to what reasonable fees and expenses are appropriate in the circumstances, and the matter is not already before the court on an application under section 63(4), the court may on the application of any party (upon notice to the other parties)—
(a) determine the matter, or
(b) order that it be determined by such means and upon such terms as the court may specify.

—(3) Subsection (1) has effect subject to any order of the court under section 24(4) or 25(3)(b) (order as to entitlement to fees or expenses in case of removal or resignation of arbitrator).

—(4) Nothing in this section affects any right of the arbitrator to payment of his fees and expenses.

65. —(1) Unless otherwise agreed by the parties, the tribunal may direct that the recoverable costs of the arbitration, or of any part of the arbitral proceedings, shall be limited to a specified amount.

—(2) Any direction may be made or varied at any stage, but this must be done sufficiently in advance of the incurring of costs to which it relates, or the taking of any steps in the proceedings which may be affected by it, for the limit to be taken into account.

Powers of the court in relation to award

66. —(1) An award made by the tribunal pursuant to an arbitration agreement may, by leave of the court, be enforced in the same manner as a judgment or order of the court to the same effect.

—(2) Where leave is so given, judgment may be entered in terms of the award.

—(3) Leave to enforce an award shall not be given where, or to the extent that, the person against whom it is sought to be enforced shows that the tribunal lacked substantive jurisdiction to make the award. The right to raise such an objection may have been lost (see section 73).

—(4) Nothing in this section affects the recognition or enforcement of an award under any other enactment or rule of law, in particular under Part II of the Arbitration Act 1950 (enforcement of awards under Geneva Convention) or the provisions of Part III of this Act relating to the recognition and enforcement of awards under the New York Convention or by an action on the award.

67. —(1) A party to arbitral proceedings may (upon notice to the other parties and to the tribunal) apply to the court—

(a) challenging any award of the arbitral tribunal as to its substantive jurisdiction; or

(b) for an order declaring an award made by the tribunal on the merits to be of no effect, in whole or in part, because the tribunal did not have substantive jurisdiction. A party may lose the right to object (see section 73) and the right to apply is subject to the restrictions in section 70(2) and (3).

—(2) The arbitral tribunal may continue the arbitral proceedings and make a further award while an application to the court under this section is pending in relation to an award as to jurisdiction.

—(3) On an application under this section challenging an award of the arbitral tribunal as to its substantive jurisdiction, the court may by order—

(a) confirm the award,

(b) vary the award, or

(c) set aside the award in whole or in part.

—(4) The leave of the court is required for any appeal from a decision of the court under this section.

68. —(1) A party to arbitral proceedings may (upon notice to the other parties and to the tribunal) apply to the court challenging an award in the proceedings on the ground of serious irregularity affecting the tribunal, the proceedings or the award. A party may lose the right to object (see section 73) and the right to apply is subject to the restrictions in section 70(2) and (3).

—(2) Serious irregularity means an irregularity of one or more of the following kinds which the court considers has caused or will cause substantial injustice to the applicant—

(a) failure by the tribunal to comply with section 33 (general duty of tribunal);
(b) the tribunal exceeding its powers (otherwise than by exceeding its substantive jurisdiction: see section 67);
(c) failure by the tribunal to conduct the proceedings in accordance with the procedure agreed by the parties;
(d) failure by the tribunal to deal with all the issues that were put to it;
(e) any arbitral or other institution or person vested by the parties with powers in relation to the proceedings or the award exceeding its powers;
(f) uncertainty or ambiguity as to the effect of the award;
(g) the award being obtained by fraud or the award or the way in which it was procured being contrary to public policy;
(h) failure to comply with the requirements as to the form of the award; or
(i) any irregularity in the conduct of the proceedings or in the award which is admitted by the tribunal or by any arbitral or other institution or person vested by the parties with powers in relation to the proceedings or the award.

—(3) If there is shown to be serious irregularity affecting the tribunal, the proceedings or the award, the court may—
(a) remit the award to the tribunal, in whole or in part, for reconsideration,
(b) set the award aside in whole or in part, or
(c) declare the award to be of no effect, in whole or in part. The court shall not exercise its power to set aside or to declare an award to be of no effect, in whole or in part, unless it is satisfied that it would be inappropriate to remit the matters in question to the tribunal for reconsideration.

—(4) The leave of the court is required for any appeal from a decision of the court under this section.

69. —(1) Unless otherwise agreed by the parties, a party to arbitral proceedings may (upon notice to the other parties and to the tribunal) appeal to the court on a question of law arising out of an award made in the proceedings. An agreement to dispense with reasons for the tribunal's award shall be considered an agreement to exclude the court's jurisdiction under this section.

—(2) An appeal shall not be brought under this section except—
(a) with the agreement of all the other parties to the proceedings, or
(b) with the leave of the court. The right to appeal is also subject to the restrictions in section 70(2) and (3).

—(3) Leave to appeal shall be given only if the court is satisfied—

(a) that the determination of the question will substantially affect the rights of one or more of the parties,

(b) that the question is one which the tribunal was asked to determine,

(c) that, on the basis of the findings of fact in the award—

(i) the decision of the tribunal on the question is obviously wrong, or

(ii) the question is one of general public importance and the decision of the tribunal is at least open to serious doubt, and

(d) that, despite the agreement of the parties to resolve the matter by arbitration, it is just and proper in all the circumstances for the court to determine the question.

—(4) An application for leave to appeal under this section shall identify the question of law to be determined and state the grounds on which it is alleged that leave to appeal should be granted.

—(5) The court shall determine an application for leave to appeal under this section without a hearing unless it appears to the court that a hearing is required.

—(6) The leave of the court is required for any appeal from a decision of the court under this section to grant or refuse leave to appeal.

—(7) On an appeal under this section the court may by order—

(a) confirm the award,

(b) vary the award,

(c) remit the award to the tribunal, in whole or in part, for reconsideration in the light of the court's determination, or

(d) set aside the award in whole or in part. The court shall not exercise its power to set aside an award, in whole or in part, unless it is satisfied that it would be inappropriate to remit the matters in question to the tribunal for reconsideration.

—(8) The decision of the court on an appeal under this section shall be treated as a judgment of the court for the purposes of a further appeal. But no such appeal lies without the leave of the court which shall not be given unless the court considers that the question is one of general importance or is one which for some other special reason should be considered by the Court of Appeal.

70. —(1) The following provisions apply to an application or appeal under section 67, 68 or 69.

—(2) An application or appeal may not be brought if the applicant or appellant has not first exhausted—

(a) any available arbitral process of appeal or review, and

(b) any available recourse under section 57 (correction of award or additional award).

—(3) Any application or appeal must be brought within 28 days of the date of the award or, if there has been any arbitral process of appeal or review, of the date when the applicant or appellant was notified of the result of that process.

—(4) If on an application or appeal it appears to the court that the award—

(a) does not contain the tribunal's reasons, or

(b) does not set out the tribunal's reasons in sufficient detail to enable the court properly to consider the application or appeal, the court may order the tribunal to state the reasons for its award in sufficient detail for that purpose.

—(5) Where the court makes an order under subsection (4), it may make such further order as it thinks fit with respect to any additional costs of the arbitration resulting from its order.

—(6) The court may order the applicant or appellant to provide security for the costs of the application or appeal, and may direct that the application or appeal be dismissed if the order is not complied with. The power to order security for costs shall not be exercised on the ground that the applicant or appellant is—

(a) an individual ordinarily resident outside the United Kingdom, or

(b) a corporation or association incorporated or formed under the law of a country outside the United Kingdom, or whose central management and control is exercised outside the United Kingdom.

—(7) The court may order that any money payable under the award shall be brought into court or otherwise secured pending the determination of the application or appeal, and may direct that the application or appeal be dismissed if the order is not complied with.

—(8) The court may grant leave to appeal subject to conditions to the same or similar effect as an order under subsection (6) or (7). This does not affect the general discretion of the court to grant leave subject to conditions.

71. —(1) The following provisions have effect where the court makes an order under section 67, 68 or 69 with respect to an award.

—(2) Where the award is varied, the variation has effect as part of the tribunal's award.

—(3) Where the award is remitted to the tribunal, in whole or in part, for reconsideration, the tribunal shall make a fresh award in respect of the matters remitted within three months of the date of the order for remission or such longer or shorter period as the court may direct.

—(4) Where the award is set aside or declared to be of no effect, in whole or in part, the court may also order that any provision that an award is a condition precedent to the bringing of legal proceedings in respect of a matter to which the arbitration agreement applies, is of no effect as regards the subject matter of the award or, as the case may be, the relevant part of the award.

Miscellaneous

72. —(1) A person alleged to be a party to arbitral proceedings but who takes no part in the proceedings may question—
(a) whether there is a valid arbitration agreement,
(b) whether the tribunal is properly constituted, or
(c) what matters have been submitted to arbitration in accordance with the arbitration agreement, by proceedings in the court for a declaration or injunction or other appropriate relief.

—(2) He also has the same right as a party to the arbitral proceedings to challenge an award—
(a) by an application under section 67 on the ground of lack of substantive jurisdiction in relation to him, or
(b) by an application under section 68 on the ground of serious irregularity (within the meaning of that section) affecting him; and section 70(2) (duty to exhaust arbitral procedures) does not apply in his case.

73. —(1) If a party to arbitral proceedings takes part, or continues to take part, in the proceedings without making, either forthwith or within such time as is allowed by the arbitration agreement or the tribunal or by any provision of this Part, any objection—
(a) that the tribunal lacks substantive jurisdiction,
(b) that the proceedings have been improperly conducted,
(c) that there has been a failure to comply with the arbitration agreement or with any provision of this Part, or
(d) that there has been any other irregularity affecting the tribunal or the proceedings, he may not raise that objection later, before the tribunal or the court, unless he shows that, at the time he took part or continued to take part in the proceedings, he did not know and could not with reasonable diligence have discovered the grounds for the objection.

—(2) Where the arbitral tribunal rules that it has substantive jurisdiction and a party to arbitral proceedings who could have questioned that ruling—
(a) by any available arbitral process of appeal or review, or
(b) by challenging the award, does not do so, or does not do so within the time allowed by the arbitration agreement or any provision of this Part, he may not object later to the tribunal's substantive jurisdiction on any ground which was the subject of that ruling.

74. —(1) An arbitral or other institution or person designated or requested by the parties to appoint or nominate an arbitrator is not liable for anything done or omitted in the discharge or purported discharge of that function unless the act or omission is shown to have been in bad faith.

—(2) An arbitral or other institution or person by whom an arbitrator is appointed or nominated is not liable, by reason of having appointed or nominated him, for anything done or omitted by the arbitrator (or his employees or agents) in the discharge or purported discharge of his functions as arbitrator.

—(3) The above provisions apply to an employee or agent of an arbitral or other institution or person as they apply to the institution or person himself.

75. The powers of the court to make declarations and orders under section 73 of the Solicitors Act 1974 or Article 71H of the Solicitors (Northern Ireland) Order 1976 (power to charge property recovered in the proceedings with the payment of solicitors' costs) may be exercised in relation to arbitral proceedings as if those proceedings were proceedings in the court.

Supplementary

76. —(1) The parties are free to agree on the manner of service of any notice or other document required or authorized to be given or served in pursuance of the arbitration agreement or for the purposes of the arbitral proceedings.

—(2) If or to the extent that there is no such agreement the following provisions apply.

—(3) A notice or other document may be served on a person by any effective means.

—(4) If a notice or other document is addressed, pre-paid and delivered by post—

(a) to the addressee's last known principal residence or, if he is or has been carrying on a trade, profession or business, his last known principal business address, or

(b) where the addressee is a body corporate, to the body's registered or principal office, it shall be treated as effectively served.

—(5) This section does not apply to the service of documents for the purposes of legal proceedings, for which provision is made by rules of court.

—(6) References in this Part to a notice or other document include any form of communication in writing and references to giving or serving a notice or other document shall be construed accordingly.

77. —(1) This section applies where service of a document on a person in the manner agreed by the parties, or in accordance with provisions of section 76 having effect in default of agreement, is not reasonably practicable.

—(2) Unless otherwise agreed by the parties, the court may make such order as it thinks fit—

(a) for service in such manner as the court may direct, or

(b) dispensing with service of the document.

—(3) Any party to the arbitration agreement may apply for an order, but only after exhausting any available arbitral process for resolving the matter.

—(4) The leave of the court is required for any appeal from a decision of the court under this section.

78. —(1) The parties are free to agree on the method of reckoning periods of time for the purposes of any provision agreed by them or any provision of this Part having effect in default of such agreement.

—(2) If or to the extent there is no such agreement, periods of time shall be reckoned in accordance with the following provisions.

—(3) Where the act is required to be done within a specified period after or from a specified date, the period begins immediately after that date.

—(4) Where the act is required to be done a specified number of clear days after a specified date, at least that number of days must intervene between the day on which the act is done and that date.

—(5) Where the period is a period of seven days or less which would include a Saturday, Sunday or a public holiday in the place where anything which has to be done within the period falls to be done, that day shall be excluded. In relation to England and Wales or Northern Ireland, a "public holiday" means Christmas Day, Good Friday or a day which under the Banking and Financial Dealings Act 1971 is a bank holiday.

79. —(1) Unless the parties otherwise agree, the court may by order extend any time limit agreed by them in relation to any matter relating to the arbitral proceedings or specified in any provision of this Part having effect in default of such agreement. This section does not apply to a time limit to which section 12 applies (power of court to extend time for beginning arbitral proceedings, & c.).

—(2) An application for an order may be made-

(a) by any party to the arbitral proceedings (upon notice to the other parties and to the tribunal), or

(b) by the arbitral tribunal (upon notice to the parties).

—(3) The court shall not exercise its power to extend a time limit unless it is satisfied—

(a) that any available recourse to the tribunal, or to any arbitral or other institution or person vested by the parties with power in that regard, has first been exhausted, and

(b) that a substantial injustice would otherwise be done.

—(4) The court's power under this section may be exercised whether or not the time has already expired.

—(5) An order under this section may be made on such terms as the court thinks fit.

—(6) The leave of the court is required for any appeal from a decision of the court under this section.

80. —(1) References in this Part to an application, appeal or other step in relation to legal proceedings being taken "upon notice" to the other parties to the arbitral proceedings, or to the tribunal, are to such notice of the originating process as is required by rules of court and do not impose any separate requirement.

—(2) Rules of court shall be made—
(a) requiring such notice to be given as indicated by any provision of this Part, and
(b) as to the manner, form and content of any such notice.

—(3) Subject to any provision made by rules of court, a requirement to give notice to the tribunal of legal proceedings shall be construed—
(a) if there is more than one arbitrator, as a requirement to give notice to each of them; and
(b) if the tribunal is not fully constituted, as a requirement to give notice to any arbitrator who has been appointed.

—(4) References in this Part to making an application or appeal to the court within a specified period are to the issue within that period of the appropriate originating process in accordance with rules of court.

—(5) Where any provision of this Part requires an application or appeal to be made to the court within a specified time, the rules of court relating to the reckoning of periods, the extending or abridging of periods, and the consequences of not taking a step within the period prescribed by the rules, apply in relation to that requirement.

—(6) Provision may be made by rules of court amending the provisions of this Part—
(a) with respect to the time within which any application or appeal to the court must be made,
(b) so as to keep any provision made by this Part in relation to arbitral proceedings in step with the corresponding provision of rules of court applying in relation to proceedings in the court, or
(c) so as to keep any provision made by this Part in relation to legal proceedings in step with the corresponding provision of rules of court applying generally in relation to proceedings in the court.

—(7) Nothing in this section affects the generality of the power to make rules of court.

81. —(1) Nothing in this Part shall be construed as excluding the operation of any rule of law consistent with the provisions of this Part, in particular, any rule of law as to—
(a) matters which are not capable of settlement by arbitration;
(b) the effect of an oral arbitration agreement; or
(c) the refusal of recognition or enforcement of an arbitral award on grounds of public policy.

—(2) Nothing in this Act shall be construed as reviving any jurisdiction of the court to set aside or remit an award on the ground of errors of fact or law on the face of the award.

82. —(1) In this Part—"arbitrator", unless the context otherwise requires, includes an umpire; "available arbitral process", in relation to any matter, includes any process of appeal to or review by an arbitral or other institution or person vested by the parties with powers in relation to

that matter; "claimant", unless the context otherwise requires, includes a counterclaimant, and related expressions shall be construed accordingly; "dispute" includes any difference; "enactment" includes an enactment contained in Northern Ireland legislation; "legal proceedings" means civil proceedings in the High Court or a county court; "peremptory order" means an order made under section 41(5) or made in exercise of any corresponding power conferred by the parties; "premises" includes land, buildings, moveable structures, vehicles, vessels, aircraft and hovercraft; "question of law" means—

(a) for a court in England and Wales, a question of the law of England and Wales, and

(b) for a court in Northern Ireland, a question of the law of Northern Ireland; "substantive jurisdiction", in relation to an arbitral tribunal, refers to the matters specified in section 30(1)(a) to (c), and references to the tribunal exceeding its substantive jurisdiction shall be construed accordingly.

—(2) References in this Part to a party to an arbitration agreement include any person claiming under or through a party to the agreement.

83. In this Part the expressions listed below are defined or otherwise explained by the provisions indicated—

agreement, agree and agreed	section 5(1)
agreement in writing	section 5(2) to (5)
arbitration agreement	sections 6 and 5(1)
arbitrator	section 82(1)
available arbitral process	section 82(1)
claimant	section 82(1)
commencement (in relation to arbitral proceedings)	section 14
costs of the arbitration	section 59
the court	section 105
dispute	section 82(1)
enactment	section 82(1)
legal proceedings	section 82(1)
Limitation Acts	section 13(4)
notice (or other document)	section 76(6)
party— —in relation to an arbitration agreement —where section 106(2) or (3) applies	 section 82(2) section 106(4)
peremptory order	section 82(1) (and see section 41(5))
premises	section 82(1)
question of law	section 82(1)
recoverable costs	sections 63 and 64
seat of the arbitration	section 3
serve and service (of notice or other document)	section 76(6)
substantive jurisdiction (in relation to an arbitral tribunal)	section 82(1) (and see section 30(1)(a) to (c))
upon notice (to the parties or the tribunal)	section 80
written and in writing	section 5(6)

84. —(1) The provisions of this Part do not apply to arbitral proceedings commenced before the date on which this Part comes into force.

—(2) They apply to arbitral proceedings commenced on or after that date under an arbitration agreement whenever made.

—(3) The above provisions have effect subject to any transitional provision made by an order under section 109(2) (power to include transitional provisions in commencement order).

PART II

OTHER PROVISIONS RELATING TO ARBITRATION

Domestic arbitration agreements

85. —(1) In the case of a domestic arbitration agreement the provisions of Part I are modified in accordance with the following sections.

—(2) For this purpose a "domestic arbitration agreement" means an arbitration agreement to which none of the parties is—

(a) an individual who is a national of, or habitually resident in, a state other than the United Kingdom, or

(b) a body corporate which is incorporated in, or whose central control and management is exercised in, a state other than the United Kingdom, and under which the seat of the arbitration (if the seat has been designated or determined) is in the United Kingdom.

—(3) In subsection (2) "arbitration agreement" and "seat of the arbitration" have the same meaning as in Part I (see sections 3, 5(1) and 6).

86. —(1) In section 9 (stay of legal proceedings), subsection (4) (stay unless the arbitration agreement is null and void, inoperative, or incapable of being performed) does not apply to a domestic arbitration agreement.

—(2) On an application under that section in relation to a domestic arbitration agreement the court shall grant a stay unless satisfied—

(a) that the arbitration agreement is null and void, inoperative, or incapable of being performed, or

(b) that there are other sufficient grounds for not requiring the parties to abide by the arbitration agreement.

—(3) The court may treat as a sufficient ground under subsection (2)(b) the fact that the applicant is or was at any material time not ready and willing to do all things necessary for the proper conduct of the arbitration or of any other dispute resolution procedures required to be exhausted before resorting to arbitration.

—(4) For the purposes of this section the question whether an arbitration agreement is a domestic arbitration agreement shall be determined by reference to the facts at the time the legal proceedings are commenced.

87. —(1) In the case of a domestic arbitration agreement any agreement to exclude the jurisdiction of the court under—

(a) section 45 (determination of preliminary point of law), or

(b) section 69 (challenging the award: appeal on point of law), is not effective unless entered into after the commencement of the arbitral proceedings in which the question arises or the award is made.

—(2) For this purpose the commencement of the arbitral proceedings has the same meaning as in Part I (see section 14).

—(3) For the purposes of this section the question whether an arbitration agreement is a domestic arbitration agreement shall be determined by reference to the facts at the time the agreement is entered into.

88. —(1) The Secretary of State may by order repeal or amend the provisions of sections 85 to 87.

—(2) An order under this section may contain such supplementary, incidental and transitional provisions as appear to the Secretary of State to be appropriate.

—(3) An order under this section shall be made by statutory instrument and no such order shall be made unless a draft of it has been laid before and approved by a resolution of each House of Parliament.

Consumer arbitration agreements

89. —(1) The following sections extend the application of the Unfair Terms in Consumer Contracts Regulations 1994 in relation to a term which constitutes an arbitration agreement. For this purpose "arbitration agreement" means an agreement to submit to arbitration present or future disputes or differences (whether or not contractual).

—(2) In those sections "the Regulations" means those regulations and includes any regulations amending or replacing those regulations.

—(3) Those sections apply whatever the law applicable to the arbitration agreement.

90. The Regulations apply where the consumer is a legal person as they apply where the consumer is a natural person.

91. —(1) A term which constitutes an arbitration agreement is unfair for the purposes of the Regulations so far as it relates to a claim for a pecuniary remedy which does not exceed the amount specified by order for the purposes of this section.

—(2) Orders under this section may make different provision for different cases and for different purposes.

—(3) The power to make orders under this section is exercisable—

(a) for England and Wales, by the Secretary of State with the concurrence of the Lord Chancellor,

(b) for Scotland, by the Secretary of State with the concurrence of the Lord Advocate, and

(c) for Northern Ireland, by the Department of Economic Development for Northern Ireland with the concurrence of the Lord Chancellor.

—(4) Any such order for England and Wales or Scotland shall be made by statutory instrument which shall be subject to annulment in pursuance of a resolution of either House of Parliament.

—(5) Any such order for Northern Ireland shall be a statutory rule for the purposes of the Statutory Rules (Northern Ireland) Order 1979 and shall be subject to negative resolution, within the meaning of section 41(6) of the Interpretation Act (Northern Ireland) 1954.

* * *

Appointment of judges as arbitrators

93. —(1) A judge of the Commercial Court or an official referee may, if in all the circumstances he thinks fit, accept appointment as a sole arbitrator or as umpire by or by virtue of an arbitration agreement.

—(2) A judge of the Commercial Court shall not do so unless the Lord Chief Justice has informed him that, having regard to the state of business in the High Court and the Crown Court, he can be made available.

—(3) An official referee shall not do so unless the Lord Chief Justice has informed him that, having regard to the state of official referees' business, he can be made available.

—(4) The fees payable for the services of a judge of the Commercial Court or official referee as arbitrator or umpire shall be taken in the High Court.

—(5) In this section—"arbitration agreement" has the same meaning as in Part I; and "official referee" means a person nominated under section 68(1)(a) of the Supreme Court Act 1981 to deal with official referees' business.

—(6) The provisions of Part I of this Act apply to arbitration before a person appointed under this section with the modifications specified in Schedule 2.

Statutory arbitrations

94. —(1) The provisions of Part I apply to every arbitration under an enactment (a "statutory arbitration"), whether the enactment was passed or made before or after the commencement of this Act, subject to the adaptations and exclusions specified in sections 95 to 98.

—(2) The provisions of Part I do not apply to a statutory arbitration if or to the extent that their application—

(a) is inconsistent with the provisions of the enactment concerned, with any rules or procedure authorized or recognized by it, or

(b) is excluded by any other enactment.

—(3) In this section and the following provisions of this Part "enactment"—

(a) in England and Wales, includes an enactment contained in subordinate legislation within the meaning of the Interpretation Act 1978;

(b) in Northern Ireland, means a statutory provision within the meaning of section 1(f) of the Interpretation Act (Northern Ireland) 1954.

95. —(1) The provisions of Part I apply to a statutory arbitration—

(a) as if the arbitration were pursuant to an arbitration agreement and as if the enactment were that agreement, and

(b) as if the persons by and against whom a claim subject to arbitration in pursuance of the enactment may be or has been made were parties to that agreement.

—(2) Every statutory arbitration shall be taken to have its seat in England and Wales or, as the case may be, in Northern Ireland.

96. —(1) The following provisions of Part I apply to a statutory arbitration with the following adaptations.

—(2) In section 30(1) (competence of tribunal to rule on its own jurisdiction), the reference in paragraph (a) to whether there is a valid arbitration agreement shall be construed as a reference to whether the enactment applies to the dispute or difference in question.

—(3) Section 35 (consolidation of proceedings and concurrent hearings) applies only so as to authorize the consolidation of proceedings, or concurrent hearings in proceedings, under the same enactment.

—(4) Section 46 (rules applicable to substance of dispute) applies with the omission of subsection (1)(b) (determination in accordance with considerations agreed by parties).

97. The following provisions of Part I do not apply in relation to a statutory arbitration—

(a) section 8 (whether agreement discharged by death of a party);

(b) section 12 (power of court to extend agreed time limits);

(c) sections 9(5), 10(2) and 71(4) (restrictions on effect of provision that award condition precedent to right to bring legal proceedings).

98. —(1) The Secretary of State may make provision by regulations for adapting or excluding any provision of Part I in relation to statutory arbitrations in general or statutory arbitrations of any particular description.

—(2) The power is exercisable whether the enactment concerned is passed or made before or after the commencement of this Act.

—(3) Regulations under this section shall be made by statutory instrument which shall be subject to annulment in pursuance of a resolution of either House of Parliament.

PART III

RECOGNITION AND ENFORCEMENT OF CERTAIN FOREIGN AWARDS

Enforcement of Geneva Convention awards

99. Part II of the Arbitration Act 1950 (enforcement of certain foreign awards) continues to apply in relation to foreign awards within the meaning of that Part which are not also New York Convention awards.

Recognition and enforcement of New York Convention awards

100. —(1) In this Part a "New York Convention award" means an award made, in pursuance of an arbitration agreement, in the territory of a state (other than the United Kingdom) which is a party to the New York Convention.

—(2) For the purposes of subsection (1) and of the provisions of this Part relating to such awards—

(a) "arbitration agreement" means an arbitration agreement in writing, and

(b) an award shall be treated as made at the seat of the arbitration, regardless of where it was signed, despatched or delivered to any of the parties. In this subsection "agreement in writing" and "seat of the arbitration" have the same meaning as in Part I.

—(3) If Her Majesty by Order in Council declares that a state specified in the Order is a party to the New York Convention, or is a party in respect of any territory so specified, the Order shall, while in force, be conclusive evidence of that fact.

—(4) In this section "the New York Convention" means the Convention on the Recognition and Enforcement of Foreign Arbitral Awards adopted by the United Nations Conference on International Commercial Arbitration on 10th June 1958.

101. —(1) A New York Convention award shall be recognized as binding on the persons as between whom it was made, and may accordingly be relied on by those persons by way of defense, set-off or otherwise in any legal proceedings in England and Wales or Northern Ireland.

—(2) A New York Convention award may, by leave of the court, be enforced in the same manner as a judgment or order of the court to the same effect. As to the meaning of "the court" see section 105.

—(3) Where leave is so given, judgment may be entered in terms of the award.

102. —(1) A party seeking the recognition or enforcement of a New York Convention award must produce—

(a) the duly authenticated original award or a duly certified copy of it, and
(b) the original arbitration agreement or a duly certified copy of it.

—(2) If the award or agreement is in a foreign language, the party must also produce a translation of it certified by an official or sworn translator or by a diplomatic or consular agent.

103. —(1) Recognition or enforcement of a New York Convention award shall not be refused except in the following cases.

—(2) Recognition or enforcement of the award may be refused if the person against whom it is invoked proves—
(a) that a party to the arbitration agreement was (under the law applicable to him) under some incapacity;
(b) that the arbitration agreement was not valid under the law to which the parties subjected it or, failing any indication thereon, under the law of the country where the award was made;
(c) that he was not given proper notice of the appointment of the arbitrator or of the arbitration proceedings or was otherwise unable to present his case;
(d) that the award deals with a difference not contemplated by or not falling within the terms of the submission to arbitration or contains decisions on matters beyond the scope of the submission to arbitration (but see subsection (4));
(e) that the composition of the arbitral tribunal or the arbitral procedure was not in accordance with the agreement of the parties or, failing such agreement, with the law of the country in which the arbitration took place;
(f) that the award has not yet become binding on the parties, or has been set aside or suspended by a competent authority of the country in which, or under the law of which, it was made.

—(3) Recognition or enforcement of the award may also be refused if the award is in respect of a matter which is not capable of settlement by arbitration, or if it would be contrary to public policy to recognize or enforce the award.

—(4) An award which contains decisions on matters not submitted to arbitration may be recognized or enforced to the extent that it contains decisions on matters submitted to arbitration which can be separated from those on matters not so submitted.

—(5) Where an application for the setting aside or suspension of the award has been made to such a competent authority as is mentioned in subsection (2)(f), the court before which the award is sought to be relied upon may, if it considers it proper, adjourn the decision on the recognition or enforcement of the award. It may also on the application of the party claiming recognition or enforcement of the award order the other party to give suitable security.

104. Nothing in the preceding provisions of this Part affects any right to rely upon or enforce a New York Convention award at common law or under section 66.

PART IV

GENERAL PROVISIONS

105. —(1) In this Act "the court" means the High Court or a county court, subject to the following provisions.

—(2) The Lord Chancellor may by order make provision—

(a) allocating proceedings under this Act to the High Court or to county courts; or

(b) specifying proceedings under this Act which may be commenced or taken only in the High Court or in a county court.

—(3) The Lord Chancellor may by order make provision requiring proceedings of any specified description under this Act in relation to which a county court has jurisdiction to be commenced or taken in one or more specified county courts. Any jurisdiction so exercisable by a specified county court is exercisable throughout England and Wales or, as the case may be, Northern Ireland.

—(4) An order under this section—

(a) may differentiate between categories of proceedings by reference to such criteria as the Lord Chancellor sees fit to specify, and

(b) may make such incidental or transitional provision as the Lord Chancellor considers necessary or expedient.

—(5) An order under this section for England and Wales shall be made by statutory instrument which shall be subject to annulment in pursuance of a resolution of either House of Parliament.

—(6) An order under this section for Northern Ireland shall be a statutory rule for the purposes of the Statutory Rules (Northern Ireland) Order 1979 which shall be subject to annulment in pursuance of a resolution of either House of Parliament in like manner as a statutory instrument and section 5 of the Statutory Instruments Act 1946 shall apply accordingly.

106. —(1) Part I of this Act applies to any arbitration agreement to which Her Majesty, either in right of the Crown or of the Duchy of Lancaster or otherwise, or the Duke of Cornwall, is a party.

—(2) Where Her Majesty is party to an arbitration agreement otherwise than in right of the Crown, Her Majesty shall be represented for the purposes of any arbitral proceedings—

(a) where the agreement was entered into by Her Majesty in right of the Duchy of Lancaster, by the Chancellor of the Duchy or such person as he may appoint, and

(b) in any other case, by such person as Her Majesty may appoint in writing under the Royal Sign Manual.

—(3) Where the Duke of Cornwall is party to an arbitration agreement, he shall be represented for the purposes of any arbitral proceedings by such person as he may appoint.

—(4) References in Part I to a party or the parties to the arbitration agreement or to arbitral proceedings shall be construed, where subsection (2) or (3) applies, as references to the person representing Her Majesty or the Duke of Cornwall.

107. —(1) The enactments specified in Schedule 3 are amended in accordance with that Schedule, the amendments being consequential on the provisions of this Act.

—(2) The enactments specified in Schedule 4 are repealed to the extent specified.

108. —(1) The provisions of this Act extend to England and Wales and, except as mentioned below, to Northern Ireland.

—(2) The following provisions of Part II do not extend to Northern Ireland—section 92 (exclusion of Part I in relation to small claims arbitration in the county court), and section 93 and Schedule 2 (appointment of judges as arbitrators).

—(3) Sections 89, 90 and 91 (consumer arbitration agreements) extend to Scotland and the provisions of Schedules 3 and 4 (consequential amendments and repeals) extend to Scotland so far as they relate to enactments which so extend, subject as follows.

—(4) The repeal of the Arbitration Act 1975 extends only to England and Wales and Northern Ireland.

109. —(1) The provisions of this Act come into force on such day as the Secretary of State may appoint by order made by statutory instrument, and different days may be appointed for different purposes.

—(2) An order under subsection (1) may contain such transitional provisions as appear to the Secretary of State to be appropriate.

110. This Act may be cited as the Arbitration Act 1996.

E. INDIAN ARBITRATION AND CONCILIATION ACT OF 1996 (SELECTED PROVISIONS)

PREAMBLE

WHEREAS the United Nations Commission on International Trade Law (UNCITRAL) has adopted the UNCITRAL Model Law on International Commercial Arbitration in 1985;

AND WHEREAS the General Assembly of the United Nations has recommended that all countries give due consideration to the said Model Law, in view of the desirability of uniformity of the law of arbitral procedures and the specific needs of international commercial arbitration practice;

AND WHEREAS the UNCITRAL has adopted the UNCITRAL Conciliation Rules in 1980;

AND WHEREAS the General Assembly of the United Nations has recommended the use of the said Rules in cases where a dispute arises in the context of international commercial relations and the parties seek an amicable settlement of that dispute by recourse to conciliation;

AND WHEREAS the said Model Law and Rules make significant contribution to the establishment of a unified legal framework for the fair and efficient settlement of disputes arising in international commercial relations;

AND WHEREAS it is expedient to make law respecting arbitration and conciliation, taking into account the aforesaid Model law and Rules;

BE it enacted by Parliament in the forty seventh year of the Republic as follows:

PRELIMINARY

1. Short title, extent and Commencement.

(1) This Act may be called the Arbitration and Conciliation Act, 1996.

(2) It extends to the whole of India:

Provided that Parts I, III and IV shall extend to the State of Jammu and Kashmir only in so far as they relate to international commercial arbitration or, as the case may be, international commercial conciliation.

Explanation. In this sub-section, the expression "international commercial conciliation" shall have the same meaning as the expression "international commercial arbitration" in clause (f) of sub-section (1) of Section 2, subject to the modification that for the word "arbitration" occurring therein, the word "conciliation" shall be substituted.

(3) It shall be deemed to have came into force on the 25th day of January, 1996.

PART I

ARBITRATION

CHAPTER I

GENERAL PROVISIONS

2. Definitions.

(1) In this Part, unless the context otherwise requires

(a) "Arbitration" means any arbitration whether or not administered by permanent arbitral institution;

(b) "Arbitration agreement" means an agreement referred to in Section 7;

(c) "Arbitral award" includes an interim award;

(d) "Arbitral tribunal" means a sole arbitrator or a panel of arbitrators;

(e) "Court" means the Principal Civil Court of original jurisdiction in a district and includes the High Court in exercise of its ordinary original civil jurisdiction having jurisdiction to decide the questions forming the subject matter of the arbitration if the same had been the subject matter of a suit, but does not include any Civil Court of a grade inferior to such principal Civil Court or any Court of Small Causes;

(f) "International commercial arbitration" means an arbitration relating to disputes arising out of legal relationships, whether contractual or not, considered as commercial under the law in force in India and where at least one of the parties is

(i) an individual who is a national of, or habitually resident in, any country other than India; or
(ii) a body corporate which is incorporated in any country other than India; or
(iii) a company or an association or a body of individuals whose central management and control is exercised in any country other than India; or
(iv) the Government of a foreign country;

(g) "legal representative" means a person who in law represents the estate of a deceased person, and includes any person who intermeddles with the estate of the deceased and, where a party acts in a representative character, the person on whom the estate devolves on the death of the party so acting;

(h) "party" means a party to an arbitration agreement.

(2) This Part shall apply where the place of arbitration is in India.

(3) This Part shall not affect any other law for the time being in force by virtue of which certain disputes may not be submitted to arbitration.

(4) This Part except sub-section (1) of Section 40, Sections 41 and 43 shall apply to every arbitration under any other enactment for the time being in force, as if the arbitration were pursuant to an arbitration agreement and as if that other enactment were an arbitration agreement, except in so far as the provisions of this part are inconsistent with that other enactment or with any rules made thereunder.

(5) Subject to the provisions of sub-section (4), and save in so far as is otherwise provided by any law for the time being in-force or in any agreement in force between India and any other country or countries, this part shall apply to all arbitrations and to all proceedings relating thereto.

Construction of References

* * *

(7) An arbitral award made under this part shall be considered as a domestic award.

* * *

CHAPTER VI
MAKING OF ARBITRAL AWARD & TERMINATION OF PROCEEDINGS

28. Rules applicable to substance of dispute.

(1) Where the place of arbitration is situate in India,

(a) in an arbitration other than an international commercial arbitration, the arbitral tribunal shall decide the dispute submitted to arbitration in accordance with the substantive law for the time being in force in India;

(b) in international commercial arbitration,

(i) the arbitral tribunal shall decide the dispute in accordance with the rules of law designated by the parties as applicable to the substance of the dispute;

(ii) any designation by the parties of the law or legal system of a given country shall be construed, unless otherwise expressed, as directly referring to the substantive law of that country and not to its conflict of laws rules;

(iii) failing any designation of the law under sub-clause (ii) by the parties, the arbitral tribunal shall apply the rules of law it considers to the appropriate given all the circumstances surrounding the dispute.

(2) The arbitral tribunal shall decide *ex aequo et bono* or as *amiable compositeur* only if the parties have expressly authorized it to do so.

(3) In all cases, the arbitral tribunal shall decide in accordance with the terms of the contract and shall take into account the usages of the trade applicable to the transaction.

* * *

CHAPTER VII
RECOURSE AGAINST ARBITRAL AWARD

34. Application for setting aside arbitral award.

(1) Recourse to a court against an arbitral award may be made only by an application for setting aside such award in accordance with sub-section (2) and sub-section (3).

(2) An arbitral award may be set aside by the court only if—

(a) the party making the application furnishes proof that—

(i) a party was under some incapacity; or

(ii) the arbitration agreement is not valid under the law to which the parties have subjected it or, failing any indication thereon, under the law for the time being in force; or

(iii) the party making the application was not given proper notice of the appointment of an arbitrator or of the arbitral proceedings or was otherwise unable to present his case; or

(iv) the arbitral award deals with a dispute not contemplated by or not falling within the terms of the submission to arbitration, or it contains decisions on matters beyond the scope of the submission to arbitrations: Provided that, if the decisions on matters submitted to arbitration can be separated from those not so submitted, only the part of the arbitral award which contains decisions on matters not submitted to arbitration may be set aside; or

(v) the composition of the arbitral tribunal or the arbitral procedure was not in accordance with the agreement of the parties, unless such agreement was in conflict with a provision of this Part from which the parties cannot derogate, or failing such agreement, was not in accordance with this Part; or

(b) the court finds that—

(i) the subject matter of the dispute is not capable of settlement by arbitration under the law for the time being in force; or

(ii) the arbitral award is in conflict with the public policy of India.

Explanation.

Without prejudice to the generality of sub-clause (ii) of clause (b), it is hereby declared, for the avoidance of any doubt, that an award is in conflict with the public policy of India. If the making of the award was induced or affected by fraud or corruption or was in violation of Section 75 or Section 81.

(3) An application for setting aside may not be made after three months have elapsed from the date on which the party making that application had received that arbitral award or, if a request had been made under Section 33, from the date on which that request had been disposed of by the arbitral tribunal:

Provided that if the court is satisfied that the applicant was prevented by sufficient cause from making the application within the said period of three months it may entertain the application within a further period of thirty days, but not thereafter.

(4) On receipt of an application under sub-section (1), the court may, where it is appropriate and it is so requested by a party, adjourn the proceedings for a period of time determined by it in order to give the arbitral tribunal an opportunity to resume the arbitral proceedings or to take such other action as in the opinion of arbitral tribunal will eliminate the grounds for setting aside the arbitral award.

CHAPTER VIII

FINALITY & ENFORCEMENT OF ARBITRAL AWARDS

35. Finality of arbitral awards.

Subject to this Part an arbitral award shall be final and binding on the parties and person claiming under them respectively.

* * *

PART II

ENFORCEMENT OF CERTAIN FOREIGN AWARDS

CHAPTER I

New York Convention awards

44. Definition.

In this Chapter, unless the context otherwise requires, "foreign award" means an arbitral award on differences between persons arising out of legal relationships, whether contractual or not, considered as commercial under the law in force in India, made on or after the 11th day of October, 1960.

(a) in pursuance of an agreement in writing for arbitration to which the Convention set forth in the First Schedule applies, and

(b) in one of such territories as the Central Government, being satisfied that reciprocal provisions have been made may, by notification in the Official Gazette, declare to be territories to which the said Convention applies.

45. Power of judicial authority to refer parties to arbitration.

Notwithstanding anything contained in Part I or in the Code of Civil Procedure, 1908, a judicial authority, when seized of an action in a matter in respect of which the parties have made an agreement referred to in Section 44, shall, at the request of one of the parties or any person claiming through or under him, refer the parties to arbitration, unless it finds that the said agreement is null and void, inoperative or incapable of being performed.

46. When foreign award binding.

Any foreign award which would be enforceable under this Chapter shall be treated as binding for all purposes on the persons as between whom it was made, and may accordingly be relied on by any of those persons by way of defense, set off or otherwise in any legal proceedings in India and any references in this Chapter to enforcing a foreign award shall be construed as including references to relying on an award.

47. Evidence.

(1) The party applying for the enforcement of a foreign award shall, at the time of the application, produce before the court—

(a) the original award or a copy thereof, duly authenticated in the manner required by the law of the country in which it was made;

(b) the original agreement for arbitration or a duly certified copy thereof; and

(c) such evidence as may be necessary to prove that the award is a foreign award.

(2) If the award or agreement to be produced under sub-section (1) is in a foreign language, the party seeking to enforce the award shall produce a translation into English certified as correct by a diplomatic or consular agent of the country to which that party belongs or certified as correct in such other manner as may be sufficient according to the law in force in India.

Explanation.

In this section and all the following sections of this Chapter, "Court" means the principal Civil Court of original jurisdiction in a district, and includes the High Court in exercise of its ordinary original civil jurisdiction, having jurisdiction over the subject matter of the award if the same had been the subject matter of a suit, but does not include any civil court of a grade inferior to such principal Civil Court, or any court of Small Causes.

48. Conditions for enforcement of foreign awards.

(1) Enforcement of a foreign award may be refused, at the request of the party against whom it is invoked, only if that party furnishes to the court proof that—

(a) the parties to the agreement referred to in Section 44 were, under the law applicable to them, under some incapacity, or the said agreement is not valid under the law to which the parties have subjected it or, failing any indication thereon, under the law of the country where the award was made; or

(b) the party against whom the award is invoked was not given proper notice of the appointment of the arbitrator or of the arbitral proceedings or was otherwise unable to present his case; or

(c) the award deals with a difference not contemplated by or not falling within the terms of the submission to arbitration, or it contains decisions on matters beyond the scope of the submission to arbitration: Provided that, if the decisions on matters submitted to arbitration can be separated from those not so submitted, that part of the award which contains decisions on matters submitted to arbitration may be enforced; or

(d) the composition of the arbitral authority or the arbitral procedure was not in accordance with the agreement of the parties, or, failing such agreement, was not in accordance with the law of the country where the arbitration took place; or

(e) the award has not yet become binding on the parties, or has been set aside or suspended by a competent authority of the country in which, or under the law of which, that award was made.

(2) Enforcement of an arbitral award may also be refused if the court finds that—

(a) the subject-matter of the difference is not capable of settlement by arbitration under the law of India; or

(b) the enforcement of the award would be contrary to the public policy of India.

Explanation.

Without prejudice to the generality of clause (b) of this section, it is hereby declared, for the avoidance of any doubt, that an award is in conflict with the public policy of India if the making of the award was induced or affected by fraud or corruption.

(3) If an application for the setting aside or suspension of the award has been made to a competent authority referred to in clause (e) of sub-section (1) the court may, if it considers it proper, adjourn the decision on the enforcement of the award and may also, on the application of the party claiming enforcement of the award, order the other party to give suitable security.

49. Enforcement of foreign awards.

Where the court is satisfied that the foreign award is enforceable under this chapter, the award shall be deemed to be a decree of that court.

50. Appealable orders.

(1) An appeal shall lie from the order refusing to

(a) refer the parties to arbitration under Section 45;

(b) enforce a foreign award under Section 48, to the court authorised by law to hear appeals from such order.

(2) No second appeal shall lie from an order passed in appeal under this section, but nothing in this section shall affect or take away any right to appeal to the Supreme Court.

51. Saving.

Nothing in this Chapter shall prejudice any rights which any person would have had of enforcing in India of any award or of availing himself in India of any award if this Chapter had not been enacted.

* * *

F. JAPAN: ARBITRATION LAW*

(Law No.138 of 2003)

Chapter I: GENERAL PROVISIONS

Article 1. (Purpose)

Arbitral proceedings where the place of arbitration is in the territory of Japan and court proceedings in connection with arbitral proceedings shall, in addition to the provisions of other laws, follow those of this Law.

Article 2. (Definitions)

(1) For the purposes of this Law, "arbitration agreement" shall mean an agreement by the parties to submit to one or more arbitrators the resolution of all or certain civil disputes which have arisen or which may arise in respect of a defined legal relationship (whether contractual or not) and to abide by their award (hereinafter referred to as "arbitral award").

(2) For the purposes of this Law, "arbitral tribunal" shall mean a sole arbitrator or a panel of two or more arbitrators, who, based on an arbitration agreement, conduct proceedings and make an arbitral award in respect of civil disputes subject thereto.

(3) For the purposes of this Law, "written statement" shall mean a document that a party prepares and submits to an arbitral tribunal in arbitral proceedings and which states the case of that party.

Article 3. (Scope of Application)

(1) The provisions of Chapters II through VII and Chapters IX and X, except the provisions specified in the following paragraph and article 8, apply only if the place of arbitration is in the territory of Japan.

(2) The provisions of article 14, paragraph (1) and article 15 apply when the place of arbitration is in or outside the territory of Japan, or when the place of arbitration is not designated.

(3) The provisions of Chapter VIII apply when the place of arbitration is in or outside the territory of Japan.

Article 4. (Court Intervention)

With respect to arbitral proceedings, no court shall intervene except where so provided in this Law.

Article 5. (Court Jurisdiction)

(1) Only the following courts have jurisdiction over cases concerning court proceedings based on the provisions of this Law:

(i) the district court designated by the agreement of the parties;

* The act can be found at http://www.jseinc.org/en/laws/new_arbitration_act.html

(ii) the district court having jurisdiction over the place of arbitration (only when the designated place of arbitration falls within the jurisdiction of a single district court); or

(iii) the district court having jurisdiction over the general forum of the counterparty in the relevant case.

(2) In the event that two or more courts have jurisdiction based on the provisions of this Law, the court to which the request was first made shall have jurisdiction.

(3) The court shall, upon determining that the whole or a part of a case concerning court proceedings based on the provisions of this Law does not fall under its jurisdiction, upon request or by its own authority, transfer such case to a court with jurisdiction.

Article 6. (Voluntary Oral Hearing)

Any decision concerning court proceedings based on the provisions of this Law may be made without an oral hearing.

Article 7. (Appeal against Court Decision)

Any party with an interest affected by the decision concerning court proceedings based on the provisions of this Law may, only if specifically provided for by this Law, file an immediate appeal against the decision within the peremptory term of two weeks from the day on which notice is given.

Article 8. (Court Intervention in the Event that the Place of Arbitration Has Not Been Designated)

(1) Even if the place of arbitration has not been designated, each of the court applications cited in the following items may be made when there is a possibility that the place of arbitration will be in the territory of Japan and the applicant or counterparty's general forum (excluding designations based on the last address) is in the territory of Japan. In such case, according to the classifications cited in the respective items, the respective provisions shall apply:

(i) an article 16, paragraph (3) application: same article;

(ii) an article 17, paragraphs (2) through (5) application: same article;

(iii) an article 19, paragraph (4) application: articles 18 and 19; or

(iv) an article 20 application: same article.

(2) Notwithstanding the provisions of article 5, paragraph (1), only the district courts having jurisdiction over the general forum described in the preceding paragraph have jurisdiction over the case relating to the applications cited in each of the items in the preceding paragraph.

Article 9. (Reading of Case Records Relating to Court Proceedings)

A party with an interest in any court proceedings based on the provisions of this Law may request any of the following from the court clerk:

(i) a reading of or a copy of the case records;

(ii) a copy of the records produced by electronic, magnetic or any other means unrecognizable by natural sensory function in the case records;

(iii) the delivery of an authenticated copy, transcript or extract thereof; or

(iv) the delivery of a certificate regarding matters relating to the case.

Article 10. (Application of the Code of Civil Procedure to Court Proceedings)

Except as otherwise provided, the provisions of the Code of Civil Procedure [Law No. 109 of 1996] shall apply to any court proceedings based on the provisions of this Law.

Article 11. (Supreme Court Rules)

In addition to those provided by this Law, particulars necessary in relation to court proceedings based on the provisions of this Law shall be as prescribed by the Rules of the Supreme Court.

Article 12. (Written Notice)

(1) Unless otherwise agreed by the parties, when notice in arbitral proceedings is given in writing, it is deemed to have been given at the time it is delivered to the addressee personally, or, at the time it is delivered to the addressee's domicile, habitual residence, place of business, office or delivery address (which hereafter in this article means the place stipulated by the addressee as the place for delivery of documents from the sender).

(2) With respect to a written notice in arbitral proceedings, where it is possible for the notice to be delivered to the addressee's domicile, habitual residence, place of business, office or delivery address, whereas it is difficult for the sender to obtain materials to certify that the delivery has been made, if the court considers it necessary, it may upon request of the sender decide to serve the notice itself. The provisions of article 104 and articles 110 through 113 of the Code of Civil Procedure shall not apply with respect to service in such an event.

(3) The provisions of the preceding paragraph shall not apply in the event the parties have agreed that the service described in the same paragraph shall not be made.

(4) The case concerning the request described in paragraph (2) shall be, notwithstanding the provisions of article 5, paragraph (1), subject only

to the jurisdiction of the courts cited in items (i) and (ii) of the same paragraph and the district court with jurisdiction over the addressee's domicile, habitual residence, place of business, office or delivery address.

(5) When notice in arbitral proceedings is given in writing, if none of the addressee's domicile, habitual residence, place of business, office or delivery address can be found after making a reasonable inquiry, unless otherwise agreed by the parties, it will suffice if the sender sends its notice to the addressee's last-known domicile, habitual residence, place of business, office or delivery address by registered letter or any other means by which the attempt to deliver it can be certified. In such case, a written notice is deemed to have been given at the normally expected time of its arrival.

(6) The provisions of paragraph (1) and the preceding paragraph shall not apply to notices in court proceedings based on the provisions of this Law.

Chapter II: ARBITRATION AGREEMENT

Article 13. (Effect of Arbitration Agreement)

(1) Unless otherwise provided by law, an arbitration agreement shall be valid only when its subject matter is a civil dispute that may be resolved by settlement between the parties (excluding that of divorce or separation).

(2) The arbitration agreement shall be in the form of a document signed by all the parties, letters or telegrams exchanged between the parties (including those sent by facsimile device or other communication device for parties at a distance which provides the recipient with a written record of the transmitted content), or other written instrument.

(3) When a written contract refers to a document that contains an arbitration clause and the reference is such as to make that clause part of the contract, the arbitration agreement shall be in writing.

(4) When an arbitration agreement is made by way of electromagnetic record (records produced by electronic, magnetic or any other means unrecognizable by natural sensory function and used for data-processing by a computer) recording its content, the arbitration agreement shall be in writing.

(5) When the parties to the arbitral proceedings exchange written statements in which the existence of an arbitration agreement is alleged by one party and not denied by another, the arbitration agreement shall be in writing.

(6) Even if in a particular contract containing an arbitration agreement, any or all of the contractual provisions, excluding the arbitration agreement, are found to be null and void, cancelled or for other reasons invalid, the validity of the arbitration agreement shall not necessarily be affected.

Article 14. (Arbitration Agreement and Substantive Claim before Court)

(1) A court before which an action is brought in respect of a civil dispute which is the subject of an arbitration agreement shall, if the defendant so requests, dismiss the action. Provided, this shall not apply in the following instances:

(i) when the arbitration agreement is null and void, cancelled, or for other reasons invalid;

(ii) when arbitration proceedings are inoperative or incapable of being performed based on the arbitration agreement; or

(iii) when the request is made by the defendant subsequent to the presentation of its statement in the oral hearing or in the preparations for argument proceedings on the substance of the dispute.

(2) An arbitral tribunal may commence or continue arbitral proceedings and make an arbitral award even while the action referred to in the preceding paragraph is pending before the court.

Article 15. (Arbitration Agreement and Interim Measures by Court)

It is not incompatible with an arbitration agreement for a party to request, before or during arbitral proceedings, from a court an interim measure of protection and for a court to grant such measure in respect of any civil dispute which is the subject of the arbitration agreement.

Chapter III: ARBITRATOR

Article 16. (Number of Arbitrators)

(1) The parties are free to determine the number of arbitrators.

(2) Failing such determination as provided for in the preceding paragraph, when there are two parties in an arbitration, the number of arbitrators shall be three.

(3) Failing such determination as provided for in paragraph (1), when there are three or more parties in an arbitration, the court shall determine the number of arbitrators upon request of a party.

Article 17. (Appointment of Arbitrators)

(1) The parties are free to agree on a procedure of appointing the arbitrators. Provided, this shall not apply to the provisions of paragraphs (5) and (6).

(2) Failing such agreement as provided for in the preceding paragraph, when there are two parties in an arbitration with three arbitrators, each party shall appoint one arbitrator, and the two arbitrators thus appointed shall appoint the third arbitrator. In such case, if a party fails to appoint an arbitrator within thirty days of a request to do so by the

other party who has appointed an arbitrator, the appointment shall be made by the court upon the request of that party, or if the two arbitrators appointed by the parties fail to agree on the third arbitrator within thirty days of their appointment, upon the request of a party.

(3) Failing such agreement as provided in paragraph (1) or any agreement on the appointment of arbitrators between the parties, when there are two parties in an arbitration with a sole arbitrator, the court shall appoint an arbitrator upon the request of a party.

(4) Failing such agreement as provided for in paragraph (1) when there are three or more parties, the court shall appoint arbitrators upon the request of a party.

(5) Where, under an appointment procedure for arbitrators agreed upon by the parties as provided for in paragraph (1), arbitrators cannot be appointed due to a failure to act as requested under such procedure or for any other reason, a party may request of the court the appointment of arbitrators.

(6) The court, in appointing arbitrators based on the provisions contained in paragraphs (2) through (5), shall have due regard to the following items:

(i) the qualifications required of the arbitrators by the agreement of the parties;

(ii) the impartiality and independence of the appointees; and

(iii) in the case of a sole arbitrator or in the case where the two arbitrators appointed by the parties are to appoint the third arbitrator, whether or not it would be appropriate to appoint an arbitrator of a nationality other than those of the parties.

Article 18. (Grounds for Challenge)

(1) A party may challenge an arbitrator:

(i) if it does not possess the qualifications agreed to by the parties; or

(ii) if circumstances exist that give rise to justifiable doubts as to its impartiality or independence.

(2) A party who appointed an arbitrator, or made recommendations with respect to the appointment of an arbitrator, or participated in any similar acts, may challenge that arbitrator only for reasons of which it becomes aware after the appointment has been made.

(3) When a person is approached in connection with its possible appointment as an arbitrator, it shall fully disclose any circumstances likely to give rise to justifiable doubts as to its impartiality or independence.

(4) An arbitrator, during the course of arbitral proceedings, shall without delay disclose any circumstances likely to give rise to justifiable

doubts as to its impartiality or independence (unless the parties have already been informed of them by the arbitrator).

Article 19. (Challenge Procedure)

(1) The parties are free to agree on a procedure for challenging an arbitrator. Provided, this shall not apply to the provisions of paragraph (4).

(2) Failing an agreement as provided for in the proceeding paragraph, upon request of a party, the arbitral tribunal shall decide on the challenge.

(3) A party who intends to make a request as provided for in the preceding paragraph shall, within fifteen days of the later of either the day on which it became aware of the constitution of the arbitral tribunal or the day on which it became aware of any circumstance referred to in any item of paragraph (1) of the preceding article, send a written request describing the reasons for the challenge to the arbitral tribunal. In such case, the arbitral tribunal shall decide that grounds for challenge exist when it finds that grounds for challenge exist with respect to the arbitrator.

(4) If a challenge of the arbitrator under the procedure for challenge prescribed in the preceding three paragraphs is not successful, the challenging party may request within thirty days after having received notice of the decision rejecting the challenge, the court to decide on the challenge. In such case, the court shall decide that grounds for challenge exist when it finds that grounds for challenge exist with respect to the arbitrator.

(5) While a case relating to a challenge as prescribed in paragraph (4) is pending before the court, the arbitral tribunal may commence or continue the arbitral proceedings and make an arbitral award.

Article 20. (Request for Removal)

Any party may request the court to decide on the removal of an arbitrator if any of the following grounds exist. In such case, if the court finds that the grounds for the request exist, it shall decide to remove the said arbitrator:

(i) if the arbitrator becomes de jure or de facto unable to perform its functions; or

(ii) for reasons other than those in the proceeding item, if the arbitrator fails to act without undue delay.

Article 21. (Termination of an Arbitrator's Mandate)

(1) An arbitrator's mandate shall terminate upon the occurrence of any of the following:

(i) the death of an arbitrator;

(ii) the resignation of an arbitrator;

(iii) the removal of an arbitrator upon the agreement of the parties;

(iv) a decision that grounds for challenge exist under the procedure for challenge described in the provisions of article 19, paragraphs (1) through (4); or

(v) a decision to remove an arbitrator based on the provisions of the preceding article.

(2) If, during the course of procedure for challenge under the provisions of article 19, paragraphs (1) through (4), or removal proceedings under the provisions of the preceding article, an arbitrator withdraws from its office or is removed upon the agreement of the parties, this alone does not imply the existence of any ground referred to in the items in article 18, paragraph (1) or the items in the preceding article with respect to the arbitrator.

Article 22. (Appointment of Substitute Arbitrator)

Unless otherwise agreed by the parties, where the mandate of an arbitrator terminates under any of the grounds described in each item of paragraph (1) of the preceding article, a substitute arbitrator shall be appointed according to the rules that were applicable to the appointment of the arbitrator being replaced.

Chapter IV: SPECIAL JURISDICTION OF ARBITRAL TRIBUNAL

Article 23. (Competence of Arbitral Tribunal to Rule on its Jurisdiction)

(1) The arbitral tribunal may rule on assertions made in respect of the existence or validity of an arbitration agreement or its own jurisdiction (which hereafter in this article means its authority to conduct arbitral proceedings and to make arbitral awards).

(2) A plea that the arbitral tribunal does not have jurisdiction shall be raised promptly in the case where the grounds for the assertion arise during the course of arbitral proceedings, or in other cases before the time at which the first written statement on the substance of the dispute is submitted to the arbitral tribunal (including the time at which initial assertions on the substance of the dispute are presented orally at an oral hearing). Provided, the arbitral tribunal may admit a later plea if it considers the delay justified.

(3) A party may raise the plea prescribed in the preceding paragraph even if it has appointed an arbitrator, or made recommendations with respect to the appointment of an arbitrator, or participated in any similar acts.

(4) The arbitral tribunal shall give the following ruling or arbitral award, as the case may be, on a plea raised in accordance with paragraph (2):

(i) a preliminary independent ruling or an arbitral award, when it considers it has jurisdiction; or

(ii) a ruling to terminate arbitral proceedings, when it considers it has no jurisdiction.

(5) If the arbitral tribunal gives a preliminary independent ruling that it has jurisdiction, any party may, within thirty days of receipt of notice of such ruling, request the court to decide the matter. In such an event, while such a request is pending before the court, the arbitral tribunal may continue the arbitral proceedings and make an arbitral award.

Article 24. (Interim Measures of Protection)

(1) Unless otherwise agreed by the parties, the arbitral tribunal may, at the request of a party, order any party to take such interim measure of protection as the arbitral tribunal may consider necessary in respect of the subject matter of the dispute.

(2) The arbitral tribunal may order any party to provide appropriate security in connection with such measure as prescribed in the preceding paragraph.

Chapter V: COMMENCEMENT AND CONDUCT OF ARBITRAL PROCEEDINGS

Article 25. (Equal Treatment of Parties)

(1) The parties shall be treated with equality in the arbitral proceedings.

(2) Each party shall be given a full opportunity of presenting its case in the arbitral proceedings.

Article 26. (Rules of Procedure)

(1) The parties are free to agree on the procedure to be followed by the arbitral tribunal in conducting the arbitral proceedings. Provided, it shall not violate the provisions of this Law relating to public policy.

(2) Failing such agreement as prescribed in the preceding paragraph, the arbitral tribunal may, subject to the provisions of this Law, conduct the arbitral proceedings in such manner as it considers appropriate.

(3) Failing such agreement as prescribed in paragraph (1), the power conferred upon the arbitral tribunal includes the power to determine the admissibility, relevance, materiality and weight of any evidence.

Article 27. (Waiver of right to object)

Unless otherwise agreed by the parties, as to arbitral proceedings, a party who knows that any provision of this Law or any arbitral proceedings rules agreed upon by the parties (to the extent that none of these relate to public policy) has not been complied with and yet fails to state its objection to such non-compliance without delay (if a time limit by which objections should be made is provided for, within such period of time), shall be deemed to have waived its right to object.

Article 28. (Place of arbitration)

(1) The parties are free to agree on the place of arbitration.

(2) Failing such agreement as prescribed in the preceding paragraph, the place of arbitration shall be determined by the arbitral tribunal having regard to the circumstances of the case, including the convenience of the parties.

(3) Notwithstanding the place of arbitration determined in accordance with the provisions of the preceding two paragraphs, the arbitral tribunal may, unless otherwise agreed by the parties, carry out the following procedures at any place it considers appropriate:

(i) consultation among the members of the arbitral tribunal;

(ii) hearing of parties, experts or witnesses; and

(iii) inspection of goods, other property or documents.

Article 29. (Commencement of arbitral proceedings and interruption of limitation)

(1) Unless otherwise agreed by the parties, the arbitral proceedings in respect of a particular civil dispute commence on the date on which one party gave the other party notice to refer that dispute to the arbitral proceedings.

(2) A claim made in arbitral proceedings shall give rise to an interruption of limitation. Provided, this shall not apply where the arbitral proceedings have been terminated for a reason other than the issuance of an arbitral award.

Article 30. (Language)

(1) The parties are free to agree on the language or languages to be used in the arbitral proceedings and the proceedings to be conducted using that language or those languages.

(2) Failing such agreement as prescribed in the preceding paragraph, the arbitral tribunal shall determine the language or languages to be used in the arbitral proceedings and the proceedings to be conducted using that language or those languages.

(3) Failing any designation of proceedings to be conducted using the designated language or languages in the agreement prescribed in paragraph (1) or the determination prescribed in the preceding paragraph, the proceedings to be conducted using such language or languages are as follows:

(i) any oral proceedings;

(ii) any statement or notice in writing by a party; or

(iii) any ruling (including an arbitral award) or notice in writing by the arbitral tribunal.

(4) The arbitral tribunal may order that any documentary evidence shall be accompanied by a translation into the language or languages designated in the agreement as prescribed in paragraph (1) or the determination prescribed in paragraph (2) (where designation has been made as to the language or languages to be used for translation, such language or languages).

Article 31. (Time Restrictions on Parties' Statements)

(1) Within the period of time determined by the arbitral tribunal, the claimant (which hereinafter means the party that carried out the act to commence the arbitral proceedings) shall state the relief or remedy sought, the facts supporting its claim and the points at issue. In such case, the claimant may submit all documentary evidence it considers to be relevant or may add a reference to the documentary evidence or other evidence it will submit.

(2) Within the period of time determined by the arbitral tribunal, the respondent (which hereinafter means any party to the arbitral proceedings other than the claimant) shall state its defense in respect of the particulars stated according to the provisions of the preceding paragraph. In such case, the provisions of the latter part of the same paragraph shall apply.

(3) Any party may amend or supplement its statement during the course of the arbitral proceedings. Provided, the arbitral tribunal may refuse to allow such amendment or supplementation if made in delay.

(4) The preceding three paragraphs shall not apply when otherwise agreed by the parties.

Article 32. (Procedure of the Hearing)

(1) The arbitral tribunal may hold oral hearings for the presentation of evidence or for oral argument by the parties. Provided, where a party makes an application for holding oral hearings, including the request in article 34, paragraph (3), the arbitral tribunal shall hold such oral hearings at an appropriate stage of the arbitral proceedings.

(2) The preceding paragraph shall not apply when otherwise agreed by the parties.

(3) When holding oral hearings for the purposes of oral argument or inspection of goods, other property or documents, the arbitral tribunal shall give sufficient advance notice to the parties of the time and place for such hearings.

(4) A party who supplied written statements, documentary evidence or any other records to the arbitral tribunal shall take necessary measures to ensure that the other party will be aware of their contents.

(5) The arbitral tribunal shall take necessary measures to ensure that all parties will be aware of the contents of any expert report or other

evidence on which the arbitral tribunal may rely in making an arbitral award or other rulings.

Article 33. (Default of a Party)

(1) If the claimant violates the provisions of article 31, paragraph (1), the arbitral tribunal shall make a ruling to terminate the arbitral proceedings. Provided, this shall not apply in the case where there is sufficient cause for the violation.

(2) If the respondent violates the provisions of article 31, paragraph (2), the arbitral tribunal shall continue the arbitral proceedings without treating such violation in itself as an admission of the claimant's allegations.

(3) If any party fails to appear at an oral hearing or to produce documentary evidence, the arbitral tribunal may make the arbitral award on the evidence before it that has been collected up until such time. Provided, this shall not apply in the case where there is sufficient cause with respect to the failure to appear at an oral hearing or to produce documentary evidence.

(4) The preceding three paragraphs shall not apply when otherwise agreed by the parties.

Article 34. (Expert Appointed by Arbitral Tribunal)

(1) The arbitral tribunal may appoint one or more experts to appraise any necessary issues and to report their findings in writing or orally.

(2) In the case of the preceding paragraph, the arbitral tribunal may require a party to do the following acts:

(i) give the expert any relevant information; or

(ii) produce, or provide access to, any relevant documents, goods or other property to the expert for inspection.

(3) If a party so requests or if the arbitral tribunal considers it necessary, the expert shall, after delivery of its report described in paragraph (1), participate in an oral hearing.

(4) A party may carry out the following acts in the oral hearing described in the preceding paragraph:

(i) put questions to the expert; or

(ii) have experts whom it has personally appointed to testify on the points at issue.

(5) Each of the preceding paragraphs shall not apply when otherwise agreed by the parties.

Article 35. (Court Assistance in Taking Evidence)

(1) The arbitral tribunal or a party may apply to a court for assistance in taking evidence by any means that the arbitral tribunal considers necessary as entrustment of investigation, examination of witnesses, ex-

pert testimony, investigation of documentary evidence (excluding documents that the parties may produce in person) or inspection (excluding that of objects the parties may produce in person) prescribed in the Code of Civil Procedure. Provided, this shall not apply in the case where the parties have agreed not to apply for all or some of these means.

(2) In making the application described in the preceding paragraph, the party shall obtain the approval of the arbitral tribunal.

(3) Notwithstanding the provisions of article 5, paragraph (1), only the following courts have jurisdiction over cases relating to the application described in paragraph (1):

(i) the court described in article 5, paragraph (1), item (ii);

(ii) the district court having jurisdiction over the domicile or place of residence of the person to be examined or the person holding the relevant documents, or the location of the object for inspection; or

(iii) the district court having jurisdiction over the general forum of the applicant or the counterparty (only if there is no court described in the preceding two items).

(4) An immediate appeal may be made against the decision regarding the application in paragraph (1).

(5) When the court carries out the examination of evidence based on the application in paragraph (1), the arbitrators may peruse the documents, inspect the objects and, with the approval of the presiding judge, put questions to the witness or expert (as prescribed in article 213 of the Code of Civil Procedure).

(6) The court clerk shall enter in the record the matters concerning the examination of evidence carried out by the court following the application prescribed in paragraph (1).

Chapter VI: ARBITRAL AWARD AND TERMINATION OF ARBITRAL PROCEEDINGS

Article 36. (Substantive Law to be Applied in Arbitral Award)

(1) The arbitral tribunal shall decide the dispute in accordance with such rules of law as are agreed by the parties as applicable to the substance of the dispute. In such case, any designation of the law or legal system of a given State shall be construed, unless otherwise expressed, as directly referring to the substantive law of that State and not to its conflict of laws rules.

(2) Failing agreement as provided in the preceding paragraph, the arbitral tribunal shall apply the substantive law of the State with which the civil dispute subject to the arbitral proceedings is most closely connected.

(3) Notwithstanding the provisions prescribed in the preceding two paragraphs, the arbitral tribunal shall decide ex aequo et bono only if the parties have expressly authorized it to do so.

(4) Where there is a contract relating to the civil dispute subject to the arbitral proceedings, the arbitral tribunal shall decide in accordance with the terms of such contract and shall take into account the usages, if any, that may apply to the civil dispute.

Article 37. (Proceedings by Panel of Arbitrators)

(1) An arbitral tribunal with more than one arbitrator shall elect a presiding arbitrator from among all its members.

(2) Any decision of the arbitral tribunal shall be made by a majority of all its members.

(3) Notwithstanding the provisions prescribed in the preceding paragraph, procedural matters in arbitral proceedings may be decided by the presiding arbitrator, if so authorized by the parties or all other members of the arbitral tribunal.

(4) The provisions of the preceding three paragraphs shall not apply when otherwise agreed by the parties.

Article 38. (Settlement)

(1) If, during arbitral proceedings, the parties settle the civil dispute subject to the arbitral proceedings and the parties so request, the arbitral tribunal may make a ruling on agreed terms.

(2) The ruling as provided for in the preceding paragraph shall have the same effect as an arbitral award.

(3) The ruling as provided for in paragraph (1) shall be made in writing in accordance with paragraphs (1) and (3) of the following article and shall state that it is an arbitral award.

(4) An arbitral tribunal or one or more arbitrators designated by it may attempt to settle the civil dispute subject to the arbitral proceedings, if consented to by the parties.

(5) Unless otherwise agreed by the parties, the consent provided for in the preceding paragraph or its withdrawal shall be made in writing.

Article 39. (Arbitral Award)

(1) The arbitral award shall be made in writing and shall be signed by the arbitrators who made it. Provided, in arbitral proceedings with more than one arbitrator, the signatures of the majority of all members of the arbitral tribunal shall suffice, if the reason for any omitted signature is stated.

(2) The arbitral award shall state the reasons upon which it is based. Provided, this shall not apply when otherwise agreed by the parties.

(3) The arbitral award shall state its date and place of arbitration.

(4) The arbitral award shall be deemed to have been made at the place of arbitration.

(5) After the arbitral award is made, the arbitral tribunal shall notify each party of the arbitral award by sending a copy of the arbitral award signed by the arbitrators.

(6) The proviso of paragraph (1) shall apply to the copy of the arbitral award described in the preceding paragraph.

Article 40. (Termination of Arbitral Proceedings)

(1) The arbitral proceedings are terminated by the arbitral award or by a ruling to terminate the arbitral proceedings.

(2) Other than rulings based on the provisions of article 23, paragraph (4), item (ii) or article 33, paragraph (1), the arbitral tribunal shall issue a ruling to terminate arbitral proceedings in the case where any of the following grounds exists:

(i) the claimant withdraws its claim. Provided, this shall not apply in the event that the respondent objects thereto and the arbitral tribunal recognizes a legitimate interest on its part in obtaining a settlement of the civil dispute subject to the arbitral proceedings;

(ii) the parties agree to on termination of the arbitral proceedings;

(iii) the parties settle the civil dispute subject to the arbitral proceedings (excluding the case where a ruling under article 38, paragraph (1) is issued); or

(iv) other than the instances in the preceding three items, the arbitral tribunal finds that the continuation of the arbitral proceedings has become unnecessary or impossible.

(3) The mandate of the arbitral tribunal terminates with the termination of the arbitral proceedings. Provided, the acts prescribed in the provisions of articles 41 through 43 may be made.

Article 41. (Correction of Arbitral Award)

(1) The arbitral tribunal may upon request of a party or by its own authority correct any errors in computation, any clerical or typographical errors or any errors of similar nature in the arbitral award.

(2) Unless otherwise agreed by the parties, the request described in the preceding paragraph shall be made within thirty days of the receipt of the notice of the arbitral award.

(3) When making the request described in paragraph (1), a party shall issue advance or simultaneous notice to the other party stating the content of the request.

(4) The arbitral tribunal shall make a ruling with respect to the request described in paragraph (1) within thirty days of such request.

(5) The arbitral tribunal may extend, if it considers it necessary, the period of time provided for in the preceding paragraph.

(6) The provisions of article 39 shall apply to any ruling to correct the arbitral award or any ruling to dismiss the request in paragraph (1).

Article 42. (Interpretation of Arbitral Award by Arbitral Tribunal)

(1) A party may request the arbitral tribunal to give an interpretation of a specific part of the arbitral award.

(2) The request described in the preceding paragraph may be made only if so agreed by the parties.

(3) The provisions of paragraphs (2) and (3) of the preceding article shall apply to the request described in paragraph (1) and the provisions of article 39 and paragraphs (4) and (5) of the preceding article shall apply to any rulings made with respect to the request described in paragraph (1).

Article 43. (Additional Arbitral Award)

(1) Unless otherwise agreed by the parties, a party may request the arbitral tribunal to make an arbitral award as to claims presented in the arbitral proceedings but omitted from the arbitral award. In such case, the provisions of article 41, paragraphs (2) and (3) shall apply.

(2) The arbitral tribunal shall make a ruling with respect to the request described in the preceding paragraph within sixty days of such request. In such case, the provisions of article 41, paragraph (5) shall apply.

(3) The provisions of article 39 shall apply to the ruling described in the preceding paragraph.

Chapter VII: SETTING ASIDE OF ARBITRAL AWARD

Article 44.

(1) A party may apply to a court to set aside the arbitral award when any of the following grounds are present:

(i) the arbitration agreement is not valid due to limits to a party's capacity;

(ii) the arbitration agreement is not valid for a reason other than limits to a party's capacity under the law to which the parties have agreed to subject it (or failing any indication thereon, under the law of Japan);

(iii) the party making the application was not given notice as required by the provisions of the laws of Japan (or where the parties have otherwise reached an agreement on matters concerning the provisions of the law that do not relate to the public policy, such agreement) in the proceedings to appoint arbitrators or in the arbitral proceedings;

(iv) the party making the application was unable to present its case in the arbitral proceedings;

(v) the arbitral award contains decisions on matters beyond the scope of the arbitration agreement or the claims in the arbitral proceedings;

(vi) the composition of the arbitral tribunal or the arbitral proceedings were not in accordance with the provisions of the laws of Japan (or where the parties have otherwise reached an agreement on matters concerning the provisions of the law that do not relate to the public policy, such agreement);

(vii) the claims in the arbitral proceedings relate to a dispute that cannot constitute the subject of an arbitration agreement under the laws of Japan; or

(viii) the content of the arbitral award is in conflict with the public policy or good morals of Japan.

(2) The application described in the preceding paragraph may not be made after three months have elapsed from the date on which the party making the application had received the notice by the sending of a copy of the arbitral award (including the document constituting the ruling of the arbitral tribunal described in the provisions of articles 41 through 43), or after an enforcement decision under article 46 has become final and conclusive.

(3) Even where the case for application described in paragraph (1) falls within its jurisdiction, a court may, upon request or by its own authority, if it finds it appropriate, transfer all or a part of said case to another competent court.

(4) An immediate appeal may be filed against a decision made under the provisions of article 5, paragraph (3) or the preceding paragraph regarding the case for application described in paragraph (1).

(5) A court may not make a decision with respect to the application described in paragraph (1), unless and until an oral hearing or oral proceeding at which the parties can attend was held.

(6) Where an application is made under paragraph (1), an arbitral award may be set aside by the court in the event that it finds any of the grounds described in each of the items under the same paragraph to be present (with respect to the grounds described in items (i) through (vi) of the same paragraph, this shall be limited to where the party making the application has proved the existence of such grounds).

(7) Where the ground described in paragraph (1), item (v) is present, and where the part relating to matters prescribed in the same item can be separated from the arbitral award, only that part of the arbitral award may be set aside by the court.

(8) An immediate appeal may be filed against the decision regarding the application in paragraph (1).

Chapter VIII: RECOGNITION AND ENFORCEMENT DECISION OF ARBITRAL AWARD

Article 45. (Recognition of Arbitral Award)

(1) An arbitral award (irrespective of whether or not the place of arbitration is in the territory of Japan; this shall apply throughout this chapter) shall have the same effect as a final and conclusive judgment. Provided, an enforcement based on the arbitral award shall be subject to an enforcement decision pursuant to the provisions of the following article.

(2) The provisions of the preceding paragraph do not apply in the case where any of the following grounds are present (with respect to the grounds described in items (i) through (vii), this shall be limited to where either of the parties has proven the existence of the ground in question):

(i) the arbitration agreement is not valid due to limits to a party's capacity;

(ii) the arbitration agreement is not valid for a reason other than limits to a party's capacity under the law to which the parties have agreed to subject it (or failing any indication thereon, the law of the country under which the place of arbitration falls);

(iii) a party was not given notice as required by the provisions of the law of the country under which the place of arbitration falls (or where the parties have otherwise reached an agreement on matters concerning the provisions of the law that do not relate to public policy, such agreement) in the proceedings to appoint arbitrators or in the arbitral proceedings;

(iv) a party was unable to present its case in the arbitral proceedings;

(v) the arbitral award contains decisions on matters beyond the scope of the arbitration agreement or the claims in the arbitral proceedings;

(vi) the composition of an arbitral tribunal or the arbitral proceedings were not in accordance with the provisions of the law of the country under which the place of arbitration falls (or where the parties have otherwise reached an agreement on matters concerning the provisions of the law that do not relate to public policy, such agreement);

(vii) according to the law of the country under which the place of arbitration falls (or where the law of a country other than the country under which the place of arbitration falls was applied to the arbitral proceedings, such country), the arbitral award has not yet become binding, or the arbitral award has been set aside or suspended by a court of such country;

(viii) the claims in the arbitral proceedings relate to a dispute that cannot constitute the subject of an arbitration agreement under the laws of Japan; or

(ix) the content of the arbitral award would be contrary to the public policy or good morals of Japan.

(3) Where the ground described in item (v) of the preceding paragraph is present, and where the part relating to matters described in the same item can be separated from the arbitral award, said part and any other parts in the arbitral award shall be deemed separate independent arbitral awards and the provisions of the preceding paragraph shall apply accordingly.

Article 46. (Enforcement Decision of Arbitral Award)

(1) A party seeking enforcement based on the arbitral award may apply to a court for an enforcement decision (which hereinafter means a decision authorizing enforcement based on an arbitral award) against the debtor as counterparty.

(2) The party making the application described in the preceding paragraph shall supply a copy of the arbitral award, a document certifying that the content of said copy is identical to the arbitral award, and a Japanese translation of the arbitral award (except where made in Japanese).

(3) If an application for setting aside or suspension of an arbitral award has been made to the court as described in paragraph (2), item (vii) of the preceding article, the court where the application described in paragraph (1) has been made may, if it considers it necessary, suspend proceedings relating to the application described in paragraph (1). In such case, the court may, upon request of the party who made the application described in the same paragraph, order the other party to provide security.

(4) The case for application described in paragraph (1) shall be, notwithstanding the provisions of article 5, paragraph (1), subject only to the jurisdiction of the courts cited in each of the items of the same paragraph and a district court with jurisdiction over the location of the object of the claim or the debtor's seizable assets.

(5) Even where the case for application described in paragraph (1) falls within its jurisdiction, a court may, upon request or by its own authority, if it finds it appropriate, transfer all or a part of said case to another competent court.

(6) An immediate appeal may be filed against a decision made under the provisions of article 5, paragraph (3) or the preceding paragraph regarding the case for application described in paragraph (1).

(7) The court shall, except where it dismisses the application described in paragraph (1) pursuant to the provisions of the following paragraph or paragraph (9), issue an enforcement decision.

(8) The court may dismiss the application described in paragraph (1) only when it finds any of the grounds described in each of the items under paragraph (2) of the preceding article present (with respect to the grounds described in items (i) through (vii) of the same paragraph, this shall be limited to where the counterparty has proved the existence of the ground in question).

(9) The provisions of paragraph (3) of the preceding article shall apply with respect to the application of the provisions of the preceding paragraph in the event that the ground described in paragraph (2), item (v) of the same article is present.

(10) The provisions of article 44, paragraphs (5) and (8) shall apply with respect to decisions regarding the application described in paragraph (1).

Chapter IX: MISCELLANEOUS

Article 47. (Remuneration of Arbitrators)

(1) The arbitrators may receive remuneration in accordance with the agreement of the parties.

(2) Failing an agreement as described in the preceding paragraph, the arbitral tribunal shall determine the remuneration of the arbitrators. In such case, the remuneration shall be for an appropriate amount.

Article 48. (Deposit for the Costs of the Arbitral Proceedings)

(1) Unless otherwise agreed by the parties, the arbitral tribunal may order that the parties deposit an amount determined by the arbitral tribunal as the roughly estimated amount for costs of the arbitral proceedings within the appropriate period of time determined by the arbitral tribunal.

(2) Where such deposits, as ordered under the provisions of the preceding paragraph, have not been made, unless otherwise agreed by the parties, the arbitral tribunal may suspend or terminate the arbitral proceedings.

Article 49. (Apportionment of the Costs of the Arbitral Proceedings)

(1) The costs disbursed by the parties with respect to the arbitral proceedings shall be apportioned between the parties in accordance with the agreement of the parties.

(2) Failing an agreement as described in the preceding paragraph, each party shall bear the costs it has disbursed with respect to the arbitral proceedings.

(3) In accordance with the agreement of the parties, if any, the arbitral tribunal may, in an arbitral award or in an independent ruling, determine the apportionment between the parties of the costs disbursed

by the parties with respect to the arbitral proceedings and the amount that one party should reimburse to the other party based thereon.

(4) If the matters described in the preceding paragraph have been determined in an independent ruling, such ruling shall have the same effect as an arbitral award.

(5) The provisions of article 39 shall apply to the ruling described in the preceding paragraph.

Chapter X: PENALTIES

Article 50. (Acceptance of Bribe; Acceptance with Request; Acceptance in Advance of Assumption of Office)

(1) An arbitrator who accepts, demands or promises to accept a bribe in relation to its duty shall be punished by imprisonment with labor for not more than five years. In such case, when the arbitrator agrees to do an act in response to a request, imprisonment with labor for not more than seven years shall be imposed.

(2) When a person to be appointed an arbitrator accepts, demands or promises to accept a bribe in relation to the duty to assume with agreement to do an act in response to a request, imprisonment with labor for not more than five years shall be imposed in the event of appointment.

Article 51. (Bribe to Third Person)

When an arbitrator with agreement to do an act in response to a request, causes a bribe in relation to its duty to be given to a third person or demands or promises such bribe to be given to a third person, imprisonment with labor for not more than five years shall be imposed.

Article 52. (Aggravated Acceptance; Acceptance after Resignation of Office)

(1) When an arbitrator commits a crime described in the preceding two articles and consequently acts illegally or refrains from acting in the exercise of its duty, imprisonment labor for a definite term of not less than one year shall be imposed.

(2) The provisions of the preceding paragraph shall apply when an arbitrator accepts, demands or promises to accept a bribe, or cause a bribe to be given to a third person or demands or promises a bribe to be given to a third person, in relation to having acted illegally or refrained from acting in the exercise of its duty.

(3) When a person who was an arbitrator accepts, demands or promises to accept a bribe in relation to having acted illegally or refrained from acting in the exercise of its duty during its tenure as an arbitrator with agreement thereof in response to a request, imprisonment with labor for not more than five years shall be imposed.

Article 53. (Confiscation and Collection of Equivalent Value)

A bribe accepted by an offender or by a third person with such knowledge shall be confiscated. When the whole or a part of the bribe cannot be confiscated, a sum of money equivalent thereto shall be collected.

Article 54. (Giving a Bribe)

A person who gives, offers or promises to give a bribe as provided for in articles 50 through 52 shall be punished by imprisonment with labor for not more than three years or a fine of not more than two million five hundred thousand yen.

Article 55. (Crimes Committed Outside Japan)

(1) The provisions of articles 50 through 53 shall apply to an offender who commits any of the crimes described in articles 50 through 52 outside Japan.

(2) The crime described in the preceding article shall be treated in the same manner as provided in article 2 of the Criminal Code [Law No. 45 of 1907].

Supplementary Provisions

Article 1. (Date of Enforcement)

This Law shall come into force from the date which shall be fixed by a Cabinet Order no later than nine months from the date of the promulgation of this Law.

Article 2. (Transitory Measures Relating to Form of Arbitration Agreement)

The existing Law shall apply to the form for arbitration agreements which have been made prior to the enforcement of this Law.

Article 3. (Exception Relating to Arbitration Agreements Concluded between Consumers and Businesses)

(1) For the time being until otherwise enacted, any arbitration agreements (excluding arbitration agreements described in the following article; hereafter in this article referred to as the "consumer arbitration agreement") concluded between consumers (which hereafter in this article shall mean consumers as described in article 2, paragraph (1) of the Consumer Contract Act [Law No. 61 of 2000]) and businesses (which hereafter in this article shall mean businesses as described in article 2, paragraph (2) of the same law) subsequent to the enforcement of this Law, the subject of which constitutes civil disputes that may arise between them in the future, shall follow the provisions described in paragraphs (2) through (7).

(2) A consumer may cancel a consumer arbitration agreement. Provided, this shall not apply in the event that the consumer is a claimant in arbitral proceedings based on the consumer arbitration agreement.

(3) In the case where a business is the claimant in arbitral proceedings based on a consumer arbitration agreement, following the constitution of an arbitral tribunal the business shall request without delay that an oral hearing be conducted under the provisions of article 32, paragraph (1). In such case the arbitral tribunal shall make a ruling to carry out the oral hearing and notify the parties of the date, time and place therefor.

(4) The arbitral tribunal shall carry out the oral hearing described in the preceding paragraph prior to any other proceedings in the arbitral proceedings.

(5) Notice to the party who is a consumer based on the provisions of paragraph (3) shall be made by the sending of a document stating the following matters. In such case, the arbitral tribunal shall make every effort to use as simple an expression as possible with respect to matters described in items (ii) through (v):

(i) date, time and place of the oral hearing;

(ii) that in the case where an arbitration agreement exists, the arbitral award with respect to the civil dispute constituting its subject shall have the same effect as a final and conclusive judgment of the court;

(iii) that in the case where an arbitration agreement exists, any suit filed with the court in respect of the civil dispute constituting its subject will be dismissed irrespective of the timing when the suit is filed before or after the arbitral award;

(iv) that the consumer may cancel the consumer arbitration agreement; and

(v) that in the event that the party who is the consumer fails to appear on the date of the oral hearing described in item (i), said party shall be deemed to have cancelled the consumer arbitration agreement.

(6) On the day of the oral hearing described in paragraph (3), the arbitral tribunal shall explain the matters described in items (ii) through (iv) of the preceding paragraph orally to the party who is a consumer. In such case, where the party does not express an intent to waive its right of cancellation described in paragraph (2), said party shall be deemed to have cancelled the consumer arbitration agreement.

(7) In the event that the party who is a consumer fails to appear on the date of the oral hearing described in paragraph (3), said party shall be deemed to have cancelled the consumer arbitration agreement.

Article 4. (Exception Relating to Arbitration Agreements Concerning Individual Labor-related Disputes)

For the time being until otherwise enacted, any arbitration agreements concluded following the enforcement of this Law, the subject of which constitutes individual labor-related disputes (which means individual labor-related disputes as described in article 1 of the Law on Promoting the Resolution of Individual Labor Disputes [Law No.112 of 2001]) that may arise in the future, shall be null and void.

Article 5. (Transitional Measures Relating to Arbitral Proceedings)

Arbitral proceedings commenced prior to the enforcement of this Law and proceedings conducted by a court relating to such arbitral proceedings (excluding proceedings commenced after the issuance of an arbitral award) shall follow the existing Law.

Article 6. (Transitional Measures Relating to Lawsuits for the Challenge against Arbitrators)

In addition to the provisions in the preceding article, the existing Law shall apply to suits for challenges against arbitrators brought prior to the enforcement of this Law.

Article 7. (Transitional Measures Relating to the Request for the Challenge against Arbitrators to the Arbitral Tribunal)

In addition to the provisions of the preceding two articles, with respect to the request of the provisions of article 19, paragraph (3) in the case where the parties, prior to the enforcement of this Law, were aware of the fact that an arbitral tribunal had been formed and of the existence of any of the grounds referred to in any of the items of article 18, paragraph (1) for any arbitrator, the words "the later of either the day on which it became aware of the constitution of the arbitral tribunal or the day on which it became aware of any circumstance referred to in any item of paragraph (1) of the preceding article" in article 19, paragraph (3) shall be read as "the date on which this Law came into force".

Article 8. (Transitional Measures Relating to the Force and Effect of Arbitral Awards)

In the case where an arbitral award had been issued prior to the enforcement of this Law, its deposit to a court, its force and effect, suits to set it aside, and enforcement based thereon, shall follow the existing Law.

Articles 9 through 22 [Omitted]

G. RUSSIAN ARBITRATION ACT OF JULY 7, 1993

The present Act shall:

proceed from the recognition of the usefulness of arbitration (mediation) as a method widely applied in the settlement of disputes arising in international trade, and the need for complex regulation of international commercial arbitration in conformity with the law; take account of the provisions on such arbitration contained in the international treaties of the RF and in the Model Law on International Commercial Arbitration adopted in 1985 by the UN Commission on International Trade Law, and approved by the UN General Assembly, for possible use by states in their legislation.

Chapter I. GENERAL

Article 1. Scope of Application

1. The present Act shall apply to international commercial arbitration, if the place of arbitration is in the territory of the RF. However, the provisions of Articles 8, 9, 35 and 36 shall also apply in the cases in which the place of arbitration is abroad.

2. The following may be referred to international commercial arbitration pursuant to agreement between the parties: disputes arising from contractual and other civil-law relations in foreign-trade and other types of international economic relationships, where any of the parties has its place of business abroad, and also disputes between enterprises with foreign investments and international associations and organizations founded on RF territory, disputes between their participants, and disputes with other subjects of RF law.

3. For the purposes of Clause 2 of this Article:

if a party has more than one place of business, the place of business is that which has the closest relationship to the arbitration agreement;

if a party does not have a place of business, reference is to be made to his habitual residence.

4. The present Act shall not affect any other law of the RF by virtue of which certain disputes may not be submitted to arbitration or may be submitted to arbitration only according to provisions other than those of this Act.

5. Where an international treaty of the RF lays down rules other than those contained in RF arbitration law, the rules of the international treaty shall apply.

Article 2. Definitions and Rules of Interpretation

For the purposes of this Act:

(a) "arbitration" means any arbitration whether or not administered by a permanent arbitral institution, notably, by the International Commercial Arbitration Court or by the Maritime Arbitration Commission under the RF Chamber of Commerce and Industry (Annexes I and II to this Act);

(b) "arbitral tribunal" (mediation) means a sole arbitrator or a panel of arbitrators;

(c) "court" means a body or organ of the judicial system of the state;

(d) where a provision of this Act, except Article 28, leaves the parties free to determine a certain issue, such freedom shall include the right of the parties to authorize a third party, including an institution, to make that determination;

(e) where a provision of this Act refers to the fact that the parties have agreed or that they may agree, or in any other way refers to an agreement of the parties, such agreement shall include any arbitration rules referred to in that agreement;

(f) where a provision of this Act, other than Articles 25(a) and 32(2)(a) refers to a claim, it shall also apply to a counter-claim, and where it refers to a defense, it shall also apply to a defense to such counter-claim.

Article 3. Receipt of Written Communications

1. Unless otherwise agreed by the parties:

(a) any written communication shall be deemed to have been received if it is delivered to the addressee personally or if it is delivered at his place of business, habitual residence or mailing address; if none of these can be found after making a reasonable inquiry, a written communication shall be deemed to have been received if it is sent to the addressee's last-known place of business, habitual residence or mailing address by registered letter or any other means which provides a record of the attempt to deliver it;

(b) the communication shall be deemed to have been received on the day it is so delivered.

2. The provisions of this Article shall not apply to communications in court proceedings.

Article 4. Waiver of Right to Object

A party who knows that any provision of this Act from which the parties may derogate or any requirement under the arbitration agreement has not been complied with, and yet proceeds with the arbitration without stating his objection to such non-compliance without undue delay or, if a time limit is provided therefore, within such period of time, shall be deemed to have waived his right to object.

Article 5. Extent of Court Intervention

In matters governed by this Act, no court shall intervene, except where such provision is contained in this Act.

Article 6. Court or Other Authority for Certain Functions of Arbitration Assistance and Supervision

1. The functions referred to in Articles 11(3), 11(4), 13(3) and 14 shall be performed by the President of the RF, Chamber of Commerce and Industry.

2. The functions referred to in Articles 16(3) and 34(2) shall be performed by the Supreme Court of the republic within the RF. Territori-

al, regional or city court, the court of the autonomous region, and the court of the autonomous area in the place of arbitration.

Chapter II. ARBITRATION AGREEMENT

Article 7. Definition and Form of Arbitration Agreement

1. "Arbitration agreement" shall be an agreement by the parties to submit to arbitration all or certain disputes which have arisen or which may arise between them in respect of a defined legal relationship, whether contractual or not. An arbitration agreement may be in the form of an arbitration clause in a contract or in the form of a separate agreement.

2. The arbitration agreement shall be in writing. An agreement is in writing if it is contained in a document signed by the parties or in an exchange of letters, telex, telegrams or other means of telecommunications which provide a record of the agreement, or in an exchange of statements of claim and defense in which the existence of an agreement is alleged by one party and not denied by another. A reference in the contract to a document containing an arbitration clause shall be an arbitration contract, provided the contract is in writing and the reference is such as to make that clause part of the contract.

Article 8. Arbitration Agreement and Substantive Claim Before Court

1. A court before which an action is brought in a matter which is the subject of an arbitration agreement shall, if a party so requests not later than when submitting his first statement on the substance of the dispute, refer the parties to arbitration unless it finds that the agreement is null and void, inoperative and incapable of being performed.

2. Where an action referred to in Paragraph 1 of this Article has been brought, arbitral proceedings may nevertheless be commenced or continued, and an award may be made, while the issue is pending before the court.

Article 9. Arbitration Agreement and Interim Measures by Court

It shall not be incompatible with an arbitration agreement for a party to request, before or during arbitral proceedings, from a court an interim measure of protection, and for a court to grant such measure.

Chapter III. COMPOSITION OF ARBITRAL TRIBUNAL

Article 10. Number of Arbitrators

1. The parties shall be free to determine the number of arbitrators.

2. Failing such determination, the number of arbitrators shall be three.

Article 11. Appointment of Arbitrators

1. No person shall be precluded by reason of his citizenship from acting as an arbitrator, unless otherwise agreed by the parties.

2. The parties shall be free to agree on a procedure of appointing the arbitrator or arbitrators, subject to the provisions of Paragraphs 4 and 5 of this Article.

3. Failing such agreement:

(a) in an arbitration with three arbitrators, each party shall appoint one arbitrator, and the two arbitrators thus appointed shall appoint the third arbitrator; if a party fails to appoint the arbitrator within thirty days of receipt of a request to do so from the other party, or if the two arbitrators fail to agree on the third arbitrator within thirty days of their appointment, the appointment shall be made, upon request of a party, by the court or other authority specified in Article 6(1);

(b) in an arbitration with a sole arbitrator, if the parties are unable to agree on the arbitrator, he shall be appointed, upon request of a party, by the court or other authority specified in Article 6(1).

4. Where, under an appointment procedure agreed upon by the parties:

(a) a party fails to act as required under such procedure, or

(b) the parties or two arbitrators are unable to reach an agreement expected of them under such procedure, or

(c) a third party, including an institution, fails to perform any function entrusted to it under such procedure,

any party may request a court or other authority specified in Article 6(1) to take the necessary measures, unless the agreement on the appointment procedure provides other means for securing the appointment.

5. A decision on a matter entrusted by Paragraph 3 or 4 of this Article to the authority specified in Article 6(1) shall be subject to no appeal. This authority, in appointing an arbitrator, shall have due regard to any qualifications required of the arbitrator by the agreement of the parties and to such considerations as are likely to secure the appointment of an independent and impartial arbitrator and, in the case of a sole or third arbitrator, shall take into account as well the advisability of appointing an arbitrator of a citizenship other than those of the parties.

Article 12. Grounds for Challenge

1. When a person is approached in connection with his possible appointment as an arbitrator, he shall disclose any circumstances likely to give rise to justifiable doubts as to his impartiality or independence. An arbitrator, from the time of his appointment and throughout the arbitral proceedings, shall without delay disclose any such circumstances to the parties unless they have already been informed of them by him.

2. An arbitrator may be challenged only if circumstances exist that give rise to justifiable doubts as to his impartiality or independence, or if

he does not possess qualifications agreed to by the parties. A party may challenge an arbitrator appointed by him, or in whose appointment he has participated, only for reasons of which he becomes aware after the appointment has been made.

Article 13. Challenge Procedure

1. The parties shall be free to agree on a procedure for challenging an arbitrator, subject to the provisions of Paragraph 3 of this Article.

2. Failing such agreement, a party who intends to challenge an arbitrator shall, within fifteen days after becoming aware of the constitution of the arbitral tribunal or after becoming aware of any circumstances referred to in Article 12(2), send a written statement of the reasons for the challenge to the arbitral tribunal. Unless the challenged arbitrator withdraws from his office or the other party agrees to the challenge, the arbitral tribunal shall decide on the challenge.

If a challenge under any procedure agreed upon by the parties or under the procedure of Paragraph 2 of this Article is not successful, the challenging party may request, within thirty days after having received notice of the decision rejecting the challenge, the authority specified in Article 6(1) to take a decision on the challenge, which decision shall be subject to no appeal; while such a request is pending, the arbitral tribunal, including the challenged arbitrator, may continue the arbitral proceedings and make an award.

Article 14. Termination of Arbitrator's Mandate

1. If an arbitrator becomes de jure or de facto unable to perform his functions or for other reasons fails to act without undue delay, his mandate terminates if he withdraws from his office or if the parties agree on the termination. Otherwise, if a controversy remains concerning any of these grounds, any party may request the authority specified in Article 6(1) to decide on the termination of the mandate, which decision shall be subject to no appeal.

2. If, under this Article or Article 13(2), an arbitrator withdraws from his office or a party agrees to the termination of the mandate of an arbitrator, this shall not imply acceptance of the validity of any ground referred to in this Article or Article 12(2).

Article 15. Appointment of Substitute Arbitrator

Where the mandate of an arbitrator terminates under Article 13 or 14, or because of his withdrawal from office for any other reason, or because of the revocation of his mandate by agreement of the parties, or in any other case of termination of his mandate, a substitute arbitrator shall be appointed according to the rules that were applicable to the appointment of the arbitrator being replaced.

Chapter IV. JURISDICTION OF ARBITRAL TRIBUNAL

Article 16. Competence of Arbitral Tribunal to Rule on Its Jurisdiction

1. The arbitral tribunal may rule on its own jurisdiction, including any objections with respect to the existence or validity of the arbitration agreement. For that purpose, an arbitration clause which forms part of a contract shall be treated as an agreement independent of the other terms of the contract. A decision by the arbitral tribunal that the contract is null and void shall not entail ipso jure the invalidity of the arbitration clause.

2. A plea that the arbitral tribunal does not have jurisdiction shall be raised not later than the submission of the statement of defense. A party shall not be precluded from raising such a plea by the fact that he has appointed, or participated in the appointment of, an arbitrator. A plea that the arbitral tribunal is exceeding the scope of its authority shall be raised as soon as the matter alleged to be beyond the scope of its authority is raised during the arbitral proceedings. The arbitral tribunal may, in either case, admit a later plea if it considers the delay justified.

3. The arbitral tribunal may rule on a plea referred to in Paragraph 2 of this Article either as a preliminary question or in an award on the merits. If the arbitral tribunal rules as a preliminary question that it has jurisdiction, any party may request, within thirty days after having received notice on that ruling, the court specified in Article 6(2) to decide the matter, which decision shall be subject to no appeal; while such a request is pending, the arbitral tribunal may continue the arbitral proceedings and make an award.

Article 17. Power of Arbitral Tribunal to Order Interim Measures

Unless otherwise agreed by the parties, the arbitral tribunal may, at the request of a party, order any party to take such interim measures of protection as the arbitral tribunal may consider necessary in respect of the subject-matter of the dispute. The arbitral tribunal may require any party to provide appropriate security in connection with such measures.

Chapter V. CONDUCT OF ARBITRAL PROCEEDINGS

Article 18. Equal Treatment of Parties

The parties shall be treated with equality and each party shall be given a full opportunity of presenting his case.

Article 19. Determination of Rules of Procedure

1. Subject to the provisions of this Act, the parties shall be free to agree on the procedure to be followed by the arbitral tribunal in conducting the proceedings.

2. Failing such agreement, the arbitral tribunal may, subject to the provisions of this Act, conduct the arbitration in such manner as it

considers appropriate. The powers conferred upon the arbitral tribunal shall include the power to determine the admissibility, relevance, materiality and weight of any evidence.

Article 20. Place of Arbitration

1. The parties shall be free to agree on the place of arbitration. Failing such agreement, the place of arbitration shall be determined by the arbitral tribunal having regard to the circumstances of the case, including the convenience of the parties.

2. Notwithstanding the provisions of Paragraph 1 of this Article, the arbitral tribunal may, unless otherwise agreed by the parties, meet at any place it considers appropriate for consultation among its members, for hearing witnesses, experts or the parties, or for inspection of goods, other property or documents.

Article 21. Commencement of Arbitral Proceedings

Unless otherwise agreed by the parties, the arbitral proceedings in respect of a particular dispute shall commence on the date on which a request for that dispute to be referred to arbitration is received by the respondent.

Article 22. Language

1. The parties shall be free to agree on the language or languages to be used in the arbitral proceedings. Failing such agreement, the arbitral tribunal shall determine the language or languages to be used in the proceedings. This agreement or determination, unless otherwise specified therein, shall apply to any written statement by a party, any hearing and any award, decision or other communication by the arbitral tribunal.

2. The arbitral tribunal may order that any documentary evidence shall be accompanied by a translation into the language or languages agreed upon by the parties or determined by the arbitral tribunal.

Article 23. Statements of Claim and Defense

1. Within the period of time agreed by the parties or determined by the arbitral tribunal, the claimant shall state the facts supporting his claim, the points at issue, and the relief or remedy sought, and the respondent shall state his defense in respect of these particulars, unless the parties have otherwise agreed as to the required elements of such statements. The parties may submit with their statements all documents they consider to be relevant or may add a reference to the document or other evidence they will submit.

2. Unless otherwise agreed by the parties, either party may amend or supplement his claim or defense during the course of the arbitral proceedings, unless the arbitral tribunal considers it inappropriate to allow such amendment, having regard to the delay in making it.

Article 24. Hearings and Written Proceedings

1. Subject to any contrary agreement by the parties, the arbitral tribunal shall decide whether to hold oral hearings for the presentation of evidence or for oral argument, or whether the proceedings shall be conducted on the basis of documents and other materials. However, unless the parties have agreed that no hearings shall be held, the arbitral tribunal shall hold such hearings at an appropriate stage of the proceedings, if so requested by a party.

2. The parties shall be given sufficient advance notice of any hearing and of any meeting of the arbitral tribunal for the purposes of inspection of goods, other property or documents.

3. All statements, documents or other information supplied to the arbitral tribunal by one party shall be communicated to the other party. Any expert report or evidentiary document on which the arbitral tribunal may rely in making its decisions shall also be communicated to the parties.

Article 25. Default of a Party

Unless otherwise agreed by the parties, if, without showing sufficient cause:

(a) the claimant fails to communicate his statement of claim in accordance with Article 23(1), the arbitral tribunal shall terminate the proceedings;

(b) the respondent fails to communicate his statement of defense in accordance with Article 23(1), the arbitral tribunal shall continue the proceedings without treating such failure in itself as an admission of the claimant's allegations;

(c) any party fails to appear at a hearing or to produce documentary evidence, the arbitral tribunal may continue the proceedings and make the award on the evidence before it.

Article 26. Expert Appointed by Arbitral Tribunal

1. Unless otherwise agreed by the parties, the arbitral tribunal:

(a) may appoint one or more experts to report to it on specific issues to be determined by the arbitral tribunal;

(b) may require a party to give the expert any relevant information or to produce, or to provide access to, any relevant documents, goods or other property for his inspection.

2. Unless otherwise agreed by the parties, if a party so requests or if the arbitral tribunal considers it necessary, the expert shall, after delivery of his written or oral report, participate in a hearing where the parties have the opportunity to put questions to him and to present expert witnesses in order to testify on the points at issue.

Article 27. Court Assistance in Taking Evidence

The arbitral tribunal or a party with the approval of the arbitral tribunal may request assistance from a competent RF court in taking evidence. The court may execute the request within its competence and according to its rules on taking evidence.

Chapter VI. MAKING OF AWARD AND TERMINATION OF PROCEEDINGS

Article 28. Rules Applicable to Substance of Dispute

1. The arbitral tribunal shall decide the dispute in accordance with such rules of law as are chosen by the parties as applicable to the substance of the dispute. Any designation of the law or legal system of a given state shall be construed as directly referring to the substantive law and not to its conflict-of-laws rules.

2. Failing any designation by the parties, the arbitral tribunal shall apply the law determined by the conflict-of-laws rules which it considers applicable.

3. In all cases, the arbitral tribunal shall decide in accordance with the terms of the contract and shall take into account the usages of the trade applicable to the transaction.

Article 29. Decision-Making by Panel of Arbitrators

In arbitral proceedings with more than one arbitrator, any decision of the arbitral tribunal shall be made, unless otherwise agreed by the parties, by a majority of all its members. However, questions of procedure may be decided by a presiding arbitrator, if so authorized by the parties or all members of the arbitral tribunal.

Article 30. Settlement

1. If, during arbitral proceedings, the parties settle the dispute, the arbitral tribunal shall terminate the proceeding and, if requested by the parties and not objected to by the arbitral tribunal, record the settlement in the form of an arbitral award on agreed terms.

2. An award on agreed terms shall be made in accordance with the provisions of Article 31 and shall state that it is an award. Such an award shall have the same status and effect as any other award on the merits of the case.

Article 31. Form and Content of Award

1. The award shall be made in writing and shall be signed by the arbitrator or arbitrators. In arbitral proceedings with more than one arbitrator, the signatures of the majority of all members of the arbitral tribunal shall suffice, provided that the reason for any omitted signature is stated.

2. The award shall state the reasons upon which it is based, the conclusion on satisfaction or denial of claim, the amount of arbitration charge, the arbitration costs, and their apportionment between the parties.

3. The award shall state its date and the place of arbitration, as determined in accordance with Article 20(1). The award shall be deemed to have been made at that place.

4. After the award is made, a copy signed by the arbitrators in accordance with Paragraph 1 of this Article shall be delivered to each party.

Article 32. Termination of Proceedings

1. The arbitral proceedings shall be terminated by the final award or by an order of the arbitral tribunal in accordance with Paragraph 2 of this Article.

2. The arbitral tribunal shall issue an order for the termination of the arbitral proceedings when:

(a) the claimant withdraws his claim, unless the respondent objects thereto and the arbitral tribunal recognizes a legitimate interest on his part in obtaining a final settlement of the dispute;

(b) the parties agree on the termination of the proceedings;

(c) the arbitral tribunal finds that the continuation of the proceedings has for any other reasons become unnecessary or impossible.

3. The mandate of the arbitral tribunal shall terminate with the termination of the arbitral proceedings, subject to the provisions of Article 33 and 34(4).

Article 33. Correction and Interpretation of Award. Additional Award

1. Within thirty days of receipt of the award, unless another period of time has been agreed upon by the parties:

(a) a party, with notice to the other party, may request the arbitral tribunal to correct in the award any errors in computation, any clerical or typographical errors, or any errors of similar nature;

(b) if so agreed by the parties, a party, with notice to the other party, may request the arbitral tribunal to give an interpretation of a specific point or part of the award.

If the arbitral tribunal considers the request to be justified, it shall make the correction or give the interpretation within thirty days of receipt of the request. The interpretation shall form part of the award.

2. The arbitral tribunal may correct any error of the type referred to in Paragraph 1(a) of this Article on its own initiative within thirty days of the date of the award.

3. Unless otherwise agreed by the parties, a party, with notice to the other party, may request, within thirty days of receipt of the award, the arbitral tribunal to make an additional award as to claims presented in the arbitral proceedings but omitted from the award. If the arbitral tribunal considers the request to be justified, it shall make the additional award within sixty days.

4. The arbitral tribunal may extend, if necessary, the period of time within which it shall make a correction, interpretation or additional award under Paragraph 1 or 3 of this Article.

5. The provisions of Article 31 shall apply to a correction or interpretation of the award or to an additional award.

Chapter VII. RECOURSE AGAINST AWARD

Article 34. Application for Setting Aside as Exclusive Recourse Against Arbitral Award

1. Recourse to a court against an arbitral award may be made only by an application for setting aside in accordance with Paragraphs 2 and 3 of this Article.

2. An arbitral award may be set aside by the court specified in Article 6(2), only if:

(a) the party making the application furnishes proof that:

(i) a party to the arbitration agreement referred to in Article 7 was under some incapacity; or the said agreement is not valid under the law to which the parties have subjected it, or, failing any indication thereon, under RF law; or

(ii) the party making the application was not given proper notice of the appointment of an arbitrator or of the arbitral proceedings, or was otherwise unable to present his case; or

(iii) the award deals with a dispute not contemplated by or not falling within the terms of the submission to arbitration, or contains decisions on matters beyond the scope of the submission to arbitration, provided that, if the decisions on matters submitted to arbitration can be separated from those not so submitted, only that part of the award which contains decisions on matters not submitted to arbitration may be set aside; or

(iv) the composition of the arbitral tribunal or the arbitral procedure was not in accordance with the agreement of the parties, unless such agreement was in conflict with a provision of this Act from which the parties cannot derogate, or, failing such agreement, was not in accordance with this Act; or

(b) the court finds that:

(i) the subject-matter of the dispute is not capable of settlement by arbitration under RF law; or

(ii) the award is in conflict with the public policy of the RF.

3. An application for setting aside may not be made after three months have elapsed from the date on which the party making that application received the award or, if a request was made under Article 33, from the date on which that request was disposed of by the arbitral tribunal.

4. The court, when asked to set aside an award, may, where appropriate and so requested by a party, suspend the setting-aside proceedings for a period of time determined by it in order to give the arbitral tribunal an opportunity to resume the arbitral proceedings or to take such other action as, in the arbitral tribunal's opinion, will eliminate the grounds for setting aside.

Chapter VIII. RECOGNITION AND ENFORCEMENT OF AWARDS

Article 35. Recognition and Enforcement

1. An arbitral award, irrespective of the country in which it was made, shall be recognized as binding and, upon application in writing to the competent court, shall be enforced, subject to the provisions of this Article and of Article 36.

2. The party relying on an award or applying for its enforcement shall supply the duly authenticated original award or a duly certified copy thereof, and the original arbitration agreement referred to in Article 7 or a duly certified copy thereof. If the award or agreement is made in a foreign language, the party shall supply a duly certified translation thereof into the Russian language.

Article 36. Grounds for Refusing Recognition or Enforcement

1. Recognition or enforcement of an arbitral award, irrespective of the country in which it was made, may be refused only:

(a) at the request of the party against whom it is invoked, if that party furnished to the competent court where recognition or enforcement is sought proof that:

(i) a party to the arbitration agreement referred to in Article 7 was under some incapacity; or the said agreement is not valid under the law to which the parties have subjected it, or, failing any indication thereon, under the law of the country where the award was made; or

(ii) the party against whom the award is invoked was not given proper notice of the appointment of an arbitrator or of the arbitral proceedings, or was otherwise unable to present his case; or

(iii) the award deals with a dispute not contemplated by or not falling within the terms of the submission to arbitration, or it contains decisions on matters beyond the scope of the submission to arbitration, provided that, if the decisions on matters submitted to arbitration can be separated from those not so submitted, that part of the award which contains decisions on matters submitted to arbitration may be recognized and enforced; or

(iv) the composition of the arbitral tribunal or the arbitral procedure was not in accordance with the agreement of the parties or, failing such agreement, was not in accordance with the law of the country where the arbitration took place; or

(v) the award has not yet become binding on the parties or has been set aside or suspended by a court of the country in which, or under the law of which, that award was made; or

(b) if the court finds that:

(i) the subject-matter of the dispute is not capable of settlement by arbitration under RF law; or

(ii) the recognition or enforcement of the award would be contrary to the public policy of the RF.

2. If an application for setting aside or suspension of an award has been made to a court referred to in Paragraph 1(a)(v) of this Article, the court where recognition or enforcement is sought may, if it considers it proper, adjourn its decision, and may also, on the application of the party claiming recognition or enforcement of the award, order the other party to provide appropriate security.

H. GERMAN ARBITRATION LAW 1998*

Act on the Reform of the Law relating to Arbitral Proceedings

The following provisions have entered into force on

1 January 1998

Book Ten of the Code of Civil Procedure[1]

Arbitration Procedure
Sections 1025–1066

Chapter I
General provisions

Section 1025
Scope of application

(1) The provisions of this Book apply if the place of arbitration as referred to in section 1043 subs. 1 is situated in Germany.

(2) The provisions of sections 1032, 1033 and 1050 also apply if the place of arbitration is situated outside Germany or has not yet been determined.

---

* Unofficial translation by the German Institution of Arbitration (DIS) and the German Federal Ministry of Justice. Reprinted with the kind permission of German Institution of Arbitration.

1. Completely revised by Article 1, No. 7 of the Act on the Reform of the Law relating to Arbitral Proceedings of 22 December 1997, Bundesgesetzblatt (Federal Law Gazette) 1997 Part I page 3224. The Act entered into force on 1 January 1998.

(3) If the place of arbitration has not yet been determined, the German courts are competent to perform the court functions specified in sections 1034, 1035, 1037 and 1038 if the respondent or the claimant has his place of business or habitual residence in Germany.

(4) Sections 1061 to 1065 apply to the recognition and enforcement of foreign arbitral awards.

Section 1026
Extent of court intervention

In matters governed by sections 1025 to 1061, no court shall intervene except where so provided in this Book.

Section 1027
Loss of right to object

A party who knows that any provision of this Book from which the parties may derogate or any agreed requirement under the arbitral procedure has not been complied with and yet proceeds with the arbitration without stating his objection to such non-compliance without undue delay or, if a time-limit is provided therefor, within such period of time, may not raise that objection later.

Section 1028
Receipt of written communications in case of unknown whereabouts

(1) Unless otherwise agreed by the parties, if the whereabouts of a party or of a person entitled to receive communications on his behalf are not known, any written communication shall be deemed to have been received on the day on which it could have been received at the addressee's last-known mailing address, place of business or habitual residence after proper transmission by registered mail/return receipt requested or any other means which provides a record of the attempt to deliver it there.

(2) Subsection 1 does not apply to communications in court proceedings.

Chapter II
Arbitration agreement

Section 1029
Definition

(1) "Arbitration agreement" is an agreement by the parties to submit to arbitration all or certain disputes which have arisen or which may arise between them in respect of a defined legal relationship, whether contractual or not.

(2) An arbitration agreement may be in the form of a separate agreement ("separate arbitration agreement") or in the form of a clause in a contract ("arbitration clause").

Section 1030
Arbitrability

(1) Any claim involving an economic interest ("vermögensrechtlicher Anspruch") can be the subject of an arbitration agreement. An arbitration agreement concerning claims not involving an economic interest shall have legal effect to the extent that the parties are entitled to conclude a settlement on the issue in dispute.

(2) An arbitration agreement relating to disputes on the existence of a lease of residential accommodation within Germany shall be null and void. This does not apply to residential accommodation as specified in section 549 subs. 1 to 3[2] of the Civil Code.

(3) Statutory provisions outside this Book by virtue of which certain disputes may not be submitted to arbitration, or may be submitted to arbitration only under certain conditions, remain unaffected.

Section 1031
Form of arbitration agreement

(1) The arbitration agreement shall be contained either in a document signed by the parties or in an exchange of letters, telefaxes, telegrams or other means of telecommunication which provide a record of the agreement.

(2) The form requirement of subsection 1 shall be deemed to have been complied with if the arbitration agreement is contained in a document transmitted from one party to the other party or by a third party to both parties and—if no objection was raised in good time—the contents of such document are considered to be part of the contract in accordance with common usage.

(3) The reference in a contract complying with the form requirements of subsection 1 or 2 to a document containing an arbitration clause constitutes an arbitration agreement provided that the reference is such as to make that clause part of the contract.

(4) An arbitration agreement is also concluded by the issuance of a bill of lading, if the latter contains an express reference to an arbitration clause in a charter party.

(5) Arbitration agreements to which a consumer[3] is a party must be contained in a document which has been personally signed by the parties. The written form pursuant to subsection 1 may be substituted by electronic form pursuant to section 126 a of the Civil Code ("Bürgerliches

2. Section 1030 subs. 2, sentence 2 was amended by Article 3 of the Act on the Reform of the Rent Law of 19 June 2001, Bundesgesetzblatt (Federal Law Gazette) 2001 Part I, p. 1149, in force as of 1 September 2001.

3. A consumer is any natural person who concludes a transaction for a purpose which can be regarded as being outside his trade or self-employed profession ("gewerbliche oder selbständige berufliche Tätigkeit")—section 13 Civil Law Code. Section 13 Civil Law Code was newly introduced by Art. 2 subs. 1 of the Act of 27 June 2000. By the same Act, section 1031 subs. 5, 3rd sentence was deleted.

Gesetzbuch–BGB").[4] No agreements other than those referring to the arbitral proceedings may be contained in such a document or electronic document; this shall not apply in the case of a notarial certification.[5]

(6) Any non-compliance with the form requirements is cured by entering into argument on the substance of the dispute in the arbitral proceedings.

Section 1032
Arbitration agreement and substantive claim before court

(1) A court before which an action is brought in a matter which is the subject of an arbitration agreement shall, if the respondent raises an objection prior to the beginning of the oral hearing on the substance of the dispute, reject the action as inadmissible unless the court finds that the arbitration agreement is null and void, inoperative or incapable of being performed.

(2) Prior to the constitution of the arbitral tribunal, an application may be made to the court to determine whether or not arbitration is admissible.

(3) Where an action or application referred to in subsection 1 or 2 has been brought, arbitral proceedings may nevertheless be commenced or continued, and an arbitral award may be made, while the issue is pending before the court.

Section 1033
Arbitration agreement and interim measures by court

It is not incompatible with an arbitration agreement for a court to grant, before or during arbitral proceedings, an interim measure of

---

4. Section 126a Civil Code ("BGB") [Electronic form]: (1) If the statutory written form is to be substituted by electronic form, the author of the statement must add his name to the statement and append a qualified electronic signature pursuant to the Signature Act.

(2) In the case of a contract, the parties must each electronically sign a document identical in wording in the manner prescribed in subsection 1.

Section 126a Civil Code was newly introduced by Art. 1 of the Act of 13 July 2001 (Bundesgesetzblatt Part I, p. 1542).

Section 2 Signature Act ("Signaturgesetz–SigG") [Qualified electronic form]: For the purpose of this Act,

1. "electronic signature" means data in electronic form which are attached to or logically associated with other electronic data and which serve as a method of authentication;

2. "advanced electronic signature" means an electronic signature pursuant to No. 1 which a) is uniquely linked to the signatory, b) is capable of identifying the signatory, c) is created using means that the signatory can maintain under his sole control, and d) is linked to the data to which it relates in such a manner that any subsequent change of the data is detectable;

3. "qualified electronic signature" means an electronic signature pursuant to No. 2 which a) is based on a qualified certificate valid at the time of the signature's creation, and b) is created with a secure signature-creation device; . . . —Act of 16 May 2001 (Signature Act), Bundesgesetzblatt Part I, p. 876.

5. Sentence 2 and 3 of section 1031 subs. 5 were amended by Art. 2 of the Act of 14 December 2001 (Electronic Commerce Act), Bundesgesetzblatt Part I, p. 3721.

protection relating to the subject-matter of the arbitration upon request of a party.

Chapter III
Constitution of arbitral tribunal

Section 1034
Composition of arbitral tribunal

(1) The parties are free to determine the number of arbitrators. Failing such determination, the number of arbitrators shall be three.

(2) If the arbitration agreement grants preponderant rights to one party with regard to the composition of the arbitral tribunal which place the other party at a disadvantage, that other party may request the court to appoint the arbitrator or arbitrators in deviation from the nomination made, or from the agreed nomination procedure. The request must be submitted at the latest within two weeks of the party becoming aware of the constitution of the arbitral tribunal. Section 1032 subs. 3 applies mutatis mutandis.

Section 1035
Appointment of arbitrators

(1) The parties are free to agree on a procedure of appointing the arbitrator or arbitrators.

(2) Unless otherwise agreed by the parties, a party shall be bound by his appointment of an arbitrator as soon as the other party has received notice of the appointment.

(3) Failing an agreement between the parties on the appointment of the arbitrators, a sole arbitrator shall, if the parties are unable to agree on his appointment, be appointed, upon request of a party, by the court. In an arbitration with three arbitrators, each party shall appoint one arbitrator, and the two arbitrators thus appointed shall appoint the third arbitrator who shall act as chairman of the arbitral tribunal. If a party fails to appoint the arbitrator within one month of receipt of a request to do so from the other party, or if the two arbitrators fail to agree on the third arbitrator within one month of their appointment, the appointment shall be made, upon request of a party, by the court.

(4) Where, under an appointment procedure agreed upon by the parties, a party fails to act as required under such procedure, or if the parties, or two arbitrators, are unable to reach an agreement expected of them under such procedure, or a third party fails to perform any function entrusted to it under such procedure, any party may request the court to take the necessary measure, unless the agreement on the appointment procedure provides other means for securing the appointment.

(5) The court, in appointing an arbitrator, shall have due regard to any qualifications required of the arbitrator by the agreement of the parties and to such considerations as are likely to secure the appointment

of an independent and impartial arbitrator. In the case of a sole or third arbitrator, the court shall take into account as well the advisability of appointing an arbitrator of a nationality other than those of the parties.

Section 1036
Challenge of an arbitrator

(1) When a person is approached in connection with his possible appointment as an arbitrator, he shall disclose any circumstances likely to give rise to justifiable doubts as to his impartiality or independence. An arbitrator, from the time of his appointment and throughout the arbitral proceedings, shall without delay disclose any such circumstances to the parties unless they have already been informed of them by him.

(2) An arbitrator may be challenged only if circumstances exist that give rise to justifiable doubts as to his impartiality or independence, or if he does not possess qualifications agreed to by the parties. A party may challenge an arbitrator appointed by him, or in whose appointment he has participated, only for reasons of which he becomes aware after the appointment has been made.

Section 1037
Challenge procedure

(1) The parties are free to agree on a procedure for challenging an arbitrator, subject to the provisions of subsection 3 of this section.

(2) Failing such agreement, a party who intends to challenge an arbitrator shall, within two weeks after becoming aware of the constitution of the arbitral tribunal or after becoming aware of any circumstance referred to in section 1036 subs. 2, send a written statement of the reasons for the challenge to the arbitral tribunal. Unless the challenged arbitrator withdraws from his office or the other party agrees to the challenge, the arbitral tribunal shall decide on the challenge.

(3) If a challenge under any procedure agreed upon by the parties or under the procedure of subsection 2 of this section is not successful, the challenging party may request, within one month after having received notice of the decision rejecting the challenge, the court to decide on the challenge; the parties may agree on a different time-limit. While such a request is pending, the arbitral tribunal, including the challenged arbitrator, may continue the arbitral proceedings and make an award.

Section 1038
Failure or impossibility to act

(1) If an arbitrator becomes de jure or de facto unable to perform his functions or for other reasons fails to act without undue delay, his mandate terminates if he withdraws from his office or if the parties agree on the termination. If the arbitrator does not withdraw from his office or if the parties cannot agree on the termination, any party may request the court to decide on the termination of the mandate.

(2) If, under subsection 1 of this section or section 1037 subs. 2, an arbitrator withdraws from his office or a party agrees to the termination of the mandate of an arbitrator, this does not imply acceptance of the validity of any ground for withdrawal referred to in subsection 1 of this section or section 1036 subs. 2.

Section 1039
Appointment of substitute arbitrator

(1) Where the mandate of an arbitrator terminates under section 1037 or 1038 or because of his withdrawal from office for any other reason or because of the revocation of his mandate by agreement of the parties, a substitute arbitrator shall be appointed according to the rules that were applicable to the appointment of the arbitrator being replaced.

(2) The parties are free to agree on another procedure.

Chapter IV
Jurisdiction of arbitral tribunal

Section 1040
Competence of arbitral tribunal to rule on its jurisdiction

(1) The arbitral tribunal may rule on its own jurisdiction and in this connection on the existence or validity of the arbitration agreement. For that purpose, an arbitration clause which forms part of a contract shall be treated as an agreement independent of the other terms of the contract.

(2) A plea that the arbitral tribunal does not have jurisdiction shall be raised not later than the submission of the statement of defense. A party is not precluded from raising such a plea by the fact that he has appointed, or participated in the appointment of, an arbitrator. A plea that the arbitral tribunal is exceeding the scope of its authority shall be raised as soon as the matter alleged to be beyond the scope of its authority is raised during the arbitral proceedings. The arbitral tribunal may, in either case, admit a later plea if it considers that the party has justified the delay.

(3) If the arbitral tribunal considers that it has jurisdiction, it rules on a plea referred to in subsection 2 of this section in general by means of a preliminary ruling. In this case, any party may request, within one month after having received written notice of that ruling, the court to decide the matter. While such a request is pending, the arbitral tribunal may continue the arbitral proceedings and make an award.

Section 1041
Interim measures of protection

(1) Unless otherwise agreed by the parties, the arbitral tribunal may, at the request of a party, order such interim measures of protection as the arbitral tribunal may consider necessary in respect of the subject-matter

of the dispute. The arbitral tribunal may require any party to provide appropriate security in connection with such measure.

(2) The court may, at the request of a party, permit enforcement of a measure referred to in subsection 1, unless application for a corresponding interim measure has already been made to a court. It may recast such an order if necessary for the purpose of enforcing the measure.

(3) The court may, upon request, repeal or amend the decision referred to in subsection 2.

(4) If a measure ordered under subsection 1 proves to have been unjustified from the outset, the party who obtained its enforcement is obliged to compensate the other party for damage resulting from the enforcement of such measure or from his providing security in order to avoid enforcement. This claim may be put forward in the pending arbitral proceedings.

Chapter V
Conduct of arbitral proceedings

Section 1042
General rules of procedure

(1) The parties shall be treated with equality and each party shall be given a full opportunity of presenting his case.

(2) Counsel may not be excluded from acting as authorized representatives.

(3) Otherwise, subject to the mandatory provisions of this Book, the parties are free to determine the procedure themselves or by reference to a set of arbitration rules.

(4) Failing an agreement by the parties, and in the absence of provisions in this Book, the arbitral tribunal shall conduct the arbitration in such manner as it considers appropriate. The arbitral tribunal is empowered to determine the admissibility of taking evidence, take evidence and assess freely such evidence.

Section 1043
Place of arbitration

(1) The parties are free to agree on the place of arbitration. Failing such agreement, the place of arbitration shall be determined by the arbitral tribunal having regard to the circumstances of the case, including the convenience of the parties.

(2) Notwithstanding the provisions of subsection 1 of this section, the arbitral tribunal may, unless otherwise agreed by the parties, meet at any place it considers appropriate for an oral hearing, for hearing witnesses, experts or the parties, for consultation among its members or for inspection of property or documents.

Section 1044
Commencement of arbitral proceedings

Unless otherwise agreed by the parties, the arbitral proceedings in respect of a particular dispute commence on the date on which a request for that dispute to be referred to arbitration is received by the respondent. The request shall state the names of the parties, the subject-matter of the dispute and contain a reference to the arbitration agreement.

Section 1045
Language of proceedings

(1) The parties are free to agree on the language or languages to be used in the arbitral proceedings. Failing such agreement, the arbitral tribunal shall determine the language or languages to be used in the proceedings. This agreement or determination, unless otherwise specified therein, shall apply to any written statement by a party, any hearing and any award, decision or other communication by the arbitral tribunal.

(2) The arbitral tribunal may order that any documentary evidence shall be accompanied by a translation into the language or languages agreed upon by the parties or determined by the arbitral tribunal.

Section 1046
Statements of claim and defense

(1) Within the period of time agreed by the parties or determined by the arbitral tribunal, the claimant shall state his claim and the facts supporting the claim, and the respondent shall state his defense in respect of these particulars. The parties may submit with their statements all documents they consider to be relevant or may add a reference to other evidence they will submit.

(2) Unless otherwise agreed by the parties, either party may amend or supplement his claim or defense during the course of the arbitral proceedings, unless the arbitral tribunal considers it inappropriate to allow such amendment having regard to the delay in making it without sufficient justification.

(3) Subsections 1 and 2 apply mutatis mutandis to counter-claims.

Section 1047
Oral hearings and written proceedings

(1) Subject to agreement by the parties, the arbitral tribunal shall decide whether to hold oral hearings or whether the proceedings shall be conducted on the basis of documents and other materials. Unless the parties have agreed that no hearings shall be held, the arbitral tribunal shall hold such hearings at an appropriate stage of the proceedings, if so requested by a party.

(2) The parties shall be given sufficient advance notice of any hearing and of any meeting of the arbitral tribunal for the purpose of taking evidence.

(3) All statements, documents or other information supplied to the arbitral tribunal by one party shall be communicated to the other party. Also, any expert report or evidentiary document on which the arbitral tribunal may rely in making its decision shall be communicated to both parties.

Section 1048
Default of a party

(1) If the claimant fails to communicate his statement of claim in accordance with section 1046 subs. 1, the arbitral tribunal shall terminate the proceedings.

(2) If the respondent fails to communicate his statement of defense in accordance with section 1046 subs. 1, the arbitral tribunal shall continue the proceedings without treating such failure in itself as an admission of the claimant's allegations.

(3) If any party fails to appear at an oral hearing or to produce documentary evidence within a set time-limit, the arbitral tribunal may continue the proceedings and make the award on the evidence before it.

(4) Any default which has been justified to the tribunal's satisfaction will be disregarded. Apart from that, the parties may agree otherwise on the consequences of default.

Section 1049
Expert appointed by arbitral tribunal

(1) Unless otherwise agreed by the parties, the arbitral tribunal may appoint one or more experts to report to it on specific issues to be determined by the arbitral tribunal. It may also require a party to give the expert any relevant information or to produce, or to provide access to, any relevant documents or property for his inspection.

(2) Unless otherwise agreed by the parties, if a party so requests or if the arbitral tribunal considers it necessary, the expert shall, after delivery of his written or oral report, participate in an oral hearing where the parties have the opportunity to put questions to him and to present expert witnesses in order to testify on the points at issue.

(3) Sections 1036 and 1037 subs. 1 and 2 apply mutatis mutandis to an expert appointed by the arbitral tribunal.

Section 1050
Court assistance in taking evidence and other judicial acts

The arbitral tribunal or a party with the approval of the arbitral tribunal may request from a court assistance in taking evidence or performance of other judicial acts which the arbitral tribunal is not empowered to carry out. Unless it regards the application as inadmissible, the court shall execute the request according to its rules on taking evidence or other judicial acts. The arbitrators are entitled to participate in any judicial taking of evidence and to ask questions.

Chapter VI
Making of award and termination of proceedings

Section 1051
Rules applicable to substance of dispute

(1) The arbitral tribunal shall decide the dispute in accordance with such rules of law as are chosen by the parties as applicable to the substance of the dispute. Any designation of the law or legal system of a given State shall be construed, unless otherwise expressed, as directly referring to the substantive law of that State and not to its conflict of laws rules.

(2) Failing any designation by the parties, the arbitral tribunal shall apply the law of the State with which the subject-matter of the proceedings is most closely connected.

(3) The arbitral tribunal shall decide ex aequo et bono or as amiable compositeur only if the parties have expressly authorized it to do so. The parties may so authorize the arbitral tribunal up to the time of its decision.

(4) In all cases, the arbitral tribunal shall decide in accordance with the terms of the contract and shall take into account the usages of the trade applicable to the transaction.

Section 1052
Decision making by panel of arbitrators

(1) In arbitral proceedings with more than one arbitrator, any decision of the arbitral tribunal shall be made, unless otherwise agreed by the parties, by a majority of all its members.

(2) If an arbitrator refuses to take part in the vote on a decision, the other arbitrators may take the decision without him, unless otherwise agreed by the parties. The parties shall be given advance notice of the intention to make an award without the arbitrator refusing to participate in the vote. In the case of other decisions, the parties shall subsequent to the decision be informed of the refusal to participate in the vote.

(3) Individual questions of procedure may be decided by a presiding arbitrator alone if so authorized by the parties or all members of the arbitral tribunal.

Section 1053
Settlement

(1) If, during arbitral proceedings, the parties settle the dispute, the arbitral tribunal shall terminate the proceedings. If requested by the parties, it shall record the settlement in the form of an arbitral award on

agreed terms, unless the contents are in violation of public policy (ordre public).

(2) An award on agreed terms shall be made in accordance with section 1054 and shall state that it is an award. Such an award has the same effect as any other award on the merits of the case.

(3) If notarial certification is required for a declaration to be effective, it will be substituted, in the case of an arbitral award on agreed terms, by recording the declaration of the parties in the award.

(4) An award on agreed terms may, upon agreement between the parties, also be declared enforceable by a notary whose notarial office is in the district of the court competent for the declaration of enforceability according to section 1062 subs. 1, no. 2. The notary shall refuse the declaration of enforceability, if the requirements of subsection 1, sentence 2 are not complied with.

Section 1054
Form and contents of award

(1) The award shall be made in writing and shall be signed by the arbitrator or arbitrators. In arbitral proceedings with more than one arbitrator, the signatures of the majority of all members of the arbitral tribunal shall suffice, provided that the reason for any omitted signature is stated.

(2) The award shall state the reasons upon which it is based, unless the parties have agreed that no reasons are to be given or the award is an award on agreed terms under section 1053.

(3) The award shall state its date and the place of arbitration as determined in accordance with section 1043 subs. 1. The award shall be deemed to have been made on that date and at that place.

(4) A copy of the award signed by the arbitrators shall be delivered to each party.

Section 1055
Effect of arbitral award

The arbitral award has the same effect between the parties as a final and binding court judgment.

Section 1056
Termination of proceedings

(1) The arbitral proceedings are terminated by the final award or by an order of the arbitral tribunal in accordance with subsection 2 of this section.

(2) The arbitral tribunal shall issue an order for the termination of the arbitral proceedings when

1. the claimant:

a. fails to state his claim according to section 1046 subs. 1 and section 1048 subs. 4 does not apply, or

b. withdraws his claim, unless the respondent objects thereto and the arbitral tribunal recognizes a legitimate interest on his part in obtaining a final settlement of the dispute, or

2. the parties agree on the termination of the proceedings, or

3. the parties fail to pursue the arbitral proceedings in spite of being so requested by the arbitral tribunal or when the continuation of the proceedings has for any other reason become impossible.

(3) The mandate of the arbitral tribunal terminates with the termination of the arbitral proceedings, subject to the provisions of sections 1057 subs. 2, 1058 and 1059 subs. 4.

Section 1057
Decision on costs

(1) Unless the parties agree otherwise, the arbitral tribunal shall allocate, by means of an arbitral award, the costs of the arbitration as between the parties, including those incurred by the parties necessary for the proper pursuit of their claim or defense. It shall do so at its discretion and take into consideration the circumstances of the case, in particular the outcome of the proceedings.

(2) To the extent that the costs of the arbitral proceedings have been fixed, the arbitral tribunal shall also decide on the amount to be borne by each party. If the costs have not been fixed or if they can only be fixed once the arbitral proceedings have been terminated, the decision shall be taken by means of a separate award.

Section 1058
Correction and interpretation of award; additional award

(1) Any party may request the arbitral tribunal

1. to correct in the award any errors in computation, any clerical or typographical errors or any errors of similar nature,

2. to give an interpretation of specific parts of the award,

3. to make an additional award as to claims presented in the arbitral proceedings but omitted from the award.

(2) Unless otherwise agreed by the parties, the request shall be made within one month of receipt of the award.

(3) The arbitral tribunal shall make the correction or give the interpretation within one month and make an additional award within two months.

(4) The arbitral tribunal may make a correction of the award on its own initiative.

(5) Section 1054 shall apply to a correction or interpretation of the award or to an additional award.

Chapter VII
Recourse against award

Section 1059
Application for setting aside

(1) Recourse to a court against an arbitral award may be made only by an application for setting aside in accordance with subsections 2 and 3 of this section.

(2) An arbitral award may be set aside only if:

1. the applicant shows sufficient cause that:

   a) a party to the arbitration agreement referred to in sections 1029 and 1031 was under some incapacity pursuant to the law applicable to him; or the said agreement is not valid under the law to which the parties have subjected it or, failing any indication thereon, under German law; or

   b) he was not given proper notice of the appointment of an arbitrator or of the arbitral proceedings or was otherwise unable to present his case; or

   c) the award deals with a dispute not contemplated by or not falling within the terms of the submission to arbitration, or contains decisions on matters beyond the scope of the submission to arbitration; provided that, if the decisions on matters submitted to arbitration can be separated from those not so submitted, only that part of the award which contains decisions on matters not submitted to arbitration may be set aside; or

   d) the composition of the arbitral tribunal or the arbitral procedure was not in accordance with a provision of this Book or with an admissible agreement of the parties and this presumably affected the award; or

2. the court finds that

   a) the subject-matter of the dispute is not capable of settlement by arbitration under German law; or

   b) recognition or enforcement of the award leads to a result which is in conflict with public policy (ordre public).

(3) Unless the parties have agreed otherwise, an application for setting aside to the court may not be made after three months have elapsed. The period of time shall commence on the date on which the party making the application had received the award. If a request had been made under section 1058, the time-limit shall be extended by not more than one month from receipt of the decision on the request. No

application for setting aside the award may be made once the award has been declared enforceable by a German court.

(4) The court, when asked to set aside an award, may, where appropriate, set aside the award and remit the case to the arbitral tribunal.

(5) Setting aside the arbitral award shall, in the absence of any indication to the contrary, result in the arbitration agreement becoming operative again in respect of the subject-matter of the dispute.

Chapter VIII
Recognition and enforcement of awards

Section 1060
Domestic awards

(1) Enforcement of the award takes place if it has been declared enforceable.

(2) An application for a declaration of enforceability shall be refused and the award set aside if one of the grounds for setting aside under section 1059 subs. 2 exists. Grounds for setting aside shall not be taken into account, if at the time when the application for a declaration of enforceability is served, an application for setting aside based on such grounds has been finally rejected. Grounds for setting aside under section 1059 subs. 2, no. 1 shall also not be taken into account if the time-limits set by section 1059 subs. 3 have expired without the party opposing the application having made an application for setting aside the award.

Section 1061
Foreign awards

(1) Recognition and enforcement of foreign arbitral awards shall be granted in accordance with the Convention on the Recognition and Enforcement of Foreign Arbitral Awards of 10 June 1958 (Bundesgesetzblatt [BGBl.] 1961 Part II p. 121). The provisions of other treaties on the recognition and enforcement of arbitral awards shall remain unaffected.

(2) If the declaration of enforceability is to be refused, the court shall rule that the arbitral award is not to be recognized in Germany.

(3) If the award is set aside abroad after having been declared enforceable, application for setting aside the declaration of enforceability may be made.

Chapter IX
Court proceedings

Section 1062
Competence

(1) The Higher Regional Court ("Oberlandesgericht") designated in the arbitration agreement or, failing such designation, the Higher Regional Court in whose district the place of arbitration is situated, is competent for decisions on applications relating to

1. the appointment of an arbitrator (sections 1034 and 1035), the challenge of an arbitrator (section 1037) or the termination of an arbitrator's mandate (section 1038);

2. the determination of the admissibility or inadmissibility of arbitration (section 1032) or the decision of an arbitral tribunal confirming its competence in a preliminary ruling (section 1040);

3. the enforcement, setting aside or amendment of an order for interim measures of protection by the arbitral tribunal (section 1041);

4. the setting aside (section 1059) or the declaration of enforceability of the award (section 1060 et seq.) or the setting aside of the declaration of enforceability (section 1061).

(2) If the place of arbitration in the cases referred to in subsection 1, no. 2, first alternative, nos. 3 and 4 is not in Germany, competence lies with the Higher Regional Court ("Oberlandesgericht") where the party opposing the application has his place of business or place of habitual residence, or where assets of that party or the property in dispute or affected by the measure is located, failing which the Berlin Higher Regional Court ("Kammergericht") shall be competent.

(3) In the cases referred to in section 1025 subs. 3, the Higher Regional Court ("Oberlandesgericht") in whose district the claimant or the respondent has his place of business or place of habitual residence is competent.

(4) For assistance in the taking of evidence and other judicial acts (section 1050), the Local Court ("Amtsgericht"), in whose district the judicial act is to be carried out, is competent.

(5) Where there are several Higher Regional Courts ("Oberlandesgerichte") in one Land, the Government of that Land may transfer by ordinance competence to one Higher Regional Court, or, where existent, to the highest Regional Court ("Oberstes Landesgericht")[6]; the Land Government may transfer such authority to the Department of Justice of the Land concerned by ordinance. Several Länder may agree on cross-border competence of a single Higher Regional Court.

Section 1063
General provisions

(1) The court shall decide by means of an order.[7] The party opposing the application shall be given an opportunity to comment before a decision is taken.

(2) The court shall order an oral hearing to be held, if the setting aside of the award has been requested or if, in an application for recogni-

6. At present existing only in Bavaria—"Bayerisches Oberstes Landesgericht".

7. Amended by Art. 2 subs. 1 no. 104 of the Act of 27 July 2001 (Civil Procedure Reform Act), Bundesgesetzblatt Part I, p. 1887. Cf. section 128 CCP [Principle of Oral Presentation]: (4) Unless provided otherwise, decisions of the court which do not constitute judgments can be rendered without oral hearing.

tion or declaration of enforceability of the award, grounds for setting aside in terms of section 1059 subs. 2 are to be considered.

(3) The presiding judge of the civil court senate ("Zivilsenat") may issue, without prior hearing of the party opposing the application, an order to the effect that, until a decision on the request has been reached, the applicant may pursue enforcement of the award or enforce the interim measure of protection of the arbitration court pursuant to section 1041. In the case of an award, enforcement of the award may not go beyond measures of protection. The party opposing the application may prevent enforcement by providing as security an amount corresponding to the amount that may be enforced by the applicant.

(4) As long as no oral hearing is ordered, applications and declarations may be put on record at the court registry.

Section 1064
Particularities regarding the enforcement of awards

(1) At the time of the application for a declaration of enforceability of an arbitral award the award or a certified copy of the award shall be supplied. The certification may also be made by counsel authorized to represent the party in the judicial proceedings.

(2) The order declaring the award enforceable shall be declared provisionally enforceable.

(3) Unless otherwise provided in treaties, subsections 1 and 2 shall apply to foreign awards.

Section 1065
Legal remedies[8]

(1) A complaint on a point of law is available against the decisions mentioned under section 1062 subs. 1, nos. 2 and 4. No recourse against other decisions in the proceedings specified in section 1062 subs. 1 may be made.

(2) The complaint on a point of law can also be based on the ground that the decision is based on a violation of a treaty. Sections 707 and 717 apply mutatis mutandis.

Chapter X
Arbitral tribunals not established by agreement

Section 1066
Mutatis mutandis application of the provisions of the Tenth Book

The provisions of this Book apply mutatis mutandis to arbitral tribunals established lawfully by disposition on death or other dispositions not based on an agreement.

---

8. Amended by Art. 2 subs. 1 no. 105 of the Act of 27 July 2001 (Civil Procedure Reform Act), Bundesgesetzblatt Part I, p. 1887.

Article 2 of the Arbitral Proceedings Reform Act:

Section 19
Amendment to the Act on Restraints of Competition

Section 91 of the Act on Restraints of Competition (Gesetz gegen Wettbewerbsbeschränkungen) as promulgated on 20 February 1990 (Bundesgesetzblatt Part I p.235), last amended by section 2 subs. 20 of the Act of 17 December 1997 (Bundesgesetzblatt Part I p. 3108), is repealed.

Note:

The repeal of section 91 of the Act on Restraints of Competition is of great relevance for economic arbitration, since the restrictions on the arbitrability of cartel disputes are thereby abolished. The arbitrability of cartel disputes is now determined solely according to the general provisions on arbitrability contained in section 1030 of the Code of Civil Procedure.

Section 91 of the Act on Restraints of Competition had provided that arbitration agreements on *future* legal disputes arising out of effective cartel agreements or decisions, which do not grant each party the right to choose between proceedings before an arbitral tribunal or a state court, are null and void.

Article 4 of the Arbitral Proceedings Reform Act:

Transitional provisions
Section 1. Arbitral proceedings

(1) The effectiveness of arbitration agreements that have been concluded prior to the entry into force of this Act, shall be determined according to the law previously in force.

(2) Arbitral proceedings that are pending but not terminated upon the entry into force of this Act are governed by the law previously in force provided that the arbitral settlement ("schiedsrichterlicher Vergleich") is substituted by the award on agreed terms. The parties may agree to apply the new law.

(3) Court proceedings pending upon the entry into force of this Act remain subject to the law previously in force.

(4) Arbitral settlements that have been concluded and declared enforceable prior to the entry into force of this Act are subject to enforcement provided that the decision on their enforceability has become final and binding or has been declared provisionally enforceable.

. . .

I. SWEDISH ARBITRATION ACT OF 1999 (SFS 1999:116)*

The Arbitration Agreement

Section 1

Disputes concerning matters in respect of which the parties may reach a settlement may, by agreement, be referred to one or several arbitrators for resolution. Such an agreement may relate to future disputes pertaining to a legal relationship specified in the agreement. The dispute may concern the existence of a particular fact. In addition to interpreting agreements, the filling of gaps in contracts can also be referred to arbitrators. Arbitrators may rule on the civil law effects of competition law as between the parties.

Section 2

The arbitrators may rule on their own jurisdiction to decide the dispute. The aforesaid shall not prevent a court from determining such a question at the request of a party. The arbitrators may continue the arbitral proceedings pending the determination by the court. Notwithstanding that the arbitrators have, in a decision during the proceedings, determined that they possess jurisdiction to resolve the dispute, such decision is not binding. The provisions of sections 34 and 36 shall apply in respect of an action to challenge an arbitration award which entails a decision in respect of jurisdiction.

Section 3

Where the validity of an arbitration agreement which constitutes part of another agreement must be determined in conjunction with a determination of the jurisdiction of the arbitrators, the arbitration agreement shall be deemed to constitute a separate agreement.

Section 4

A court may not, over an objection of a party, rule on an issue which, pursuant to an arbitration agreement, shall be decided by arbitrators. A party must invoke an arbitration agreement on the first occasion that a party pleads his case on the merits in the court. The invocation of an arbitration agreement raised on a later occasion shall have no effect unless the party had a legal excuse and invoked such as soon as the excuse ceased to exist. The invocation of an arbitration agreement shall be considered notwithstanding that the party who invoked the agreement has allowed an issue which is covered by the arbitration agreement to be determined by the Debt Enforcement Authority in a case concerning expedited collection procedures. During the pendency of a dispute before arbitrators or prior thereto, a court may, irrespective of the arbitration agreement, issue such

* Available at http://www.chamber.se/arbitration/english/laws/skiljedomsvlagen_eng.html

decisions in respect of security measures as the court has jurisdiction to issue.

Section 5

A party shall forfeit his right to invoke the arbitration agreement as a bar to court proceedings where the party:

1. has opposed a request for arbitration;
2. failed to appoint an arbitrator in due time; or
3. fails, within due time, to provide his share of the requested security for compensation to the arbitrators.

Section 6

Where a dispute between a business enterprise and a consumer concerns goods, services, or any other products supplied principally for private use, an arbitration agreement may not be invoked where such was entered into prior to the dispute. However, such agreements shall apply with respect to rental or lease relationships where, through the agreement, a regional rent tribunal or a regional tenancies tribunal is appointed as an arbitral tribunal and the provisions of Chapter 8, section 28 or Chapter 12, section 66 of the Real Estate Code do not prescribe otherwise. The first paragraph shall not apply where the dispute concerns an agreement between an insurer and a policy-holder concerning insurance based on a collective agreement or group agreement and handled by representatives of the group. Nor shall the first paragraph apply where Sweden's international obligations provide to the contrary.

The Arbitrators

Section 7

Any person who possesses full legal capacity in regard to his actions and his property may act as an arbitrator.

Section 8

An arbitrator shall be impartial. If a party so requests, an arbitrator shall be discharged if there exists any circumstance which may diminish confidence in the arbitrator's impartiality. Such a circumstance shall always be deemed to exist:

1. where the arbitrator or a person closely associated to him is a party, or otherwise may expect benefit or detriment worth attention, as a result of the outcome of the dispute;
2. where the arbitrator or a person closely associated to him is the director of a company or any other association which is a party, or otherwise represents a party or any other person who may expect benefit or detriment worth attention as a result of the outcome of the dispute;

3. where the arbitrator has taken a position in the dispute, as an expert or otherwise, or has assisted a party in the preparation or conduct of his case in the dispute; or

4. where the arbitrator has received or demanded compensation in violation of section 39, second paragraph.

Section 9

A person who is asked to accept an appointment as arbitrator shall immediately disclose all circumstances which, pursuant to sections 7 or 8, might be considered to prevent him from serving as arbitrator. An arbitrator shall inform the parties and the other arbitrators of such circumstances as soon as all arbitrators have been appointed and thereafter in the course of the arbitral proceedings as soon as he has learned of any new circumstance.

Section 10

A challenge of an arbitrator on account of a circumstance set forth in section 8 shall be presented within fifteen days commencing on the date on which the party became aware both of the appointment of the arbitrator and of the existence of the circumstance. The challenge shall be adjudicated by the arbitrators, unless the parties have decided that it shall be determined by another party. If the challenge is successful, the decision shall be subject to no appeal. A party who is dissatisfied with a decision denying a motion or dismissing a motion on the grounds that the motion was not timely filed may file an application with the District Court that the arbitrator be removed from his post. The application must be submitted within thirty days commencing on the date on which the party receives the decision. The arbitrators may continue with the arbitral proceedings pending the determination of the District Court.

Section 11

The parties may agree that a motion as referred to in section 10, first paragraph shall be conclusively determined by an arbitration institution.

Section 12

The parties may determine the number of arbitrators and the manner in which they shall be appointed. Sections 13–16 shall apply unless the parties have agreed otherwise. Where the parties have so agreed, and any of the parties so requests, the District Court shall appoint arbitrators also in situations other than those stated in sections 14–17.

Section 13

The arbitrators shall be three in number. Each party shall appoint one arbitrator, and the arbitrators so appointed shall appoint the third.

Section 14

Where each party is required to appoint an arbitrator and one party has notified the opposing party of his choice of arbitrator in a request for arbitration pursuant to section 19, the opposing party must, within thirty days of receipt of the notice, notify the first party in writing in respect of his choice of arbitrator. A party who, in this manner, has notified the opposing party of his choice of arbitrator may not revoke the appointment without the consent of the other party. If the opposing party fails to appoint an arbitrator within the stipulated time, the District Court shall appoint an arbitrator upon request by the first party.

Section 15

Where an arbitrator shall be appointed by other arbitrators, but they fail to do so within thirty days commencing on the date on which the last arbitrator was appointed, the District Court shall appoint the arbitrator upon request by a party. Where an arbitrator shall be appointed by someone other than a party or arbitrators, but such is not done within thirty days of the date on which a party desiring the appointment of an arbitrator requested that the person responsible for the appointment make such appointment, the District Court shall, upon the request by a party, appoint the arbitrator. The same shall apply where an arbitrator shall be appointed by the parties jointly, but they have failed to agree within thirty days commencing on the date on which the question was raised through receipt by one party of notice from the opposing party.

Section 16

Where an arbitrator resigns or is discharged, the District Court shall, upon request by a party, appoint a new arbitrator. Where the arbitrator cannot fulfil his duties due to circumstances which arise after his appointment, the person who originally was required to make the appointment shall, instead, appoint a new arbitrator. Sections 14 and 15 shall apply in conjunction with such an appointment. The period of time within which a new arbitrator shall be appointed, even for the party who requested the arbitration, is thirty days calculated, with respect to all parties, from the date on which the person who shall appoint the arbitrator became aware thereof.

Section 17

Where an arbitrator has delayed the proceedings, the District Court shall, upon request by a party, discharge the arbitrator and appoint another arbitrator. The parties may decide that such a request shall, instead, be conclusively determined by an arbitration institution.

Section 18

Where a party has requested that the District Court appoint an arbitrator pursuant to section 12, third paragraph or sections 14–17, the

Court may reject the request on the grounds that the arbitration is not legally permissible only where such is manifest.

The Proceedings
Section 19

Unless otherwise agreed by the parties, the arbitral proceedings are initiated when a party receives a request for arbitration in accordance with the second paragraph hereof. A request for arbitration must be in writing and include:

1. an express and unconditional request for arbitration;
2. a statement of the issue which is covered by the arbitration agreement and which is to be resolved by the arbitrators; and
3. a statement of the party's choice of arbitrator where the party is required to appoint an arbitrator.

Section 20

Where the arbitral tribunal is composed of more than one arbitrator, one of them shall be appointed chairman. Unless the parties or the arbitrators have decided otherwise, the chairman shall be the arbitrator appointed by the other arbitrators or the District Court, in their stead.

Section 21

The arbitrators shall handle the dispute in an impartial, practical, and speedy manner. They shall thereupon act in accordance with the decisions of the parties insofar as there is no impediment to so doing.

Section 22

The parties shall determine the place of arbitration. Where this is not the case, the arbitrators shall determine the place of arbitration. The arbitrators may hold hearings and other meetings elsewhere in Sweden, or abroad, unless otherwise agreed by the parties.

Section 23

Within the period of time determined by the arbitrators, the claimant shall state his claims in respect of the issue stated in the request for arbitration, as well as the circumstances invoked by the party in support thereof. Thereafter, within the period of time determined by the arbitrators, the respondent shall state his position in relation to the claims, and the circumstances invoked by the respondent in support thereof. The claimant may submit new claims, and the respondent his own claims, provided that the claims fall within the scope of the arbitration agreement and, taking into consideration the time at which they are submitted or other circumstances, the arbitrators do not consider it inappropriate to adjudicate such claims. Subject to the same conditions, during the proceedings, each party may amend or supplement previously presented claims and may invoke new circumstances in support of his case. The first and second paragraphs hereof shall not apply where the parties have decided otherwise.

Section 24

The arbitrators shall afford the parties, to the extent necessary, an opportunity to present their respective cases in writing or orally. Where a party so requests, and provided that the parties have not otherwise agreed, an oral hearing shall be held prior to the determination of an issue referred to the arbitrators for resolution. A party shall be given an opportunity to review all documents and all other materials pertaining to the dispute which are supplied to the arbitrators by the opposing party or another person. Where one of the parties, without valid cause, fails to appear at a hearing or otherwise fails to comply with an order of the arbitrators, such failure shall not prevent a continuation of the proceedings and a resolution of the dispute on the basis of the existing materials.

Section 25

The parties shall supply the evidence. However, the arbitrators may appoint experts, unless both parties are opposed thereto. The arbitrators may refuse to admit evidence which is offered where such evidence is manifestly irrelevant to the case or where such refusal is justified having regard to the time at which the evidence is offered. The arbitrators may not administer oaths or truth affirmations. Nor may they impose conditional fines or otherwise use compulsory measures in order to obtain requested evidence. Unless the parties have agreed otherwise, the arbitrators may, at the request of a party, decide that, during the proceedings, the opposing party must undertake a certain interim measure to secure the claim which is to be adjudicated by the arbitrators. The arbitrators may prescribe that the party requesting the interim measure must provide reasonable security for the damage which may be incurred by the opposing party as a result of the interim measure.

Section 26

Where a party wishes a witness or an expert to testify under oath, or a party to be examined under truth affirmation, the party may, after obtaining the consent of the arbitrators, submit an application to such effect to the District Court. The aforementioned shall apply where a party wishes that a party or other person be ordered to produce as evidence a document or an object. If the arbitrators consider that the measure is justified having regard to the evidence in the case, they shall approve the request. Where the measure may lawfully be taken, the District Court shall grant the application. The provisions of the Code of Judicial Procedure shall apply with respect to a measure as referred to in the first paragraph. The arbitrators shall be summoned to hear the testimony of a witness, an expert, or a party, and be afforded the opportunity to ask questions. The absence of an arbitrator from the giving of testimony shall not prevent the hearing from taking place.

The Award
Section 27

The issues which have been referred to the arbitrators shall be decided in an award. Where the arbitrators terminate the arbitral proceedings without deciding such issues, such shall also take place through an award. Where the parties enter into a settlement agreement, the arbitrators may, at the request of the parties, confirm it in an award. Other determinations, which are not embodied in an award, are designated as decisions. The mandate of the arbitrators shall be deemed to be completed when they have delivered a final award, unless otherwise provided in sections 32 or 35.

Section 28

Where a party withdraws a claim, the arbitrators shall dismiss that part of the dispute, unless the opposing party requests that the arbitrators rule on the claim.

Section 29

A part of the dispute, or a certain issue which is of significance to the resolution of the dispute, may be decided through a separate award, unless opposed by both parties. However, a claim invoked as a defense by way of set off shall be adjudicated in the same award as the main claim. Where a party has admitted a claim, in whole or in part, a separate award may be rendered in respect of that which has been admitted.

Section 30

Where an arbitrator fails, without valid cause, to participate in the determination of an issue by the arbitral tribunal, such failure will not prevent the other arbitrators from ruling on the matter. Unless the parties have decided otherwise, the opinion agreed upon by the majority of the arbitrators participating in the determination shall prevail. If no majority is attained for any opinion, the opinion of the chairman shall prevail.

Section 31

An award shall be made in writing, signed by the arbitrators. It suffices that the award is signed by a majority of the arbitrators, provided that the reason why all of the arbitrators have not signed the award is noted therein. The parties may decide that the chairman of the arbitral tribunal alone shall sign the award. The award shall state the place of arbitration and the date when the award is made. The award shall be delivered to the parties immediately.

Section 32

If the arbitrators find that an award contains any obvious inaccuracy as a consequence of a typographical, computational, or other similar mistake by the arbitrators or any another person, or if the arbitrators by oversight have failed to decide an issue which should have been dealt with in the award, they may, within thirty days of the date of the announcement of the award, decide to correct or supplement the award. They may also correct or supplement an award, or interpret the decision in an award, where any of the parties so requests within thirty days of receipt of the award by that party. Where, upon request by any of the parties, the arbitrators decide to correct an award or interpret the decision in an award, such shall take place within thirty days from the date of receipt by the arbitrators of the party's request. Where the arbitrators decide to supplement the award, such shall take place within sixty days. Before any decision is made pursuant to this section, the parties should be afforded an opportunity to express their views with respect to the measure.

Invalidity of Awards and Setting Aside Awards

Section 33

An award is invalid:

1. if it includes determination of an issue which, in accordance with Swedish law, may not be decided by arbitrators;

2. if the award, or the manner in which the award arose, is clearly incompatible with the basic principles of the Swedish legal system; or

3. if the award does not fulfil the requirements with regard to the written form and signature in accordance with section 31, first paragraph. The invalidity may apply to a certain part of the award.

Section 34

An award which may not be challenged in accordance with section 36 shall, following an application, be wholly or partially set aside upon motion of a party:

1. if it is not covered by a valid arbitration agreement between the parties;

2. if the arbitrators have made the award after the expiration of the period decided on by the parties, or where the arbitrators have otherwise exceeded their mandate;

3. if arbitral proceedings, according to section 47, should not have taken place in Sweden;

4. if an arbitrator has been appointed contrary to the agreement between the parties or this Act;

5. if an arbitrator was unauthorized due to any circumstance set forth in sections 7 or 8; or

6. if, without fault of the party, there otherwise occurred an irregularity in the course of the proceedings which probably influenced the outcome of the case.

A party shall not be entitled to rely upon a circumstance which, through participation in the proceedings without objection, or in any other manner, he may be deemed to have waived. A party shall not be regarded as having accepted the arbitrators' jurisdiction to determine the issue referred to arbitration solely by having appointed an arbitrator. Pursuant to sections 10 and 11, a party may lose the right in accordance with the first paragraph, sub-section 5 to rely upon a circumstance as set forth in section 8. An action must be brought within three months from the date upon which the party received the award or, where correction, supplementation, or interpretation has taken place pursuant to section 32, within a period of three months from the date when the party received the award in its final wording. Following the expiration of the time limit, a party may not invoke a new ground of objection in support of his claim.

Section 35

A court may stay proceedings concerning the invalidity or setting aside of an award for a certain period of time in order to provide the arbitrators with an opportunity to resume the arbitral proceedings or to take some other measure which, in the opinion of the arbitrators, will eliminate the ground for the invalidity or setting aside:

1. provided the court holds that the claim in the case shall be accepted and either of the parties requests a stay; or

2. both parties request a stay. Where the arbitrators make a new award, a party may, within the period of time determined by the court and without issuing a writ of summons, challenge the award insofar as it was based upon the resumed arbitral proceedings or an amendment to the first award. Notwithstanding Chapter 43, section 11, second paragraph of the Code of Judicial Procedure, a trial may continue even where the period of the stay exceeds fifteen days.

Section 36

An award whereby the arbitrators concluded the proceedings without ruling on the issues submitted to them for resolution may be amended, in whole or in part, upon the application of a party. An action must be brought within three months from the date upon which the party received the award or, where correction, supplementation, or interpretation has taken place in accordance with section 32, within a period of three months from the date upon which the party received the award in its final wording. The award shall contain clear instructions as to what must be done by a party who wishes to challenge the award. An action in accordance with the first paragraph which only concerns an issue as referred to in section 42 is permissible where the award means that the arbitrators have considered themselves to lack jurisdiction to determine the dispute. Where the award entails another matter, a party who desires to challenge the award may do so in accordance with the provisions of section 34.

Costs of Arbitration

Section 37

The parties shall be jointly and severally liable to pay reasonable compensation to the arbitrators for work and expenses. However, where the arbitrators have stated in the award that they lack jurisdiction to determine the dispute, the party that did not request arbitration shall be liable to make payment only insofar as required due to special circumstances. In a final award, the arbitrators may order the parties to pay compensation to them, together with interest from the date occurring one month following the date of the announcement of the award. The compensation shall be stated separately for each arbitrator.

Section 38

The arbitrators may request security for the compensation. They may fix separate security for individual claims. Where a party fails to provide its share of the requested security within the period specified by the arbitrators, the opposing party may provide the entire security. Where the requested security is not provided, the arbitrators may terminate the proceedings, in whole or in part. During the proceedings, the arbitrators may decide to realise security in order to cover expenses. Following the determination of the arbitrators' compensation in a final award and where the award in that respect has become enforceable, the arbitrators may realise their payment from the security, in the event the parties fail to fulfil their payment obligations in accordance with the award. The right to security also includes income from the property.

Section 39

The provisions of sections 37 and 38 shall apply unless otherwise jointly decided by the parties in a manner that is binding upon the arbitrators. An agreement regarding compensation to the arbitrators that is not entered into with the parties jointly is void. Where one of the parties has provided the entire security, such party may, however, solely consent to the realization of the security by the arbitrators in order to cover the compensation for work expended.

Section 40

The arbitrators may not withhold the award pending the payment of compensation.

Section 41

A party or an arbitrator may bring an action in the District Court against the award regarding the payment of compensation to the arbitrators. Such action must be brought within three months from the date upon which the party received the award and, in the case of an arbitrator, within the same period from the announcement of the award. Where correction, supplementation, or interpretation has taken place in accordance with section 32, the action must be brought by a party within three months from the date upon which the party received the award in its final wording and, in the case of an arbitrator, within the same period from the date when the award was announced in its final wording. The award shall contain clear instructions as to what must be done by a party who wishes to bring an action against the award in this respect. A judgment pursuant to which the compensation to an arbitrator is reduced shall also apply to the party who did not bring the action.

Section 42

Unless otherwise agreed by the parties, the arbitrators may, upon request by a party, order the opposing party to pay compensation for the party's costs and determine the manner in which the compensation to the arbitrators shall be finally allocated between the parties. The arbitrators' order may also include interest, if a party has so requested.

Forum and Limitation Periods

Section 43

An action against an award pursuant to sections 33, 34, and 36 shall be considered by the Court of Appeal within the jurisdiction where the arbitral proceedings were held. Where the place of arbitration is not stated in the award, the action may be brought before the Svea Court of Appeal. The determination of the Court of Appeal may not be appealed. However, the Court of Appeal may grant leave to appeal the determination where it is of importance as a matter of precedent that the appeal be considered by the Supreme Court. An action regarding compensation to an arbitrator shall be considered by the District Court at the place of arbitration. Where the place of arbitration is not stated in the award, the action may be brought before the Stockholm District Court.

Section 44

Applications to appoint or discharge an arbitrator shall be considered by the District Court at the place where one of the parties is domiciled or by the District Court at the place of arbitration. The application may also be considered by the Stockholm District Court. Where possible the opposing party shall be afforded the opportunity to express his opinion upon the application before it is granted. Where the application concerns the removal of an arbitrator, the arbitrator should also be heard. Applications concerning the taking of evidence in accordance with section 26 shall be considered by the District Court determined by the arbitrators. In the absence of such decision, the application shall be considered by the Stockholm District Court. Where the District Court has granted an application to appoint or remove an arbitrator, such decision may not appealed. Nor may a determination of the District Court in accordance with section 10, third paragraph otherwise be appealed.

Section 45

Where, according to law or by agreement, an action by a party must be brought within a certain period, but the action is covered by an arbitration agreement, the party must request arbitration in accordance with section 19 within the stated period. Where arbitration has been requested in due time but the arbitral proceedings are terminated without a legal determination of the issue which was submitted to the arbitrators, and this is not due to the negligence of the party, the action shall be deemed to have been instituted in due time where a party requests arbitration or institutes court proceedings within thirty days of receipt of the award, or where the award has been set aside or declared invalid or an action against the award in accordance with section 36 has been dismissed, from the time that this decision becomes final.

International Matters
Section 46

This Act shall apply to arbitral proceedings which take place in Sweden notwithstanding that the dispute has an international connection.

Section 47

Arbitral proceedings in accordance with this Act may be commenced in Sweden, where the arbitration agreement provides that the proceedings shall take place in Sweden, or where the arbitrators or an arbitration institution pursuant to the agreement have determined that the proceedings shall take place in Sweden, or the opposing party otherwise consents thereto. Arbitral proceedings in accordance with this Act may also be commenced in Sweden against a party which is domiciled in Sweden or is otherwise subject to the jurisdiction of the Swedish courts with regard to the matter in dispute, unless the arbitration agreement provides that the proceedings shall take place abroad. In other cases, arbitral proceedings in accordance with this Act may not take place in Sweden.

Section 48

Where an arbitration agreement has an international connection, the agreement shall be governed by the law agreed upon by the parties. Where the parties have not reached such an agreement, the arbitration agreement shall be governed by the law of the country in which, by virtue of the agreement, the proceedings have taken place or shall take place. The first paragraph shall not apply to the issue of whether a party was authorized to enter into an arbitration agreement or was duly represented.

Section 49

Where foreign law is applicable to the arbitration agreement, section 4 shall apply to issues which are covered by the agreement, except when:

1. in accordance with the applicable law, the agreement is invalid, inoperative, or incapable of being performed; or

2. in accordance with Swedish law, the dispute may not be determined by arbitrators. The jurisdiction of a court to issue such decisions regarding security measures as the court is entitled to issue in accordance with law, notwithstanding the arbitration agreement, is set forth in section 4, third paragraph.

Section 50

The provisions of sections 26 and 44 regarding the taking of evidence during the arbitral proceedings in Sweden shall also apply in respect of arbitral proceedings which take place abroad, where the proceedings are based upon an arbitration agreement and, pursuant to Swedish law, the issues which are referred to the arbitrators may be resolved by arbitrators.

Section 51

Where none of the parties is domiciled or has its place of business in Sweden, such parties may in a commercial relationship through an express written agreement exclude or limit the application of the grounds for setting aside an award as are set forth in section 34. An award which is subject to such an agreement shall be recognized and enforced in Sweden in accordance with the rules applicable to a foreign award.

Recognition and Enforcement of Foreign Awards, etc.

Section 52

An award made abroad shall be deemed to be a foreign award. In conjunction with the application of this Act, an award shall be deemed to have been made in the country in which the place of arbitration is situated.

Section 53

Unless otherwise stated in sections 54–60, a foreign award which is based on an arbitration agreement shall be recognized and enforced in Sweden.

Section 54

A foreign award shall not be recognized and enforced in Sweden where the party against whom the award is invoked proves:

1. that the parties to the arbitration agreement, pursuant to the law applicable to them, lacked capacity to enter into the agreement or were not properly represented, or that the arbitration agreement was not valid under the law to which the parties have subjected it or, failing any indication thereon, under the law of the country where the award was made;

2. that the party against whom the award is invoked was not given proper notice of the appointment of the arbitrator or of the arbitration proceedings, or was otherwise unable to present his case;

3. that the award deals with a dispute not contemplated by, or not falling within, the terms of the submission to arbitration, or contains decisions on matters which are beyond the scope of the arbitration agreement, provided that, if the decision on a matter which falls within the mandate can be separated from those which fall outside the mandate, that part of the award which contains decisions on matters falling within the mandate may be recognized and enforced;

4. that the composition of the arbitral tribunal, or the arbitral procedure, was not in accordance with the agreement of the parties or, failing such agreement, was not in accordance with the law of the country where the arbitration took place; or

5. that the award has not yet become binding on the parties, or has been set aside or suspended by a competent authority of the country in which, or under the law of which, the award was made.

Section 55

Recognition and enforcement of a foreign award shall also be refused where a court finds:

1. that the award includes determination of an issue which, in accordance with Swedish law, may not be decided by arbitrators; or

2. that it would be clearly incompatible with the basic principles of the Swedish legal system to recognize and enforce the award.

Section 56

An application for the enforcement of a foreign award shall be lodged with the Svea Court of Appeal. The original award or a certified copy of the award must be appended to the application. Unless the Court of Appeal decides otherwise, a certified translation into the Swedish language of the entire award must also be submitted.

Section 57

An application for enforcement shall not be granted unless the opposing party has been afforded an opportunity to express his opinion upon the application.

Section 58

Where the opposing party objects that an arbitration agreement was not entered into, the applicant must submit the arbitration agreement in an original or a certified copy and, unless otherwise decided by the Court of Appeal, must submit a certified translation into the Swedish language, or in some other manner prove that an arbitration agreement was entered into. Where the opposing party objects that a petition has been lodged to set aside the award or a motion for a stay of execution has been submitted to the competent authority as referred to in section 54, sub-section 5, the Court of Appeal may postpone its decision and, upon request by the applicant, order the opposing party to provide reasonable security in default of which enforcement might otherwise be ordered.

Section 59

Where the Court of Appeal grants the application, the award shall be enforced as a final judgment of a Swedish court, unless otherwise determined by the Supreme Court following an appeal of the Court of Appeal's decision.

Section 60

Where a security measure has been granted in accordance with Chapter 15 of the Code of Judicial Procedure, in conjunction with the application of section 7 of the same Chapter, a request for arbitration abroad which might result in an award which is recognized and may be enforced in Sweden shall be equated with the commencement of an action. Where an application for the enforcement of a foreign award has been lodged, the Court of Appeal shall examine a request for a security measure or a request to set aside such decision.

1. This Act shall enter into force on 1 April 1999, at which time the Arbitration Act (SFS 1929:145) and the Foreign Arbitration Agreements and Awards Act (SFS 1929:147) shall be repealed.

2. The previous Act shall apply to arbitral proceedings which have been commenced prior to the entry into force or, with respect to enforcement of a foreign award, when the application for enforcement was lodged prior to the entry into force.

3. Where an arbitration agreement has been concluded prior to the entry into force, the provisions of section 18, second paragraph, section 21, first paragraph, sub-section 1, and section 26, second and third paragraphs of the Arbitration Act (SFS 1929:145) shall apply, with respect to the period within which the award shall be rendered, to proceedings that are commenced within two years from the date of the entry into force of the new Act.

4. In the circumstances set forth in sub-sections 2 and 3, the parties may agree that only the new Act shall apply.

5. References in statutes or other legislation to the Arbitration Act (SFS 1929:145) shall refer instead to the new Act.

IV. ARBITRATION RULES

■ ■ ■

A. INTERNATIONAL CHAMBER OF COMMERCE 1998 ARBITRATION RULES*

RULES OF ARBITRATION OF THE INTERNATIONAL CHAMBER OF COMMERCE

The current Rules of Arbitration of the International Chamber of Commerce came into effect on 1 January 1998. They include the costs scales effective as of 1 January 2008.

FOREWORD

The closing decades of the twentieth century saw international commercial arbitration gain worldwide acceptance as the normal means of resolving international commercial disputes. National laws on arbitration have been modernized on all continents. International treaties on arbitration have been signed or adhered to with impressive success. Arbitration has become part of the curricula of large numbers of law schools. With the gradual removal of political and trade barriers and the rapid globalization of the world economy, new challenges have been created for arbitration institutions in response to the growing demand of parties for certainty and predictability, greater rapidity and flexibility as well as neutrality and efficacy in the resolution of international disputes.

Since the International Court of Arbitration was established in 1923, ICC arbitration has been constantly nourished by the experience gathered by the ICC International Court of Arbitration in the course of administering more than thirteen thousand international arbitration cases, now involving each year parties and arbitrators from over 100 countries and from a diversity of legal, economic, cultural and linguistic backgrounds.

The present ICC Rules of Arbitration came into effect on 1 January 1998. They are the result of an intensive, worldwide consultation process and constitute the first major revision of the Rules in more than 20 years.

---

* ICC Rules of Arbitration (1998); ICC Publication No. 808, ISBN 92.842.1302.0; Published in its official English version by the International Chamber of Commerce. Copyright 1997, 2001 International Chamber of Commerce (ICC), Paris. Available from: ICC International Court of Arbitration, 38 cours Albert 1er, 75008 Paris, France; ICC Publishing, Inc., 156 Fifth Avenue, New York 10010; and on the web site: http//www.iccdrl.com/ Reprinted with permission of the International Chamber of Commerce.

The changes made are designed to reduce delays and ambiguities and to fill certain gaps, taking into account the evolution of arbitration practice. The basic features of the ICC arbitration system have not been altered, however, notably its universality and flexibility, as well as the central role played by the ICC Court in the administration of arbitral cases.

Every ICC arbitration is conducted by an arbitral tribunal with responsibility for examining the merits of the case and rendering a final award. Each year, ICC arbitrations are held in numerous countries, in most major languages and with arbitrators from all over the world. The work of those arbitral tribunals is monitored by the ICC Court, which meets weekly all year round. Composed of members from over 80 countries, the Court organizes and supervises arbitrations held under the ICC Rules of Arbitration. The Court must remain constantly alert to changes in the law and the practice of arbitration in all parts of the world and must adapt its working methods to the evolving needs of parties and arbitrators. For the day-to-day management of cases in many languages, the ICC Court is supported by a Secretariat based at the headquarters of the International Chamber of Commerce, in Paris.

Although the ICC Rules of Arbitration have been especially designed for arbitrations in an international context, they may also be used for non-international cases.

STANDARD ICC ARBITRATION CLAUSE

The ICC recommends that all parties wishing to make reference to ICC arbitration in their contracts use the following standard clause.

Parties are reminded that it may be desirable for them to stipulate in the arbitration clause itself the law governing the contract, the number of arbitrators and the place and language of the arbitration. The parties' free choice of the law governing the contract and of the place and language of the arbitration is not limited by the ICC Rules of Arbitration.

Attention is called to the fact that the laws of certain countries require that parties to contracts expressly accept arbitration clauses, sometimes in a precise and particular manner.

The ICC Rules of arbitration have been translated into several [languages]*. . . . These translations are available on the web site of the ICC International Court of Arbitration:

www.iccarbitration.org

ENGLISH

"All disputes arising out of or in connection with the present contract shall be finally settled under the Rules of Arbitration of the International Chamber of Commerce by one or more arbitrators appointed in accordance with the said Rules."

* Arabic, Brazilian Portuguese, Chinese, Czech, Dutch, English, French, German, Italian, Japanese, Polish, Russian, Spanish, and Turkish.

RULES OF ARBITRATION OF THE INTERNATIONAL CHAMBER OF COMMERCE

In force as from 1 January 1998
Costs scales effective as of 1 July 2003

INTRODUCTORY PROVISIONS

Article 1
International Court of Arbitration

1

The International Court of Arbitration (the "Court") of the International Chamber of Commerce (the "ICC") is the arbitration body attached to the ICC. The statutes of the Court are set forth in Appendix I. Members of the Court are appointed by the World Council of the ICC. The function of the Court is to provide for the settlement by arbitration of business disputes of an international character in accordance with the Rules of Arbitration of the International Chamber of Commerce (the "Rules"). If so empowered by an arbitration agreement, the Court shall also provide for the settlement by arbitration in accordance with these Rules of business disputes not of an international character.

2

The Court does not itself settle disputes. It has the function of ensuring the application of these Rules. It draws up its own Internal Rules (Appendix II).

3

The Chairman of the Court, or, in the Chairman's absence or otherwise at his request, one of its Vice–Chairmen shall have the power to take urgent decisions on behalf of the Court, provided that any such decision is reported to the Court at its next session.

4

As provided for in its Internal Rules, the Court may delegate to one or more committees composed of its members the power to take certain decisions, provided that any such decision is reported to the Court at its next session.

5

The Secretariat of the Court (the "Secretariat") under the direction of its Secretary General (the "Secretary General") shall have its seat at the headquarters of the ICC.

Article 2
Definitions

In these Rules:

(i) "Arbitral Tribunal" includes one or more arbitrators.

(ii) "Claimant" includes one or more claimants and "Respondent" includes one or more respondents.

(iii) "Award" includes, *inter alia*, an interim, partial or final Award.

Article 3
Written Notifications or Communications; Time Limits

1

All pleadings and other written communications submitted by any party, as well as all documents annexed thereto, shall be supplied in a number of copies sufficient to provide one copy for each party, plus one for each arbitrator, and one for the Secretariat. A copy of any communication from the Arbitral Tribunal to the parties shall be sent to the Secretariat.

2

All notifications or communications from the Secretariat and the Arbitral Tribunal shall be made to the last address of the party or its representative for whom the same are intended, as notified either by the party in question or by the other party. Such notification or communication may be made by delivery against receipt, registered post, courier, facsimile transmission, telex, telegram or any other means of telecommunication that provides a record of the sending thereof.

3

A notification or communication shall be deemed to have been made on the day it was received by the party itself or by its representative, or would have been received if made in accordance with the preceding paragraph.

4

Periods of time specified in or fixed under the present Rules, shall start to run on the day following the date a notification or communication is deemed to have been made in accordance with the preceding paragraph. When the day next following such date is an official holiday, or a non-business day in the country where the notification or communication is deemed to have been made, the period of time shall commence on the first following business day. Official holidays and non-business days are included in the calculation of the period of time. If the last day of the relevant period of time granted is an official holiday or a non-business day in the country where the notification or communication is deemed to have been made, the period of time shall expire at the end of the first following business day.

COMMENCING THE ARBITRATION

Article 4
Request for Arbitration

1

A party wishing to have recourse to arbitration under these Rules shall submit its Request for Arbitration (the "Request") to the Secretariat, which shall notify the Claimant and Respondent of the receipt of the Request and the date of such receipt.

2

The date on which the Request is received by the Secretariat shall, for all purposes, be deemed to be the date of the commencement of the arbitral proceedings.

3

The Request shall, *inter alia*, contain the following information:

a) the name in full, description and address of each of the parties;

b) a description of the nature and circumstances of the dispute giving rise to the claim(s);

c) a statement of the relief sought, including, to the extent possible, an indication of any amount(s) claimed;

d) the relevant agreements and, in particular, the arbitration agreement;

e) all relevant particulars concerning the number of arbitrators and their choice in accordance with the provisions of Articles 8, 9 and 10, and any nomination of an arbitrator required thereby; and

f) any comments as to the place of arbitration, the applicable rules of law and the language of the arbitration.

4

Together with the Request, the Claimant shall submit the number of copies thereof required by Article 3(1) and shall make the advance payment on administrative expenses required by Appendix III ("Arbitration Costs and Fees") in force on the date the Request is submitted. In the event that the Claimant fails to comply with either of these requirements, the Secretariat may fix a time limit within which the Claimant must comply, failing which the file shall be closed without prejudice to the right of the Claimant to submit the same claims at a later date in another Request.

5

The Secretariat shall send a copy of the Request and the documents annexed thereto to the Respondent for its Answer to the Request once the

Secretariat has sufficient copies of the Request and the required advance payment.

6

When a party submits a Request in connection with a legal relationship in respect of which arbitration proceedings between the same parties are already pending under these Rules, the Court may, at the request of a party, decide to include the claims contained in the Request in the pending proceedings provided that the Terms of Reference have not been signed or approved by the Court. Once the Terms of Reference have been signed or approved by the Court, claims may only be included in the pending proceedings subject to the provisions of Article 19.

Article 5
Answer to the Request; Counterclaims

1

Within 30 days from the receipt of the Request from the Secretariat, the Respondent shall file an Answer (the "Answer") which shall, *inter alia*, contain the following information:

a) its name in full, description and address;

b) its comments as to the nature and circumstances of the dispute giving rise to the claim(s);

c) its response to the relief sought;

d) any comments concerning the number of arbitrators and their choice in light of the Claimant's proposals and in accordance with the provisions of Articles 8, 9 and 10, and any nomination of an arbitrator required thereby; and

e) any comments as to the place of arbitration, the applicable rules of law and the language of the arbitration.

2

The Secretariat may grant the Respondent an extension of the time for filing the Answer, provided the application for such an extension contains the Respondent's comments concerning the number of arbitrators and their choice and, where required by Articles 8, 9 and 10, the nomination of an arbitrator. If the Respondent fails to do so, the Court shall proceed in accordance with these Rules.

3

The Answer shall be supplied to the Secretariat in the number of copies specified by Article 3(1).

4

A copy of the Answer and the documents annexed thereto shall be communicated by the Secretariat to the Claimant.

5

Any counterclaim(s) made by the Respondent shall be filed with its Answer and shall provide:

a) a description of the nature and circumstances of the dispute giving rise to the counterclaim(s); and

b) a statement of the relief sought, including, to the extent possible, an indication of any amount(s) counterclaimed.

6

The Claimant shall file a Reply to any counterclaim within 30 days from the date of receipt of the counterclaim(s) communicated by the Secretariat. The Secretariat may grant the Claimant an extension of time for filing the Reply.

Article 6
Effect of the Arbitration Agreement

1

Where the parties have agreed to submit to arbitration under the Rules, they shall be deemed to have submitted *ipso facto* to the Rules in effect on the date of commencement of the arbitration proceedings, unless they have agreed to submit to the Rules in effect on the date of their arbitration agreement.

2

If the Respondent does not file an Answer, as provided by Article 5, or if any party raises one or more pleas concerning the existence, validity or scope of the arbitration agreement, the Court may decide, without prejudice to the admissibility or merits of the plea or pleas, that the arbitration shall proceed if it is *prima facie* satisfied that an arbitration agreement under the Rules may exist. In such a case, any decision as to the jurisdiction of the Arbitral Tribunal shall be taken by the Arbitral Tribunal itself. If the Court is not so satisfied, the parties shall be notified that the arbitration cannot proceed. In such a case, any party retains the right to ask any court having jurisdiction whether or not there is a binding arbitration agreement.

3

If any of the parties refuses or fails to take part in the arbitration or any stage thereof, the arbitration shall proceed notwithstanding such refusal or failure.

4

Unless otherwise agreed, the Arbitral Tribunal shall not cease to have jurisdiction by reason of any claim that the contract is null and void or allegation that it is non-existent, provided that the Arbitral Tribunal upholds the validity of the arbitration agreement. The Arbitral Tribunal shall continue to have jurisdiction to determine the respective rights of the parties and to adjudicate their claims and pleas even though the contract itself may be non-existent or null and void.

THE ARBITRAL TRIBUNAL

Article 7
General Provisions

1

Every arbitrator must be and remain independent of the parties involved in the arbitration.

2

Before appointment or confirmation, a prospective arbitrator shall sign a statement of independence and disclose in writing to the Secretariat any facts or circumstances which might be of such a nature as to call into question the arbitrator's independence in the eyes of the parties. The Secretariat shall provide such information to the parties in writing and fix a time limit for any comments from them.

3

An arbitrator shall immediately disclose in writing to the Secretariat and to the parties any facts or circumstances of a similar nature which may arise during the arbitration.

4

The decisions of the Court as to the appointment, confirmation, challenge or replacement of an arbitrator shall be final and the reasons for such decisions shall not be communicated.

5

By accepting to serve, every arbitrator undertakes to carry out his responsibilities in accordance with these Rules.

6

Insofar as the parties have not provided otherwise, the Arbitral Tribunal shall be constituted in accordance with the provisions of Articles 8, 9 and 10.

Article 8
Number of Arbitrators

1

The disputes shall be decided by a sole arbitrator or by three arbitrators.

2

Where the parties have not agreed upon the number of arbitrators, the Court shall appoint a sole arbitrator, save where it appears to the Court that the dispute is such as to warrant the appointment of three arbitrators. In such case, the Claimant shall nominate an arbitrator within a period of 15 days from the receipt of the notification of the decision of the Court, and the Respondent shall nominate an arbitrator within a period of 15 days from the receipt of the notification of the nomination made by the Claimant.

3

Where the parties have agreed that the dispute shall be settled by a sole arbitrator, they may, by agreement, nominate the sole arbitrator for confirmation. If the parties fail to nominate a sole arbitrator within 30 days from the date when the Claimant's Request for Arbitration has been received by the other party, or within such additional time as may be allowed by the Secretariat, the sole arbitrator shall be appointed by the Court.

4

Where the dispute is to be referred to three arbitrators, each party shall nominate in the Request and the Answer, respectively, one arbitrator for confirmation. If a party fails to nominate an arbitrator, the appointment shall be made by the Court. The third arbitrator, who will act as chairman of the Arbitral Tribunal, shall be appointed by the Court, unless the parties have agreed upon another procedure for such appointment, in which case the nomination will be subject to confirmation pursuant to Article 9. Should such procedure not result in a nomination within the time limit fixed by the parties or the Court, the third arbitrator shall be appointed by the Court.

Article 9
Appointment and Confirmation of the Arbitrators

1

In confirming or appointing arbitrators, the Court shall consider the prospective arbitrator's nationality, residence and other relationships with the countries of which the parties or the other arbitrators are nationals and the prospective arbitrator's availability and ability to conduct the arbitration in accordance with these Rules. The same shall apply where the Secretary General confirms arbitrators pursuant to Article 9(2).

2

The Secretary General may confirm as co-arbitrators, sole arbitrators and chairmen of Arbitral Tribunals persons nominated by the parties or pursuant to their particular agreements, provided they have filed a statement of independence without qualification or a qualified statement of independence has not given rise to objections. Such confirmation shall be reported to the Court at its next session. If the Secretary General considers that a co-arbitrator, sole arbitrator or chairman of an Arbitral Tribunal should not be confirmed, the matter shall be submitted to the Court.

3

Where the Court is to appoint a sole arbitrator or the chairman of an Arbitral Tribunal, it shall make the appointment upon a proposal of a National Committee of the ICC that it considers to be appropriate. If the Court does not accept the proposal made, or if the National Committee fails to make the proposal requested within the time limit fixed by the Court, the Court may repeat its request or may request a proposal from another National Committee that it considers to be appropriate.

4

Where the Court considers that the circumstances so demand, it may choose the sole arbitrator or the chairman of the Arbitral Tribunal from a country where there is no National Committee, provided that neither of the parties objects within the time limit fixed by the Court.

5

The sole arbitrator or the chairman of the Arbitral Tribunal shall be of a nationality other than those of the parties. However, in suitable circumstances and provided that neither of the parties objects within the time limit fixed by the Court, the sole arbitrator or the chairman of the Arbitral Tribunal may be chosen from a country of which any of the parties is a national.

6

Where the Court is to appoint an arbitrator on behalf of a party which has failed to nominate one, it shall make the appointment upon a proposal of the National Committee of the country of which that party is a national. If the Court does not accept the proposal made, or if the National Committee fails to make the proposal requested within the time limit fixed by the Court, or if the country of which the said party is a national has no National Committee, the Court shall be at liberty to choose any person whom it regards as suitable. The Secretariat shall inform the National Committee, if one exists, of the country of which such person is a national.

Article 10
Multiple Parties

1

Where there are multiple parties, whether as Claimant or as Respondent, and where the dispute is to be referred to three arbitrators, the multiple Claimants, jointly, and the multiple Respondents, jointly, shall nominate an arbitrator for confirmation pursuant to Article 9.

2

In the absence of such a joint nomination and where all parties are unable to agree to a method for the constitution of the Arbitral Tribunal, the Court may appoint each member of the Arbitral Tribunal and shall designate one of them to act as chairman. In such case, the Court shall be at liberty to choose any person it regards as suitable to act as arbitrator, applying Article 9 when it considers this appropriate.

Article 11
Challenge of Arbitrators

1

A challenge of an arbitrator, whether for an alleged lack of independence or otherwise, shall be made by the submission to the Secretariat of a written statement specifying the facts and circumstances on which the challenge is based.

2

For a challenge to be admissible, it must be sent by a party either within 30 days from receipt by that party of the notification of the appointment or confirmation of the arbitrator, or within 30 days from the date when the party making the challenge was informed of the facts and circumstances on which the challenge is based if such date is subsequent to the receipt of such notification.

3

The Court shall decide on the admissibility, and, at the same time, if necessary, on the merits of a challenge after the Secretariat has afforded an opportunity for the arbitrator concerned, the other party or parties and any other members of the Arbitral Tribunal to comment in writing within a suitable period of time. Such comments shall be communicated to the parties and to the arbitrators.

Article 12
Replacement of Arbitrators

1

An arbitrator shall be replaced upon his death, upon the acceptance by the Court of the arbitrator's resignation, upon acceptance by the Court of a challenge or, upon the request of all the parties.

2

An arbitrator shall also be replaced on the Court's own initiative when it decides that he is prevented *de jure* or *de facto* from fulfilling his functions, or that he is not fulfilling his functions in accordance with the Rules or within the prescribed time limits.

3

When, on the basis of information that has come to its attention, the Court considers applying Article 12(2), it shall decide on the matter after the arbitrator concerned, the parties and any other members of the Arbitral Tribunal have had an opportunity to comment in writing within a suitable period of time. Such comments shall be communicated to the parties and to the arbitrators.

4

When an arbitrator is to be replaced, the Court has discretion to decide whether or not to follow the original nominating process. Once reconstituted, and after having invited the parties to comment, the Arbitral Tribunal shall determine if and to what extent prior proceedings shall be repeated before the reconstituted Arbitral Tribunal.

5

Subsequent to the closing of the proceedings, instead of replacing an arbitrator who has died or been removed by the Court pursuant to Articles 12(1) and 12(2), the Court may decide, when it considers it appropriate, that the remaining arbitrators shall continue the arbitration. In making such determination, the Court shall take into account the views of the remaining arbitrators and of the parties and such other matters that it considers appropriate in the circumstances.

THE ARBITRAL PROCEEDINGS

Article 13
Transmission of the File to the Arbitral Tribunal

The Secretariat shall transmit the file to the Arbitral Tribunal as soon as it has been constituted, provided the advance on costs requested by the Secretariat at this stage has been paid.

Article 14
Place of the Arbitration

1

The place of the arbitration shall be fixed by the Court unless agreed upon by the parties.

2

The Arbitral Tribunal may, after consultation with the parties, conduct hearings and meetings at any location it considers appropriate unless otherwise agreed by the parties.

3

The Arbitral Tribunal may deliberate at any location it considers appropriate.

Article 15
Rules Governing the Proceedings

1

The proceedings before the Arbitral Tribunal shall be governed by these Rules, and, where these Rules are silent by any rules which the parties or, failing them, the Arbitral Tribunal may settle on, whether or not reference is thereby made to the rules of procedure of a national law to be applied to the arbitration.

2

In all cases, the Arbitral Tribunal shall act fairly and impartially and ensure that each party has a reasonable opportunity to present its case.

Article 16
Language of the Arbitration

In the absence of an agreement by the parties, the Arbitral Tribunal shall determine the language or languages of the arbitration, due regard being given to all relevant circumstances, including the language of the contract.

Article 17
Applicable Rules of Law

1

The parties shall be free to agree upon the rules of law to be applied by the Arbitral Tribunal to the merits of the dispute. In the absence of any such agreement, the Arbitral Tribunal shall apply the rules of law which it determines to be appropriate.

2

In all cases the Arbitral Tribunal shall take account of the provisions of the contract and the relevant trade usages.

3

The Arbitral Tribunal shall assume the powers of an *amiable compositeur* or decide *ex aequo et bono* only if the parties have agreed to give it such powers.

Article 18
Terms of Reference; Procedural Timetable

1

As soon as it has received the file from the Secretariat, the Arbitral Tribunal shall draw up, on the basis of documents or in the presence of the parties and in the light of their most recent submissions, a document defining its Terms of Reference. This document shall include the following particulars:

a) the full names and descriptions of the parties;

b) the addresses of the parties to which notifications and communications arising in the course of the arbitration may be made;

c) a summary of the parties' respective claims and of the relief sought by each party, with an indication to the extent possible of the amounts claimed or counterclaimed;

d) unless the Arbitral Tribunal considers it inappropriate, a list of issues to be determined;

e) the full names, descriptions and addresses of the arbitrators;

f) the place of the arbitration; and

g) particulars of the applicable procedural rules and, if such is the case, reference to the power conferred upon the Arbitral Tribunal to act as *amiable compositeur* or to decide *ex aequo et bono*.

2

The Terms of Reference shall be signed by the parties and the Arbitral Tribunal. Within two months of the date on which the file has been transmitted to it, the Arbitral Tribunal shall transmit to the Court the Terms of Reference signed by it and by the parties. The Court may extend this time limit pursuant to a reasoned request from the Arbitral Tribunal or on its own initiative if it decides it is necessary to do so.

3

If any of the parties refuses to take part in the drawing up of the Terms of Reference or to sign the same, they shall be submitted to the Court for approval. When the Terms of Reference have been signed in accordance with Article 18(2) or approved by the Court, the arbitration shall proceed.

4

When drawing up the Terms of Reference, or as soon as possible thereafter, the Arbitral Tribunal, after having consulted the parties, shall establish in a separate document a provisional timetable that it intends to follow for the conduct of the arbitration and shall communicate it to the Court and the parties. Any subsequent modifications of the provisional timetable shall be communicated to the Court and the parties.

Article 19
New Claims

After the Terms of Reference have been signed or approved by the Court, no party shall make new claims or counterclaims which fall outside the limits of the Terms of Reference unless it has been authorized to do so by the Arbitral Tribunal, which shall consider the nature of such new claims or counterclaims, the stage of the arbitration and other relevant circumstances.

Article 20
Establishing the Facts of the Case

1

The Arbitral Tribunal shall proceed within as short a time as possible to establish the facts of the case by all appropriate means.

2

After studying the written submissions of the parties and all documents relied upon, the Arbitral Tribunal shall hear the parties together in person if any of them so requests or, failing such a request, it may of its own motion decide to hear them.

3

The Arbitral Tribunal may decide to hear witnesses, experts appointed by the parties or any other person, in the presence of the parties, or in their absence provided they have been duly summoned.

4

The Arbitral Tribunal, after having consulted the parties, may appoint one or more experts, define their terms of reference and receive their reports. At the request of a party, the parties shall be given the opportunity to question at a hearing any such expert appointed by the Tribunal.

5

At any time during the proceedings, the Arbitral Tribunal may summon any party to provide additional evidence.

6

The Arbitral Tribunal may decide the case solely on the documents submitted by the parties unless any of the parties requests a hearing.

7

The Arbitral Tribunal may take measures for protecting trade secrets and confidential information.

Article 21
Hearings

1

When a hearing is to be held, the Arbitral Tribunal, giving reasonable notice, shall summon the parties to appear before it on the day and at the place fixed by it.

2

If any of the parties, although duly summoned, fails to appear without valid excuse, the Arbitral Tribunal shall have the power to proceed with the hearing.

3

The Arbitral Tribunal shall be in full charge of the hearings, at which all the parties shall be entitled to be present. Save with the approval of the Arbitral Tribunal and the parties, persons not involved in the proceedings shall not be admitted.

4

The parties may appear in person or through duly authorized representatives. In addition, they may be assisted by advisers.

Article 22
Closing of the Proceedings

1

When it is satisfied that the parties have had a reasonable opportunity to present their cases, the Arbitral Tribunal shall declare the proceedings closed. Thereafter, no further submission or argument may be made, or evidence produced, unless requested or authorized by the Arbitral Tribunal.

2

When the Arbitral Tribunal has declared the proceedings closed, it shall indicate to the Secretariat an approximate date by which the draft Award will be submitted to the Court for approval pursuant to Article 27. Any postponement of that date shall be communicated to the Secretariat by the Arbitral Tribunal.

Article 23
Conservatory and Interim Measures

1

Unless the parties have otherwise agreed, as soon as the file has been transmitted to it, the Arbitral Tribunal may, at the request of a party, order any interim or conservatory measure it deems appropriate. The Arbitral Tribunal may make the granting of any such measure subject to appropriate security being furnished by the requesting party. Any such measure shall take the form of an order, giving reasons, or of an Award, as the Arbitral Tribunal considers appropriate.

2

Before the file is transmitted to the Arbitral Tribunal, and in appropriate circumstances even thereafter, the parties may apply to any competent judicial authority for interim or conservatory measures. The application of a party to a judicial authority for such measures or for the implementation of any such measures ordered by an Arbitral Tribunal shall not be deemed to be an infringement or a waiver of the arbitration agreement and shall not affect the relevant powers reserved to the Arbitral Tribunal. Any such application and any measures taken by the judicial authority must be notified without delay to the Secretariat. The Secretariat shall inform the Arbitral Tribunal thereof.

AWARDS

Article 24
Time Limit for the Award

1

The time limit within which the Arbitral Tribunal must render its final Award is six months. Such time limit shall start to run from the date of the last signature by the Arbitral Tribunal or of the parties of the Terms of Reference, or, in the case of application of Article 18(3), the date of the notification to the Arbitral Tribunal by the Secretariat of the approval of the Terms of Reference by the Court.

2

The Court may extend this time limit pursuant to a reasoned request from the Arbitral Tribunal or on its own initiative if it decides it is necessary to do so.

Article 25
Making of the Award

1

When the Arbitral Tribunal is composed of more than one arbitrator, an Award is given by a majority decision. If there be no majority, the Award shall be made by the chairman of the Arbitral Tribunal alone.

2

The Award shall state the reasons upon which it is based.

3

The Award shall be deemed to be made at the place of the arbitration and on the date stated therein.

Article 26
Award by Consent

If the parties reach a settlement after the file has been transmitted to the Arbitral Tribunal in accordance with Article 13, the settlement shall be recorded in the form of an Award made by consent of the parties if so requested by the parties and if the Arbitral Tribunal agrees to do so.

Article 27
Scrutiny of the Award by the Court

Before signing any Award, the Arbitral Tribunal shall submit it in draft form to the Court. The Court may lay down modifications as to the form of the Award and, without affecting the Arbitral Tribunal's liberty of decision, may also draw its attention to points of substance. No Award shall be rendered by the Arbitral Tribunal until it has been approved by the Court as to its form.

Article 28
Notification, Deposit and Enforceability of the Award

1

Once an Award has been made, the Secretariat shall notify to the parties the text signed by the Arbitral Tribunal, provided always that the costs of the arbitration have been fully paid to the ICC by the parties or by one of them.

2

Additional copies certified true by the Secretary General shall be made available on request and at any time to the parties, but to no one else.

3

By virtue of the notification made in accordance with Paragraph 1 of this Article, the parties waive any other form of notification or deposit on the part of the Arbitral Tribunal.

4

An original of each Award made in accordance with the present Rules shall be deposited with the Secretariat.

5

The Arbitral Tribunal and the Secretariat shall assist the parties in complying with whatever further formalities may be necessary.

6

Every Award shall be binding on the parties. By submitting the dispute to arbitration under these Rules, the parties undertake to carry out any Award without delay and shall be deemed to have waived their right to any form of recourse insofar as such waiver can validly be made.

Article 29
Correction and Interpretation of the Award

1

On its own initiative, the Arbitral Tribunal may correct a clerical, computational or typographical error, or any errors of similar nature contained in an Award, provided such correction is submitted for approval to the Court within 30 days of the date of such Award.

2

Any application of a party for the correction of an error of the kind referred to in Article 29(1), or for the interpretation of an Award, must be made to the Secretariat within 30 days of the receipt of the Award by such party, in a number of copies as stated in Article 3(1). After transmittal of the application to the Arbitral Tribunal, it shall grant the other party a short time limit, normally not exceeding 30 days, from the receipt of the application by that party to submit any comments thereon. If the Arbitral Tribunal decides to correct or interpret the Award, it shall submit its decision in draft form to the Court not later than 30 days following the expiration of the time limit for the receipt of any comments from the other party or within such other period as the Court may decide.

3

The decision to correct or to interpret the Award shall take the form of an addendum and shall constitute part of the Award. The provisions of Articles 25, 27 and 28 shall apply *mutatis mutandis*.

COSTS

Article 30
Advance to Cover the Costs of the Arbitration

1

After receipt of the Request, the Secretary General may request the Claimant to pay a provisional advance in an amount intended to cover the costs of arbitration until the Terms of Reference have been drawn up.

2

As soon as practicable, the Court shall fix the advance on costs in an amount likely to cover the fees and expenses of the arbitrators and the ICC administrative costs for the claims and counterclaims which have been referred to it by the parties. This amount may be subject to readjustment at any time during the arbitration. Where, apart from the claims, counterclaims are submitted, the Court may fix separate advances on costs for the claims and the counterclaims.

3

The advance on costs fixed by the Court shall be payable in equal shares by the Claimant and the Respondent. Any provisional advance paid on the basis of Article 30(1) will be considered as a partial payment thereof. However, any party shall be free to pay the whole of the advance on costs in respect of the principal claim or the counterclaim should the other party fail to pay its share. When the Court has set separate advances on costs in accordance with Article 30(2), each of the parties shall pay the advance on costs corresponding to its claims.

4

When a request for an advance on costs has not been complied with, and after consultation with the Arbitral Tribunal, the Secretary General may direct the Arbitral Tribunal to suspend its work and set a time limit, which must be not less than 15 days, on the expiry of which the relevant claims, or counterclaims, shall be considered as withdrawn. Should the party in question wish to object to this measure, it must make a request within the aforementioned period for the matter to be decided by the Court. Such party shall not be prevented, on the ground of such withdrawal, from reintroducing the same claims or counterclaims at a later date in another proceeding.

5

If one of the parties claims a right to a set-off with regard to either claims or counterclaims, such set-off shall be taken into account in determining the advance to cover the costs of arbitration in the same way as a separate claim insofar as it may require the Arbitral Tribunal to consider additional matters.

Article 31
Decision as to the Costs of the Arbitration

1

The costs of the arbitration shall include the fees and expenses of the arbitrators and the ICC administrative expenses fixed by the Court, in accordance with the scale in force at the time of the commencement of the arbitral proceedings, as well as the fees and expenses of any experts appointed by the Arbitral Tribunal and the reasonable legal and other costs incurred by the parties for the arbitration.

2

The Court may fix the fees of the arbitrators at a figure higher or lower than that which would result from the application of the relevant scale should this be deemed necessary due to the exceptional circumstances of the case. Decisions on costs other than those fixed by the Court may be taken by the Arbitral Tribunal at any time during the proceedings.

3

The final Award shall fix the costs of the arbitration and decide which of the parties shall bear them or in what proportion they shall be borne by the parties.

MISCELLANEOUS

Article 32
Modified Time Limits

1

The parties may agree to shorten the various time limits set out in these Rules. Any such agreement entered into subsequent to the constitution of an Arbitral Tribunal shall become effective only upon the approval of the Arbitral Tribunal.

2

The Court, on its own initiative, may extend any time limit which has been modified pursuant to Article 32(1) if it decides that it is necessary to do so in order that the Arbitral Tribunal or the Court may fulfil their responsibilities in accordance with these Rules.

Article 33
Waiver

A party which proceeds with the arbitration without raising its objection to a failure to comply with any provision of these Rules, or of any other rules applicable to the proceedings, any direction given by the Arbitral Tribunal, or any requirement under the arbitration agreement relating to the constitution of the Arbitral Tribunal, or to the conduct of the proceedings, shall be deemed to have waived its right to object.

Article 34
Exclusion of Liability

Neither the arbitrators, nor the Court and its members, nor the ICC and its employees, nor the ICC National Committees shall be liable to any person for any act or omission in connection with the arbitration.

Article 35
General Rule

In all matters not expressly provided for in these Rules, the Court and the Arbitral Tribunal shall act in the spirit of these Rules and shall make every effort to make sure that the Award is enforceable at law.

APPENDIX I

STATUTES OF THE INTERNATIONAL COURT OF ARBITRATION OF THE ICC

Article 1
Function

1

The function of the International Court of Arbitration of the International Chamber of Commerce (the "Court") is to ensure the application of the Rules of Arbitration of the International Chamber of Commerce, and it has all the necessary powers for that purpose.

2

As an autonomous body, it carries out these functions in complete independence from the ICC and its organs.

3

Its members are independent from the ICC National Committees.

Article 2
Composition of the Court

The Court shall consist of a Chairman, Vice–Chairmen, and members and alternate members (collectively designated as members). In its work it is assisted by its Secretariat (Secretariat of the Court).

Article 3
Appointment

1

The Chairman is elected by the ICC World Council upon the recommendation of the Executive Board of the ICC.

2

The ICC World Council appoints the Vice–Chairmen of the Court from among the members of the Court or otherwise.

3

Its members are appointed by the ICC World Council on the proposal of National Committees, one member for each Committee.

4

On the proposal of the Chairman of the Court, the World Council may appoint alternate members.

5

The term of office of all members is three years. If a member is no longer in a position to exercise his functions, his successor is appointed by the World Council for the remainder of the term.

Article 4
Plenary Session of the Court

The Plenary Sessions of the Court are presided over by the Chairman or, in his absence, by one of the Vice–Chairmen designated by him. The deliberations shall be valid when at least six members are present. Decisions are taken by a majority vote, the Chairman having a casting vote in the event of a tie.

Article 5
Committees

The Court may set up one or more Committees and establish the functions and organization of such Committees.

Article 6
Confidentiality

The work of the Court is of a confidential nature which must be respected by everyone who participates in that work in whatever capacity. The Court lays down the rules regarding the persons who can attend the meetings of the Court and its Committees and who are entitled to have access to the materials submitted to the Court and its Secretariat.

Article 7
Modification of the Rules of Arbitration

Any proposal of the Court for a modification of the Rules is laid before the Commission on Arbitration before submission to the Executive Board and the World Council of the ICC for approval.

APPENDIX II

INTERNAL RULES OF THE INTERNATIONAL COURT OF ARBITRATION OF THE ICC

Article 1
Confidential Character of the Work of the International Court of Arbitration

1

The sessions of the Court, whether plenary or those of a Committee of the Court, are open only to its members and to the Secretariat.

2

However, in exceptional circumstances, the Chairman of the Court may invite other persons to attend. Such persons must respect the confidential nature of the work of the Court.

3

The documents submitted to the Court, or drawn up by it in the course of its proceedings, are communicated only to the members of the Court and to the Secretariat and to persons authorized by the Chairman to attend Court sessions.

4

The Chairman or the Secretary General of the Court may authorize researchers undertaking work of a scientific nature on international trade law to acquaint themselves with awards and other documents of general interest, with the exception of memoranda, notes, statements and documents remitted by the parties within the framework of arbitration proceedings.

5

Such authorization shall not be given unless the beneficiary has undertaken to respect the confidential character of the documents made available and to refrain from any publication in their respect without having previously submitted the text for approval to the Secretary General of the Court.

6

The Secretariat will in each case submitted to arbitration under the Rules retain in the archives of the Court all Awards, Terms of Reference, and decisions of the Court, as well as copies of the pertinent correspondence of the Secretariat.

7

Any documents, communications or correspondence submitted by the parties or the arbitrators may be destroyed unless a party or an arbitrator requests in writing within a period fixed by the Secretariat the return of such documents. All related costs and expenses for the return of those documents shall be paid by such party or arbitrator.

Article 2
Participation of Members of the International Court of Arbitration in ICC Arbitration

1

The Chairman and the members of the Secretariat of the Court may not act as arbitrators or as counsel in cases submitted to ICC arbitration.

2

The Court shall not appoint Vice–Chairmen or members of the Court as arbitrators. They may, however, be proposed for such duties by one or more of the parties, or, pursuant to any other procedure agreed upon by the parties, subject to confirmation.

3

When the Chairman, a Vice–Chairman or a member of the Court or of the Secretariat is involved in any capacity whatsoever in proceedings pending before the Court, such person must inform the Secretary General of the Court upon becoming aware of such involvement.

4

Such person must refrain from participating in the discussions or in the decisions of the Court concerning the proceedings and must be absent from the courtroom whenever the matter is considered.

5

Such person will not receive any material documentation or information pertaining to such proceedings.

Article 3
Relations between the Members of the Court and the ICC National Committees

1

By virtue of their capacity, the members of the Court are independent of the ICC National Committees which proposed them for appointment by the ICC World Council.

2

Furthermore, they must regard as confidential, vis-à-vis the said National Committees, any information concerning individual cases with which they have become acquainted in their capacity as members of the Court, except when they have been requested by the Chairman of the Court or by its Secretary General to communicate specific information to their respective National Committee.

Article 4
Committee of the Court

1

In accordance with the provisions of Article 1 (4) of the Rules and Article 5 of its Statutes (Appendix I), the Court hereby establishes a Committee of the Court.

2

The members of the Committee consist of a Chairman and at least two other members. The Chairman of the Court acts as the Chairman of the Committee. If absent, the Chairman may designate a Vice–Chairman of the Court or, in exceptional circumstances, another member of the Court as Chairman of the Committee.

3

The other two members of the Committee are appointed by the Court from among the Vice–Chairmen or the other members of the Court. At each Plenary Session the Court appoints the members who are to attend the meetings of the Committee to be held before the next Plenary Session.

4

The Committee meets when convened by its Chairman. Two members constitute a quorum.

5

(a) The Court shall determine the decisions that may be taken by the Committee.

(b) The decisions of the Committee are taken unanimously.

(c) When the Committee cannot reach a decision or deems it preferable to abstain, it transfers the case to the next Plenary Session, making any suggestions it deems appropriate.

(d) The Committee's decisions are brought to the notice of the Court at its next Plenary Session.

Article 5
Court Secretariat

1

In case of absence, the Secretary General may delegate to the General Counsel and Deputy Secretary General the authority to confirm arbitrators, to certify true copies of Awards and to request the payment of a provisional advance, respectively provided for in Articles 9(2), 28(2) and 30(1) of the Rules.

2

The Secretariat may, with the approval of the Court, issue notes and other documents for the information of the parties and the arbitrators, or as necessary for the proper conduct of the arbitral proceedings.

Article 6
Scrutiny of Arbitral Awards

When the Court scrutinizes draft Awards in accordance with Article 27 of the Rules, it considers, to the extent practicable, the requirements of mandatory law at the place of arbitration.

APPENDIX III

ARBITRATION COSTS AND FEES

Article 1
Advance on Costs

1

Each request to commence an arbitration pursuant to the Rules must be accompanied by an advance payment of US$2500 on the administrative expenses. Such payment is nonrefundable, and shall be credited to the Claimant's portion of the advance on costs.

2

The provisional advance fixed by the Secretary General according to Article 30(1) of the Rules shall normally not exceed the amount obtained by adding together the administrative expenses, the minimum of the fees (as set out in the scale hereinafter) based upon the amount of the claim and the expected reimbursable expenses of the Arbitral Tribunal incurred with respect to the drafting of the Terms of Reference. If such amount is not quantified, the provisional advance shall be fixed at the discretion of the Secretary General. Payment by the Claimant shall be credited to its share of the advance on costs fixed by the Court.

3

In general, after the Terms of Reference have been signed or approved by the Court and the provisional timetable has been established, the Arbitral Tribunal shall, in accordance with Article 30(4) of the Rules, proceed only with respect to those claims or counterclaims in regard to which the whole of the advance on costs has been paid.

4

The advance on costs fixed by the Court according to Article 30(2) of the Rules comprises the fees of the arbitrator or arbitrators (hereinafter referred to as "arbitrator"), any arbitration-related expenses of the arbitrator and the administrative expenses.

5

Each party shall pay in cash its share of the total advance on costs. However, if its share exceeds an amount fixed from time to time by the Court, a party may post a bank guarantee for this additional amount.

6

A party that has already paid in full its share of the advance on costs fixed by the Court may, in accordance with Article 30(3) of the Rules, pay the unpaid portion of the advance owed by the defaulting party by posting a bank guarantee.

7

When the Court has fixed separate advances on costs pursuant to Article 30(2) of the Rules, the Secretariat shall invite each party to pay the amount of the advance corresponding to its respective claim(s).

8

When, as a result of the fixing of separate advances on costs, the separate advance fixed for the claim of either party exceeds one half of such global advance as was previously fixed (in respect of the same claims and counterclaims that are the subject of separate advances), a bank guarantee may be posted to cover any such excess amount. In the event that the amount of the separate advance is subsequently increased, at least one half of the increase shall be paid in cash.

9

The Secretariat shall establish the terms governing all bank guarantees which the parties may post pursuant to the above provisions.

10

As provided in Article 30(2) of the Rules, the advance on costs may be subject to readjustment at any time during the arbitration, in particular to take into account fluctuations in the amount in dispute, changes in the amount of the estimated expenses of the arbitrator, or the evolving difficulty or complexity of arbitration proceedings.

11

Before any expertise ordered by the Arbitral Tribunal can be commenced, the parties, or one of them, shall pay an advance on costs fixed by the Arbitral Tribunal sufficient to cover the expected fees and expenses of the expert as determined by the Arbitral Tribunal. The Arbitral Tribunal shall be responsible for ensuring the payment by the parties of such fees and expenses.

Article 2
Costs and Fees

1

Subject to Article 31(2) of the Rules, the Court shall fix the fees of the arbitrator in accordance with the scale hereinafter set out or, where the sum in dispute is not stated, at its discretion.

2

In setting the arbitrator's fees, the Court shall take into consideration the diligence of the arbitrator, the time spent, the rapidity of the proceedings, and the complexity of the dispute so as to arrive at a figure within the limits specified or, in exceptional circumstances (Article 31(2) of the Rules), at a figure higher or lower than those limits.

3

When a case is submitted to more than one arbitrator, the Court, at its discretion, shall have the right to increase the total fees up to a maximum which shall normally not exceed three times the fees of one arbitrator.

4

The arbitrator's fees and expenses shall be fixed exclusively by the Court as required by the Rules. Separate fee arrangements between the parties and the arbitrator are contrary to the Rules.

5

The Court shall fix the administrative expenses of each arbitration in accordance with the scale hereinafter set out or, where the sum in dispute is not stated, at its discretion. In exceptional circumstances, the Court may fix the administrative expenses at a lower or higher figure than that which would result from the application of such scale, provided that such expenses shall normally not exceed the maximum amount of the scale. Further, the Court may require the payment of administrative expenses in addition to those provided in the scale of administrative expenses as a condition to holding an arbitration in abeyance at the request of the parties or of one of them with the acquiescence of the other.

6

If an arbitration terminates before the rendering of a final Award, the Court shall fix the costs of the arbitration at its discretion, taking into account the stage attained by the arbitral proceedings and any other relevant circumstances.

7

In the case of an application under Article 29(2) of the Rules, the Court may fix an advance to cover additional fees and expenses of the Arbitral Tribunal and may make the transmission of such application to the Arbitral Tribunal subject to the prior cash payment in full to the ICC of such advance. The Court shall fix at its discretion any possible fees of the arbitrator when approving the decision of the Arbitral Tribunal.

8

When an arbitration is preceded by an attempt at amicable resolution pursuant to the ICC ADR Rules, one half of the administrative expenses paid for such ADR proceedings shall be credited to the administrative expenses of the arbitration.

9

Amounts paid to the arbitrator do not include any possible value added taxes (VAT) or other taxes or charges and imposts applicable to the arbitrator's fees. Parties have a duty to pay any such taxes or charges; however, the recovery of any such charges or taxes is a matter solely between the arbitrator and the parties.

Article 3
ICC as Appointing Authority

Any request received for an authority of the ICC to act as appointing authority will be treated in accordance with the Rules of ICC as Appointing Authority in UNCITRAL or Other Ad Hoc Arbitration Proceedings and shall be accompanied by a non-refundable sum of US$2,500. No request shall be processed unless accompanied by the said sum. For additional services, ICC may at its discretion fix administrative expenses, which shall be commensurate with the services provided and shall not exceed the maximum sum of US$10,000.

Article 4
Scales of Administrative Expenses and Arbitrator's Fees

1

The Scales of Administrative Expenses and Arbitrator's Fees set forth below shall be effective as of 1 January 2008 in respect of all arbitrations commenced on or after such date, irrespective of the version of the Rules applying to such arbitrations.

2

To calculate the administrative expenses and the arbitrator's fees, the amounts calculated for each successive slice of the sum in dispute must be added together, except that where the sum in dispute is over US$80 million, a flat amount of US$88,800 shall constitute the entirety of the administrative expenses.

ADMINISTRATIVE EXPENSES

Sum in dispute (in US Dollars)				Administrative expenses(*)
up to	50,000			$ 2,500
from	50,001	to	100,000	4.30%
from	100,001	to	200,000	2.30%
from	200,001	to	500,000	1.90%
from	500,001	to	1,000,000	1.37%
from	1,000,001	to	2,000,000	0.86%
from	2,000,001	to	5,000,000	0.41%
from	5,000,001	to	10,000,000	0.22%
from	10,000,001	to	30,000,000	0.09%
from	30,000,001	to	50,000,000	0.08%
from	50,000,001	to	80,000,000	0.01%
over	80,000,000			$88,800

(*) For illustrative purposes only, the table on the following page indicates the resulting administrative expenses in US$ when the proper calculations have been made.

B. ARBITRATOR'S FEES

Sum in dispute (in US Dollars)				Fees(**) minimum	maximum
up to	50,000			$2,500	17.00%
from	50,001	to	100,000	2.50%	12.80%
from	100,001	to	200,000	1.35%	7.25%
from	200,001	to	500,000	1.29%	6.45%
from	500,001	to	1,000,000	0.90%	3.80%
from	1,000,001	to	2,000,000	0.65%	3.40%
from	2,000,001	to	5,000,000	0.35%	1.30%
from	5,000,001	to	10,000,000	0.12%	0.85%
from	10,000,001	to	30,000,000	0.06%	0.225%
from	30,000,001	to	50,000,000	0.056%	0.215%
from	50,000,001	to	80,000,000	0.031%	0.152%
from	80,000,001	to	100,000,000	0.02%	0.112%
over	100,000,000			0.01%	0.056%

(**) For illustrative purposes only, the table on the following page indicates the resulting range of fees when the proper calculations have been made.

SUM IN DISPUTE (in US Dollars)	A. ADMINISTRATIVE EXPENSES (in US Dollars)
up to 50,000	2500
from 50,001 to 100,000	2500 + 4.30% of amt. over 50,000
from 100,001 to 200,000	4650 + 2.30% of amt. over 100,000
from 200,001 to 500,000	6950 + 1.90% of amt. over 200,000
from 500,001 to 1,000,000	12,650 + 1.37% of amt. over 500,000
from 1,000,001 to 2,000,000	19,500 + 0.86% of amt. over 1,000,000
from 2,000,001 to 5,000,000	28,100 + 0.41% of amt. over 2,000,000
from 5,000,001 to 10,000,000	40,400 + 0.22% of amt. over 5,000,000
from 10,000,001 to 30,000,000	51,400 + 0.09% of amt. over 10,000,000
from 30,000,001 to 50,000,000	69,400 + 0.08% of amt. over 30,000,000
from 50,000,001 to 80,000,000	85,400 + 0.01% of amt. over 50,000,000
from 80,000,001 to 100,000,000	88,800
over 100,000,000	88,800

SUM IN DISPUTE (in US Dollars)	B. ARBITRATOR'S FEES (in US Dollars)	
	Minimum	Maximum
up to 50,000	2500	17.00% of amount in dispute
from 50,001 to 100,000	2,500 + 2.50% of amt. over 50,000	8,500 + 12.80% of amt. over 50,000
from 100,001 to 200,000	3,750 + 1.35% of amt. over 100,000	14,900 + 7.25% of amt. over 100,000
from 200,001 to 500,000	5,100 + 1.29% of amt. over 200,000	22,150 + 6.45% of amt. over 200,000
from 500,001 to 1,000,000	8,970 + 0.90% of amt. over 500,000	41,500 + 3.80% of amt. over 500,000
from 1,000,001 to 2,000,000	13,470 + 0.65% of amt. over 1,000,000	60,500 + 3.40% of amt. over 1,000,000
from 2,000,001 to 5,000 000	19,970 + 0.35% of amt. over 2,000,000	94,500 + 1.30% of amt. over 2,000,000
from 5,000,001 to 10,000,000	30,470 + 0.12% of amt. over 5,000,000	133,500 + 0.85% of amt. over 5,000,000
from 10,000,001 to 30,000,000	36,470 + 0.06% of amt. over 10,000,000	176,000 + 0.225% of amt. over 10,000,000
from 30,000,001 to 50,000,000	48,470 + 0.056% of amt. over 30,000,000	221,000 + 0.215% of amt. over 30,000,000
from 50,000,001 to 80,000,000	59,670 + 0.031% of amt. over 50,000,000	264,000 + 0.152% of amt. over 50,000,000
from 80,000,001 to 100,000,000	68,970 + 0.02% of amt. over 80,000,000	309,600+ 0.112% of amt. over 80,000,000
over 100,000,000	72,970 + 0.01% of amt. over 100,000,000	332,000 + 0.056% of amt. over 100,000,000

B. RULES OF ICC AS APPOINTING AUTHORITY IN UNCITRAL OR OTHER *AD HOC* ARBITRATION PROCEEDINGS*

Effective as of 1 January 2004, the Rules of ICC as Appointing Authority chiefly cover the appointment and challenge of arbitrators in proceedings conducted under the UNCITRAL Arbitration Rules and in other *ad hoc* proceedings.

Foreword

One of the key steps in any arbitration is the constitution of the arbitral tribunal. Whilst this gives the parties the opportunity to designate arbitrators of their choice, especial care is required to ensure the independence and competence of the persons chosen, particularly in international proceedings. For this reason, parties may prefer to leave the task to a specialized institution, such as ICC.

During more than eighty years of administering international arbitrations, ICC has acquired exceptional experience in appointing arbitrators. In addition, it enjoys the support of a worldwide network of national committees able to identify arbitrators with appropriate qualifications of many different nationalities and from various spheres of activity.

The present rules supersede the rules ICC as Appointing Authority under the UNCITRAL Arbitration Rules, which have been in force for some twenty years and applied only to cases conducted under the UNCITRAL Arbitration Rules. The scope of the new rules extends also to ad hoc proceedings not conducted under the UNCITRAL Arbitration Rules. In both cases, in addition to making appointments, the ICC International Court of Arbitration may be given other powers, including the power to decide upon challenges of arbitrators, whether or not appointed by ICC.

Article 1
ICC as Appointing Authority in UNCITRAL or Other *Ad Hoc* Arbitration Proceedings

1

If so empowered by an arbitration clause, a subsequent agreement of the parties, a designation by the Secretary–General of the Permanent Court of Arbitration in The Hague, or otherwise, the International Chamber of Commerce ('ICC') shall act as appointing authority in accordance with the parties' agreement and/or the UNCITRAL Arbitration Rules.

* The Rules can be found at the ICC Court of Arbitration website at http://www.iccdrl.com/ The Rules are available from the ICC International Court of Arbitration, 38 Cours Albert 1er, 75008 Paris, France: ICC Publication No. 826, ISBN 92–842–1335–5, copyright 2003. Reprinted with permission of the International Chamber of Commerce.

2

The present Rules shall also apply where an authority within ICC[1] is requested to act as appointing authority in accordance with the parties' agreement or is designated by the Secretary–General of the Permanent Court of Arbitration in The Hague. References to ICC in these Rules include such other authorities.

3

Where ICC is empowered or requested to act as appointing authority under Articles 1(1) or 1(2), the function shall be carried out by the ICC International Court of Arbitration (the 'Court'). To fulfil this role, the Court shall create a special committee (the 'Special Committee') consisting of the Chairman of the Court and two other members of the Court. The Chairman may designate a Vice–Chairman of the Court to replace him at a meeting of the Special Committee. Unless otherwise provided, the Special Committee shall carry out the functions of the Court under these Rules. The Special Committee's decisions shall be taken unanimously. In the event that a unanimous decision cannot be reached, the matter shall be referred to the Court sitting as a special plenary session (the 'Special Plenary Session'). When making decisions upon challenges pursuant to these Rules, the Court shall do so at a Special Plenary Session.

Article 2
Request for ICC to Act as Appointing Authority

1

In cases referred to in Article 1 of these Rules, a party wishing ICC to act as appointing authority shall submit a request (the 'Request') to the Secretariat of the Court (the 'Secretariat'), which shall notify the other party or parties of the receipt of the Request and the date of such receipt.

2

The Request shall contain all the information that the requesting party deems appropriate to allow the Court to make the requested appointment.

3

The Request and all documents annexed thereto shall be supplied in a sufficient number of copies to provide one for each party and one for the Secretariat. When submitting its Request, the requesting party shall make the payment required by Article 6 of these Rules. Should the requesting party fail to comply with either of these requirements, the Secretariat may set a time limit for compliance. Failing compliance within the time limit, the file shall be closed without prejudice to the right of the requesting party to resubmit its Request at a later date.

1. Such as the Chairman or Secretary General of ICC or the Chairman or Secretary General of the ICC International Court of Arbitration.

Article 3
The Court Acting as Appointing Authority under the UNCITRAL Arbitration Rules

1

When acting as the appointing authority for the purpose of appointing a sole or presiding (third) arbitrator pursuant to Articles 6(2) and 7(3) of the UNCITRAL Arbitration Rules, the Court shall follow the list-procedure set forth in Article 6(3) of the UNCITRAL Arbitration Rules, unless all parties agree that the list-procedure should not be used or the Court determines in its discretion that the use of the list-procedure is not appropriate for the case.

2

When following the list-procedure, the Court shall prepare a list of at least three candidates which shall be communicated to the parties by the Secretariat. Within 15 days of receiving this list, each party may return the list to the Secretariat after deleting the name or names to which it objects and numbering the remaining names on the list in the order of its preference. After expiration of the aforementioned 15–day time limit, the Court shall appoint the sole or presiding arbitrator from among the names approved on the list returned to the Secretariat and in accordance with the order of preference indicated by the parties. If for any reason the appointment cannot be made according to this procedure, the Court may exercise its discretion in appointing the sole or presiding arbitrator.

3

In accordance with Article 6(4) of the UNCITRAL Arbitration Rules, when making the appointment, the Court shall have regard to such considerations as are likely to secure the appointment of an independent and impartial arbitrator and shall take into account as well the advisability of appointing an arbitrator of a nationality other than that of the parties.

4

When appointing an arbitrator on behalf of a party in default under Article 7 of the UNCITRAL Arbitration Rules, the Court may exercise its discretion in making the appointment.

5

When making decisions upon challenges submitted by any party under Article 12 of the UNCITRAL Arbitration Rules, the Court will do so at a Special Plenary Session after the Secretariat has afforded an opportunity for the arbitrator concerned, the other party or parties and any other members of the arbitral tribunal to comment in writing within a suitable period of time. Such comments shall be communicated to the parties and to the arbitrators, before being submitted to the Court.

6

When appointing a substitute arbitrator under Articles 12(2) and 13 of the UNCITRAL Arbitration Rules, the Court shall follow the procedure set forth in the preceding paragraphs.

7

At the request of any party and pursuant to Article 39(4) of the UNCITRAL Arbitration Rules, the Court may, on a consultative basis, provide a statement concerning the fees of the arbitrators, taking into account the ICC Scale of Arbitrator's Fees for cases conducted under the ICC Rules of Arbitration.

8

At the request of any party and pursuant to Article 41(3) of the UNCITRAL Arbitration Rules, the Court may, on a consultative basis, give the arbitral tribunal any comments it deems appropriate concerning the amount of any deposit or supplementary deposit to be made under Article 41 of the UNCITRAL Arbitration Rules.

Article 4
The Court Acting as Appointing Authority in *Ad Hoc*, Non–UNCITRAL Arbitration Proceedings

1

Where the parties have agreed or where an applicable text provides that ICC shall act as appointing authority in ad hoc, non-UNCITRAL (hereafter, non-UNCITRAL) arbitral proceedings, the Court, exercising its discretion within the limits fixed by the parties in their agreement(s), or the limits contained in the applicable text, shall appoint an arbitrator independent of the parties involved in the arbitration.

2

The parties to non-UNCITRAL arbitral proceedings may agree that the Court, as appointing authority, shall have the power to decide upon a challenge made by any of the parties against any member of the arbitral tribunal. A challenge shall be made by submitting to the Secretariat a written statement specifying the facts and circumstances on which the challenge is based.

3

The Court shall decide on the challenge at a Special Plenary Session after the Secretariat has afforded an opportunity for the arbitrator concerned, the other party or parties and any other members of the arbitral tribunal to comment in writing within a suitable period of time. Such comments shall be communicated to the parties and to the arbitrators, before being submitted to the Court.

Article 5
General Provisions

1

When requested to act under these Rules, the Court shall proceed if it is satisfied that an agreement authorizing it to act as appointing authority may exist.

2

If so empowered by an arbitration clause, a subsequent agreement of the parties, or otherwise, the Court shall consider providing services, besides those specifically indicated in these Rules, in accordance with the parties' agreement.

3

Before appointment in cases provided for under Articles 3 and 4 of these Rules, a prospective arbitrator shall sign a declaration of acceptance and a statement of independence and disclose in writing to the Secretariat any facts or circumstances which might be of such a nature as to call into question the arbitrator's independence in the eyes of the parties.

4

The reasons for the decisions taken by the Court under these Rules shall not be communicated.

5

Neither the Court and its members, nor the International Chamber of Commerce and its employees shall be liable to any person for any act or omission in connection with the activities performed under these Rules.

Article 6
ICC Costs for Services Rendered as Appointing Authority

1

Each Request submitted to the Secretariat must be accompanied by payment to ICC of a non-refundable sum, the amount of which shall be determined according to the Appendix to these Rules.

2

For services provided pursuant to Article 5(2) of these Rules, the Court may fix administrative expenses commensurate with these services, which shall be paid by the requesting party or parties.

APPENDIX
ICC COSTS FOR SERVICES RENDERED AS APPOINTING AUTHORITY

Article 1

The non-refundable amount referred to in Article 6(1) of these Rules is US$2,500. The non-refundable amount is payable by the party or parties submitting the Request. No Request shall be processed unless accompanied by the requisite payment.

Article 2

The administrative expenses of ICC for the services rendered pursuant to Article 5(2) of these Rules shall be fixed at ICC's discretion depending on the tasks carried out by ICC. Such administrative expenses shall be commensurate with said services and shall not exceed the maximum sum of US$10,000.

C. AMERICAN ARBITRATION ASSOCIATION INTERNATIONAL RULES OF 2008*

International Dispute Resolution Procedures

Amended and Effective 1 March, 2008

Introduction

The international business community uses arbitration to resolve commercial disputes arising in the global marketplace. Supportive laws are in place. The New York Convention of 1958 has been widely adopted, providing a favorable legislative climate that enables the enforcement of arbitration clauses. International commercial arbitration awards are recognized by national courts in most parts of the world, even more than foreign court judgments. A key component to the successful resolution of an international commercial dispute is the role played by the administrative institution. The International Centre for Dispute Resolution ® (ICDR) is the international division of the American Arbitration Association (AAA) charged with the exclusive administration of all of the AAA's international matters. The ICDR's experience, international expertise and multilingual staff forms an integral part of the dispute resolution process. The ICDR's international system is premised on its ability to move the matter forward, facilitate communications, ensure that qualified arbitrators and mediators are appointed, control costs, understand cultural sensitivities, resolve procedural impasses and properly interpret and apply its International Mediation and Arbitration Rules. Additionally, the ICDR has many cooperative agreements with arbitral institutions around the world for facilitating the administration of its international cases.

International Arbitration

As the ICDR is a division of the AAA, parties can arbitrate future disputes under these rules by inserting either of the following clauses into their contracts:

"Any controversy or claim arising out of or relating to this contract, or the breach thereof, shall be determined by arbitration administered by

* Reprinted by permission of the American Arbitration Association.

the International Centre for Dispute Resolution in accordance with its International Arbitration Rules."

or

"Any controversy or claim arising out of or relating to this contract, or the breach thereof, shall be determined by arbitration administered by the American Arbitration Association in accordance with its International Arbitration Rules."

The parties may wish to consider adding:

(a) "The number of arbitrators shall be (one or three)";

(b) "The place of arbitration shall be (city and/or country)"; or

(c) "The language(s) of the arbitration shall be ______."

Parties are encouraged, when writing their contracts or when a dispute arises, to request a conference, in person or by telephone, with the ICDR, to discuss an appropriate method for selection of arbitrators or any other matter that might facilitate efficient arbitration of the dispute.

Under these Rules, the parties are free to adopt any mutually agreeable procedure for appointing arbitrators, or may designate arbitrators upon whom they agree. Parties can reach agreements concerning appointing arbitrators either when writing their contracts or after a dispute has arisen. This flexible procedure permits parties to utilize whatever method they consider best suits their needs. For example, parties may choose to have a sole arbitrator or a tribunal of three or more. They may agree that arbitrators shall be appointed by the ICDR, or that each side shall designate one arbitrator and those two shall name a third, with the ICDR making appointments if the tribunal is not promptly formed by that procedure. Parties may mutually request the ICDR to submit to them a list of arbitrators from which each can delete names not acceptable to it, or the parties may instruct the ICDR to appoint arbitrators without the submission of lists, or may leave that matter to the sole discretion of the ICDR. Parties also may agree on a variety of other methods for establishing the tribunal. In any event, if parties are unable to agree on a procedure for appointing arbitrators or on the designation of arbitrators, the ICDR, after inviting consultation by the parties, will appoint the arbitrators. The Rules thus provide for the fullest exercise of party autonomy, while assuring that the ICDR is available to act if the parties cannot reach mutual agreement. By providing for arbitration under these Rules, parties can avoid the uncertainty of having to petition a local court to resolve procedural impasses. These Rules, as administered by the IDCR, are intended to provide prompt, effective and economical arbitration services to the global business community.

Whenever a singular term is used in the Rules, such as "party," "claimant" or "arbitrator," that term shall include the plural if there is more than one such entity.

Parties filing an international case with the International Centre for Dispute Resolution, or the American Arbitration Association, may file online via AAAWebFile ® at www.adr.org. or by directly contacting the ICDR in New York, Dublin or Singapore. Parties can also file a case at any one of the AAA's regional offices.

Further information about these Rules can be secured by contacting the International Centre for Dispute Resolution at 212.484.4181 or by visiting the ICDR's Web site at www.icdr.org.

INTERNATIONAL ARBITRATION RULES

Article 1

a. Where parties have agreed in writing to arbitrate disputes under these International Arbitration Rules or have provided for arbitration of an international dispute by the International Centre for Dispute Resolution or the American Arbitration Association without designating particular Rules, the arbitration shall take place in accordance with these Rules, as in effect at the date of commencement of the arbitration, subject to whatever modifications the parties may adopt in writing.

b. These Rules govern the arbitration, except that, where any such rule is in conflict with any provision of the law applicable to the arbitration from which the parties cannot derogate, that provision shall prevail.

c. These Rules specify the duties and responsibilities of the administrator, the International Centre for Dispute Resolution, a division of the American Arbitration Association. The administrator may provide services through its Centre, located in New York, or through the facilities of arbitral institutions with which it has agreements of cooperation.

Commencing the Arbitration

Notice of Arbitration and Statement of Claim

Article 2

1. The party initiating arbitration ("claimant") shall give written notice of arbitration to the administrator and at the same time to the party against whom a claim is being made ("respondent").

2. Arbitral proceedings shall be deemed to commence on the date on which the administrator receives the notice of arbitration.

3. The notice of arbitration shall contain a statement of claim including the following:

(a) a demand that the dispute be referred to arbitration;

(b) the names, addresses and telephone numbers of the parties;

(c) a reference to the arbitration clause or agreement that is invoked;

(d) a reference to any contract out of or in relation to which the dispute arises;

(e) a description of the claim and an indication of the facts supporting it;

(f) the relief or remedy sought and the amount claimed; and

(g) may include proposals as to the means of designating and the number of arbitrators, the place of arbitration and the language(s) of the arbitration.

4. Upon receipt of the notice of arbitration, the administrator shall communicate with all parties with respect to the arbitration and shall acknowledge the commencement of the arbitration.

Statement of Defense and Counterclaim

Article 3

1. Within 30 days after the commencement of the arbitration, a respondent shall submit a written statement of defense, responding to the issues raised in the notice of arbitration, to the claimant and any other parties, and to the administrator.

2. At the time a respondent submits its statement of defense, a respondent may make counterclaims or assert setoffs as to any claim covered by the agreement to arbitrate, as to which the claimant shall within 30 days submit a written statement of defense to the respondent and any other parties and to the administrator.

3. A respondent shall respond to the administrator, the claimant and other parties within 30 days after the commencement of the arbitration as to any proposals the claimant may have made as to the number of arbitrators, the place of the arbitration or the language(s) of the arbitration, except to the extent that the parties have previously agreed as to these matters.

4. The arbitral tribunal, or the administrator if the arbitral tribunal has not yet been formed, may extend any of the time limits established in this article if it considers such an extension justified.

Amendments to Claims

Article 4

During the arbitral proceedings, any party may amend or supplement its claim, counterclaim or defense, unless the tribunal considers it inappropriate to allow such amendment or supplement because of the party's delay in making it, prejudice to the other parties or any other circumstances. A party may not amend or supplement a claim or counterclaim if the amendment or supplement would fall outside the scope of the agreement to arbitrate.

The Tribunal

Number of Arbitrators

Article 5

If the parties have not agreed on the number of arbitrators, one arbitrator shall be appointed unless the administrator determines in its discretion that three arbitrators are appropriate because of the large size, complexity or other circumstances of the case.

Appointment of Arbitrators

Article 6

1. The parties may mutually agree upon any procedure for appointing arbitrators and shall inform the administrator as to such procedure.

2. The parties may mutually designate arbitrators, with or without the assistance of the administrator. When such designations are made, the parties shall notify the administrator so that notice of the appointment can be communicated to the arbitrators, together with a copy of these Rules.

3. If within 45 days after the commencement of the arbitration, all of the parties have not mutually agreed on a procedure for appointing the arbitrator(s) or have not mutually agreed on the designation of the arbitrator(s), the administrator shall, at the written request of any party, appoint the arbitrator(s) and designate the presiding arbitrator. If all of the parties have mutually agreed upon a procedure for appointing the arbitrator(s), but all appointments have not been made within the time limits provided in that procedure, the administrator shall, at the written request of any party, perform all functions provided for in that procedure that remain to be performed.

4. In making such appointments, the administrator, after inviting consultation with the parties, shall endeavor to select suitable arbitrators. At the request of any party or on its own initiative, the administrator may appoint nationals of a country other than that of any of the parties.

5. Unless the parties have agreed otherwise no later than 45 days after the commencement of the arbitration, if the notice of arbitration names two or more claimants or two or more respondents, the administrator shall appoint all the arbitrators.

Impartiality and Independence of Arbitrators

Article 7

1. Arbitrators acting under these Rules shall be impartial and independent. Prior to accepting appointment, a prospective arbitrator shall disclose to the administrator any circumstance likely to give rise to justifiable doubts as to the arbitrator's impartiality or independence. If, at any stage during the arbitration, new circumstances arise that may give rise to such doubts, an arbitrator shall promptly disclose such circumstances to the parties and to the administrator. Upon receipt of such information from an arbitrator or a party, the administrator shall communicate it to the other parties and to the tribunal.

2. No party or anyone acting on its behalf shall have any ex parte communication relating to the case with any arbitrator, or with any candidate for appointment as party-appointed arbitrator except to advise

the candidate of the general nature of the controversy and of the anticipated proceedings and to discuss the candidate's qualifications, availability or independence in relation to the parties, or to discuss the suitability of candidates for selection as a third arbitrator where the parties or party designated arbitrators are to participate in that selection. No party or anyone acting on its behalf shall have any ex parte communication relating to the case with any candidate for presiding arbitrator.

Challenge of Arbitrators

Article 8

1. A party may challenge any arbitrator whenever circumstances exist that give rise to justifiable doubts as to the arbitrator's impartiality or independence. A party wishing to challenge an arbitrator shall send notice of the challenge to the administrator within 15 days after being notified of the appointment of the arbitrator or within 15 days after the circumstances giving rise to the challenge become known to that party.

2. The challenge shall state in writing the reasons for the challenge.

3. Upon receipt of such a challenge, the administrator shall notify the other parties of the challenge. When an arbitrator has been challenged by one party, the other party or parties may agree to the acceptance of the challenge and, if there is agreement, the arbitrator shall withdraw. The challenged arbitrator may also withdraw from office in the absence of such agreement. In neither case does withdrawal imply acceptance of the validity of the grounds for the challenge.

Article 9

If the other party or parties do not agree to the challenge or the challenged arbitrator does not withdraw, the administrator in its sole discretion shall make the decision on the challenge.

Replacement of an Arbitrator

Article 10

If an arbitrator withdraws after a challenge, or the administrator sustains the challenge, or the administrator determines that there are sufficient reasons to accept the resignation of an arbitrator, or an arbitrator dies, a substitute arbitrator shall be appointed pursuant to the provisions of Article 6, unless the parties otherwise agree.

Article 11

1. If an arbitrator on a three-person tribunal fails to participate in the arbitration for reasons other than those identified in Article 10, the two other arbitrators shall have the power in their sole discretion to continue the arbitration and to make any decision, ruling or award, notwithstanding the failure of the third arbitrator to participate. In determining whether to continue the arbitration or to render any decision, ruling or award without the participation of an arbitrator, the two other

arbitrators shall take into account the stage of the arbitration, the reason, if any, expressed by the third arbitrator for such nonparticipation, and such other matters as they consider appropriate in the circumstances of the case. In the event that the two other arbitrators determine not to continue the arbitration without the participation of the third arbitrator, the administrator on proof satisfactory to it shall declare the office vacant, and a substitute arbitrator shall be appointed pursuant to the provisions of Article 6, unless the parties otherwise agree.

2. If a substitute arbitrator is appointed under either Article 10 or Article 11, the tribunal shall determine at its sole discretion whether all or part of any prior hearings shall be repeated.

General Conditions

Representation

Article 12

Any party may be represented in the arbitration. The names, addresses and telephone numbers of representatives shall be communicated in writing to the other parties and to the administrator. Once the tribunal has been established, the parties or their representatives may communicate in writing directly with the tribunal.

Place of Arbitration

Article 13

1. If the parties disagree as to the place of arbitration, the administrator may initially determine the place of arbitration, subject to the power of the tribunal to determine finally the place of arbitration within 60 days after its constitution. All such determinations shall be made having regard for the contentions of the parties and the circumstances of the arbitration.

2. The tribunal may hold conferences or hear witnesses or inspect property or documents at any place it deems appropriate. The parties shall be given sufficient written notice to enable them to be present at any such proceedings.

Language

Article 14

If the parties have not agreed otherwise, the language(s) of the arbitration shall be that of the documents containing the arbitration agreement, subject to the power of the tribunal to determine otherwise based upon the contentions of the parties and the circumstances of the arbitration. The tribunal may order that any documents delivered in another language shall be accompanied by a translation into the language(s) of the arbitration.

Pleas as to Jurisdiction

Article 15

1. The tribunal shall have the power to rule on its own jurisdiction, including any objections with respect to the existence, scope or validity of the arbitration agreement.

2. The tribunal shall have the power to determine the existence or validity of a contract of which an arbitration clause forms a part. Such an arbitration clause shall be treated as an agreement independent of the other terms of the contract. A decision by the tribunal that the contract is null and void shall not for that reason alone render invalid the arbitration clause.

3. A party must object to the jurisdiction of the tribunal or to the arbitrability of a claim or counterclaim no later than the filing of the statement of defense, as provided in Article 3, to the claim or counterclaim that gives rise to the objection. The tribunal may rule on such objections as a preliminary matter or as part of the final award.

Conduct of the Arbitration

Article 16

1. Subject to these Rules, the tribunal may conduct the arbitration in whatever manner it considers appropriate, provided that the parties are treated with equality and that each party has the right to be heard and is given a fair opportunity to present its case.

2. The tribunal, exercising its discretion, shall conduct the proceedings with a view to expediting the resolution of the dispute. It may conduct a preparatory conference with the parties for the purpose of organizing, scheduling and agreeing to procedures to expedite the subsequent proceedings.

3. The tribunal may in its discretion direct the order of proof, bifurcate proceedings, exclude cumulative or irrelevant testimony or other evidence, and direct the parties to focus their presentations on issues the decision of which could dispose of all or part of the case.

4. Documents or information supplied to the tribunal by one party shall at the same time be communicated by that party to the other party or parties.

Further Written Statements

Article 17

1. The tribunal may decide whether the parties shall present any written statements in addition to statements of claims and counterclaims and statements of defense, and it shall fix the periods of time for submitting any such statements.

2. The periods of time fixed by the tribunal for the communication of such written statements should not exceed 45 days. However, the

tribunal may extend such time limits if it considers such an extension justified.

Notices

Article 18

1. Unless otherwise agreed by the parties or ordered by the tribunal, all notices, statements and written communications may be served on a party by air mail, air courier, facsimile transmission, telex, telegram or other written forms of electronic communication addressed to the party or its representative at its last known address or by personal service.

2. For the purpose of calculating a period of time under these Rules, such period shall begin to run on the day following the day when a notice, statement or written communication is received. If the last day of such period is an official holiday at the place received, the period is extended until the first business day which follows. Official holidays occurring during the running of the period of time are included in calculating the period.

Evidence

Article 19

1. Each party shall have the burden of proving the facts relied on to support its claim or defense.

2. The tribunal may order a party to deliver to the tribunal and to the other parties a summary of the documents and other evidence which that party intends to present in support of its claim, counterclaim or defense.

3. At any time during the proceedings, the tribunal may order parties to produce other documents, exhibits or other evidence it deems necessary or appropriate.

Hearings

Article 20

1. The tribunal shall give the parties at least 30 days advance notice of the date, time and place of the initial oral hearing. The tribunal shall give reasonable notice of subsequent hearings.

2. At least 15 days before the hearings, each party shall give the tribunal and the other parties the names and addresses of any witnesses it intends to present, the subject of their testimony and the languages in which such witnesses will give their testimony.

3. At the request of the tribunal or pursuant to mutual agreement of the parties, the administrator shall make arrangements for the interpretation of oral testimony or for a record of the hearing.

4. Hearings are private unless the parties agree otherwise or the law provides to the contrary. The tribunal may require any witness or wit-

nesses to retire during the testimony of other witnesses. The tribunal may determine the manner in which witnesses are examined.

5. Evidence of witnesses may also be presented in the form of written statements signed by them.

6. The tribunal shall determine the admissibility, relevance, materiality and weight of the evidence offered by any party. The tribunal shall take into account applicable principles of legal privilege, such as those involving the confidentiality of communications between a lawyer and client.

Interim Measures of Protection

Article 21

1. At the request of any party, the tribunal may take whatever interim measures it deems necessary, including injunctive relief and measures for the protection or conservation of property.

2. Such interim measures may take the form of an interim award, and the tribunal may require security for the costs of such measures.

3. A request for interim measures addressed by a party to a judicial authority shall not be deemed incompatible with the agreement to arbitrate or a waiver of the right to arbitrate.

4. The tribunal may in its discretion apportion costs associated with applications for interim relief in any interim award or in the final award.

Experts

Article 22

1. The tribunal may appoint one or more independent experts to report to it, in writing, on specific issues designated by the tribunal and communicated to the parties.

2. The parties shall provide such an expert with any relevant information or produce for inspection any relevant documents or goods that the expert may require. Any dispute between a party and the expert as to the relevance of the requested information or goods shall be referred to the tribunal for decision.

3. Upon receipt of an expert's report, the tribunal shall send a copy of the report to all parties and shall give the parties an opportunity to express, in writing, their opinion on the report. A party may examine any document on which the expert has relied in such a report.

4. At the request of any party, the tribunal shall give the parties an opportunity to question the expert at a hearing. At this hearing, parties may present expert witnesses to testify on the points at issue.

Default

Article 23

1. If a party fails to file a statement of defense within the time established by the tribunal without showing sufficient cause for such

failure, as determined by the tribunal, the tribunal may proceed with the arbitration.

2. If a party, duly notified under these Rules, fails to appear at a hearing without showing sufficient cause for such failure, as determined by the tribunal, the tribunal may proceed with the arbitration.

3. If a party, duly invited to produce evidence or take any other steps in the proceedings, fails to do so within the time established by the tribunal without showing sufficient cause for such failure, as determined by the tribunal, the tribunal may make the award on the evidence before it.

Closure of Hearing

Article 24

1. After asking the parties if they have any further testimony or evidentiary submissions and upon receiving negative replies or if satisfied that the record is complete, the tribunal may declare the hearings closed.

2. The tribunal in its discretion, on its own motion or upon application of a party, may reopen the hearings at any time before the award is made.

Waiver of Rules

Article 25

A party who knows that any provision of the Rules or requirement under the Rules has not been complied with, but proceeds with the arbitration without promptly stating an objection in writing thereto, shall be deemed to have waived the right to object.

Awards, Decisions and Rulings

Article 26

1. When there is more than one arbitrator, any award, decision or ruling of the arbitral tribunal shall be made by a majority of the arbitrators. If any arbitrator fails to sign the award, it shall be accompanied by a statement of the reason for the absence of such signature.

2. When the parties or the tribunal so authorize, the presiding arbitrator may make decisions or rulings on questions of procedure, subject to revision by the tribunal.

Form and Effect of the Award

Article 27

1. Awards shall be made in writing, promptly by the tribunal, and shall be final and binding on the parties. The parties undertake to carry out any such award without delay.

2. The tribunal shall state the reasons upon which the award is based, unless the parties have agreed that no reasons need be given.

3. The award shall contain the date and the place where the award was made, which shall be the place designated pursuant to Article 13.

4. An award may be made public only with the consent of all parties or as required by law.

5. Copies of the award shall be communicated to the parties by the administrator.

6. If the arbitration law of the country where the award is made requires the award to be filed or registered, the tribunal shall comply with such requirement.

7. In addition to making a final award, the tribunal may make interim, interlocutory or partial orders and awards.

8. Unless otherwise agreed by the parties, the administrator may publish or otherwise make publicly available selected awards, decisions and rulings that have been edited to conceal the names of the parties and other identifying details or that have been made publicly available in the course of enforcement or otherwise.

Applicable Laws and Remedies

Article 28

1. The tribunal shall apply the substantive law(s) or Rules of law designated by the parties as applicable to the dispute. Failing such a designation by the parties, the tribunal shall apply such law(s) or Rules of law as it determines to be appropriate.

2. In arbitrations involving the application of contracts, the tribunal shall decide in accordance with the terms of the contract and shall take into account usages of the trade applicable to the contract.

3. The tribunal shall not decide as amiable compositeur or ex aequo et bono unless the parties have expressly authorized it to do so.

4. A monetary award shall be in the currency or currencies of the contract unless the tribunal considers another currency more appropriate, and the tribunal may award such pre-award and post-award interest, simple or compound, as it considers appropriate, taking into consideration the contract and applicable law.

5. Unless the parties agree otherwise, the parties expressly waive and forego any right to punitive, exemplary or similar damages unless a statute requires that compensatory damages be increased in a specified manner. This provision shall not apply to any award of arbitration costs to a party to compensate for dilatory or bad faith conduct in the arbitration.

Settlement or Other Reasons for Termination

Article 29

1. If the parties settle the dispute before an award is made, the tribunal shall terminate the arbitration and, if requested by all parties,

may record the settlement in the form of an award on agreed terms. The tribunal is not obliged to give reasons for such an award.

2. If the continuation of the proceedings becomes unnecessary or impossible for any other reason, the tribunal shall inform the parties of its intention to terminate the proceedings. The tribunal shall thereafter issue an order terminating the arbitration, unless a party raises justifiable grounds for objection.

Interpretation or Correction of the Award

Article 30

1. Within 30 days after the receipt of an award, any party, with notice to the other parties, may request the tribunal to interpret the award or correct any clerical, typographical or computation errors or make an additional award as to claims presented but omitted from the award.

2. If the tribunal considers such a request justified, after considering the contentions of the parties, it shall comply with such a request within 30 days after the request.

Costs

Article 31

The tribunal shall fix the costs of arbitration in its award. The tribunal may apportion such costs among the parties if it determines that such apportionment is reasonable, taking into account the circumstances of the case.

Such costs may include:

(a) the fees and expenses of the arbitrators;

(b) the costs of assistance required by the tribunal, including its experts;

(c) the fees and expenses of the administrator;

(d) the reasonable costs for legal representation of a successful party; and

(e) any such costs incurred in connection with an application for interim or emergency relief pursuant to Article 21.

Compensation of Arbitrators

Article 32

Arbitrators shall be compensated based upon their amount of service, taking into account their stated rate of compensation and the size and complexity of the case. The administrator shall arrange an appropriate daily or hourly rate, based on such considerations, with the parties and with each of the arbitrators as soon as practicable after the commencement of the arbitration. If the parties fail to agree on the terms of compensation, the administrator shall establish an appropriate rate and communicate it in writing to the parties.

Deposit of Costs

Article 33

1. When a party files claims, the administrator may request the filing party to deposit appropriate amounts as an advance for the costs referred to in Article 31, paragraphs (a), (b) and (c).

2. During the course of the arbitral proceedings, the tribunal may request supplementary deposits from the parties.

3. If the deposits requested are not paid in full within 30 days after the receipt of the request, the administrator shall so inform the parties, in order that one or the other of them may make the required payment. If such payments are not made, the tribunal may order the suspension or termination of the proceedings.

4. After the award has been made, the administrator shall render an accounting to the parties of the deposits received and return any unexpended balance to the parties.

Confidentiality

Article 34

Confidential information disclosed during the proceedings by the parties or by witnesses shall not be divulged by an arbitrator or by the administrator. Except as provided in Article 27, unless otherwise agreed by the parties, or required by applicable law, the members of the tribunal and the administrator shall keep confidential all matters relating to the arbitration or the award.

Exclusion of Liability

Article 35

The members of the tribunal and the administrator shall not be liable to any party for any act or omission in connection with any arbitration conducted under these Rules, except that they may be liable for the consequences of conscious and deliberate wrongdoing.

Interpretation of Rules

Article 36

The tribunal shall interpret and apply these Rules insofar as they relate to its powers and duties. The administrator shall interpret and apply all other Rules.

Emergency Measures of Protection

Article 37

1. Unless the parties agree otherwise, the provisions of this Article 37 shall apply to arbitrations conducted under arbitration clauses or agreements entered on or after May 1, 2006.

2. A party in need of emergency relief prior to the constitution of the tribunal shall notify the administrator and all other parties in writing of the nature of the relief sought and the reasons why such relief is required on an emergency basis. The application shall also set forth the reasons why the party is entitled to such relief. Such notice may be given by e-mail, facsimile transmission or other reliable means, but must include a statement certifying that all other parties have been notified or an explanation of the steps taken in good faith to notify other parties.

3. Within one business day of receipt of notice as provided in paragraph 2, the administrator shall appoint a single emergency arbitrator from a special panel of emergency arbitrators designated to rule on emergency applications. Prior to accepting appointment, a prospective emergency arbitrator shall disclose to the administrator any circumstance likely to give rise to justifiable doubts to the arbitrator's impartiality or independence. Any challenge to the appointment of the emergency arbitrator must be made within one business day of the communication by the administrator to the parties of the appointment of the emergency arbitrator and the circumstances disclosed.

4. The emergency arbitrator shall as soon as possible, but in any event within two business days of appointment, establish a schedule for consideration of the application for emergency relief. Such schedule shall provide a reasonable opportunity to all parties to be heard, but may provide for proceedings by telephone conference or on written submissions as alternatives to a formal hearing. The emergency arbitrator shall have the authority vested in the tribunal under Article 15, including the authority to rule on her/his own jurisdiction, and shall resolve any disputes over the applicability of this Article 37.

5. The emergency arbitrator shall have the power to order or award any interim or conservancy measure the emergency arbitrator deems necessary, including injunctive relief and measures for the protection or conservation of property. Any such measure may take the form of an interim award or of an order. The emergency arbitrator shall give reasons in either case. The emergency arbitrator may modify or vacate the interim award or order for good cause shown.

6. The emergency arbitrator shall have no further power to act after the tribunal is constituted. Once the tribunal has been constituted, the tribunal may reconsider, modify or vacate the interim award or order of emergency relief issued by the emergency arbitrator. The emergency arbitrator may not serve as a member of the tribunal unless the parties agree otherwise.

7. Any interim award or order of emergency relief may be conditioned on provision by the party seeking such relief of appropriate security.

8. A request for interim measures addressed by a party to a judicial authority shall not be deemed incompatible with this Article 37 or with the agreement to arbitrate or a waiver of the right to arbitrate. If the administrator is directed by a judicial authority to nominate a special master to consider and report on an application for emergency relief, the administrator shall proceed as in Paragraph 2 of this article and the references to the emergency arbitrator shall be read to mean the special master, except that the special master shall issue a report rather than an interim award.

9. The costs associated with applications for emergency relief shall initially be apportioned by the emergency arbitrator or special master, subject to the power of the tribunal to determine finally the apportionment of such costs.

ADMINISTRATIVE FEES

The administrative fees of the ICDR are based on the amount of the claim or counterclaim. Arbitrator compensation is not included in this schedule. Unless the parties agree otherwise, arbitrator compensation and administrative fees are subject to allocation by the arbitrator in the award.

Fees

An initial filing fee is payable in full by a filing party when a claim, counterclaim or additional claim is filed. A case service fee will be incurred for all cases that proceed to their first hearing. This fee will be payable in advance at the time that the first hearing is scheduled. This fee will be refunded at the conclusion of the case if no hearings have occurred.

However, if the administrator is not notified at least 24 hours before the time of the scheduled hearing, the case service fee will remain due and will not be refunded.

These fees will be billed in accordance with the following schedule:

Amount of Claim	Initial Filing Fee	Case Service Fee
Above $0 to $10,000	$ 750	$ 200
Above $10,000 to $75,000	$ 950	$ 300
Above $75,000 to $150,000	$ 1,800	$ 750
Above $150,000 to $300,000	$ 2,750	$1,250
Above $300,000 to $500,000	$ 4,250	$1,750
Above $500,000 to $1,000,000	$ 6,000	$2,500
Above $1,000,000 to $5,000,000	$ 8,000	$3,250
Above $5,000,000 to $10,000,000	$10,000	$4,000
Above $10,000,000	Base fee of 12,500 plus .01% of the amount of claim above $10 million	$6,000

Nonmonetary Claims*	$ 3,250	$1,250
	Filing fees capped at $ 65,000	

* This fee is applicable only when a claim or counterclaim is not for a monetary amount. Where a monetary claim amount is not known, parties will be required to state a range of claims or be subject to the highest possible filing fee.

Fees are subject to increase if the amount of a claim or counterclaim is modified after the initial filing date. Fees are subject to decrease if the amount of a claim or counterclaim is modified before the first hearing.

The minimum fees for any case having three or more arbitrators are $2,750 for the filing fee, plus a $1,250 case service fee.

Parties on cases held in abeyance for one year by agreement, will be assessed an annual abeyance fee of $300. If a party refuses to pay the assessed fee, the other party or parties may pay the entire fee on behalf of all parties, otherwise the matter will be closed.

Refund Schedule

The ICDR offers a refund schedule on filing fees. For cases with claims up to $75,000, a minimum filing fee of $300 will not be refunded. For all other cases, a minimum fee of $500 will not be refunded. Subject to the minimum fee requirements, refunds will be calculated as follows:

'100% of the filing fee, above the minimum fee, will be refunded if the case is settled or withdrawn within five calendar days of filing.

'50% of the filing fee will be refunded if the case is settled or withdrawn between six and 30 calendar days of filing. Where the filing fee is $500, the refund will be $200.

'25% of the filing fee will be refunded if the case is settled or withdrawn between 31 and 60 calendar days of filing. No refund will be made once an arbitrator has been appointed (this includes one arbitrator on a three-arbitrator panel). No refunds will be granted on awarded cases.

Note: the date of receipt of the demand for arbitration with the ICDR will be used to calculate refunds of filing fees for both claims and counterclaims.

Suspension for Nonpayment

If arbitrator compensation or administrative charges have not been paid in full, the administrator may so inform the parties in order that one of them may advance the required payment. If such payments are not made, the tribunal may order the suspension or termination of the proceedings. If no arbitrator has yet been appointed, the ICDR may suspend the proceedings.

Hearing Room Rental

The fees described above do not cover the rental of hearing rooms, which are available on a rental basis. Check with the ICDR for availability and rates.

D. ARBITRATION RULES OF THE LONDON COURT OF INTERNATIONAL ARBITRATION OF 1998[2]

THE LCIA RULES

(Adopted to take effect for arbitrations commencing on or after 1 January 1998)

Where any agreement, submission or reference provides in writing and in whatsoever manner for arbitration under the rules of the LCIA or by the Court of the LCIA ("the LCIA Court"), the parties shall be taken to have agreed in writing that the arbitration shall be conducted in accordance with the following rules ("the Rules") or such amended rules as the LCIA may have adopted hereafter to take effect before the commencement of the arbitration. The Rules include the Schedule of Costs in effect at the commencement of the arbitration, as separately amended from time to time by the LCIA Court.

Article 1

The Request for Arbitration

1.1 Any party wishing to commence an arbitration under these Rules ("the Claimant") shall send to the Registrar of the LCIA Court ("the Registrar") a written request for arbitration ("the Request"), containing or accompanied by:

(a) the names, addresses, telephone, facsimile, telex and e-mail numbers (if known) of the parties to the arbitration and of their legal representatives;

(b) a copy of the written arbitration clause or separate written arbitration agreement invoked by the Claimant ("the Arbitration Agreement"), together with a copy of the contractual documentation in which the arbitration clause is contained or in respect of which the arbitration arises;

(c) a brief statement describing the nature and circumstances of the dispute, and specifying the claims advanced by the Claimant against another party to the arbitration ("the Respondent");

(d) a statement of any matters (such as the seat or language(s) of the arbitration, or the number of arbitrators, or their qualifications or identities) on which the parties have already agreed in writing for the arbitration or in respect of which the Claimant wishes to make a proposal;

(e) if the Arbitration Agreement calls for party nomination of arbitrators, the name, address, telephone, facsimile, telex and e-mail numbers (if known) of the Claimant's nominee;

---

2. The LCIA Rules can be found at the LCIA Website at http://www.lcia-arbitration.com/ Reprinted by permission of the LCIA.

(f) the fee prescribed in the Schedule of Costs (without which the Request shall be treated as not having been received by the Registrar and the arbitration as not having been commenced);

(g) confirmation to the Registrar that copies of the Request (including all accompanying documents) have been or are being served simultaneously on all other parties to the arbitration by one or more means of service to be identified in such confirmation.

1.2 The date of receipt by the Registrar of the Request shall be treated as the date on which the arbitration has commenced for all purposes. The Request (including all accompanying documents) should be submitted to the Registrar in two copies where a sole arbitrator should be appointed, or, if the parties have agreed or the Claimant considers that three arbitrators should be appointed, in four copies.

Article 2
The Response

2.1 Within 30 days of service of the Request on the Respondent, (or such lesser period fixed by the LCIA Court), the Respondent shall send to the Registrar a written response to the Request ("the Response"), containing or accompanied by:

(a) confirmation or denial of all or part of the claims advanced by the Claimant in the Request;

(b) a brief statement describing the nature and circumstances of any counterclaims advanced by the Respondent against the Claimant;

(c) comment in response to any statements contained in the Request, as called for under Article 1.1(d), on matters relating to the conduct of the arbitration;

(d) if the Arbitration Agreement calls for party nomination of arbitrators, the name, address, telephone, facsimile, telex and e-mail numbers (if known) of the Respondent's nominee; and

(e) confirmation to the Registrar that copies of the Response (including all accompanying documents) have been or are being served simultaneously on all other parties to the arbitration by one or more means of service to be identified in such confirmation.

2.2 The Response (including all accompanying documents) should be submitted to the Registrar in two copies, or if the parties have agreed or the Respondent considers that three arbitrators should be appointed, in four copies.

2.3 Failure to send a Response shall not preclude the Respondent from denying any claim or from advancing a counterclaim in the arbitration. However, if the Arbitration Agreement calls for party nomination of arbitrators, failure to send a Response or to nominate an arbitrator within time or at all shall constitute an irrevocable waiver of that party's opportunity to nominate an arbitrator.

Article 3

The LCIA Court and Registrar

3.1 The functions of the LCIA Court under these Rules shall be performed in its name by the President or a Vice–President of the LCIA Court or by a division of three or five members of the LCIA Court appointed by the President or a Vice–President of the LCIA Court, as determined by the President.

3.2 The functions of the Registrar under these Rules shall be performed by the Registrar or any deputy Registrar of the LCIA Court under the supervision of the LCIA Court.

3.3 All communications from any party or arbitrator to the LCIA Court shall be addressed to the Registrar.

Article 4

Notices and Periods of Time

4.1 Any notice or other communication that may be or is required to be given by a party under these Rules shall be in writing and shall be delivered by registered postal or courier service or transmitted by facsimile, telex, e-mail or any other means of telecommunication that provide a record of its transmission.

4.2 A party's last-known residence or place of business during the arbitration shall be a valid address for the purpose of any notice or other communication in the absence of any notification of a change to such address by that party to the other parties, the Arbitral Tribunal and the Registrar.

4.3 For the purpose of determining the date of commencement of a time limit, a notice or other communication shall be treated as having been received on the day it is delivered or, in the case of telecommunications, transmitted in accordance with Articles 4.1 and 4.2.

4.4 For the purpose of determining compliance with a time limit, a notice or other communication shall be treated as having been sent, made or transmitted if it is dispatched in accordance with Articles 4.1 and 4.2 prior to or on the date of the expiration of the time-limit.

4.5 Notwithstanding the above, any notice or communication by one party may be addressed to another party in the manner agreed in writing between them or, failing such agreement, according to the practice followed in the course of their previous dealings or in whatever manner ordered by the Arbitral Tribunal.

4.6 For the purpose of calculating a period of time under these Rules, such period shall begin to run on the day following the day when a notice or other communication is received. If the last day of such period is an official holiday or a non-business day at the residence or place of business of the addressee, the period is extended until the first business day which follows. Official holidays or non-business days occurring during the running of the period of time are included in calculating that period.

4.7 The Arbitral Tribunal may at any time extend (even where the period of time has expired) or abridge any period of time prescribed under these Rules or under the Arbitration Agreement for the conduct of the arbitration, including any notice or communication to be served by one party on any other party.

Article 5

Formation of the Arbitral Tribunal

5.1 The expression "the Arbitral Tribunal" in these Rules includes a sole arbitrator or all the arbitrators where more than one. All references to an arbitrator shall include the masculine and feminine. (References to the President, Vice–President and members of the LCIA Court, the Registrar or deputy Registrar, expert, witness, party and legal representative shall be similarly understood).

5.2 All arbitrators conducting an arbitration under these Rules shall be and remain at all times impartial and independent of the parties; and none shall act in the arbitration as advocates for any party. No arbitrator, whether before or after appointment, shall advise any party on the merits or outcome of the dispute.

5.3 Before appointment by the LCIA Court, each arbitrator shall furnish to the Registrar a written résumé of his past and present professional positions; he shall agree in writing upon fee rates conforming to the Schedule of Costs; and he shall sign a declaration to the effect that there are no circumstances known to him likely to give rise to any justified doubts as to his impartiality or independence, other than any circumstances disclosed by him in the declaration. Each arbitrator shall thereby also assume a continuing duty forthwith to disclose any such circumstances to the LCIA Court, to any other members of the Arbitral Tribunal and to all the parties if such circumstances should arise after the date of such declaration and before the arbitration is concluded.

5.4 The LCIA Court shall appoint the Arbitral Tribunal as soon as practicable after receipt by the Registrar of the Response or after the expiry of 30 days following service of the Request upon the Respondent if no Response is received by the Registrar (or such lesser period fixed by the LCIA Court). The LCIA Court may proceed with the formation of the Arbitral Tribunal notwithstanding that the Request is incomplete or the Response is missing, late or incomplete. A sole arbitrator shall be appointed unless the parties have agreed in writing otherwise, or unless the LCIA Court determines that in view of all the circumstances of the case a three-member tribunal is appropriate.

5.5 The LCIA Court alone is empowered to appoint arbitrators. The LCIA Court will appoint arbitrators with due regard for any particular method or criteria of selection agreed in writing by the parties. In selecting arbitrators consideration will be given to the nature of the transaction, the nature and circumstances of the dispute, the nationality, location and languages of the parties and (if more than two) the number of parties.

5.6 In the case of a three-member Arbitral Tribunal, the chairman (who will not be a party-nominated arbitrator) shall be appointed by the LCIA Court.

Article 6

Nationality of Arbitrators

6.1 Where the parties are of different nationalities, a sole arbitrator or chairman of the Arbitral Tribunal shall not have the same nationality as any party unless the parties who are not of the same nationality as the proposed appointee all agree in writing otherwise.

6.2 The nationality of parties shall be understood to include that of controlling shareholders or interests.

6.3 For the purpose of this Article, a person who is a citizen of two or more states shall be treated as a national of each state; and citizens of the European Union shall be treated as nationals of its different Member States and shall not be treated as having the same nationality.

Article 7

Party and Other Nominations

7.1 If the parties have agreed that any arbitrator is to be appointed by one or more of them or by any third person, that agreement shall be treated as an agreement to nominate an arbitrator for all purposes. Such nominee may only be appointed by the LCIA Court as arbitrator subject to his prior compliance with Article 5.3. The LCIA Court may refuse to appoint any such nominee if it determines that he is not suitable or independent or impartial.

7.2 Where the parties have howsoever agreed that the Respondent or any third person is to nominate an arbitrator and such nomination is not made within time or at all, the LCIA Court may appoint an arbitrator notwithstanding the absence of the nomination and without regard to any late nomination. Likewise, if the Request for Arbitration does not contain a nomination by the Claimant where the parties have howsoever agreed that the Claimant or a third person is to nominate an arbitrator, the LCIA Court may appoint an arbitrator notwithstanding the absence of the nomination and without regard to any late nomination.

Article 8

Three or More Parties

8.1 Where the Arbitration Agreement entitles each party howsoever to nominate an arbitrator, the parties to the dispute number more than two and such parties have not all agreed in writing that the disputant parties represent two separate sides for the formation of the Arbitral Tribunal as Claimant and Respondent respectively, the LCIA Court shall appoint the Arbitral Tribunal without regard to any party's nomination.

8.2 In such circumstances, the Arbitration Agreement shall be treated for all purposes as a written agreement by the parties for the appointment of the Arbitral Tribunal by the LCIA Court.

Article 9
Expedited Formation

9.1 In exceptional urgency, on or after the commencement of the arbitration, any party may apply to the LCIA Court for the expedited formation of the Arbitral Tribunal, including the appointment of any replacement arbitrator under Articles 10 and 11 of these Rules.

9.2 Such an application shall be made in writing to the LCIA Court, copied to all other parties to the arbitration; and it shall set out the specific grounds for exceptional urgency in the formation of the Arbitral Tribunal.

9.3 The LCIA Court may, in its complete discretion, abridge or curtail any time-limit under these Rules for the formation of the Arbitral Tribunal, including service of the Response and of any matters or documents adjudged to be missing from the Request. The LCIA Court shall not be entitled to abridge or curtail any other time-limit.

Article 10
Revocation of Arbitrator's Appointment

10.1 If either (a) any arbitrator gives written notice of his desire to resign as arbitrator to the LCIA Court, to be copied to the parties and the other arbitrators (if any) or (b) any arbitrator dies, falls seriously ill, refuses, or becomes unable or unfit to act, either upon challenge by a party or at the request of the remaining arbitrators, the LCIA Court may revoke that arbitrator's appointment and appoint another arbitrator. The LCIA Court shall decide upon the amount of fees and expenses to be paid for the former arbitrator's services (if any) as it may consider appropriate in all the circumstances.

10.2 If any arbitrator acts in deliberate violation of the Arbitration Agreement (including these Rules) or does not act fairly and impartially as between the parties or does not conduct or participate in the arbitration proceedings with reasonable diligence, avoiding unnecessary delay or expense, that arbitrator may be considered unfit in the opinion of the LCIA Court.

10.3 An arbitrator may also be challenged by any party if circumstances exist that give rise to justifiable doubts as to his impartiality or independence. A party may challenge an arbitrator it has nominated, or in whose appointment it has participated, only for reasons of which it becomes aware after the appointment has been made.

10.4 A party who intends to challenge an arbitrator shall, within 15 days of the formation of the Arbitral Tribunal or (if later) after becoming aware of any circumstances referred to in Article 10.1, 10.2 or 10.3, send a written statement of the reasons for its challenge to the LCIA Court, the Arbitral Tribunal and all other parties. Unless the challenged arbitrator withdraws or all other parties agree to the challenge within 15 days of receipt of the written statement, the LCIA Court shall decide on the challenge.

Article 11

Nomination and Replacement of Arbitrators

11.1 In the event that the LCIA Court determines that any nominee is not suitable or independent or impartial or if an appointed arbitrator is to be replaced for any reason, the LCIA Court shall have a complete discretion to decide whether or not to follow the original nominating process.

11.2 If the LCIA Court should so decide, any opportunity given to a party to make a re-nomination shall be waived if not exercised within 15 days (or such lesser time as the LCIA Court may fix), after which the LCIA Court shall appoint the replacement arbitrator.

Article 12

Majority Power to Continue Proceedings

12.1 If any arbitrator on a three-member Arbitral Tribunal refuses or persistently fails to participate in its deliberations, the two other arbitrators shall have the power, upon their written notice of such refusal or failure to the LCIA Court, the parties and the third arbitrator, to continue the arbitration (including the making of any decision, ruling or award), notwithstanding the absence of the third arbitrator.

12.2 In determining whether to continue the arbitration, the two other arbitrators shall take into account the stage of the arbitration, any explanation made by the third arbitrator for his non-participation and such other matters as they consider appropriate in the circumstances of the case. The reasons for such determination shall be stated in any award, order or other decision made by the two arbitrators without the participation of the third arbitrator.

12.3 In the event that the two other arbitrators determine at any time not to continue the arbitration without the participation of the third arbitrator missing from their deliberations, the two arbitrators shall notify in writing the parties and the LCIA Court of such determination; and in that event, the two arbitrators or any party may refer the matter to the LCIA Court for the revocation of that third arbitrator's appointment and his replacement under Article 10.

Article 13
Communications between Parties and the Arbitral Tribunal

13.1 Until the Arbitral Tribunal is formed, all communications between parties and arbitrators shall be made through the Registrar.

13.2 Thereafter, unless and until the Arbitral Tribunal directs that communications shall take place directly between the Arbitral Tribunal and the parties (with simultaneous copies to the Registrar), all written communications between the parties and the Arbitral Tribunal shall continue to be made through the Registrar.

13.3 Where the Registrar sends any written communication to one party on behalf of the Arbitral Tribunal, he shall send a copy to each of the other parties. Where any party sends to the Registrar any communication (including Written Statements and Documents under Article 15), it shall include a copy for each arbitrator; and it shall also send copies direct to all other parties and confirm to the Registrar in writing that it has done or is doing so.

Article 14
Conduct of the Proceedings

14.1 The parties may agree on the conduct of their arbitral proceedings and they are encouraged to do so, consistent with the Arbitral Tribunal's general duties at all times:

(i) to act fairly and impartially as between all parties, giving each a reasonable opportunity of putting its case and dealing with that of its opponent; and

(ii) to adopt procedures suitable to the circumstances of the arbitration, avoiding unnecessary delay or expense, so as to provide a fair and efficient means for the final resolution of the parties' dispute.

Such agreements shall be made by the parties in writing or recorded in writing by the Arbitral Tribunal at the request of and with the authority of the parties.

14.2 Unless otherwise agreed by the parties under Article 14.1, the Arbitral Tribunal shall have the widest discretion to discharge its duties allowed under such law(s) or rules of law as the Arbitral Tribunal may determine to be applicable; and at all times the parties shall do everything necessary for the fair, efficient and expeditious conduct of the arbitration.

14.3 In the case of a three-member Arbitral Tribunal the chairman may, with the prior consent of the other two arbitrators, make procedural rulings alone.

Article 15

Submission of Written Statements and Documents

15.1 Unless the parties have agreed otherwise under Article 14.1 or the Arbitral Tribunal should determine differently, the written stage of the proceedings shall be as set out below.

15.2 Within 30 days of receipt of written notification from the Registrar of the formation of the Arbitral Tribunal, the Claimant shall send to the Registrar a Statement of Case setting out in sufficient detail the facts and any contentions of law on which it relies, together with the relief claimed against all other parties, save and insofar as such matters have not been set out in its Request.

15.3 Within 30 days of receipt of the Statement of Case or written notice from the Claimant that it elects to treat the Request as its Statement of Case, the Respondent shall send to the Registrar a Statement of Defence setting out in sufficient detail which of the facts and contentions of law in the Statement of Case or Request (as the case may be) it admits or denies, on what grounds and on what other facts and contentions of law it relies. Any counterclaims shall be submitted with the Statement of Defence in the same manner as claims are to be set out in the Statement of Case.

15.4 Within 30 days of receipt of the Statement of Defence, the Claimant shall send to the Registrar a Statement of Reply which, where there are any counterclaims, shall include a Defence to Counterclaim in the same manner as a defence is to be set out in the Statement of Defence.

15.5 If the Statement of Reply contains a Defence to Counterclaim, within 30 days of its receipt the Respondent shall send to the Registrar a Statement of Reply to Counterclaim.

15.6 All Statements referred to in this Article shall be accompanied by copies (or, if they are especially voluminous, lists) of all essential documents on which the party concerned relies and which have not previously been submitted by any party, and (where appropriate) by any relevant samples and exhibits.

15.7 As soon as practicable following receipt of the Statements specified in this Article, the Arbitral Tribunal shall proceed in such manner as has been agreed in writing by the parties or pursuant to its authority under these Rules.

15.8 If the Respondent fails to submit a Statement of Defence or the Claimant a Statement of Defence to Counterclaim, or if at any point any party fails to avail itself of the opportunity to present its case in the manner determined by Article 15.2 to 15.6 or directed by the Arbitral Tribunal, the Arbitral Tribunal may nevertheless proceed with the arbitration and make an award.

Article 16

Seat of Arbitration and Place of Hearings

16.1 The parties may agree in writing the seat (or legal place) of their arbitration. Failing such a choice, the seat of arbitration shall be London, unless and until the LCIA Court determines in view of all the circumstances, and after having given the parties an opportunity to make written comment, that another seat is more appropriate.

16.2 The Arbitral Tribunal may hold hearings, meetings and deliberations at any convenient geographical place in its discretion; and if elsewhere than the seat of the arbitration, the arbitration shall be treated as an arbitration conducted at the seat of the arbitration and any award as an award made at the seat of the arbitration for all purposes.

16.3 The law applicable to the arbitration (if any) shall be the arbitration law of the seat of arbitration, unless and to the extent that the parties have expressly agreed in writing on the application of another arbitration law and such agreement is not prohibited by the law of the arbitral seat.

Article 17

Language of Arbitration

17.1 The initial language of the arbitration shall be the language of the Arbitration Agreement, unless the parties have agreed in writing otherwise and providing always that a non-participating or defaulting party shall have no cause for complaint if communications to and from the Registrar and the arbitration proceedings are conducted in English.

17.2 In the event that the Arbitration Agreement is written in more than one language, the LCIA Court may, unless the Arbitration Agreement provides that the arbitration proceedings shall be conducted in more than one language, decide which of those languages shall be the initial language of the arbitration.

17.3 Upon the formation of the Arbitral Tribunal and unless the parties have agreed upon the language or languages of the arbitration, the Arbitration Tribunal shall decide upon the language(s) of the arbitration, after giving the parties an opportunity to make written comment and taking into account the initial language of the arbitration and any other matter it may consider appropriate in all the circumstances of the case.

17.4 If any document is expressed in a language other than the language(s) of the arbitration and no translation of such document is submitted by the party relying upon the document, the Arbitral Tribunal or (if the Arbitral Tribunal has not been formed) the LCIA Court may order that party to submit a translation in a form to be determined by the Arbitral Tribunal or the LCIA Court, as the case may be.

Article 18

Party Representation

18.1 Any party may be represented by legal practitioners or any other representatives.

18.2 At any time the Arbitral Tribunal may require from any party proof of authority granted to its representative(s) in such form as the Arbitral Tribunal may determine.

Article 19

Hearings

19.1 Any party which expresses a desire to that effect has the right to be heard orally before the Arbitral Tribunal on the merits of the dispute, unless the parties have agreed in writing on documents-only arbitration.

19.2 The Arbitral Tribunal shall fix the date, time and physical place of any meetings and hearings in the arbitration, and shall give the parties reasonable notice thereof.

19.3 The Arbitral Tribunal may in advance of any hearing submit to the parties a list of questions which it wishes them to answer with special attention.

19.4 All meetings and hearings shall be in private unless the parties agree otherwise in writing or the Arbitral Tribunal directs otherwise.

19.5 The Arbitral Tribunal shall have the fullest authority to establish time-limits for meetings and hearings, or for any parts thereof.

Article 20

Witnesses

20.1 Before any hearing, the Arbitral Tribunal may require any party to give notice of the identity of each witness that party wishes to call (including rebuttal witnesses), as well as the subject matter of that witness's testimony, its content and its relevance to the issues in the arbitration.

20.2 The Arbitral Tribunal may also determine the time, manner and form in which such materials should be exchanged between the parties and presented to the Arbitral Tribunal; and it has a discretion to allow, refuse, or limit the appearance of witnesses (whether witness of fact or expert witness).

20.3 Subject to any order otherwise by the Arbitral Tribunal, the testimony of a witness may be presented by a party in written form, either as a signed statement or as a sworn affidavit.

20.4 Subject to Article 14.1 and 14.2, any party may request that a witness, on whose testimony another party seeks to rely, should attend for oral questioning at a hearing before the Arbitral Tribunal. If the Arbitral Tribunal orders that other party to produce the witness and the witness fails to attend the oral hearing without good cause, the Arbitral Tribunal may place such weight on the written testimony (or exclude the same altogether) as it considers appropriate in the circumstances of the case.

20.5 Any witness who gives oral evidence at a hearing before the Arbitral Tribunal may be questioned by each of the parties under the control of the Arbitral Tribunal. The Arbitral Tribunal may put questions at any stage of his evidence.

20.6 Subject to the mandatory provisions of any applicable law, it shall not be improper for any party or its legal representatives to interview any witness or potential witness for the purpose of presenting his testimony in written form or producing him as an oral witness.

20.7 Any individual intending to testify to the Arbitral Tribunal on any issue of fact or expertise shall be treated as a witness under these Rules notwithstanding that the individual is a party to the arbitration or was or is an officer, employee or shareholder of any party.

Article 21

Experts to the Arbitral Tribunal

21.1 Unless otherwise agreed by the parties in writing, the Arbitral Tribunal:

(a) may appoint one or more experts to report to the Arbitral Tribunal on specific issues, who shall be and remain impartial and independent of the parties throughout the arbitration proceedings; and

(b) may require a party to give any such expert any relevant information or to provide access to any relevant documents, goods, samples, property or site for inspection by the expert.

21.2 Unless otherwise agreed by the parties in writing, if a party so requests or if the Arbitral Tribunal considers it necessary, the expert shall, after delivery of his written or oral report to the Arbitral Tribunal and the parties, participate in one or more hearings at which the parties shall have the opportunity to question the expert on his report and to present expert witnesses in order to testify on the points at issue.

21.3 The fees and expenses of any expert appointed by the Arbitral Tribunal under this Article shall be paid out of the deposits payable by the parties under Article 24 and shall form part of the costs of the arbitration.

Article 22

Additional Powers of the Arbitral Tribunal

22.1 Unless the parties at any time agree otherwise in writing, the Arbitral Tribunal shall have the power, on the application of any party or of its own motion, but in either case only after giving the parties a reasonable opportunity to state their views:

(a) to allow any party, upon such terms (as to costs and otherwise) as it shall determine, to amend any claim, counterclaim, defence and reply;

(b) to extend or abbreviate any time-limit provided by the Arbitration Agreement or these Rules for the conduct of the arbitration or by the Arbitral Tribunal's own orders;

(c) to conduct such enquiries as may appear to the Arbitral Tribunal to be necessary or expedient, including whether and to what extent the Arbitral Tribunal should itself take the initiative in identifying the issues and ascertaining the relevant facts and the law(s) or rules of law applicable to the arbitration, the merits of the parties' dispute and the Arbitration Agreement;

(d) to order any party to make any property, site or thing under its control and relating to the subject matter of the arbitration available for inspection by the Arbitral Tribunal, any other party, its expert or any expert to the Arbitral Tribunal;

(e) to order any party to produce to the Arbitral Tribunal, and to the other parties for inspection, and to supply copies of, any documents or classes of documents in their possession, custody or power which the Arbitral Tribunal determines to be relevant;

(f) to decide whether or not to apply any strict rules of evidence (or any other rules) as to the admissibility, relevance or weight of any material tendered by a party on any matter of fact or expert opinion; and to determine the time, manner and form in which such material should be exchanged between the parties and presented to the Arbitral Tribunal;

(g) to order the correction of any contract between the parties or the Arbitration Agreement, but only to the extent required to rectify any mistake which the Arbitral Tribunal determines to be common to the parties and then only if and to the extent to which the law(s) or rules of law applicable to the contract or Arbitration Agreement permit such correction; and

(h) to allow, only upon the application of a party, one or more third persons to be joined in the arbitration as a party provided any such third person and the applicant party have consented thereto in writing, and thereafter to make a single final award, or separate awards, in respect of all parties so implicated in the arbitration;

22.2 By agreeing to arbitration under these Rules, the parties shall be treated as having agreed not to apply to any state court or other judicial authority for any order available from the Arbitral Tribunal under Article 22.1, except with the agreement in writing of all parties.

22.3 The Arbitral Tribunal shall decide the parties' dispute in accordance with the law(s) or rules of law chosen by the parties as applicable to the merits of their dispute. If and to the extent that the Arbitral Tribunal determines that the parties have made no such choice, the Arbitral Tribunal shall apply the law(s) or rules of law which it considers appropriate.

22.4 The Arbitral Tribunal shall only apply to the merits of the dispute principles deriving from "ex aequo et bono", "amiable composition" or "honorable engagement" where the parties have so agreed expressly in writing.

Article 23

Jurisdiction of the Arbitral Tribunal

23.1 The Arbitral Tribunal shall have the power to rule on its own jurisdiction, including any objection to the initial or continuing existence, validity or effectiveness of the Arbitration Agreement. For that purpose, an arbitration clause which forms or was intended to form part of another agreement shall be treated as an arbitration agreement independent of that other agreement. A decision by the Arbitral Tribunal that such other agreement is non-existent, invalid or ineffective shall not entail ipso jure the non-existence, invalidity or ineffectiveness of the arbitration clause.

23.2 A plea by a Respondent that the Arbitral Tribunal does not have jurisdiction shall be treated as having been irrevocably waived unless it is raised not later than the Statement of Defence; and a like plea by a Respondent to Counterclaim shall be similarly treated unless it is raised no later than the Statement of Defence to Counterclaim. A plea that the Arbitral Tribunal is exceeding the scope of its authority shall be raised promptly after the Arbitral Tribunal has indicated its intention to decide on the matter alleged by any party to be beyond the scope of its authority, failing which such plea shall also be treated as having been waived irrevocably. In any case, the Arbitral Tribunal may nevertheless admit an untimely plea if it considers the delay justified in the particular circumstances.

23.3 The Arbitral Tribunal may determine the plea to its jurisdiction or authority in an award as to jurisdiction or later in an award on the merits, as it considers appropriate in the circumstances.

23.4 By agreeing to arbitration under these Rules, the parties shall be treated as having agreed not to apply to any state court or other judicial authority for any relief regarding the Arbitral Tribunal's jurisdiction or authority, except with the agreement in writing of all parties to the arbitration or the prior authorization of the Arbitral Tribunal or following the latter's award ruling on the objection to its jurisdiction or authority.

Article 24

Deposits

24.1 The LCIA Court may direct the parties, in such proportions as it thinks appropriate, to make one or several interim or final payments on account of the costs of the arbitration. Such deposits shall be made to and held by the LCIA and from time to time may be released by the LCIA Court to the arbitrator(s), any expert appointed by the Arbitral Tribunal and the LCIA itself as the arbitration progresses.

24.2 The Arbitral Tribunal shall not proceed with the arbitration without ascertaining at all times from the Registrar or any deputy Registrar that the LCIA is in requisite funds.

24.3 In the event that a party fails or refuses to provide any deposit as directed by the LCIA Court, the LCIA Court may direct the other party or parties to effect a substitute payment to allow the arbitration to proceed (subject to any award on costs). In such circumstances, the party paying the substitute payment shall be entitled to recover that amount as a debt immediately due from the defaulting party.

24.4 Failure by a claimant or counterclaiming party to provide promptly and in full the required deposit may be treated by the LCIA Court and the Arbitral Tribunal as a withdrawal of the claim or counterclaim respectively.

Article 25

Interim and Conservatory Measures

25.1 The Arbitral Tribunal shall have the power, unless otherwise agreed by the parties in writing, on the application of any party:

(a) to order any respondent party to a claim or counterclaim to provide security for all or part of the amount in dispute, by way of deposit or bank guarantee or in any other manner and upon such terms as the Arbitral Tribunal considers appropriate. Such terms may include the provision by the claiming or counterclaiming party of a cross-indemnity, itself secured in such manner as the Arbitral Tribunal considers appropriate, for any costs or losses incurred by such respondent in providing security. The amount of any costs and losses payable under such cross-indemnity may be determined by the Arbitral Tribunal in one or more awards;

(b) to order the preservation, storage, sale or other disposal of any property or thing under the control of any party and relating to the subject matter of the arbitration; and

(c) to order on a provisional basis, subject to final determination in an award, any relief which the Arbitral Tribunal would have power to grant in an award, including a provisional order for the payment of money or the disposition of property as between any parties.

25.2 The Arbitral Tribunal shall have the power, upon the application of a party, to order any claiming or counterclaiming party to provide security for the legal or other costs of any other party by way of deposit or bank guarantee or in any other manner and upon such terms as the Arbitral Tribunal considers appropriate. Such terms may include the provision by that other party of a cross-indemnity, itself secured in such manner as the Arbitral Tribunal considers appropriate, for any costs and losses incurred by such claimant or counterclaimant in providing security. The amount of any costs and losses payable under such cross-indemnity may be determined by the Arbitral Tribunal in one or more awards. In the event that a claiming or counterclaiming party does not comply with any order to provide security, the Arbitral Tribunal may stay that party's claims or counterclaims or dismiss them in an award.

25.3 The power of the Arbitral Tribunal under Article 25.1 shall not prejudice howsoever any party's right to apply to any state court or other judicial authority for interim or conservatory measures before the formation of the Arbitral Tribunal and, in exceptional cases, thereafter. Any application and any order for such measures after the formation of the Arbitral Tribunal shall be promptly communicated by the applicant to the Arbitral Tribunal and all other parties. However, by agreeing to arbitration under these Rules, the parties shall be taken to have agreed not to apply to any state court or other judicial authority for any order for security for its legal or other costs available from the Arbitral Tribunal under Article 25.2.

Article 26

The Award

26.1 The Arbitral Tribunal shall make its award in writing and, unless all parties agree in writing otherwise, shall state the reasons upon which its award is based. The award shall also state the date when the award is made and the seat of the arbitration; and it shall be signed by the Arbitral Tribunal or those of its members assenting to it.

26.2 If any arbitrator fails to comply with the mandatory provisions of any applicable law relating to the making of the award, having been given a reasonable opportunity to do so, the remaining arbitrators may proceed in his absence and state in their award the circumstances of the other arbitrator's failure to participate in the making of the award.

26.3 Where there are three arbitrators and the Arbitral Tribunal fails to agree on any issue, the arbitrators shall decide that issue by a majority. Failing a majority decision on any issue, the chairman of the Arbitral Tribunal shall decide that issue.

26.4 If any arbitrator refuses or fails to sign the award, the signatures of the majority or (failing a majority) of the chairman shall be sufficient, provided that the reason for the omitted signature is stated in the award by the majority or chairman.

26.5 The sole arbitrator or chairman shall be responsible for delivering the award to the LCIA Court, which shall transmit certified copies to the parties provided that the costs of arbitration have been paid to the LCIA in accordance with Article 28.

26.6 An award may be expressed in any currency. The Arbitral Tribunal may order that simple or compound interest shall be paid by any party on any sum awarded at such rates as the Arbitral Tribunal determines to be appropriate, without being bound by legal rates of interest imposed by any state court, in respect of any period which the Arbitral Tribunal determines to be appropriate ending not later than the date upon which the award is complied with.

26.7 The Arbitral Tribunal may make separate awards on different issues at different times. Such awards shall have the same status and effect as any other award made by the Arbitral Tribunal.

26.8 In the event of a settlement of the parties' dispute, the Arbitral Tribunal may render an award recording the settlement if the parties so request in writing (a "Consent Award"), provided always that such award contains an express statement that it is an award made by the parties' consent. A Consent Award need not contain reasons. If the parties do not require a consent award, then on written confirmation by the parties to the LCIA Court that a settlement has been reached, the Arbitral Tribunal shall be discharged and the arbitration proceedings concluded, subject to payment by the parties of any outstanding costs of the arbitration under Article 28.

26.9 All awards shall be final and binding on the parties. By agreeing to arbitration under these Rules, the parties undertake to carry out any award immediately and without any delay (subject only to Article 27); and the parties also waive irrevocably their right to any form of appeal, review or recourse to any state court or other judicial authority, insofar as such waiver may be validly made.

Article 27

Correction of Awards and Additional Awards

27.1 Within 30 days of receipt of any award, or such lesser period as may be agreed in writing by the parties, a party may by written notice to the Registrar (copied to all other parties) request the Arbitral

Tribunal to correct in the award any errors in computation, clerical or typographical errors or any errors of a similar nature. If the Arbitral Tribunal considers the request to be justified, it shall make the corrections within 30 days of receipt of the request. Any correction shall take the form of separate memorandum dated and signed by the Arbitral Tribunal or (if three arbitrators) those of its members assenting to it; and such memorandum shall become part of the award for all purposes.

27.2 The Arbitral Tribunal may likewise correct any error of the nature described in Article 27.1 on its own initiative within 30 days of the date of the award, to the same effect.

27.3 Within 30 days of receipt of the final award, a party may by written notice to the Registrar (copied to all other parties), request the Arbitral Tribunal to make an additional award as to claims or counterclaims presented in the arbitration but not determined in any award. If the Arbitral Tribunal considers the request to be justified, it shall make the additional award within 60 days of receipt of the request. The provisions of Article 26 shall apply to any additional award.

Article 28

Arbitration and Legal Costs

28.1 The costs of the arbitration (other than the legal or other costs incurred by the parties themselves) shall be determined by the LCIA Court in accordance with the Schedule of Costs. The parties shall be jointly and severally liable to the Arbitral Tribunal and the LCIA for such arbitration costs.

28.2 The Arbitral Tribunal shall specify in the award the total amount of the costs of the arbitration as determined by the LCIA Court. Unless the parties agree otherwise in writing, the Arbitral Tribunal shall determine the proportions in which the parties shall bear all or part of such arbitration costs. If the Arbitral Tribunal has determined that all or any part of the arbitration costs shall be borne by a party other than a party which has already paid them to the LCIA, the latter party shall have the right to recover the appropriate amount from the former party.

28.3 The Arbitral Tribunal shall also have the power to order in its award that all or part of the legal or other costs incurred by a party be paid by another party, unless the parties agree otherwise in writing. The Arbitral Tribunal shall determine and fix the amount of each item comprising such costs on such reasonable basis as it thinks fit.

28.4 Unless the parties otherwise agree in writing, the Arbitral Tribunal shall make its orders on both arbitration and legal costs on the general principle that costs should reflect the parties' relative success and failure in the award or arbitration, except where it appears to the Arbitral Tribunal that in the particular circumstances this general approach is inappropriate. Any order for costs shall be made with reasons in the award containing such order.

28.5 If the arbitration is abandoned, suspended or concluded, by agreement or otherwise, before the final award is made, the parties shall remain jointly and severally liable to pay to the LCIA and the Arbitral Tribunal the costs of the arbitration as determined by the LCIA Court in accordance with the Schedule of Costs. In the event that such arbitration costs are less than the deposits made by the parties, there shall be a refund by the LCIA in such proportion as the parties may agree in writing, or failing such agreement, in the same proportions as the deposits were made by the parties to the LCIA.

Article 29

Decisions by the LCIA Court

29.1 The decisions of the LCIA Court with respect to all matters relating to the arbitration shall be conclusive and binding upon the parties and the Arbitral Tribunal. Such decisions are to be treated as administrative in nature and the LCIA Court shall not be required to give any reasons.

29.2 To the extent permitted by the law of the seat of the arbitration, the parties shall be taken to have waived any right of appeal or review in respect of any such decisions of the LCIA Court to any state court or other judicial authority. If such appeals or review remain possible due to mandatory provisions of any applicable law, the LCIA Court shall, subject to the provisions of that applicable law, decide whether the arbitral proceedings are to continue, notwithstanding an appeal or review.

Article 30

Confidentiality

30.1 Unless the parties expressly agree in writing to the contrary, the parties undertake as a general principle to keep confidential all awards in their arbitration, together with all materials in the proceedings created for the purpose of the arbitration and all other documents produced by another party in the proceedings not otherwise in the public domain-save and to the extent that disclosure may be required of a party by legal duty, to protect or pursue a legal right or to enforce or challenge an award in bona fide legal proceedings before a state court or other judicial authority.

30.2 The deliberations of the Arbitral Tribunal are likewise confidential to its members, save and to the extent that disclosure of an arbitrator's refusal to participate in the arbitration is required of the other members of the Arbitral Tribunal under Articles 10, 12 and 26.

30.3 The LCIA Court does not publish any award or any part of an award without the prior written consent of all parties and the Arbitral Tribunal.

Article 31

Exclusion of Liability

31.1 None of the LCIA, the LCIA Court (including its President, Vice–Presidents and individual members), the Registrar, any deputy Registrar, any arbitrator and any expert to the Arbitral Tribunal shall be liable to any party howsoever for any act or omission in connection with any arbitration conducted by reference to these Rules, save where the act or omission is shown by that party to constitute conscious and deliberate wrongdoing committed by the body or person alleged to be liable to that party.

31.2 After the award has been made and the possibilities of correction and additional awards referred to in Article 27 have lapsed or been exhausted, neither the LCIA, the LCIA Court (including its President, Vice–Presidents and individual members), the Registrar, any deputy Registrar, any arbitrator or expert to the Arbitral Tribunal shall be under any legal obligation to make any statement to any person about any matter concerning the arbitration, nor shall any party seek to make any of these persons a witness in any legal or other proceedings arising out of the arbitration.

Article 32

General Rules

32.1 A party who knows that any provision of the Arbitration Agreement (including these Rules) has not been complied with and yet proceeds with the arbitration without promptly stating its objection to such non-compliance, shall be treated as having irrevocably waived its right to object.

32.2 In all matters not expressly provided for in these Rules, the LCIA Court, the Arbitral Tribunal and the parties shall act in the spirit of these Rules and shall make every reasonable effort to ensure that an award is legally enforceable.

RECOMMENDED ARBITRATION CLAUSES

Future Disputes

Parties to an international contract who wish to have any disputes referred to arbitration under the LCIA Rules are recommended to insert in the contract an arbitration clause in the following form:

"Any dispute arising out of or in connection with this contract, including any question regarding its existence, validity or termination, shall be referred to and finally resolved by arbitration under the Rules of the London Court of International Arbitration, which Rules are deemed to be incorporated by reference into this clause."

Parties are also reminded that difficulties and expenses may be avoided if they expressly specify the law governing their contract. The parties may if they wish also specify the number of arbitrators, and the place and language of the arbitration. The following provisions may be suitable:

'The governing law of this contract shall be the substantive law of . . .'

'The tribunal shall consist of . . . (a sole or three) arbitrator(s).'

In the case of a three-member tribunal, the following words may be added:

'. . . two of them shall be nominated by the respective parties'

'The place* of the arbitration shall be . . . (city)

"The language of the arbitration shall be . . ."

Existing Disputes

If a dispute has arisen when the contract or agreement does not contain an arbitration clause, or when the parties wish to change a clause to provide for LCIA arbitration, the following form of agreement is recommended:

"A dispute having arisen between the parties concerning . . . the parties hereby agree that the matter shall be referred to and finally resolved by arbitration under the Rules of the London Court of International Arbitration."

Further provisions as suggested above relating to the governing law, number of arbitrators, place and language, may be added as appropriate to the case.

SCHEDULE OF ARBITRATION FEES AND COSTS

(Effective 1 June 2003)

For arbitrations under the LCIA Rules; under UNCITRAL Rules when administered by the LCIA; when the LCIA acts as Appointing Authority only; and when the LCIA is appointed to decide challenges.

1. Administrative charges under LCIA and UNCITRAL Rules**

a. Registration Fee (payable in advance with Request for Arbitration non-refundable). £1,500

b. Time spent*** by the Registrar and his/her deputy, and by the Secretariat of the LCIA in the administration of the arbitration.****

* (Note: The Tribunal may hold hearings or meetings anywhere convenient providing the Award is made at the place of arbitration.)

** Charges may be subject to Value Added Tax at the prevailing rate.

*** Minimum unit of time in all cases: 15 minutes.

**** Items 1(b), 1(c), and 1(d) * * *, are payable on interim invoice; with the award, or as directed by the LCIA Court under Article 24.1 of the Rules.

Registrar and his/her deputy	£150 per hour
Secretariat	£75 per hour

c. A sum equivalent to 5% of the fees of the Tribunal (excluding expenses) in respect of the LCIA's general overhead. * * *

d. Expenses incurred by the Secretariat in connection with the arbitration (such as postage, telephone, facsimile, travel etc.), and additional arbitration support services, whether provided by the Secretariat from its own resources or otherwise. * * * at applicable hourly rates or at cost

e. The LCIA's fees and expenses will be invoiced in sterling, but may be paid in other convertible currencies, at rates prevailing at the time of payment, provided that any transfer and/or currency exchange charges shall be borne by the payer.

2. Request to Act as Appointing Authority only

a. Appointment Fee (payable in advance with request—non-refundable). £1,000

b. As for 1(b) and 1(d), above.

3. Request to act in deciding challenges to arbitrators in non-LCIA arbitrations

a. As for 2(a) and 2(b), above; plus

b. Time spent by members of the LCIA Court in carrying out their functions in deciding the challenges. at hourly rates advised by members of the LCIA Court.

4. Fees and Expenses of the Tribunal

a. The Tribunal's fees will be calculated by reference to work done by its members in connection with the arbitration and will be charged at rates appropriate to the particular circumstances of the case, including its complexity and the special qualifications of the arbitrators. The Tribunal shall agree in writing upon fee rates conforming to this Schedule of Fees and Costs prior to its appointment by the LCIA Court. The rates will be advised by the Registrar to the parties at the time of the appointment of the Tribunal, but may be reviewed annually if the duration of the arbitration requires.

The fee rates shall be within the following range: £150 to £350 per hour.

However, in exceptional cases, the rate may be higher or lower, provided that, in such cases, (a) the fees of the Tribunal shall be fixed by the LCIA Court on the recommendation of the Registrar, following consultations with the arbitrator(s), and (b) the fees shall be agreed expressly by all parties.

b. The Tribunal's fees may include a charge for time spent travelling.

The Tribunal's fees may also include a charge for time reserved but not used as a result of late postponement or cancellation, provided that the basis for such charge shall be advised in writing to, and approved by, the LCIA Court.

c. The Tribunal may also recover such expenses as are reasonably incurred in connection with the arbitration, and as are in a reasonable amount, provided that claims for expenses should be supported by invoices or receipts.

d. The Tribunal's fees may be invoiced either in the currency of account between the Tribunal and the parties, or in sterling. The Tribunal's expenses may be invoiced in the currency in which they were incurred, or in sterling.

e. In the event of the revocation of the appointment of any arbitrator, pursuant to the provisions of Article 10 of the LCIA Rules, the LCIA Court shall decide upon the amount of fees and expenses to be paid for the former arbitrator's services (if any) as it may consider appropriate in all the circumstances.

5. Deposits

a. The LCIA Court may direct the parties, in such proportions as it thinks appropriate, to make one or several interim or final payments on account of the costs of the arbitration. The LCIA Court may limit such payments to a sum sufficient to cover fees, expenses and costs for the next stage of the arbitration.

b. The Tribunal shall not proceed with the arbitration without ascertaining at all times from the Registrar or any deputy Registrar that the LCIA is in requisite funds.

c. In the event that a party fails or refuses to provide any deposit as directed by the LCIA Court, the LCIA Court may direct the other party or parties to effect a substitute payment to allow the arbitration to proceed (subject to any award on costs). In such circumstances, the party paying the substitute payment shall be entitled to recover that amount as a debt immediately due from the defaulting party.

d. Failure by a claimant or counterclaiming party to provide promptly and in full the required deposit may be treated by the LCIA Court and the Arbitral Tribunal as a withdrawal of the claim or counterclaim, respectively.

e. Funds lodged by the parties on account of the fees and expenses of the Tribunal and of the LCIA are held on trust in client bank accounts which are controlled by reference to each individual case and are disbursed by the LCIA, in accordance with the LCIA Rules and with this Schedule of Arbitration Fees and Costs. In the event that funds lodged by the parties exceed the costs of the arbitration at the conclusion of the arbitration, surplus monies will be returned to the parties as the ultimate default beneficiaries under the trust.

6. Interest on Deposits

Interest on sums deposited shall be credited to the account of each party depositing them, at the rate applicable to an amount equal to the amount so credited.

7. Interim Payments

a. When interim payments are required to cover the LCIA's administrative costs or the Tribunal's fees or expenses, including the fees or expenses of any expert appointed by the Tribunal, such payments may be made out of deposits held, upon the approval of the LCIA Court.

b. The LCIA may, in any event, submit interim invoices in respect of all current arbitrations, in March, June, September and December of each year, for payment direct by the parties or from funds held on deposit.

8. Registrar's Authority

a. For the purposes of sections 5(a) and 5(c) above, and of Articles 24.1 and 24.3 of the LCIA Rules, the Registrar has the authority of the LCIA Court to make the directions referred to, under the supervision of the Court.

b. For the purposes of section 7(a) above, and of Article 24.1 of the LCIA Rules, the Registrar has the authority of the LCIA Court to approve the payments referred to.

c. Any request by an arbitrator for payment on account of his fees shall be supported by a fee note, which shall include, or be accompanied by, details of the time spent at the rates that have been advised to the parties by the LCIA.

d. Any dispute regarding administration costs or the fees and expenses of the Tribunal shall be determined by the LCIA Court.

9. Notes

a. The parties shall be jointly and severally liable to the Arbitral Tribunal and the LCIA for the arbitration costs (other than the legal or other costs incurred by the parties themselves).

b. The Tribunal's Award(s) shall be transmitted to the parties by the LCIA Court provided that the costs of the arbitration have been paid in accordance with Article 28 of the LCIA Rules.

E. CHINA INTERNATIONAL ECONOMIC AND TRADE ARBITRATION COMMISSION (CIETAC)*

ARBITRATION RULES

(Revised and Adopted by the China Council for the Promotion of International Trade /China Chamber of International Commerce on January 11, 2005. Effective as from May 1, 2005.)

Chapter I. General Provisions

Article 1. The Rules

These Rules are formulated in accordance with the Arbitration Law of the People's Republic of China and the provisions of other relevant laws, as well as the "Decision" of the former Administration Council of the Central People's Government and the "Notice" and the "Official Reply" of the State Council.

Article 2. Name and Structure

1. The China International Economic and Trade Arbitration Commission (originally named the Foreign Trade Arbitration Commission of the China Council for the Promotion of International Trade, later renamed the Foreign Economic and Trade Arbitration Commission of the China Council for the Promotion of International Trade, and currently called the China International Economic and Trade Arbitration Commission, hereinafter referred to as the "CIETAC") independently and impartially resolves, by means of arbitration, disputes arising from economic and trade transactions of a contractual or non-contractual nature.

2. The CIETAC concurrently uses the "Court of Arbitration of the China Chamber of International Commerce" as its name.

3. Where an arbitration agreement or an arbitration clause contained in a contract provides for arbitration by the CIETAC or one of its Sub-Commissions or by the CIETAC using one of its prior names, the parties shall be deemed to have unanimously agreed that the arbitration shall be administered by the CIETAC or by one of its Sub-Commissions.

4. Where an arbitration agreement or an arbitration clause contained in a contract provides for arbitration by the China Council for the Promotion of International Trade/China Chamber of International Commerce or by the Arbitration Commission or the Court of Arbitration of the China Council for the Promotion of International Trade/China Chamber of International Commerce, the parties shall be deemed to have unanimously agreed that the arbitration shall be administered by the CIETAC.

5. The Chairman of the CIETAC shall perform the functions and duties vested in him/her by these Rules while a Vice-Chairman may

* The CIETAC Rules can be found at http://www.cietac.org.cn/epop_1.htm

perform the Chairman's functions and duties with the Chairman's authorization.

6. The CIETAC has a Secretariat, which handles its day-to-day work under the direction of its Secretary–General.

7. The CIETAC is based in Beijing, and has a South China Sub–Commission (formerly known as Shenzhen Sub–Commission) in Shenzhen Special Economic Zone and a Shanghai Sub–Commission in Shanghai. These Sub–Commissions are integral parts of the CIETAC. The Sub–Commissions have their respective secretariats, which handle their day-to-day work under the direction of the Secretaries–General of the respective Sub–Commissions.

8. The parties may agree to have their disputes arbitrated by the CIETAC in Beijing, the South China Sub–Commission in Shenzhen or the Shanghai Sub–Commission in Shanghai. In the absence of such an agreement, the Claimant shall have the option to submit the case for arbitration by the CIETAC in Beijing, the South China Sub–Commission in Shenzhen or the Shanghai Sub–Commission in Shanghai. When such option is exercised, the first choice by the party shall prevail. In case of any dispute, the final decision shall be made by the CIETAC.

9. The CIETAC may, in its discretion, establish arbitration centers for specific business sectors and issue arbitration rules therefor.

10. The CIETAC shall establish a Panel of Arbitrators, and may, in its discretion, establish Panels of Arbitrators for specific business sectors.

Article 3. Jurisdiction

The CIETAC accepts cases involving:

1. international or foreign-related disputes;

2. disputes related to the Hong Kong Special Administrative Region or the Macao Special Administrative Region or the Taiwan region; and

3. domestic disputes.

Article 4. Scope of Application

1. These Rules uniformly apply to the CIETAC and its Sub–Commissions. When arbitration proceedings are administered by a Sub–Commission, the functions and duties under these Rules allocated to the Chairman, the secretariat and the Secretary–General of the CIETAC shall be performed, respectively, by a Vice–Chairman authorized by the Chairman, a secretariat and a Secretary–General of the relevant Sub–Commission except for the power to make decisions on challenges to arbitrators.

2. The parties shall be deemed to have agreed to arbitrate in accordance with these Rules whenever they have provided for arbitration by the CIETAC. Where the parties have agreed on the application of other arbitration rules, or any modification of these Rules, the parties' agreement shall prevail except where such agreement is inoperative or in conflict with a mandatory provision of the law of the place of arbitration.

3. Where the parties agree to refer their disputes to arbitration under these Rules without providing the name of an arbitration institution, they shall be deemed to have agreed to refer the dispute to arbitration by the CIETAC.

4. Where the parties agree to refer their dispute to arbitration under the CIETAC's arbitration rules for a specific business sector or profession and the dispute falls within the scope of such rules, the parties' agreement shall prevail; otherwise, these Rules shall apply.

Article 5. Arbitration Agreement

1. The CIETAC shall, upon the written application of a party, accept a case in accordance with an arbitration agreement concluded between the parties, either before or after the occurrence of the dispute, in which it is provided that disputes are to be referred to arbitration by the CIETAC.

2. An arbitration agreement means an arbitration clause in a contract concluded between the parties or any other form of written agreement providing for the settlement of disputes by arbitration.

3. The arbitration agreement shall be in writing. An arbitration agreement is in writing if it is contained in a tangible form of a document such as a contract, letter, telegram, telex, facsimile, EDI, or Email. An arbitration agreement shall be deemed to exist where its existence is asserted by one party and not denied by the other during the exchange of the Request for Arbitration and the Statement of Defense.

4. An arbitration clause contained in a contract shall be treated as a clause independent and separate from all other clauses of the contract, and an arbitration agreement attached to a contract shall also be treated as independent and separate from all other clauses of the contract. The validity of an arbitration clause or an arbitration agreement shall not be affected by any modification, rescission, termination, transfer, expiry, invalidity, ineffectiveness, revocation or nonexistence of the contract.

Article 6. Objection to an Arbitration Agreement and/or Jurisdiction

1. The CIETAC shall have the power to determine the existence and validity of an arbitration agreement and its jurisdiction over an arbitration case. The CIETAC may, if necessary, delegate such power to the arbitral tribunal.

2. Where the CIETAC is satisfied by prima facie evidence that an arbitration agreement providing for arbitration by the CIETAC exists, it may make a decision based on such evidence that it has jurisdiction over the arbitration case, and the arbitration shall proceed. Such a decision shall not prevent the CIETAC from making a new decision on jurisdiction based on facts and/or evidence found by the arbitral tribunal during the arbitration proceedings that are inconsistent with the prima facie evidence.

3. An objection to an arbitration agreement and/or jurisdiction over an arbitration case shall be raised in writing before the first oral hearing is held by the arbitral tribunal. Where a case is to be decided on the basis of documents only, such an objection shall be raised before the submission of the first substantive defense.

4. The arbitration shall proceed notwithstanding an objection to the arbitration agreement and/or jurisdiction over the arbitration case.

5. The aforesaid objections to and/or decisions on jurisdiction by the CIETAC shall include objections to and/or decisions on a party's standing to participate in the arbitration.

Article 7. Bona Fide Cooperation

The parties shall proceed with the arbitration in bona fide cooperation.

Article 8. Waiver of Right to Object

A party shall be deemed to have waived its right to object where it knows or should have known that any provision of, or requirement under, these Rules has not been complied with and yet participates in or proceeds with the arbitration proceedings without promptly and explicitly submitting its objection in writing to such non-compliance.

Chapter II. Arbitral Proceedings

Section 1. Request for Arbitration, Defense and Counterclaim

Article 9. Commencement of Arbitration

The arbitral proceedings shall commence on the date on which the CIETAC or one of its Sub–Commissions receives a Request for Arbitration.

Article 10. Application for Arbitration

A party applying for arbitration under these Rules shall:

1. Submit a Request for Arbitration in writing signed by and/or affixed with the seal of the Claimant and/or its authorized representative(s), which shall, inter alia, include:

(a) the names and addresses of the Claimant and the Respondent, including the zip code, telephone, telex, fax and telegraph numbers, Email addresses or any other means of electronic telecommunications;

(b) a reference to the arbitration agreement that is invoked;

(c) a statement of the facts of the case and the main issues in dispute;

(d) the claim of the Claimant; and

(e) the facts and grounds on which the claim is based.

2. Attach to the Request for Arbitration the relevant evidence supporting the facts on which the Claimant's claim is based.

3. Make payment of the arbitration fee in advance to the CIETAC according to its Arbitration Fee Schedule.

Article 11. Acceptance of a Case

1. Upon receipt of the Request for Arbitration and its attachments, if the CIETAC after examination finds the formalities required for arbitration application to be incomplete, it may request the Claimant to complete them. Where the formalities are found to be complete, the CIETAC shall send a Notice of Arbitration to both parties together with one copy each of the CIETAC Arbitration Rules, the Panel of Arbitrators and the Arbitration Fee Schedule. The Request for Arbitration and its attachments submitted by the Claimant shall be sent to the Respondent under the same cover.

2. The CIETAC or its Sub–Commission shall, after accepting a case, appoint a staff-member of its secretariat to assist the arbitral tribunal in the procedural administration of the case.

Article 12. Statement of Defense

1. Within forty-five (45) days from the date of receipt of the Notice of Arbitration, the Respondent shall file a Statement of Defense in writing with the Secretariat of the CIETAC or its Sub–Commission. The arbitral tribunal may extend that time period if it believes that there are justified reasons. The Statement of Defense shall be signed by and/or affixed with the seal of the Respondent and/or its authorized representative(s), and shall, inter alia, include:

(a) the names and addresses of the Respondent, including the zip code, telephone, telex, fax and telegraph numbers, Email addresses or any other means of electronic telecommunications;

(b) the defense to the Request for Arbitration setting forth the facts and grounds on which the defense is based; and

(c) the relevant evidence supporting the defense.

2. The arbitral tribunal has the power to decide whether to accept a Statement of Defense submitted after expiration of the above time limit.

3. Failure of the Respondent to file a Statement of Defense shall not operate to affect the arbitral proceedings.

Article 13. Counterclaim

1. Within forty-five (45) days from the date of receipt of the Notice of Arbitration, the Respondent shall file with the CIETAC its counterclaim in writing, if any. The arbitral tribunal may extend that time period if it believes that there are justified reasons.

2. When filing a counterclaim, the Respondent shall specify its counterclaim in its written Statement of Counterclaim and state the facts and grounds upon which its counterclaim is based with relevant evidence attached thereto.

3. When filing a counterclaim, the Respondent shall pay an arbitration fee in advance according to the Arbitration Fee Schedule of the CIETAC within a specified time period.

4. Where the formalities required for filing a counterclaim are found to be complete, the CIETAC shall send the Statement of Counterclaim and its attachments to the Claimant. The Claimant shall, within thirty (30) days from the date of receipt of the Statement of Counterclaim and the attachment, submit in writing its Statement of Defense to the Respondent's counterclaim.

5. The arbitral tribunal has the power to decide whether to accept a Statement of Defense submitted after expiration of the above time limit.

6. Failure of the Claimant to file a Statement of Defense to the Respondent's counterclaim shall not operate to affect the arbitral proceedings.

Article 14. Amendments to the Claim or Counterclaim

The Claimant may amend its claim and the Respondent may amend its counterclaim. However, the arbitral tribunal may not permit any such amendment if it considers that the amendment is too late and may delay the arbitral proceedings.

Article 15. Copies of Submissions

When submitting the Request for Arbitration, the Statement of Defense, the Statement of Counterclaim, evidence and other documents, the parties shall make the submissions in quintuplicate. Where there are more than two parties, additional copies shall be provided accordingly. Where the arbitral tribunal is composed of a sole arbitrator, the number of copies submitted may be reduced by two. Where the preservation of property or protection of evidence is applied for, the party shall forward one additional copy accordingly.

Article 16. Representation

1. A party may be represented by its authorized representative(s) in handling matters relating to the arbitration. In such a case, a Power of Attorney shall be forwarded to the CIETAC by the party or its authorized representative(s).

2. Either Chinese or foreign citizens may be authorized by a party to act as its representative(s).

Article 17. Preservation of Property

When any party applies for the preservation of property, the CIETAC shall forward the party's application for a ruling to the competent court at the place where the domicile of the party against whom the preservation of property is sought is located or where the property of the said party is located.

Article 18. Protection of Evidence

When a party applies for the protection of evidence, the CIETAC shall forward the party's application for a ruling to the competent court at the place where the evidence is located.

Section 2. The Arbitral Tribunal

Article 19. Duties of Arbitrator

An arbitrator shall not represent either party and shall remain independent of the parties and treat them equally.

Article 20. Number of Arbitrators

1. The arbitral tribunal shall be composed of one or three arbitrators.

2. Unless otherwise agreed by the parties or provided by these Rules, the arbitral tribunal shall be composed of three arbitrators.

Article 21. Panel of Arbitrators

1. The parties shall appoint arbitrators from the Panel of Arbitrators provided by the CIETAC.

2. Where the parties have agreed to appoint arbitrators from outside of the CIETAC's Panel of Arbitrators, the arbitrators so appointed by the parties or nominated according to the agreement of the parties may act as co-arbitrator, presiding arbitrator or sole arbitrator after the appointment has been confirmed by the Chairman of the CIETAC in accordance with the law.

Article 22. Three Arbitrators

1. Within fifteen (15) days from the date of receipt of the Notice of Arbitration, the Claimant and the Respondent shall each appoint one arbitrator or entrust the Chairman of the CIETAC to make such appointment. Where a party fails to appoint or to entrust the Chairman of the CIETAC to appoint an arbitrator within the specified time period, the arbitrator shall be appointed by the Chairman of the CIETAC.

2. Within fifteen (15) days from the date of the Respondent's receipt of the Notice of Arbitration, the presiding arbitrator shall be jointly appointed by the parties or appointed by the Chairman of the CIETAC upon the parties' joint authorization.

3. The parties may each recommend one to three arbitrators as candidates for the presiding arbitrator and shall submit the list of recommended candidates to the CIETAC within the time period specified in paragraph 2. Where there is only one common candidate in the lists, such candidate shall be the presiding arbitrator jointly appointed by the parties. Where there are more than one common candidate in the lists, the Chairman of the CIETAC shall choose a presiding arbitrator from among the common candidates based on the specific nature and circumstances of

the case, who shall act as the presiding arbitrator jointly appointed by the parties. Where there is no common candidate in the lists, the presiding arbitrator shall be appointed by the Chairman of the CIETAC from outside of the lists of recommended candidates.

4. Where the parties have failed to jointly appoint the presiding arbitrator according to the above provisions, the presiding arbitrator shall be appointed by the Chairman of the CIETAC.

Article 23. Sole Arbitrator

Where the arbitral tribunal is composed of one arbitrator, the sole arbitrator shall be appointed pursuant to the procedure stipulated in Paragraphs 2, 3 and 4 of Article 22.

Article 24. Multi–Party

1. Where there are two or more Claimants and/or Respondents in an arbitration case, the Claimant side and/or the Respondent side each shall, through consultation, jointly appoint or jointly entrust the Chairman of the CIETAC to appoint one arbitrator from the CIETAC's Panel of Arbitrators.

2. Where the Claimant side and/or the Respondent side fail to jointly appoint or jointly entrust the Chairman of the CIETAC to appoint one arbitrator within fifteen (15) days from the date of receipt of the Notice of Arbitration, the arbitrator shall be appointed by the Chairman of the CIETAC.

3. The presiding arbitrator or the sole arbitrator shall be appointed in accordance with the procedure stipulated in Paragraphs 2, 3 and 4 of Article 22. When appointing the presiding arbitrator or the sole arbitrator pursuant to Paragraph 3 of Article 22, the Claimant side and/or the Respondent side each shall, through consultation, submit a list of their jointly agreed candidates to the CIETAC.

Article 25. Disclosure

1. An arbitrator appointed by the parties or by the Chairman of the CIETAC shall sign a Declaration and disclose to the CIETAC in writing any facts or circumstances likely to give rise to justifiable doubts as to his/her impartiality or independence.

2. If circumstances that need to be disclosed arise during the arbitral proceedings, the arbitrator shall promptly disclose such circumstances in writing to the CIETAC.

3. The CIETAC shall communicate the Declaration and/or the disclosure of the arbitrator to the parties.

Article 26. Challenge of Arbitrators

1. Upon receipt of the Declaration and/or written disclosure of an arbitrator communicated by the CIETAC, a party who intends to challenge the arbitrator on the grounds of the facts or circumstances disclosed

by the arbitrator shall forward the challenge in writing to the CIETAC within ten (10) days from the date of such receipt. If a party fails to file a challenge within the above time limit, it shall not challenge an arbitrator later on the basis of matters disclosed by the arbitrator.

2. A party who has justifiable doubts as to the impartiality or independence of an appointed arbitrator may make a request in writing to the CIETAC for that arbitrator's withdrawal. In the request, the facts and reasons on which the request is based shall be stated with supporting evidence.

3. A party may challenge an arbitrator in writing within fifteen (15) days from the date of its receipt of the Notice of Formation of the Arbitral Tribunal. Where a party becomes aware of the reasons for a challenge after the said receipt, the party may challenge the arbitrator in writing within fifteen (15) days after such reasons become known, but no later than the conclusion of the last oral hearing.

4. The CIETAC shall promptly communicate the challenge to the other party, the arbitrator being challenged and the other members of the arbitral tribunal.

5. Where an arbitrator is challenged by one party and the other party agrees to the challenge, or the arbitrator being challenged withdraws from his/her office, such arbitrator shall no longer be on the arbitral tribunal. Neither case implies that the challenge made by the party is sustainable.

6. In circumstances other than those specified in Paragraph 5, the Chairman of the CIETAC shall make a final decision on the challenge with or without stating the reasons therefor.

7. An arbitrator who has been challenged shall continue to fulfill the functions of arbitrator until a decision on the challenge has been made by the Chairman of the CIETAC.

Article 27. Replacement of Arbitrator

1. In the event that an arbitrator is prevented de jure or de facto from fulfilling his/her functions, or he/she fails to fulfill his/her functions in accordance with the requirements of these Rules or within the time period specified in these Rules, the Chairman of the CIETAC shall have the power to decide whether the arbitrator shall be replaced. The arbitrator may also withdraw form his/her office.

2. In the event that an arbitrator is unable to fulfill his/her functions owing to his/her demise, removal from the CIETAC's Panel of Arbitrators, withdrawal, resignation or any other reasons, a substitute arbitrator shall be appointed within a time period specified by the CIETAC pursuant to the procedure applied to the appointment of the arbitrator being replaced.

3. After the replacement of the arbitrator, the arbitral tribunal shall decide whether the whole or a part of the previous proceedings of the case shall be repeated.

4. The Chairman of the CIETAC shall make a final decision on whether an arbitrator should be replaced or not with or without stating the reasons therefor.

Article 28. Majority to Continue Arbitration

In the event that, after the conclusion of the last oral hearing, an arbitrator on a three-member arbitral tribunal is unable to participate in the deliberation and/or render the award owing to his/ her demise or removal from the CIETAC's Panel of Arbitrators, the other two arbitrators may request the Chairman of the CIETAC to replace the arbitrator pursuant to Article 27. After consulting with the parties and upon the approval of the Chairman of the CIETAC, the other two arbitrators may continue the arbitration and make decisions, rulings or the award. The Secretariat of the CIETAC shall notify the parties of the above circumstances.

Section 3. Hearing

Article 29. Conduct of Hearing

1. The arbitral tribunal shall examine the case in any way that it deems appropriate unless otherwise agreed by the parties. Under any circumstance, the arbitral tribunal shall act impartially and fairly and shall afford reasonable opportunities to all parties for presentations and debates.

2. The arbitral tribunal shall hold oral hearings when examining the case. However, oral hearings may be omitted and the case shall be examined on the basis of documents only if the parties so request or agree and the arbitral tribunal also deems that oral hearings are unnecessary.

3. Unless otherwise agreed by the parties, the arbitral tribunal may adopt an inquisitorial or adversarial approach when examining the case, having regard to the circumstances of the case.

4. The arbitral tribunal may hold deliberation at any place or in any manner that it considers appropriate.

5. The arbitral tribunal may, if it considers it necessary, issue procedural directions and lists of questions, hold pre-hearing meetings and preliminary hearings, and produce terms of reference, etc., unless otherwise agreed by the parties.

Article 30. Notice of Oral Hearings

1. The date of the first oral hearing shall be fixed by the arbitral tribunal and notified to the parties by the Secretariat of the CIETAC at least twenty (20) days in advance of the oral hearing date. A party having justified reasons may request a postponement of the oral hearing. Howev-

er, such request must be communicated to the arbitral tribunal at least ten (10) days in advance of the oral hearing date. The arbitral tribunal shall decide whether to postpone the oral hearing or not.

2. A notice of oral hearing subsequent to the first oral hearing and a notice of a postponed oral hearing shall not be subject to the twenty (20)-day time limit provided for in the foregoing paragraph.

Article 31. Place of Arbitration

1. Where the parties have agreed on the place of arbitration in writing, the parties' agreement shall prevail.

2. Where the parties have not agreed on the place of arbitration, the place of arbitration shall be the domicile of the CIETAC or its Sub–Commission.

3. The arbitral award shall be deemed as being made at the place of arbitration.

Article 32. Place of Oral Hearing

1. Where the parties have agreed on the place of oral hearings, the case shall be heard at that agreed place except for circumstances stipulated in Paragraph 3 of Article 69 of these Rules.

2. Unless the parties agree otherwise, a case accepted by the CIETAC shall be heard in Beijing, or if the arbitral tribunal considers it necessary, at other places with the approval of the Secretary General of the CIETAC. A case accepted by a Sub–Commission of the CIETAC shall be heard at the place where the Sub–Commission is located, or if the arbitral tribunal considers it necessary, at other places with the approval of the Secretary–General of the Sub–Commission.

Article 33. Confidentiality

1. Hearings shall be held in camera. Where both parties request an open hearing, the arbitral tribunal shall make a decision.

2. For cases heard in camera, the parties, their representatives, witnesses, interpreters, arbitrators, experts consulted by the arbitral tribunal and appraisers appointed by the arbitral tribunal and the relevant staff-members of the Secretariat of the CIETAC shall not disclose to any outsiders any substantive or procedural matters of the case.

Article 34. Default

1. If the Claimant fails to appear at an oral hearing without showing sufficient cause for such failure, or withdraws from an on-going oral hearing without the permission of the arbitral tribunal, the Claimant may be deemed to have withdrawn its Request for Arbitration. In such a case, if the Respondent has filed a counterclaim, the arbitral tribunal shall proceed with the hearing of the counterclaim and make a default award.

2. If the Respondent fails to appear at an oral hearing without showing sufficient cause for such failure, or withdraws from an on-going oral hearing without the permission of the arbitral tribunal, the arbitral tribunal may proceed with the arbitration and make a default award. In such a case, if the Respondent has filed a counterclaim, the Respondent may be deemed to have withdrawn its counterclaim.

Article 35. Record of Oral Hearing

1. During the oral hearing, the arbitral tribunal may arrange a stenographic and/or audio-visual record. The arbitral tribunal may, when it considers it necessary, take minutes stating the main points of the oral hearing and request the parties and/or their representatives, witnesses and/or other persons involved to sign and/or affix their seals to the minutes.

2. The stenographic and/or audio-visual record of the oral hearing shall be available for the use and reference by the arbitral tribunal.

Article 36. Evidence

1. Each party shall have the burden of proving the facts relied on to support its claim, defense or counterclaim.

2. The arbitral tribunal may specify a time period for the parties to produce evidence and the parties shall produce evidence within the specified time period. The arbitral tribunal may refuse to admit any evidence produced beyond the period. If a party has difficulties to produce evidence within the specified time period, it may apply for an extension before the expiration of the period.

The arbitral tribunal shall decide whether or not to extend the time period.

3. If a party having the burden of proof fails to produce evidence within the specified time period, or the produced evidence is not sufficient to support its claim or counterclaim, it shall bear the consequences thereof.

Article 37. Investigation by the Arbitral Tribunal

1. The arbitral tribunal may, on its own initiative, undertake investigations and collect evidence as it considers necessary.

2. When investigating and collecting evidence by itself, the arbitral tribunal shall promptly notify the parties to be present at such investigation if it considers it necessary. In the event that one or both parties fail to be present, the investigation and collection shall proceed without being affected.

3. The arbitral tribunal shall, through the Secretariat of the CIETAC, transmit the evidence collected by itself to the parties and afford them an opportunity to comment.

Article 38. Expert's Report and Appraiser's Report

1. The arbitral tribunal may consult or appoint experts and appraisers for clarification on specific issues of a case. Such an expert or appraiser may either be a Chinese or foreign organization or citizen.

2. The arbitral tribunal has the power to request the parties to deliver or produce to the expert or appraiser any relevant materials, documents, or property and goods for checking, inspection and/ or appraisal. The parties shall be obliged to comply.

3. Copies of the expert's report and the appraiser's report shall be communicated to the parties, who shall be given an opportunity to comment on the report. At the request of either party and with the approval of the arbitral tribunal, the expert and appraiser may be heard at an oral hearing where, if considered necessary and appropriate by the arbitral tribunal, they may give explanations on their reports.

Article 39. Examination of Evidence

1. All evidence submitted by a party shall be filed with the Secretariat of the CIETAC for transmission to the other party.

2. Where a case is examined by way of an oral hearing, the evidence shall be exhibited at the hearing and examined by the parties.

3. In the event that evidence is submitted after the hearing and the arbitral tribunal decides to admit the evidence without holding further hearings, the arbitral tribunal may require the parties to submit their opinions thereon in writing within a specified time period.

Article 40. Combination of Conciliation with Arbitration

1. Where the parties have reached a settlement agreement by themselves through negotiation or conciliation without involving the CIETAC, either party may, based on an arbitration agreement concluded between them that provides for arbitration by the CIETAC and the settlement agreement, request the CIETAC to constitute an arbitral tribunal to render an arbitral award in accordance with the terms of the settlement agreement. Unless the parties agree otherwise, the Chairman of the CIETAC shall appoint a sole arbitrator to form such arbitral tribunal, which shall examine the case in the procedure it considers appropriate and render an award in due course. The specific procedure and the time limit for rendering the award shall not be subject to other provisions of these Rules.

2. Where both parties have the desire for conciliation or one party so desires and the other party agrees when approached by the arbitral tribunal, the arbitral tribunal may conciliate the case during the course of the arbitration proceedings.

3. The arbitral tribunal may conciliate the case in the manner it considers appropriate.

4. The arbitral tribunal shall terminate the conciliation and continue the arbitration proceedings if one of the parties requests a termination of the conciliation or if the arbitral tribunal believes that further efforts to conciliate will be futile.

5. A settlement agreement reached between the parties during the course of conciliation by the arbitral tribunal but without the involvement of the arbitral tribunal shall be deemed as one reached through the conciliation by the arbitral tribunal.

6. Where settlement is reached through conciliation by the arbitral tribunal, the parties shall sign a written settlement agreement. Unless otherwise agreed by the parties, the arbitral tribunal will close the case and render an arbitral award in accordance with the terms of the settlement agreement.

7. Where conciliation fails, the arbitral tribunal shall proceed with the arbitration and render an arbitral award.

8. Where conciliation fails, any opinion, view or statement and any proposal or proposition expressing acceptance or opposition by either party or by the arbitral tribunal in the process of conciliation shall not be invoked as grounds for any claim, defense or counterclaim in the subsequent arbitration proceedings, judicial proceedings or any other proceedings.

Article 41. Withdrawal and Dismissal

1. A party may file a request with the CIETAC to withdraw its claim or counterclaim in its entirety. In the event that the Claimant withdraws its claim in its entirety, the arbitral tribunal shall proceed with its examination of the counterclaim and render an arbitral award thereon. In the event that the Respondent withdraws its counterclaim in its entirety, the arbitral tribunal shall proceed with the examination of the claim and render an arbitral award thereon.

2. Where a case is to be dismissed before the formation of the arbitral tribunal, the decision shall be made by the Secretary–General of the CIETAC. Where the case is to be dismissed after the formation of the arbitral tribunal, the decision shall be made by the arbitral tribunal.

3. Where a party files with the CIETAC a request for arbitration for a claim which has been withdrawn, the CIETAC shall decide whether or not to accept the request anew.

Chapter III. Arbitral Award

Article 42. Time Limits

1. The arbitral tribunal shall render an arbitral award within six (6) months as from the date on which the arbitral tribunal is formed.

2. Upon the request of the arbitral tribunal, the Chairman of the CIETAC may extend said time period if he/she considers it truly necessary and the reasons for the extension truly justified.

Article 43. Making Award

1. The arbitral tribunal shall independently and impartially make its arbitral award on the basis of the facts, in accordance with the law and the terms of the contracts, with reference to international practices and in compliance with the principle of fairness and reasonableness.

2. The arbitral tribunal shall state in the award the claims, the facts of the dispute, the reasons on which the award is based, the result of the award, the allocation of the arbitration costs and the date on which and the place at which the award is made. The facts of the dispute and the reasons on which the award is based may not be stated in the award if the parties have agreed so, or if the award is made in accordance with the terms of a settlement agreement between the parties. The arbitral tribunal has the power to determine in the arbitral award the specific time period for the parties to execute the award and the liabilities to be borne by a party failing to execute the award within the specified time.

3. The CIETAC's stamp shall be affixed to the award.

4. Where a case is examined by an arbitral tribunal composed of three arbitrators, the award shall be rendered by all three arbitrators or a majority of the arbitrators. A written dissenting opinion shall be docketed into the file and may be attached to the award, but it shall not form a part of the award.

5. Where the arbitral tribunal cannot reach a majority opinion, the award shall be rendered in accordance with the presiding arbitrator's opinion. The written opinion of other arbitrators shall be docketed into the file and may be attached to the award, but it shall not form a part of the award.

6. Unless the award is made in accordance with the opinion of the presiding arbitrator or the sole arbitrator, the arbitral award shall be signed by a majority of arbitrators. An arbitrator who has a dissenting opinion may or may not sign his/her name on the award.

7. The date on which the award is made shall be the date on which the award comes into legal effect.

8. The arbitral award is final and binding upon both parties. Neither party may bring a suit before a law court or make a request to any other organization for revising the award.

Article 44. Interlocutory Award and Partial Award

An interlocutory arbitral award or partial award may be made by the arbitral tribunal on any issue of the case at any time during the arbitration before the final award is made if considered necessary by the arbitral tribunal, or if the parties request and the arbitral tribunal accepts. Either party's failure to perform the interlocutory award will not affect the continuation of the arbitration proceedings, nor will it prevent the arbitral tribunal from making a final award.

Article 45. Scrutiny of Draft Award

The arbitral tribunal shall submit its draft award to the CIETAC for scrutiny before signing the award. The CIETAC may remind the arbitral tribunal of issues in the award on condition that the arbitral tribunal's independence in rendering the award is not affected.

Article 46. Fees

1. The arbitral tribunal has the power to determine in the arbitral award the arbitration fee and other expenses to be paid by the parties to the CIETAC.

2. The arbitral tribunal has the power to decide in the award, according to the specific circumstances of the case, that the losing party shall compensate the winning party for the expenses reasonably incurred by it in pursuing its case. In deciding whether the winning party's expenses incurred in pursuing its case are reasonable, the arbitral tribunal shall consider such factors as the outcome and complexity of the case, the workload of the winning party and/or its representative(s), and the amount in dispute, etc.

Article 47. Correction of Award

Within thirty (30) days from its receipt of the arbitral award, either party may request in writing for a correction of any clerical, typographical, or calculation errors or any errors of a similar nature contained in the award; if such an error does exist in the award, the arbitral tribunal shall make a correction in writing within thirty (30) days from the date of receipt of the written request for the correction. The arbitral tribunal may likewise correct any such errors in writing on its own initiative within a reasonable time after the award is issued. Such correction in writing shall form a part of the arbitral award.

Article 48. Additional Award

Within thirty (30) days from the date on which the arbitral award is received, either party may request the arbitral tribunal in writing for an additional award on any claim or counterclaim which was advanced in the arbitration proceedings but was omitted from the award. If such omission does exist, the arbitral tribunal shall make an additional award within thirty (30) days from the date of receipt of the written request. The arbitral tribunal may also make an additional award on its own initiative within a reasonable period of time after the arbitral award is issued. Such additional award shall form a part of the arbitral award previously rendered.

Article 49. Execution of Award

1. The parties must automatically execute the arbitral award within the time period specified in the award. If no time limit is specified in the award, the parties shall execute the arbitral award immediately.

2. Where one party fails to execute the award, the other party may apply to a competent Chinese court for enforcement of the award pursuant to Chinese laws, or apply to a competent court for enforcement of the award according to the 1958 United Nations Convention on Recognition and Enforcement of Foreign Arbitral Awards or other international treaties that China has concluded or acceded to.

Chapter IV. Summary Procedure

Article 50. Application

1. Unless otherwise agreed by the parties, this Summary Procedure shall apply to any case where the amount in dispute does not exceeded RMB 500,000 yuan, or to any case where the amount in dispute exceeds RMB 500,000 yuan, yet one party applies for arbitration under this Summary Procedure and the other party agrees in writing.

2. Where no monetary claim is specified or the amount in dispute is not clear, the CIETAC shall determine whether or not to apply the Summary Procedure after a full consideration of such factors as the complexity of the case and the interests involved, etc.

Article 51. Notice of Arbitration

Where a Request for Arbitration is submitted to the CIETAC and is found to be acceptable for arbitration under the Summary Procedure, the Secretariat of the CIETAC or its Sub–Commission shall send a Notice of Arbitration to the parties.

Article 52. Formation of Arbitral Tribunal

An arbitral tribunal of a sole arbitrator shall be formed in accordance with Article 23 of these Rules to hear a case under the Summary Procedure.

Article 53. Statement of Defense and Counterclaim

1. Within twenty (20) days from the date of receipt of the Notice of Arbitration, the Respondent shall submit its Statement of Defense and relevant evidence to the Secretariat of the CIETAC; counterclaims, if any, shall also be filed with supporting evidence within the said time period. The arbitral tribunal may extend this time period if it considers it justified.

2. Within twenty (20) days from the date of receipt of the counterclaim and its attachments, the Claimant shall file its Statement of Defense to the Respondent's counterclaim.

Article 54. Conduct of Hearing

The arbitral tribunal may examine the case in the manner it considers appropriate. The arbitral tribunal may in its full discretion decide to examine the case only on the basis of the written materials and evidence submitted by the parties or to hold oral hearings.

Article 55. Oral Hearing

1. For a case examined by way of an oral hearing, the Secretariat of the CIETAC shall, after the arbitral tribunal has fixed a date for the oral hearing, notify the parties of the date at least fifteen (15) days in advance of the oral hearing date. A party having justified reasons may request the arbitral tribunal for a postponement of the oral hearing. However, such request must be communicated to the arbitral tribunal at least seven (7) days in advance of the oral hearing date. The arbitral tribunal shall decide whether to postpone the oral hearing or not.

2. Where the arbitral tribunal decides to hear the case orally, only one oral hearing shall be held unless it is otherwise truly necessary.

3. A notice of oral hearing subsequent to the first oral hearing and a notice of a postponed oral hearing shall not be subject to the fifteen (15)-day time limit provided for in the foregoing Paragraph 1.

Article 56. Time Limits for Rendering Award

1. The arbitral tribunal shall render an arbitral award within three (3) months from the date on which the arbitral tribunal is formed.

2. Upon the request of the arbitral tribunal, the Chairman of the CIETAC may extend the time period if he/she considers it truly necessary and the reasons for the extension truly justified.

Article 57. Change of Procedure

The application of the Summary Procedure shall not be affected by any amendment to the claim or by the filing of a counterclaim. Where the amount in dispute of the amended claim or that of the counterclaim exceeds RMB 500,000 Yuan, the procedure of the case shall be changed from the Summary Procedure to the general procedure unless the parties have agreed to the continuous application of the Summary Procedure.

Article 58. Context Reference

As to matters not covered in this Chapter, the relevant provisions in the other Chapters of these Rules shall apply.

Chapter V. Special Provisions for Domestic Arbitration

Article 59. Application

1. The provisions of this Chapter shall apply to domestic arbitration cases accepted by the CIETAC.

2. The provisions of the Summary Procedure of Chapter IV shall apply if a domestic arbitration case falls within the scope of Article 50 of these Rules.

Article 60. Acceptance

1. Where a Request for Arbitration is found to meet the formality requirements specified in Article 10 of these Rules, the CIETAC shall

accept the Request and notify the parties accordingly within five (5) days from its receipt of the Request or immediately upon its receipt of the Request. Where a Request for Arbitration is found not in conformity with the formality requirements, the CIETAC shall notify the party in writing of its refusal of the Request with reasons stated.

2. Upon receipt of a Request for Arbitration, the CIETAC may request the party to make corrections within a specified time period if it finds the Request is not in conformity with the provisions of Article 10 of these Rules.

Article 61. Formation of Arbitral Tribunal

The arbitral tribunal shall be formed in accordance with the provisions of Articles 21, 22, 23 and 24 of these Rules.

Article 62. Statement of Defense and Counterclaim

1. Within twenty (20) days from the date of receipt of the Notice of Arbitration, the Respondent shall submit its Statement of Defense and relevant evidence to the CIETAC; counterclaims, if any, shall also be filed with supporting evidence within the said time period. The arbitral tribunal may extend this time period if it considers it justified.

2. Within twenty (20) days from the date of receipt of the counterclaim and its attachments, the Claimant shall file its Statement of Defense to the Respondent's counterclaim.

Article 63. Notice of Oral Hearing

1. For a case examined by way of an oral hearing, the Secretariat of the CIETAC or its Sub–Commission shall notify the parties of the date of oral hearing at least fifteen (15) days in advance of the oral hearing date. The arbitral tribunal may hold the oral hearing ahead of the schedule with consent from both parties. A party having justified reasons may request the arbitral tribunal for a postponement of the oral hearing. However, such request must be communicated to the arbitral tribunal seven (7) days in advance of the oral hearing date. The arbitral tribunal shall decide whether to postpone the oral hearing or not.

2. A notice of oral hearing subsequent to the first oral hearing and a notice of a postponed oral hearing shall not be subject to the fifteen (15)-day time limit provided in the foregoing Paragraph 1.

Article 64. Record of Oral Hearing

1. The arbitral tribunal shall make a brief written record of the oral hearing. Any party or participant in the arbitration may apply for a correction of the record if any omission or mistake is found in the record regarding its own statement. If the application is refused by the arbitral tribunal, it shall nevertheless be recorded into the file.

2. The written record shall be signed or sealed by the arbitrator(s), the recorder, the parties, and other participants in the arbitration, if any.

Article 65. Time Limits for Rendering Award

1. The arbitral tribunal shall render an award within four (4) months from the date on which the arbitral tribunal is formed.

2. Upon the request of the arbitral tribunal, the Chairman of the CIETAC may extend this time period if he/she considers it truly necessary and the reasons truly justified.

Article 66. Context Reference

As to matters not covered in this Chapter, the relevant provisions in the other Chapters of these Rules shall apply.

Chapter VI. Supplementary Provisions

Article 67. Language

1. Where the parties have agreed on the arbitration language, their agreement shall prevail. Absent such agreement, the Chinese language shall be the official language to be used in the arbitration proceedings.

2. At an oral hearing, if a party or its representative(s) or witness requires language interpretation, the Secretariat of the CIETAC or its Sub–Commission may provide an interpreter, or the party may bring its own interpreter.

3. The arbitral tribunal and/or the Secretariat of the CIETAC or its Sub–Commission may, if it considers necessary, request the parties to submit a corresponding version of the documents and evidence by the parties in Chinese or in other languages.

Article 68. Service of Documents

1. All documents, notices and written materials in relation to the arbitration may be sent to the parties and/or their representatives in person, or by registered mail or express mail, facsimile, telex, cable, or by any other means considered proper by the Secretariat of the CIETAC or its Sub–Commission.

2. Any written correspondence to a party and/or its representative(s) shall be deemed to have been properly served on the party if delivered to the addressee or delivered at his place of business, registration, domicile, habitual residence or mailing address, or where, after reasonable inquiries by the other party, none of the aforesaid addresses can be found, the written correspondence is sent by the Secretariat of the CIETAC or its Sub–Commission to the addressee's last known place of business, registered address, domicile, habitual residence or mailing address by registered mail or by any other means that provides a record of the attempt of delivery.

Article 69. Arbitration Fees and Actual Expenses

1. Apart from charging arbitration fees to the parties according to the Fee Schedule of the CIETAC, the CIETAC may collect from the

parties other extra, reasonable and actual expenses including arbitrators' special remuneration and their travel and accommodation expenses incurred in dealing with the case, as well as the costs and expenses of experts, appraisers and interpreters appointed by the arbitral tribunal, etc.

2. Where a party has appointed an arbitrator who will incur extra expenses, such as travel and accommodation expenses, and fails to pay in advance as a deposit within a time period specified by the CIETAC, the party shall be deemed not to have appointed the arbitrator. In such event, the Chairman of the CIETAC may appoint an arbitrator for the party pursuant to Article 22 or Article 23 of these Rules.

3. Where the parties have agreed to hold an oral hearing at a place other than the CIETAC's domicile, extra expenses including travel and accommodation expenses incurred thereby shall be paid in advance as a deposit by the parties. In the event that the parties fail to do so, the oral hearing shall be held at the domicile of the CIETAC.

Article 70. Interpretation

1. The headings of the articles in these Rules shall not serve as interpretations of the contents of the provisions contained herein.

2. These Rules shall be interpreted by the CIETAC.

Article 71. Coming into Force

These Rules shall be effective as from May 1st, 2005. For cases accepted by the CIETAC or by its Sub–Commissions before these Rules become effective, the Arbitration Rules effective at the time of acceptance shall apply, or these Rules shall apply where both parties agree.

F. SWISS RULES OF INTERNATIONAL ARBITRATION (SWISS RULES)*

July 2004

MODEL ARBITRATION CLAUSE

Any dispute, controversy or claim arising out of or in relation to this contract, including the validity, invalidity, breach or termination thereof, shall be resolved by arbitration in accordance with the Swiss Rules of International Arbitration of the Swiss Chambers of Commerce in force on the date when the Notice of Arbitration is submitted in accordance with these Rules.

The number of arbitrators[3] shall be . . . (one or three);

The seat of the arbitration shall be . . . (name of city in Switzerland, unless the parties agree on a city abroad);

* The Swiss Rules can be found at https://www.sccam.org/sa/en/rules.php

3. For the sake of convenience only the masculine form is used within these Rules.

The arbitral proceedings shall be conducted in (insert desired language).

INTRODUCTION

(a) In the past, six Chambers of Commerce and Industry in Switzerland had their own different rules of arbitration for the resolution of international commercial disputes.

(b) In order to promote institutional arbitration in Switzerland and to harmonise the existing rules of arbitration, the Chambers of Commerce and Industry of Basel, Bern, Geneva, Ticino, Vaud and Zurich (hereinafter collectively "the Chambers") have adopted the present uniform rules, the Swiss Rules of International Arbitration (hereinafter the "Rules"), which replace the Chambers' former rules of international arbitration.

These Rules are based on the UNCITRAL Arbitration Rules, to which two types of changes and additions have been made:

i. Changes and additions required to adapt the UNCITRAL Arbitration Rules to institutional arbitration;

ii. Changes and additions reflecting modern practice and comparative law in the field of international arbitration. These changes and additions have been deliberately kept to a minimum. A comparative version of these Rules, in which the modifications to the UNCITRAL Arbitration Rules are italicised, is available on the website of the Chambers:

(c) When a Notice of Arbitration is submitted to one of the Chambers listed in Appendix A, an arbitral tribunal shall be constituted in accordance with these Rules.

(d) In order to ensure the administration of arbitrations under these Rules, the Chambers have appointed an Arbitration Committee (hereinafter the "Arbitration Committee"), which shall exercise the powers vested in the Chambers under these Rules, so that any reference to the Chambers in these Rules shall be deemed to refer to the Arbitration Committee.

(e) The Arbitration Committee is comprised of experienced practitioners of international arbitration. The Arbitration Committee shall designate from among its members the person or persons who will assist the Chambers in the administration and monitoring of the arbitral proceedings. In addition, the Arbitration Committee has designated from among its members a Special Committee (hereinafter the "Special Committee"), which shall render decisions under Articles 11 and 12 on the challenge and revocation of arbitrators and under Article 16 on the seat of arbitration, and advise the Chambers on other procedural matters that may arise in relation to the application of these Rules.

Section I. Introductory rules

SCOPE OF APPLICATION

Article 1

1. These Rules shall govern international arbitrations, where an agreement to arbitrate refers to these Rules, or to the arbitration rules of the Chambers of Commerce and Industry of Basel, Bern, Geneva, Ticino, Vaud, Zurich and any further Chamber of Commerce and Industry that may adhere to these Rules.

2. The parties are free to designate the seat of the arbitration in Switzerland or elsewhere.

3. These Rules shall come into force on January 1st, 2004 and, unless the parties have agreed otherwise, shall apply to all arbitral proceedings in which the Notice of Arbitration is submitted on or after that date.

NOTICE, CALCULATION OF PERIODS OF TIME

Article 2

1. For the purposes of these Rules, any notice, including a notification, communication or proposal, is deemed to have been received if it is physically delivered to the addressee or if it is delivered to its habitual residence, place of business or mailing address, or, if none of these can be found after making reasonable inquiry, then at the addressee's last-known residence or place of business. Notice shall be deemed to have been received on the day it is so delivered.

2. For the purposes of calculating a period of time under these Rules, such period shall begin to run on the day following the day when a notice, notification, communication or proposal is received. If the last day of such period is an official holiday or a non-business day at the residence or place of business of the addressee, the period is extended until the first business day which follows. Official holidays or non-business days occurring during the running of the period of time are included in calculating the period.

3. If the circumstances so justify, the Chambers may extend the time-limits provided in Section I (Introductory Rules) and Section II (Composition of the arbitral tribunal), as well as any time-limits that they have set.

NOTICE OF ARBITRATION AND ANSWER TO THE NOTICE OF ARBITRATION

Article 3

1. The party initiating recourse to arbitration (hereinafter called the "Claimant" or, where applicable, "Claimants") shall submit a Notice of Arbitration to the Chambers at any of the addresses listed in Appendix A.

2. Arbitral proceedings shall be deemed to commence on the date on which the Notice of Arbitration is received by the Chambers.

3. The Notice of Arbitration shall be submitted in as many copies as there are other parties (hereinafter called the "Respondent" or, where applicable, "Respondents"), together with an additional copy for each arbitrator and one copy for the Chambers, and shall include the following:

(a) A demand that the dispute be referred to arbitration;

(b) The names, addresses, telephone and fax numbers and e-mail addresses (if any) of the parties and of their counsel;

(c) A copy of the arbitration clause or the separate arbitration agreement that is invoked;

(d) A reference to the contract or other legal instrument(s) out of or in relation to which the dispute arises;

(e) The general nature of the claim and an indication of the amount involved, if any;

(f) The relief or remedy sought;

(g) A proposal as to the number of arbitrators (i.e. one or three), if the parties have not previously agreed thereon;

(h) The payment, by check or transfer to the account of the Chamber to which the Notice of Arbitration is submitted as listed in Appendix A, of the Registration Fee as required by Appendix B (Schedule of the Costs of Arbitration) in force on the date when the Notice of Arbitration is submitted.

4. The Notice of Arbitration may also include:

(a) The Claimant's proposals for the appointment of a sole arbitrator referred to in Article 7;

(b) The Claimant's designation of an arbitrator, for the purpose of constituting a three-member arbitral tribunal referred to in Article 8;

(c) The Statement of Claim referred to in Article 18.

5. If the Notice of Arbitration is incomplete or if the copies or attachments are not submitted in the required number, or if the Registration Fee is not paid, the Chambers may request the Claimant to remedy the defect within an appropriate period of time. The Chambers may also request within such time-limit a translation of the Notice of Arbitration if it is not submitted in English, German, French or Italian. If the Claimant complies with such directions within the applicable time-limit, the Notice of Arbitration shall be deemed to have been validly filed on the date when the initial version was received by the Chambers.

6. The Chambers shall provide without delay a copy of the Notice of Arbitration and of any exhibits included therewith to the Respondent, unless the Chambers decide, after consultation with the Special Committee, that there is manifestly no agreement to arbitrate referring to these Rules.

7. Within thirty days from receipt of the Notice of Arbitration, the Respondent shall submit to the Chambers an Answer to the Notice of Arbitration. This Answer to the Notice of Arbitration shall be submitted in as many copies as there are other parties, together with an additional copy for each arbitrator and one copy for the Chambers, and shall, to the extent possible, include the following:

(a) The name, address, telephone and fax numbers and e-mail address (if any) of the Respondent and of its counsel (if different from the description contained in the Notice of Arbitration);

(b) Any plea that an arbitral tribunal constituted under these Rules lacks jurisdiction;

(c) The Respondent's comments on the particulars set forth in the Notice of Arbitration, pursuant to Article 3, paragraph 3(e);

(d) The Respondent's answer to the relief or remedy sought in the Notice of Arbitration, pursuant to Article 3, paragraph 3(f);

(e) The Respondent's proposal as to the number of arbitrators (i.e. one or three), if the parties have not previously agreed thereon, pursuant to Article 3, paragraph 3(g).

8. The Answer to the Notice of Arbitration may also include:

(a) The Respondent's proposals for the appointment of a sole arbitrator referred to in Article 7;

(b) The Respondent's designation of an arbitrator for the purpose of constituting a three-member arbitral tribunal referred to in Article 8;

(c) The Statement of Defence referred to in Article 19.

9. Any counterclaim or set-off defence shall in principle be raised with the Respondent's Answer to the Notice of Arbitration. The provisions of Article 3, paragraph 3 are applicable to the counterclaim or set-off defence.

10. If no counterclaim or set-off defence is raised with the Respondent's Answer to the Notice of Arbitration, or if there is no indication of the amount of the counterclaim or set-off defence, the Chambers may rely exclusively on paragraph 3 (e) of the present Article 3 in order to determine the possible application of Article 42, paragraph 2 (Expedited Procedure).

11. The Chambers shall provide without delay a copy of the Answer to the Notice of Arbitration and of any exhibits included therewith to the Claimant.

12. Once the Registration Fee has been paid and all arbitrators have been confirmed, the Chambers shall transmit without delay the file to the sole arbitrator or to the arbitral tribunal.

13. The parties may be represented or assisted by persons of their choice. The names and addresses of such persons must be communicated in writing to the other party and the Chambers; such communication

must specify whether the appointment is being made for purposes of representation or assistance.

CONSOLIDATION OF ARBITRAL PROCEEDINGS (JOINDER), PARTICIPATION OF THIRD PARTIES

Article 4

1. Where a Notice of Arbitration is submitted between parties already involved in other arbitral proceedings pending under these Rules, the Chambers may decide, after consulting with the parties to all proceedings and the Special Committee, that the new case shall be referred to the arbitral tribunal already constituted for the existing proceedings. The Chambers may proceed likewise where a Notice of Arbitration is submitted between parties that are not identical to the parties in the existing arbitral proceedings. When rendering their decision, the Chambers shall take into account all circumstances, including the links between the two cases and the progress already made in the existing proceedings. Where the Chambers decide to refer the new case to the existing arbitral tribunal, the parties to the new case shall be deemed to have waived their right to designate an arbitrator.

2. Where a third party requests to participate in arbitral proceedings already pending under these Rules or where a party to arbitral proceedings under these Rules intends to cause a third party to participate in the arbitration, the arbitral tribunal shall decide on such request, after consulting with all parties, taking into account all circumstances it deems relevant and applicable.

Section II. Composition of the arbitral tribunal

CONFIRMATION OF ARBITRATORS

Article 5

1. All designations of a sole arbitrator or of the arbitrators composing a three-member arbitral tribunal, made by the parties or the arbitrators, are subject to confirmation by the Chambers, upon which the appointments shall become effective. The Chambers have no obligation to give reasons when they do not confirm an arbitrator.

2. Where a designation is not confirmed, the Chambers may

(a) either invite the party or parties concerned, or the arbitrators, as the case may be, to make a new designation within a reasonable time-limit; or

(b) proceed directly with the appointment.

NUMBER OF ARBITRATORS

Article 6

1. If the parties have not agreed upon the number of arbitrators, the Chambers shall decide whether the case shall be referred to a sole

arbitrator or to a three-member arbitral tribunal, taking into account all relevant circumstances.

2. As a rule, the Chambers shall refer the case to a sole arbitrator, unless the complexity of the subject matter and/or the amount in dispute justify that the case be referred to a three-member arbitral tribunal.

3. If the arbitration agreement provides for a three-member arbitral tribunal and if this appears inappropriate in view of the amount in dispute or of other circumstances, the Chambers shall advise the parties that they may wish to agree to refer the dispute to a sole arbitrator.

4. Where the amount in dispute does not exceed CHF 1'000'000 (one million Swiss francs), the provisions of Article 42, paragraph 2 (Expedited Procedure), shall apply.

APPOINTMENT OF A SOLE ARBITRATOR

Article 7

1. Where two or more parties have agreed that the dispute shall be referred to a sole arbitrator, they shall jointly designate the sole arbitrator within thirty days from the date when the Notice of Arbitration was received by the Respondent(s) unless the parties' agreement provides otherwise.

2. Where the parties have not agreed upon the number of arbitrators, they shall jointly designate the sole arbitrator within thirty days from the date when the Chambers' decision that the dispute shall be referred to a sole arbitrator was received by them.

3. If the parties fail to designate the sole arbitrator within the applicable time-limit, the Chambers shall proceed with the appointment.

APPOINTMENT OF ARBITRATORS IN BI-PARTY OR MULTI-PARTY PROCEEDINGS

Article 8

1. Where a dispute between two adverse parties is referred to a three-member arbitral tribunal, each party shall designate one arbitrator, unless the parties have agreed otherwise.

2. If a party fails to designate an arbitrator within the time-limit set by the Chambers or resulting from the arbitration agreement, the Chambers shall appoint the arbitrator. Unless the parties' agreement provides otherwise, the two arbitrators so appointed shall designate, within thirty days from the confirmation of the second arbitrator, a third arbitrator who shall act as the presiding arbitrator of the arbitral tribunal. Failing such designation, the Chambers shall appoint the presiding arbitrator.

3. In multi-party proceedings, the arbitral tribunal shall be constituted in accordance with the parties' agreement.

4. If the parties have not agreed upon a procedure for the constitution of the arbitral tribunal in multi-party proceedings, the Chambers

shall set an initial thirty-day time-limit for the Claimant or group of Claimants to designate an arbitrator and set a subsequent thirty-day time-limit for the Respondent or group of Respondents to designate an arbitrator. If the group or groups of parties have each designated an arbitrator, Article 8, paragraph 2 shall apply by analogy to the designation of the presiding arbitrator.

5. Where a party or group of parties fail(s) to designate an arbitrator in multiparty proceedings, the Chambers may appoint all three arbitrators and shall specify the presiding arbitrator.

INDEPENDENCE AND CHALLENGE OF ARBITRATORS (Articles 9 to 12)

Article 9

1. All arbitrators conducting an arbitration under these Rules shall be and remain at all times impartial and independent of the parties.

2. A prospective arbitrator shall disclose to those who approach him in connection with his possible appointment any circumstances likely to give rise to justifiable doubts as to his impartiality or independence. An arbitrator, once appointed or chosen, shall disclose such circumstances to the parties unless they have already been informed by him of these circumstances.

Article 10

1. Any arbitrator may be challenged if circumstances exist that give rise to justifiable doubts as to the arbitrator's impartiality or independence.

2. A party may challenge the arbitrator appointed by it only for reasons of which it becomes aware after the appointment has been made.

Article 11

1. If the arbitrator being challenged does not withdraw, the Special Committee shall decide on the challenge.

2. The decision of the Special Committee is final. The Special Committee has no obligation to give reasons.

Article 12

1. If an arbitrator fails to perform his functions despite a written warning from the other arbitrators or from the Chambers, the Special Committee may revoke the appointment of that arbitrator.

2. The arbitrator shall have an opportunity to present his position to the Special Committee. The decision of the Special Committee is final. The Special Committee has no obligation to give reasons.

REPLACEMENT OF AN ARBITRATOR

Article 13

1. If an arbitrator designated by a party deceases or becomes unable to perform his functions due to any reasons beyond his control, the

Chambers shall set a time-limit for the party having designated that arbitrator to designate a replacement arbitrator. This rule also applies if an arbitrator has been successfully challenged, has been otherwise removed or has resigned.

2. If the party concerned fails to designate a replacement arbitrator within the applicable time limit, the Chambers shall appoint a replacement arbitrator.

CONSEQUENCES OF THE REPLACEMENT OF AN ARBITRATOR

Article 14

If an arbitrator is replaced, the proceedings shall as a rule resume at the stage where the arbitrator who was replaced ceased to perform his functions, unless the arbitral tribunal decides otherwise.

Section III. Arbitral proceedings

GENERAL PROVISIONS

Article 15

1. Subject to these Rules, the arbitral tribunal may conduct the arbitration in such manner as it considers appropriate, provided that it ensures equal treatment of the parties and their right to be heard.

2. At any stage of the proceedings, the arbitral tribunal may hold hearings for the presentation of evidence by witnesses, including expert witnesses, or for oral argument. After consulting with the parties, the arbitral tribunal may also decide to conduct the proceedings on the basis of documents and other materials.

3. At an early stage of the arbitral proceedings and in consultation with the parties, the arbitral tribunal shall prepare a provisional timetable for the arbitral proceedings, which shall be provided to the parties and, for information, to the Chambers.

4. All documents or information supplied to the arbitral tribunal by one party shall at the same time be communicated by that party to the other party.

5. The arbitral tribunal may, after consulting with the parties, appoint a secretary. Article 9 of these Rules shall apply by analogy to the secretary.

6. All participants in the arbitral proceedings shall act in accordance with the requirements of good faith.

SEAT OF THE ARBITRATION

Article 16

1. If the parties have not determined the seat of the arbitration, or if such designation is unclear or incomplete, the Special Committee shall

determine the seat of the arbitration taking into account all relevant circumstances, or shall request the arbitral tribunal to determine the seat.

2. Without prejudice to the determination of the seat of the arbitration, the arbitral tribunal may decide where the proceedings shall be conducted. In particular, it may hear witnesses and hold meetings for consultation among its members at any place it deems appropriate, having regard to the circumstances of the arbitration.

3. The arbitral tribunal may meet at any place it deems appropriate for the inspection of goods, other property or documents. The parties shall be given sufficient notice to enable them to be present at such inspection.

4. The award shall be deemed to be made at the seat of the arbitration.

LANGUAGE

Article 17

1. Subject to an agreement by the parties, the arbitral tribunal shall, promptly after its appointment, determine the language or languages to be used in the proceedings. This determination shall apply to the Statement of Claim, the Statement of Defence, and any further written statements and, if oral hearings take place, to the language or languages to be used in such hearings.

2. The arbitral tribunal may order that any documents annexed to the Statement of Claim or Statement of Defence, and any supplementary documents or exhibits submitted in the course of the proceedings, delivered in their original language, shall be accompanied by a translation into the language or languages agreed upon by the parties or determined by the arbitral tribunal.

STATEMENT OF CLAIM

Article 18

1. Unless the Statement of Claim was contained in the Notice of Arbitration, within a period of time to be determined by the arbitral tribunal, the Claimant shall communicate its Statement of Claim in writing to the Respondent and to each of the arbitrators. A copy of the contract, and of the arbitration agreement if not contained in the contract, shall be annexed thereto.

2. The Statement of Claim shall include the following particulars:

(a) The names and addresses of the parties;

(b) A statement of the facts supporting the claim;

(c) The points at issue;

(d) The relief or remedy sought.

3. As a rule, the Claimant shall annex to its Statement of Claim all documents it deems relevant.

STATEMENT OF DEFENCE

Article 19

1. Within a period of time to be determined by the arbitral tribunal and unless the Statement of Defence was contained in the Answer to the Notice of Arbitration, the Respondent shall communicate its Statement of Defence in writing to the Claimant and to each of the arbitrators.

2. The Statement of Defence shall reply to the particulars (b), (c) and (d) of the Statement of Claim (Article 18, paragraph 2). If the Respondent has raised an objection to the jurisdiction or to the proper constitution of the arbitral tribunal, the Statement of Defence shall contain the factual and legal basis of such objection. As a rule, the Respondent shall annex to its Statement of Defence all documents on which it relies for its defence.

3. The provisions of Article 18, paragraphs 2 (b)–(d), shall apply to a counterclaim and a claim relied on for the purpose of a set-off.

AMENDMENTS TO THE CLAIM OR DEFENCE

Article 20

1. During the course of the arbitral proceedings either party may amend or supplement its claim or defence unless the arbitral tribunal considers it inappropriate to allow such amendment having regard to the delay in making it or prejudice to the other party or any other circumstances. However, a claim may not be amended in such a manner that the amended claim falls outside the scope of the arbitration clause or separate arbitration agreement.

2. The arbitral tribunal may adjust the costs of the arbitration if a party amends or supplements its claims, counterclaims or defences.

PLEAS AS TO THE JURISDICTION OF THE ARBITRAL TRIBUNAL

Article 21

1. The arbitral tribunal shall have the power to rule on objections that it has no jurisdiction, including any objections with respect to the existence or validity of the arbitration clause or of the separate arbitration agreement.

2. The arbitral tribunal shall have the power to determine the existence or the validity of the contract of which an arbitration clause forms a part. For the purposes of Article 21, an arbitration clause which forms part of a contract and which provides for arbitration under these Rules shall be treated as an agreement independent of the other terms of the contract. A decision by the arbitral tribunal that the contract is null and void shall not entail *ipso jure* the invalidity of the arbitration clause.

3. As a rule, a plea that the arbitral tribunal does not have jurisdiction shall be raised in the Answer to the Notice of Arbitration, but in no

event later than in the Statement of Defence referred to in Article 19, or, with respect to a counterclaim, in the reply to the counterclaim.

4. In general, the arbitral tribunal should rule on a plea concerning its jurisdiction as a preliminary question. However, the arbitral tribunal may proceed with the arbitration and rule on such a plea in its final award.

5. The arbitral tribunal shall have jurisdiction to hear a set-off defence even when the relationship out of which this defence is said to arise is not within the scope of the arbitration clause or is the object of another arbitration agreement or forum-selection clause.

FURTHER WRITTEN STATEMENTS

Article 22

The arbitral tribunal shall decide which further written statements, in addition to the Statement of Claim and the Statement of Defence, shall be required from the parties or may be presented by them and shall set the periods of time for communicating such statements.

PERIODS OF TIME

Article 23

The periods of time set by the arbitral tribunal for the communication of written statements (including the Statement of Claim and Statement of Defence) should not exceed forty-five days. However, the arbitral tribunal may extend the time-limits if it concludes that an extension is justified.

EVIDENCE AND HEARINGS (Articles 24 and 25)

Article 24

1. Each party shall have the burden of proving the facts relied on to support its claim or defence.

2. The arbitral tribunal may, if it considers it appropriate, require a party to deliver to the tribunal and to the other party, within such a period of time as the arbitral tribunal shall decide, a summary of the documents and other evidence which that party intends to present in support of the facts in issue set out in its Statement of Claim or Statement of Defence.

3. At any time during the arbitral proceedings the arbitral tribunal may require the parties to produce documents, exhibits or other evidence within such a period of time as the tribunal shall determine.

Article 25

1. In the event of an oral hearing, the arbitral tribunal shall give the parties adequate advance notice of the date, time and place thereof.

2. Any person may be a witness or an expert witness. If witnesses or expert witnesses are to be heard, at least fifteen days before the hearing

each party shall communicate to the arbitral tribunal and to the other party the names and addresses of the witnesses or expert witnesses it intends to present, the subject upon and the languages in which such witnesses or expert witnesses will give their testimony.

3. The arbitral tribunal shall make arrangements for the translation of oral statements made at a hearing and for a record of the hearing if either is deemed necessary by the tribunal under the circumstances of the case, or if the parties have agreed thereto and have communicated such agreement to the tribunal at least fifteen days before the hearing.

4. Hearings shall be held *in camera* unless the parties agree otherwise. The arbitral tribunal may require the retirement of any witness or witnesses or expert witnesses during the testimony of other witnesses or expert witnesses. The arbitral tribunal is free to determine the manner in which witnesses or expert witnesses are examined.

5. Evidence of witnesses or expert witnesses may also be presented in the form of written statements or reports signed by them.

6. It shall not be improper for a party, its officers, employees, legal advisors or counsel to interview witnesses, potential witnesses or expert witnesses.

7. The arbitral tribunal shall determine the admissibility, relevance, materiality and weight of the evidence offered.

INTERIM MEASURES OF PROTECTION

Article 26

1. At the request of either party, the arbitral tribunal may take any interim measures it deems necessary or appropriate.

2. Such interim measures may be established in the form of an interim award. The arbitral tribunal shall be entitled to order the provision of appropriate security.

3. A request for interim measures addressed by any party to a judicial authority shall not be deemed incompatible with the agreement to arbitrate, or as a waiver of that agreement.

4. The arbitral tribunal shall have discretion to apportion the costs relating to a request for interim measures in the interim award or in the final award.

TRIBUNAL-APPOINTED EXPERTS

Article 27

1. The arbitral tribunal, after consulting with the parties, may appoint one or more experts to report to it, in writing, on specific issues to be determined by the tribunal. A copy of the expert's terms of reference, established by the arbitral tribunal, shall be communicated to the parties.

2. The parties shall give the expert any relevant information or produce for his inspection any relevant documents or goods that he may

require of them. Any dispute between a party and such expert as to the relevance of the required information or production shall be referred to the arbitral tribunal for decision.

3. Upon receipt of the expert's report, the arbitral tribunal shall communicate a copy of the report to the parties who shall be given the opportunity to express, in writing, their opinion on the report. A party shall be entitled to examine any document on which the expert has relied in his report.

4. At the request of either party the expert, after delivery of the report, may be heard at a hearing where the parties shall have the opportunity to be present and to interrogate the expert. At this hearing either party may present expert witnesses in order to testify on the points at issue. The provisions of Article 25 shall be applicable to such proceedings.

5. The provisions of Article 9 shall apply by analogy to any expert appointed by the arbitral tribunal.

DEFAULT

Article 28

1. If, within the period of time set by the arbitral tribunal, the Claimant has failed to communicate its claim without showing sufficient cause for such failure, the arbitral tribunal shall issue an order for the termination of the arbitral proceedings. If, within the period of time set by the arbitral tribunal, the Respondent has failed to communicate its Statement of Defence without showing sufficient cause for such failure, the arbitral tribunal shall order that the proceedings continue.

2. If one of the parties, duly notified under these Rules, fails to appear at a hearing, without showing sufficient cause for such failure, the arbitral tribunal may proceed with the arbitration.

3. If one of the parties, duly invited to produce documentary evidence, fails to do so within the established period of time, without showing sufficient cause for such failure, the arbitral tribunal may make the award on the evidence before it.

CLOSURE OF PROCEEDINGS

Article 29

1. The arbitral tribunal may inquire of the parties if they have any further proof to offer or witnesses to be heard or submissions to make and, if there are none, it may declare the proceedings closed.

2. The arbitral tribunal may, if it considers it necessary owing to exceptional circumstances, decide, on its own motion or upon application of a party, to reopen the proceedings at any time before the award is made.

WAIVER OF RULES

Article 30

A party who knows that any provision of, or requirement under, these Rules has not been complied with and yet proceeds with the arbitration without promptly stating its objection to such non-compliance, shall be deemed to have waived its right to object.

Section IV. The Award

DECISIONS

Article 31

1. When there are three arbitrators, any award or other decision of the arbitral tribunal shall be made by a majority of the arbitrators. If there is no majority, the award shall be made by the presiding arbitrator alone.

2. In the case of questions of procedure, when the arbitral tribunal so authorises, the presiding arbitrator may decide on his own, subject to revision, if any, by the arbitral tribunal.

FORM AND EFFECT OF THE AWARD

Article 32

1. In addition to making a final award, the arbitral tribunal shall be entitled to make interim, interlocutory, or partial awards. If appropriate, the arbitral tribunal may also award costs in awards that are not final.

2. The award shall be made in writing and shall be final and binding on the parties. The parties undertake to carry out the award without delay.

3. The arbitral tribunal shall state the reasons upon which the award is based, unless the parties have agreed that no reasons are to be given.

4. An award shall be signed by the arbitrators and it shall contain the date on which and the place where the award was made. Where there are three arbitrators and one or two of them fail(s) to sign, the award shall state the reason for the absence of the signature(s).

5. Publication of the award is governed by Article 43.

6. Originals of the award signed by the arbitrators shall be communicated to the parties and to the Chambers by the arbitral tribunal. The Chambers shall retain a copy of the award.

APPLICABLE LAW, AMIABLE COMPOSITEUR

Article 33

1. The arbitral tribunal shall decide the case in accordance with the rules of law agreed upon by the parties or, in the absence of a choice of

law, by applying the rules of law with which the dispute has the closest connection.

2. The arbitral tribunal shall decide as *amiable compositeur* or *ex aequo et bono* only if the parties have expressly authorised the arbitral tribunal to do so.

3. In all cases, the arbitral tribunal shall decide in accordance with the terms of the contract and shall take into account the usages of the trade applicable to the transaction.

SETTLEMENT OR OTHER GROUNDS FOR TERMINATION

Article 34

1. If, before the award is made, the parties agree on a settlement of the dispute, the arbitral tribunal shall either issue an order for the termination of the arbitral proceedings or, if requested by both parties and accepted by the tribunal, record the settlement in the form of an arbitral award on agreed terms. The arbitral tribunal is not obliged to give reasons for such an award.

2. If, before the award is made, the continuation of the arbitral proceedings becomes unnecessary or impossible for any reason not mentioned in paragraph 1, the arbitral tribunal shall inform the parties of its intention to issue an order for the termination of the proceedings. The arbitral tribunal shall have the power to issue such an order unless a party raises justifiable grounds for objection.

3. Copies of the order for termination of the arbitral proceedings or of the arbitral award on agreed terms, signed by the arbitrators, shall be communicated by the arbitral tribunal to the parties and to the Chambers. Where an arbitral award on agreed terms is made, the provisions of Article 32, paragraphs 2 and 4 to 6, shall apply.

INTERPRETATION OF THE AWARD

Article 35

1. Within thirty days after the receipt of the award, either party, with notice to the other party, may request that the arbitral tribunal give an interpretation of the award. The arbitral tribunal may set a time-limit, normally not exceeding thirty days, for the other party to comment on such request.

2. The interpretation shall be given in writing within forty-five days after the receipt of the request. The interpretation shall form part of the award and the provisions of Article 32, paragraphs 2 to 6, shall apply.

CORRECTION OF THE AWARD

Article 36

1. Within thirty days after the receipt of the award, either party, with notice to the other party, may request the arbitral tribunal to correct in the award any errors in computation, any clerical or typographical

errors, or any errors of similar nature. The arbitral tribunal may set a time limit, normally not exceeding thirty days, for the other party to comment on such request.

2. The arbitral tribunal may within thirty days after the communication of the award make such corrections on its own initiative.

3. Such corrections shall be in writing, and the provisions of Article 32, paragraphs 2 to 6, shall apply.

ADDITIONAL AWARD

Article 37

1. Within thirty days after the receipt of the award, either party, with notice to the other party, may request the arbitral tribunal to make an additional award as to claims presented in the arbitral proceedings but omitted from the award. The arbitral tribunal may set a time-limit, normally not exceeding thirty days, for the other party to comment on such request.

2. If the arbitral tribunal considers the request for an additional award to be justified and considers that the omission can be rectified without any further hearings or evidence, it shall complete its award within sixty days after the receipt of the request.

3. When an additional award is made, the provisions of Article 32, paragraphs 2 to 6, shall apply.

COSTS (Articles 38 to 40)

Article 38

The arbitral tribunal shall determine the costs of arbitration in its award. The term "costs" includes only:

(a) The fees of the arbitral tribunal to be stated separately as to each arbitrator and to be determined by the tribunal itself in accordance with Article 39;

(b) The travel and other expenses incurred by the arbitrators;

(c) The costs of expert advice and of other assistance required by the arbitral tribunal;

(d) The travel and other expenses of witnesses to the extent such expenses are approved by the arbitral tribunal;

(e) The costs for legal representation and assistance of the successful party if such costs were claimed during the arbitral proceedings, and only to the extent that the arbitral tribunal determines that the amount of such costs is reasonable;

(f) The costs for the administration of the arbitration payable to the Chambers in accordance with Appendix B (Schedule of the Costs of Arbitration).

Article 39

1. The fees of the arbitral tribunal shall be reasonable in amount, taking into account the amount in dispute, the complexity of the subject-matter, the time spent by the arbitrators and any other relevant circumstances of the case, including, but not limited to, the discontinuation of the arbitral proceedings in case of settlement or other reasons. In the event of such discontinuation, the fees of the arbitral tribunal may be less than the minimum amount resulting from Appendix B (Schedule of the Costs of Arbitration).

2. The fees of the arbitral tribunal shall be determined in conformity with Appendix B (Schedule of the Costs of Arbitration).

3. The arbitral tribunal shall decide on the allocation of the fees among its members. As a rule, the Chairman shall receive between 40% and 50% and each co-arbitrator between 25% and 30% of the total fees, in view of the time and efforts spent by each arbitrator.

Article 40

1. Except as provided in paragraph 2, the costs of arbitration shall in principle be borne by the unsuccessful party. However, the arbitral tribunal may apportion each of such costs between the parties if it determines that apportionment is reasonable, taking into account the circumstances of the case.

2. With respect to the costs of legal representation and assistance referred to in Article 38, paragraph (e), the arbitral tribunal, taking into account the circumstances of the case, shall be free to determine which party shall bear such costs or may apportion such costs between the parties if it determines that apportionment is reasonable.

3. When the arbitral tribunal issues an order for the termination of the arbitral proceedings or makes an award on agreed terms, it shall determine the costs of arbitration referred to in Article 38 and Article 39, paragraph 1, in the text of that order or award.

4. Before rendering the award, the arbitral tribunal shall submit its draft award to the Chambers for consultation on the decision as to the assessment and apportionment of the costs.

5. No additional fees may be charged by an arbitral tribunal for interpretation or correction or completion of its award under Articles 35 to 37.

DEPOSIT OF COSTS

Article 41

1. The arbitral tribunal, on its establishment, shall request each party to deposit an equal amount as an advance for the costs referred to in Article 38, paragraphs (a), (b), (c) and (f). The arbitral tribunal shall provide a copy of such request for information to the Chambers.

2. Where a Respondent submits a counterclaim, or it otherwise appears appropriate in the circumstances, the arbitral tribunal may in its discretion establish separate deposits.

3. During the course of the arbitral proceedings the arbitral tribunal may request supplementary deposits from the parties. The arbitral tribunal shall provide a copy of such request for information to the Chambers.

4. If the required deposits are not paid in full within thirty days after the receipt of the request, the arbitral tribunal shall so inform the parties in order that one or another of them may make the required payment. If such payment is not made, the arbitral tribunal may order the suspension or termination of the arbitral proceedings.

5. In its final award, the arbitral tribunal shall render an accounting to the parties of the deposits received. Any unexpended balance shall be returned to the parties.

Section V. Expedited Procedure

Article 42

1. If the parties so agree, or if the provisions of Article 42, paragraph 2 are applicable, the arbitral proceedings shall be conducted in accordance with an Expedited Procedure based upon the foregoing provisions of these Rules, subject to the following changes:

(a) The Chambers may shorten the time-limits for the appointment of arbitrators;

(b) After the submission of the Answer to the Notice of Arbitration, the parties shall in principle be entitled to submit one Statement of Claim and one Statement of Defence (and Counterclaim) and, where applicable, one Statement of Defence in reply to the Counterclaim;

(c) Unless the parties agree that the dispute shall be decided on the basis of documentary evidence only, the arbitral tribunal shall hold a single hearing for the examination of the witnesses and expert witnesses as well as for oral argument;

(d) The award shall be made within six months from the date when the Chambers transmitted the file to the arbitral tribunal. In exceptional circumstances, the Chambers may extend this time-limit;

(e) The arbitral tribunal shall state the reasons upon which the award is based in summary form, unless the parties have agreed that no reasons are to be given.

2. The following provisions shall apply to all cases in which the amount in dispute representing the aggregate of the claim and the counterclaim (or any set-off defence) does not exceed CHF 1'000'000 (one million Swiss francs), unless the Chambers decide otherwise taking into account all relevant circumstances:

(a) The arbitral proceedings shall be conducted in accordance with the Expedited Procedure set forth in Article 42, paragraph 1;

(b) The case shall be referred to a sole arbitrator, unless the arbitration agreement provides for a three-member arbitral tribunal;

(c) If the arbitration agreement provides for a three-member arbitral tribunal, the Chambers shall invite the parties to agree to refer the case to a sole arbitrator. If the parties do not agree to refer the case to a sole arbitrator, the fees of the three arbitrators shall be determined in accordance with Appendix B (Schedule of the Costs of Arbitration), but shall in no event be less than the fees resulting from the hourly rate of Section 2.8 of Appendix B.

Section VI. Confidentiality and exclusion of liability

Article 43

1. Unless the parties expressly agree in writing to the contrary, the parties undertake as a general principle to keep confidential all awards and orders as well as all materials submitted by another party in the framework of the arbitral proceedings not otherwise in the public domain, save and to the extent that a disclosure may be required of a party by a legal duty, to protect or pursue a legal right or to enforce or challenge an award in legal proceedings before a judicial authority. This undertaking also applies to the arbitrators, the tribunal-appointed experts, the secretary of the arbitral tribunal and the Chambers.

2. The deliberations of the arbitral tribunal are confidential.

3. An award may be published, whether in its entirety or in the form of excerpts or a summary, only under the following conditions:

(a) A request for publication is addressed to the Chambers;

(b) All references to the parties' names are deleted; and

(c) No party objects to such publication within the time–limit fixed for that purpose by the Chambers.

Article 44

1. None of the Chambers or their staff, arbitrators, tribunal-appointed experts or the secretary of the arbitral tribunal shall be liable for any act or omission in connection with an arbitration conducted under these Rules, save where the act or omission is shown to constitute deliberate wrongdoing or extremely serious negligence.

2. After the award has been made and the possibilities of correction, interpretation and additional awards referred to in Articles 35 to 37 have lapsed or been exhausted, neither the Chambers nor the arbitrators, the tribunal-appointed experts or the secretary of the arbitral tribunal shall be under an obligation to make statements to any person about any matter concerning the arbitration, nor shall a party seek to make any of these persons a witness in any legal or other proceedings arising out of the arbitration.

APPENDIX A: Addresses of the Chambers of Commerce

Basel Chamber of Commerce
Aeschenvorstadt 67
P.O. Box
CH–4010 Basel
Telephone: +41 61 270 60 50
Fax: +41 61 270 60 05
E-mail: schiedsgericht@hkbb.ch
Bank details: UBS AG, CH–4002 Basel
Account No: 292–10157720.0
Clearing No: 292
Iban: CH98 0029 2292 10157720 0

Chamber of Commerce and Industry of Bern
Gutenbergstrasse 1
P.O. Box 5464
CH–3001 Bern
Telephone: +41 31 388 87 87
Fax: +41 31 388 87 88
E-mail: info@bern-cci.ch
Bank details: BEKB
Account No: KK 16 166.151.0.44 HIV Kanton Bern
Clearing No: 790
Swift Code: KBBECH22
Iban: CH35 0079 0016 1661 5104 4

Chamber of Commerce and Industry of Geneva
4, Boulevard du Théâtre
P.O. Box 5039
CH–1211 Geneva 11
Telephone: +41 22 819 91 11
Fax: +41 22 819 91 36
E-mail: arbitration@ccig.ch
Bank details: UBS SA, Rue du Rhône 8, 1204 Genève
Account No: 279–HU108533.1
Clearing No: 279
Swift code: UBSWCHZH12A
Iban: CH13 0027 9279 HU1085331

Chamber of Commerce and Industry of Ticino
Corso Elvezia 16
P.O. Box 2378CH–6901 Lugano
Telephone: +41 91 911 51 11
Fax: +41 91 911 51 12
E-mail: cciati@cci.ch
Bank details: Banca della Svizzera Italiana
(BSI), Via Magatti 2, CH–6901 Lugano
Account No: A201021A 8465

Clearing No: 8475
Iban: CH64 0846 5000 0A20 1021 A

Chamber of Commerce and Industry of Vaud
Avenue d'Ouchy 47
P.O. Box 205
CH–1000 Lausanne 13
Telephone: +41 21 613 35 35
Fax: +41 21 613 35 05
E-mail: direction@cvci.ch
Bank details: Banque Cantonale Vaudoise,
1001 Lausanne
Account No: C. 308.53.47
Clearing No: 767
Swift Code: BCVLCH2 L
Iban: CH96 0076 7001 U030 8534 7

Zurich Chamber of Commerce
Bleicherweg 5
P.O. Box 3058
CH–8022 Zurich
Telephone: +41 1 217 40 50
Fax: +41 1 217 40 51
E-mail: direktion@zurichcci.ch
Bank details: Credit Suisse, CH–8070 Zurich
Account No: 497380–01
Clearing No: 4835
Swift Code: CRES CH ZZ 80A
Iban: CH62 0483 5049 7380 0100 0

APPENDIX B: Schedule of the Costs of Arbitration

(All amounts in this Appendix B are in Swiss francs, hereinafter "CHF")

1. Registration Fee

1.1 When submitting a Notice of Arbitration, the Claimant shall pay a Registration Fee of

- CHF 4'500 for arbitrations where the amount in dispute does not exceed CHF 2'000'000;
- CHF 6'000 for arbitrations where the amount in dispute is between CHF 2'000'001 and CHF 10'000'000;
- CHF 8'000 for arbitrations where the amount in dispute exceeds CHF10'000'000.

1.2 If the amount in dispute is not quantified, the Claimant shall pay a Registration Fee of CHF 6'000.

1.3 If the Claimant fails to pay the Registration Fee, the Chambers shall not proceed with the arbitration.

1.4 The Registration Fee is not refundable.

1.5 The above provisions shall apply to any counterclaim.

2. Arbitrators' fees and the Chambers' Administrative Costs

2.1 The arbitrators' fees (Article 38, paragraph a) shall cover the activities of the arbitral tribunal from the moment the file is transmitted until the last award.

2.2 Where the amount in dispute exceeds the threshold specified in Section 2.3 of this Appendix B, Administrative Costs shall be payable to the Chambers, in addition to the Registration Fee.

2.3 As a rule, the arbitrators' fees and the Chambers' Administrative Costs shall be computed on the basis of the following scale, taking into account the criteria of Article 39, paragraph 1:

Amount in dispute (in Swiss francs)	Fee of Sole Arbitrator[2]		Fee of three-member arbitral tribunal		Administrative Costs[3] fixed by the Chambers
	min.	max.	min.	max.	
up to CHF 300'000	4%	12%	10%	30%	
CHF 300'001 to CHF 600'000	2%	8%	5%	20%	
CHF 600'001 to CHF 1'000'000	1.5%	6%	3.75%	15%	
CHF 1'000'001 to CHF 2'000'000	0.6%	3.6%	1.5%	9%	
CHF 2'000'001 to CHF 10'000'000	0.38%	1.5%	0.95%	3.75%	CHF 4'000 +0.2%
CHF 10'000'001 to CHF 20'000'000	0.3%	0.6%	0.75%	1.5%	0.1%
CHF 20'000'001 to CHF 50'000'000	0.1%	0.2%	0.25%	0.5%	0.05%
CHF 50'000'001 to CHF 100'000'000	0.06%	0.18%	0.15%	0.45%	0.01%
CHF 100'000'001 to CHF 250'000'000	0.02%	0.1%	0.05%	0.25%	CHF 50'000
over CHF 250'000'000	0.01%	0.06%	0.025%	0.15%	CHF 50'000

2. The fees for a sole arbitrator represent 40% of the fees for a three-member arbitral tribunal.

3. This is a contribution, in the maximum amount of CHF 50'000, to the administrative costs of the Chambers, in addition to the Registration Fee. In the event of discontinuation of the arbitral proceedings (Article 39, paragraph 1), the Chambers may, in their discretion, reimburse all or part of the Administrative Costs.

The fees and administrative costs payable for each successive range in this chart are **added together**.

The arbitrators' fees and the Chambers' Administrative Costs may exceed the amounts set out in the scale above only in exceptional circumstances and with prior approval by the Chambers.

2.4 Claims and counterclaims are added for the determination of the amount in dispute. The same rule applies to set-off defences, unless the arbitral tribunal, after consulting with the parties, concludes that such set-off claims will not require significant additional work.

2.5 Interest claims shall not be taken into account for the calculation of the amount in dispute. However, when the interest claims exceed the amounts claimed in principal, the interest claims alone shall be considered in calculating the amount in dispute.

2.6 Currencies other than the Swiss franc shall be converted into Swiss francs at the average rate of exchange between the date when the Notice of Arbitration is received by the Chambers and the date when the final award is made. For the purpose of determining the Registration Fee under Section 1 of this Appendix B, the rate of exchange shall be that of the date when the Notice of Arbitration is received by the Chambers.

2.7 If the amount in dispute is not quantified, the Arbitrators' fees and the Chambers' Administrative costs shall be fixed by the arbitral tribunal, taking into account all relevant circumstances.

2.8 Where the parties do not agree to refer the case to a Sole arbitrator as provided for by Article 42, paragraph 2 (Expedited Procedure), the fees of the three arbitrators shall be determined in accordance with the above Schedule of the Costs of Arbitration but shall in no event be less than the fees resulting from the application of an hourly rate of CHF 350 (three hundred fifty Swiss francs).

3. Arbitrators' expenses

The expenses of the arbitrators shall relate to the actual disbursements for the arbitration, such as expenses relating to: travel (first class airfare accepted only for distances exceeding 4000 kilometers), accommodation, meals (if in home city, only meals among arbitrators are taken into account), taxi, communications costs, and any other costs related to the conduct of the proceedings (such as rental of hearing rooms, court reporting services, interpreters, etc.). The Chambers may issue general guidelines to the arbitrators for the accounting of their expenses.

4. Income earned on deposits made by the parties

In consultation with the parties, the arbitral tribunal may invest the deposits made by the parties, taking into account market conditions and criteria of prudent and secure investment. When deciding whether to make such investments, the arbitral tribunal shall also have due regard to the possible need to make the deposited funds available immediately. Any income earned shall be included in the final computation of the costs of the arbitration in favour of the party or parties having made the deposit or deposits so invested.

APPENDIX C: Arbitrators' fees

Sole Arbitrator

Amount in dispute (in Swiss francs)		**Administrative costs**	**Sole Arbitrator**	
			Minimum	Maximum
0 -	300'000	-	4% of amount	12% of amount
300'001 -	600'000	-	12'000 + 2% of amount over 300'000	36'000 + 8% of amount over 300'000
600'001 -	1'000'000	-	18'000 + 1.5% of amount over 600'000	60'000 + 6% of amount over 600'000
1'000'001 -	2'000'000	-	24'000 + 0.6% of amount over 1'000'000	84'000 + 3.6% of amount over 1'000'000
2'000'001 -	10'000'000	4'000 + 0.2% of amount over 2'000'000	30'000 + 0.38% of amount over 2'000'000	120'000 + 1.5% of amount over 2'000'000
10'000'001	20'000'000	20'000 + 0.1% of amount over 10'000'000	60'400 + 0.3% of amount over 10'000'000	240'000 + 0.6% of amount over 10'000'000
20'000'001 -	50'000'000	30'000 + 0.05% of amount over 20'000'000	90'400 + 0.1% of amount over 20'000'000	300'000 + 0.2% of amount over 20'000'000
50'000'001 -	100'000'000	45'000 + 0.01% of amount over 50'000'000	120'400 + 0.06% of amount over 50'000'000	360'000 + 0.18% of amount over 50'000'000
100'000'001	250'000'000	50'000	150'400 + 0.02% of amount over 100'000'000	450'000 + 0,1% of amount over 100'000'000
> 250'000'000		50'000	180'400 + 0.01% of amount over 250'000'000	600'000 + 0.06% of amount over 250'000'000

APPENDIX C: Arbitrators' fees

Three Arbitrators

Amount in dispute (in Swiss francs)		**Administrative costs**	**Sole Arbitrator**	
			Minimum	Maximum
0 -	300'000	-	10% of amount	30% of amount
300'001 -	600'000	-	30'000 + 5% of amount over 300'000	90'000 + 20% of amount over 300'000
600'001 -	1'000'000	-	45'000 + 3.75% of amount over 600'000	150'000 + 15% of amount over 600'000
1'000'001 -	2'000'000	-	65'000 + 1.5% of amount over 1'000'000	210'000 + 9% of amount over 1'000'000
2'000'001 -	10'000'000	4'000 + 0.2% of amount over 2'000'000	75'000 + 0.95% of amount over 2'000'000	300'000 + 3.75% of amount over 2'000'000
10'000'001 -	20'000'000	20'000 + 0.1% of amount over 10'000'000	151'000 + 0.75% of amount over 10'000'000	600'000 + 1.5% of amount over 10'000'000
20'000'001 -	50'000'000	30'000 + 0.05% of amount over 20'000'000	226'000 + 0.25% of amount over 20'000'000	750'000 + 0.5% of amount over 20'000'000
50'000'001 -	100'000'000	45'000 + 0.01% of amount over 50'000'000	301'000 + 0.15% of amount over 50'000'000	900'000 + 0.45% of amount over 50'000'000
100'000'001-	250'000'000	50'000	376'000 + 0.05% of amount over 100'000'000	1'125'000 + 0,25% of amount over 100'000'000
> 250'000'000		50'000	451'000 + 0.025% of amount over 250'000'000	1'500'000 + 0.15% of amount over 250'000'000

V. Specialized Arbitration Rules

■ ■ ■

A. STOCKHOLM RULES FOR EXPEDITED ARBITRATIONS

RULES FOR EXPEDITED ARBITRATIONS OF THE STOCKHOLM CHAMBER OF COMMERCE*

Adopted by the Stockholm Chamber of Commerce and in force as of 1 January 2007

Article 1. The SCC Institute

The Arbitration Institute of the Stockholm Chamber of Commerce (the CC Institute is the body responsible for the administration of disputes in accordance with the Rules for Expedited Arbitrations of the Arbitration Institute of the Stockholm Chamber of Commerce (the CC Rules and other procedures or rules agreed upon by the parties. The SCC Institute is composed of a board of directors (the "Board") and a secretariat (the "Secretariat"). Detailed provisions regarding the organization of the SCC Institute are set out in Appendix I.

INITIATION OF PROCEEDINGS

Article 2. Request for Arbitration

Arbitration is initiated by the Claimant filing a Request for Arbitration with the SCC Institute, which shall include:

(i) a statement of the names, addresses, telephone and facsimile numbers and e-mail addresses of the parties and their counsel;

(ii) a summary of the dispute;

(iii) a preliminary statement of the relief sought by the Claimant;

(iv) a copy or description of the arbitration agreement or clause under which the dispute is to be settled; and

(v) any comments on the seat of arbitration.

Article 3. Registration Fee

(1) Upon filing the Request for Arbitration, the Claimant shall pay a Registration Fee. The amount of the Registration Fee shall be determined

* Available at http://www.sccinstitute.com/_upload/shared_files/regler/2007_expedited_rules_eng.pdf Reprinted With Permission of the Arbitration Institute of the Stockholm Chamber of Commerce.

in accordance with the Schedule of Costs (Appendix II) in force on the date of the Request for Arbitration.

(2) If the Registration Fee is not paid upon filing the Request for Arbitration, the Secretariat shall set a time period within which the Claimant shall pay the Registration Fee. If the Registration Fee is not paid within this time period, the Secretariat shall dismiss the Request for Arbitration.

Article 4. Date of commencement

The arbitration shall be deemed to commence on the date on which the Request for Arbitration is received by the SCC Institute.

Article 5. Answer

(1) The Secretariat shall send a copy of the Request for Arbitration and the documents attached thereto to the Respondent. The Secretariat shall set a time period within which the Respondent shall submit an Answer to the SCC Institute. The Answer shall include:

(i) any objections concerning the existence, validity, or applicability of the arbitration agreement; however, failure to raise any objections shall not preclude the Respondent from subsequently raising such objections at any time up to and including the submission of the Statement of Defence;

(ii) an admission or denial of the relief sought in the Request for Arbitration;

(iii) a preliminary statement of any counterclaims or set-offs; and

(iv) any comments on the seat of arbitration.

(2) The Secretariat shall send the Answer to the Claimant. The Claimant shall be given an opportunity to submit comments on the Answer.

(3) Failure by the Respondent to submit an Answer shall not prevent the arbitration from proceeding.

Article 6. Request for further details

The Board may request further details from either party regarding any of their written submissions to the SCC Institute. If the Claimant fails to comply with a request for further details, the Board may dismiss the case. If the Respondent fails to comply with a request for further details regarding its counterclaim or set-off, the Board may dismiss the counterclaim or set-off. Failure by the Respondent to otherwise comply with a request for further details shall not prevent the arbitration from proceeding.

Article 7. Time periods

The Board may, on application by either party or on its own motion, extend any time period which has been set for a party to comply with a particular direction.

Article 8. Notices

(1) Any notice or other communication from the Secretariat or the Board shall be delivered to the last known address of the addressee.

(2) Any notice or other communication shall be delivered by courier or registered mail, facsimile transmission, e-mail or any other means of communication that provides a record of the sending thereof.

(3) A notice or communication sent in accordance with paragraph (2) shall be deemed to have been received by the addressee on the date it would normally have been received given the chosen means of communication.

Article 9. Decisions by the Board

When the exchange of written submissions pursuant to Articles 2–6 has been concluded, the Board shall, if necessary:

(i) decide whether the SCC Institute manifestly lacks jurisdiction over the dispute pursuant to Article 10(i);

(ii) make any appointment of arbitrator pursuant to Article 13, and

(iii) decide the seat of arbitration pursuant to Article 20.

The Board shall also determine the Advance on Costs pursuant to Article 44.

Article 10. Dismissal

The Board shall dismiss a case, in whole or in part, if:

i) the SCC Institute manifestly lacks jurisdiction over the dispute; or

ii) the Advance on Costs is not paid pursuant to Article 44.

Article 11. Consolidation

Upon the submission of a Request for Arbitration concerning a legal relationship in respect of which an arbitration between the same parties is already pending under these Rules, the Board may, at the request of a party, decide to include the claims contained in the Request for Arbitration in the pending proceedings. Such decision will only be made after consulting the parties and the Arbitrator.

Article 12. Number of arbitrators

The Arbitral Tribunal shall consist of a sole arbitrator.

Article 13. Appointment of arbitrator

(1) The parties are free to agree on a different procedure for appointment of the Arbitrator than as provided under this Article. In such cases, if the Arbitrator has not been appointed within the time period agreed by the parties or, where the parties have not agreed on a time period, within the time period set by the Board, the appointment shall be made pursuant to paragraphs (2)–(4).

(2) The parties shall be given ten days within which to jointly appoint the Arbitrator. If the parties fail to make the appointment within this time period, the Arbitrator shall be appointed by the Board.

(3) If the parties are of different nationalities, the Arbitrator shall be of a different nationality than the parties, unless the parties have agreed otherwise or unless otherwise deemed appropriate by the Board.

(4) When appointing arbitrator, the Board shall consider the nature and circumstances of the dispute, the applicable law, the seat and language of the arbitration and the nationality of the parties.

Article 14. Impartiality and independence

(1) The Arbitrator must be impartial and independent.

(2) Before being appointed as arbitrator, a person shall disclose any circumstances which may give rise to justifiable doubts as to his/her impartiality or independence. If the person is appointed as arbitrator, he/she shall submit to the Secretariat a signed statement of impartiality and independence disclosing any circumstances which may give rise to justifiable doubts as to that person impartiality or independence. The Secretariat will provide the parties with a copy of the statement of impartiality and independence.

(3) The Arbitrator shall immediately inform the parties in writing where any circumstances referred to in paragraph (2) arise during the course of the arbitration.

Article 15. Challenge to arbitrator

(1) A party may challenge the Arbitrator if circumstances exist which give rise to justifiable doubts as to the Arbitrator impartiality or independence or if he/she does not possess qualifications agreed by the parties.

(2) A challenge to the Arbitrator shall be made by submitting a written statement to the Secretariat setting forth the reasons for the challenge within 15 days from when the circumstances giving rise to the challenge became known to the party. Failure by a party to challenge the Arbitrator within the stipulated time period constitutes a waiver of the right to make the challenge.

(3) The Secretariat shall notify the parties and the Arbitrator of the challenge and give them an opportunity to submit comments on the challenge.

(4) If the other party agrees to the challenge, the Arbitrator shall resign. In all other cases, the Board shall make the final decision on the challenge.

Article 16. Release from appointment

(1) The Board shall release the Arbitrator from appointment where:

(i) the Board accepts the resignation of the Arbitrator;

(ii) a challenge to the Arbitrator under Article 15 is sustained; or

(iii) the Arbitrator is otherwise prevented from fulfilling his/her duties or fails to perform his/her functions in an adequate manner.

(2) Before the Board releases an Arbitrator, the Secretariat may give the parties and the Arbitrator an opportunity to submit comments.

Article 17. Replacement of arbitrator

(1) The Board shall appoint a new arbitrator where the Arbitrator has been released from his/her appointment pursuant to Article 16, or where the Arbitrator has died.

(2) Where the Arbitrator has been replaced, the new Arbitrator shall decide whether and to what extent the proceedings are to be repeated.

THE PROCEEDINGS BEFORE THE ARBITRATOR

Article 18. Referral to the Arbitrator

When the Arbitrator has been appointed and the Advance on Costs has been paid, the Secretariat shall refer the case to the Arbitrator.

Article 19. Conduct of the Arbitration

(1) Subject to these Rules and any agreement between the parties, the Arbitrator may conduct the arbitration in such manner as the Arbitrator considers appropriate.

(2) In all cases, the Arbitrator shall conduct the arbitration in an impartial, practical and expeditious manner, giving each party an equal and reasonable opportunity to present its case.

(3) The following shall apply to the proceedings, unless the Arbitrator, for special reasons, decides otherwise:

(i) in addition to the Statement of Claim and the Statement of Defence, the parties each may only submit one written statement, including statements of evidence;

(ii) the statements must be brief; and

(iii) the time limits within which the documents shall be submitted may not exceed 10 working days.

(4) The Arbitrator may order a party to finally state its claims for relief and the facts relied on as grounds thereof, and the evidence on which the party relies. At the expiration of the time period for such statement, the party may not amend its claim for relief nor adduce additional facts or evidence, unless the Arbitrator, for special reasons, so permits.

Article 20. Seat of arbitration

(1) Unless agreed upon by the parties, the Board shall decide the seat of arbitration in accordance with Article 9.

(2) The Arbitrator may, after consultation with the parties, conduct hearings or meetings at any place which the Arbitrator considers appropriate. If any hearing or meeting is held elsewhere than at the seat of arbitration, the arbitration shall be deemed to have taken place at the seat of arbitration.

(3) The award shall be deemed to have been made at the seat of arbitration.

Article 21. Language

(1) Unless agreed upon by the parties, the Arbitrator shall determine the language or languages of the arbitration. In so determining, the Arbitrator shall have due regard to all relevant circumstances and shall give the parties an opportunity to submit comments.

(2) The Arbitrator may order that any documents submitted in languages other than the language(s) of the arbitration be accompanied by a translation into the language(s) of the arbitration.

Article 22. Applicable law

(1) The Arbitrator shall decide the merits of the dispute on the basis of the law or rules of law agreed upon by the parties. In the absence of such agreement, the Arbitrator shall apply the law or rules of law which the Arbitrator considers to be most appropriate.

(2) Any designation made by the parties of the law of a given state shall be deemed to refer to the substantive law of that state and not to its conflict of laws rules.

(3) The Arbitrator shall decide the dispute *ex aequo et bono* or as *amiable compositeur* only if the parties have expressly authorised it to do so.

Article 23. Timetable

After the referral of the case to the Arbitrator, the Arbitrator shall promptly establish a timetable for the conduct of the arbitration. The Arbitrator shall send the timetable to the parties and to the Secretariat.

Article 24. Written submissions

(1) The Claimant shall, within the period of time determined by the Arbitrator, submit a Statement of Claim which shall include, unless previously submitted:

(i) the specific relief sought;

(ii) the material circumstances on which the Claimant relies; and

(iii) copies of documents relied upon in the Statement of Claim.

(2) The Respondent shall, within the period of time determined by the Arbitrator, submit a Statement of Defence which shall include, unless previously submitted:

(i) a statement whether, and to what extent, the Respondent admits or denies the relief sought by the Claimant;

(ii) any objections concerning the existence, validity or applicability of the arbitration agreement;

(iii) the material circumstances relied on by the Respondent;

(iv) any counterclaim or set-off and the grounds on which it is based; and

(v) copies of documents relied upon in the Statement of Defence.

(3) The Arbitrator may direct the parties to submit additional written submissions.

Article 25. Amendments

At any time prior to the close of proceedings pursuant to Article 34, a party may amend or supplement its claim, counterclaim, defence or set-off provided its case, as amended or supplemented, is still comprised by the arbitration agreement, unless the Arbitrator considers it inappropriate to allow such amendment or supplement having regard to the delay in making it, the prejudice to the other party or any other circumstances.

Article 26. Evidence

(1) The admissibility, relevance, materiality and weight of evidence shall be for the Arbitrator to determine.

(2) The Arbitrator may require a party to identify the documentary evidence it intends to rely on and specify the circumstances intended to be proved by such evidence.

(3) At the request of a party, the Arbitrator may order a party to produce any documents or other evidence which may be relevant to the outcome of the case.

Article 27. Hearings

(1) A hearing will be held if requested by a party and if deemed necessary by the Arbitrator.

(2) The Arbitrator will, in consultation with the parties, determine the date, time and location of any hearing and will provide the parties with reasonable notice thereof.

(3) Unless otherwise agreed by the parties, hearings will be in private.

Article 28. Witnesses

(1) In advance of any hearing, the Arbitrator may request the parties to identify each witness or expert they intend to call and specify the circumstances intended to be proved by each testimony.

(2) The testimony of witnesses or party-appointed experts may be submitted in the form of signed statements.

(3) Any witness or expert, on whose testimony a party seeks to rely, shall attend a hearing for examination, unless otherwise agreed by the parties.

Article 29. Experts appointed by the Arbitrator

(1) After consultation with the parties, the Arbitrator may appoint one or more experts to report to the Arbitrator on specific issues set out by the Arbitrator in writing.

(2) Upon receipt of a report from an expert appointed by the Arbitrator, the Arbitrator shall deliver a copy of the report to the parties and shall give the parties an opportunity to submit written comments on the report.

(3) Upon the request of a party, the parties shall be given an opportunity to examine any expert appointed by the Arbitrator at a hearing.

Article 30. Default

(1) If the Claimant, without showing good cause, fails to submit a Statement of Claim in accordance with Article 24, the Arbitrator shall terminate the proceedings provided the Respondent has not filed a counterclaim.

(2) If a party, without showing good cause, fails to submit a Statement of Defence or other written statement in accordance with Article 24, or fails to appear at a hearing, or otherwise fails to avail itself of the opportunity to present its case, the Arbitrator may proceed with the arbitration and make an award.

(3) If a party without good cause fails to comply with any provision of, or requirement under, these Rules or any procedural order given by the Arbitrator, the Arbitrator may draw such inferences as it considers appropriate.

Article 31. Waiver

A party, who during the arbitration fails to object without delay to any failure to comply with the arbitration agreement, these Rules or other rules applicable to the proceedings, shall be deemed to have waived the right to object to such failure.

Article 32. Interim measures

(1) The Arbitrator may, at the request of a party, grant any interim measures it deems appropriate.

(2) The Arbitrator may order the party requesting an interim measure to provide appropriate security in connection with the measure.

(3) An interim measure may take the form of an order or an award.

(4) A request for interim measures made by a party to a judicial authority is not incompatible with the arbitration agreement or with these Rules.

Article 33. Communications from the Arbitrator

Article 8 shall apply to communications from the Arbitrator.

Article 34. Close of proceedings

The Arbitrator shall declare the proceedings closed when it is satisfied that the parties have had a reasonable opportunity to present their cases. In exceptional circumstances, prior to the making of the final award, the Arbitrator may reopen the proceedings on its own motion, or upon the application of a party.

AWARDS AND DECISIONS

Article 35. Making of awards

(1) The Arbitrator shall make the award in writing and sign the award. A party may request a reasoned award no later than at the closing statement.

(2) An award shall include the date of the award and the seat of arbitration in accordance with Article 20.

(3) The Arbitrator shall deliver copies of the award to each of the parties and to the SCC Institute without delay.

Article 36. Time limit for final award

The final award shall be made not later than three months from the date upon which the arbitration was referred to the Arbitrator pursuant to Article 18. The Board may extend this time limit upon a reasoned request from the Arbitrator, or if otherwise deemed necessary.

Article 37. Separate award

The Arbitrator may decide a separate issue or part of the dispute in a separate award.

Article 38. Settlement or other grounds for termination of the arbitration

(1) If the parties reach a settlement before the final award is made, the Arbitrator may, upon the request of both parties, record the settlement in the form of a consent award.

(2) If the arbitration for any other reason is terminated before the final award is made, the Arbitrator shall issue an award recording the termination.

Article 39. Effect of an award

An award shall be final and binding on the parties when rendered. By agreeing to arbitration under these Rules, the parties undertake to carry out any award without delay.

Article 40. Correction and interpretation of an award

(1) Within 30 days of receiving an award, a party may, upon notice to the other party, request that the Arbitrator correct any clerical, typographical or computational errors in the award, or provide an interpretation of a

specific point or part of the award. If the Arbitrator considers the request justified, the Arbitrator shall make the correction or provide the interpretation within 30 days of receiving the request.

(2) The Arbitrator may correct any error of the type referred to in paragraph (1) above on its own initiative within 30 days of the date of an award.

(3) Any correction or interpretation of an award shall be in writing and shall comply with the requirements of Article 35.

Article 41. Additional award

Within 30 days of receiving an award, a party may, upon notice to the other party, request the Arbitrator to make an additional award on claims presented in the arbitration but not determined in the award. If the Arbitrator considers the request justified, the Arbitrator shall make the additional award within 30 days of receipt of the request. When deemed necessary, the Board may extend this 30 day time limit.

COSTS OF THE ARBITRATION

Article 42. Costs of the Arbitration

(1) The Costs of the Arbitration consist of:

i) the Fee of the Arbitrator;

ii) the Administrative Fee of the SCC Institute; and

iii) the expenses of the Arbitrator and the SCC Institute.

(2) Before making the final award, the Arbitrator shall request the Board to finally determine the Costs of the Arbitration. The Board shall finally determine the Costs of the Arbitration in accordance with the Schedule of Costs (Appendix II) in force on the date of commencement of the arbitration pursuant to Article 4.

(3) The Arbitrator shall include in the final award the Costs of the Arbitration as finally determined by the Board and specify the fees and expenses of the Arbitrator.

(4) If the arbitration is terminated before the final award is made, the Board shall finally determine the Costs of the Arbitration having regard to when the arbitration terminates, the work performed by the Arbitrator and other relevant circumstances.

(5) Unless otherwise agreed by the parties, the Arbitrator shall, at the request of a party, apportion the Costs of the Arbitration between the parties, having regard to the outcome of the case and other relevant circumstances.

(6) The parties are jointly and severally liable to the arbitrator and the SCC Institute for the Costs of the Arbitration.

Article 43. Costs incurred by a party

Unless otherwise agreed by the parties, the Arbitrator may in the final award, or an award under Article 38, upon the request of a party, order one party to pay any reasonable costs incurred by another party, including costs for legal representation, having regard to the outcome of the case and other relevant circumstances.

Article 44. Advance on Costs

(1) In accordance with Article 9, the Board shall determine an amount to be paid by the parties as an Advance on Costs.

(2) The Advance on Costs shall correspond to the estimated amount of the Costs of Arbitration pursuant to Article 42.

(3) Each party shall pay half of the Advance on Costs, unless separate advances are determined. Where counterclaims or set-offs are submitted, the Board may determine separate advances on costs for the claims, the counterclaims and the set-offs, and each of the parties shall pay the advances on costs corresponding to its claim. Upon a request from the Arbitrator, the Board may order parties to pay additional advances during the course of the arbitration.

(4) If a party fails to make a required payment, the Secretariat shall give the other party an opportunity to do so within a specified period of time. If the required payment is not made, the Board shall dismiss the case in whole or in part pursuant to Article 10. If the other party makes the required payment, the Arbitrator may, at the request of such party, make a separate award for reimbursement of the payment.

(5) At any stage during the arbitration or after the Award has been made, the Board may draw on the Advance on Costs to cover the Costs of the Arbitration.

(6) The Board may decide that part of the Advance on Costs shall be provided in the form of a bank guarantee or other form of security.

CONFIDENTIALITY

Article 45. Confidentiality

Unless otherwise agreed by the parties, the SCC Institute and the Arbitrator shall maintain the confidentiality of the arbitration and the award.

GENERAL RULE

Article 46. General rule

In all matters not expressly provided for in these Rules, the SCC Institute, the Arbitrator and the parties shall act in the spirit of these Rules and shall make every reasonable effort to ensure that all awards are legally enforceable.

EXCLUSION OF LIABILITY

Article 47. Exclusion of liability

Neither the SCC Institute nor the arbitrator are liable to any party for any act or omission in connection with the arbitration unless such act or omission constitutes willful misconduct or gross negligence.

ENTRY INTO FORCE

These Rules enter into force on 1 January 2007 and will replace the former Rules for Expedited Arbitrations. These Rules will be applied to any arbitration commenced on or after 1 January 2007, unless otherwise agreed by the parties.

* * *

B. ICC RULES FOR EXPERTISE

INTERNATIONAL CHAMBER OF COMMERCE, CENTRE FOR EXPERTISE (2003)*

Rules for Expertise
In force as from 1 January 2003

FOREWORD

Experts with specialized knowledge in technical, legal, financial and other fields may be useful in a variety of situations. The ICC International Centre for Expertise responds to this need by offering three distinct services: the proposal of experts, the appointment of experts, and the administration of expertise proceedings.

The selection of competent experts, especially in an international context, is a delicate task. The Centre's privileged position at the heart of a worldwide business organization makes it particularly well-placed to fulfil this role. The Centre has proposed and appointed experts to give opinions on a wide range of subjects from accounting and contractual matters to the assessment of industrial processes and equipment.

Business needs and expertise have evolved since the ICC International Centre for Expertise was created in 1976. This makes it necessary periodically to revise the ICC Rules for Expertise under which the Centre operates. The present Rules, in force as from 1 January 2003, replace the previous revision of 1993 and introduce greater clarity and flexibility in the conduct of proceedings. Each of the Centre's three services is clearly distinguished and systematically described. Two appendices deal respectively with the Standing Committee of the International Centre for Expertise and costs.

* The ICC International Centre for Expertise, ICC Publication No. 649, entitled Rules of Expertise, ISBN 92–842–1318–5, copyright 2002 International Chamber of Commerce. Reprinted with permission of ICC. Available from: ICC Dispute Resolution Service—Expertise, 38 cours Albert ler, 75008 Paris, France, and at www.iccexpertise.org. http://www.iccwbo.org/drs/english/expertise/pdf_documents/rules/rules_expert_english

ICC expertise is part of the wide-ranging services offered by the world business organization to facilitate international commercial relations. Expertise may be used in a variety of contexts: to remove uncertainty in business operations, to assist the amicable settlement of disputes, or in connection with litigation or arbitration. It is valuable both as a service in its own right and as a complement to other dispute resolution services. In this regard, a notable feature of the new Rules is the waiver of the non-refundable charge for the proposal of an expert when requested by an arbitral tribunal acting under the ICC Rules of Arbitration.

SUGGESTED ICC EXPERTISE CLAUSES

OPTIONAL ICC EXPERTISE

'The parties may at any time, without prejudice to any other proceedings, agree to submit any dispute arising out of or in connection with clause [X] of the present contract to administered expertise proceedings in accordance with the Rules for Expertise of the International Chamber of Commerce.'

OBLIGATION TO SUBMIT DISPUTE TO ICC EXPERTISE

'In the event of any dispute arising out of or in connection with clause [X] of the present contract, the parties agree to submit the matter to administered expertise proceedings in accordance with the Rules for Expertise of the International Chamber of Commerce. [The findings of the expert shall be binding upon the parties.]'

OBLIGATION TO SUBMIT DISPUTE TO ICC EXPERTISE, FOLLOWED BY ICC ARBITRATION AS REQUIRED

'In the event of any dispute arising out of or in connection with clause [X] of the present contract, the parties agree to submit the matter, in the first instance, to administered expertise proceedings in accordance with the Rules for Expertise of the International Chamber of Commerce. If the dispute has not been resolved through such administered expertise proceedings it shall, after the Centre's notification of the termination of the expertise proceedings, be finally settled under the Rules of Arbitration of the International Chamber of Commerce by one or more arbitrators appointed in accordance with the said Rules of Arbitration.'

ICC ACTING AS APPOINTING AUTHORITY IN PARTY-ADMINISTERED EXPERTISE

'In the event of any dispute arising out of or in connection with clause [X] of the present contract, the parties agree to submit the matter to an expertise as defined in clause [Y] of the present contract. The expert shall be appointed by the International Centre for Expertise in accordance with the provisions for the appointment of experts under the Rules for Expertise of the International Chamber of Commerce.'

RULES FOR EXPERTISE OF THE INTERNATIONAL CHAMBER OF COMMERCE*

In force as from 1 January 2003

SECTION I
GENERAL PROVISIONS

Article 1
The International Centre for Expertise

1

The International Centre for Expertise (the "Centre") is a service centre of the International Chamber of Commerce (ICC). The Centre can perform one or more of the following functions in connection with domestic or international business matters:

A) Proposal of experts

Upon the request of any physical or legal person(s) or any court or tribunal (a "Person"), the Centre can provide the name of one or more experts in a particular field of activity, pursuant to Section II of these Rules. The Centre's role is limited to proposing the name of one or more experts. The Person requesting a proposal may then contact directly the proposed expert(s), and, as the case may be, agree with such expert(s) on the scope of the appropriate mission and fees. There is no obligation to make use of the services of an expert proposed by the Centre. The proposal of an expert may be useful in many different contexts. A person may require an expert in connection with its ongoing business activities or in connection with contractual relations. A party to an arbitration may wish to obtain the name of a potential expert witness. A court or arbitral tribunal which has decided to appoint an expert may seek a proposal from the Centre.

B) Appointment of experts

The Centre will appoint an expert, pursuant to Section III of these Rules, in situations where the parties have agreed to the appointment of an expert and have agreed to use the Centre as the appointing authority or where the Centre is otherwise satisfied that there is a sufficient basis for appointing an expert. In such cases the appointment by the Centre shall be binding on the parties. The Centre's role is limited to appointing the expert in question.

C) Administration of expertise proceedings

When the parties have agreed upon the administration of expertise proceedings by the Centre or when the Centre is otherwise satisfied that there is a sufficient basis for administering expertise proceedings, the Centre will administer the proceedings pursuant to Section IV of these Rules.

* Available at http://www.iccdrl.com/

2

The Centre consists of a Standing Committee and a Secretariat which is provided by ICC. The statutes of the Standing Committee are set forth in Appendix I.

SECTION II
PROPOSAL OF EXPERTS

Article 2
Recourse to the Centre

1

Any Person may ask the Centre to propose one or more experts by submitting a request for proposal of experts (the "Request for Proposal") to the Centre at the ICC International Secretariat in Paris.

2

The Request for Proposal shall include:

a) the name, address, telephone and facsimile numbers and e-mail address of each Person filing the Request for Proposal;

b) a statement that the requesting Person is seeking the proposal of an expert by the Centre;

c) a description of the field of activity of the expert to be proposed along with any desired qualifications of the expert, including but not limited to education, language skills and professional experience, and any undesired attributes of the expert;

d) a description of any matters which would disqualify a potential expert; and

e) a description of the work to be carried out by the expert and the desired time frame for completing such work.

3

Unless requested to do so by the Person seeking the proposal of an expert, the Centre will not notify any other person of the filing of a Request for Proposal.

Article 3
The Expert

1

Any proposal of an expert by the Centre shall be made by the Centre either through an ICC national committee or otherwise. The Centre's role normally ends on notification of the proposal unless the Centre is asked to appoint the proposed expert and/or administer the procedure pursuant to Sections III and IV.

2

Prior to the proposal of an expert, the Centre shall consider in particular the prospective expert's qualifications relevant to the circumstances of the case, and the expert's availability, place of residence, and language skills.

3

Before a proposal, a prospective expert shall sign a statement of independence and disclose in writing to the Centre any facts or circumstances which might be of such a nature as to call into question the expert's independence in the eyes of the Person filing the Request for Proposal. The Centre shall provide such information in writing to such Person and shall fix a time limit for any comments from such Person.

Article 4
Costs for the Proposal of an Expert

1

Each Request for Proposal must be accompanied by the non-refundable amount specified in Article 1 of Appendix II. This amount represents the total cost for the proposal of one expert by the Centre. No Request for Proposal shall be processed unless accompanied by the requisite payment.

2

When the Centre is requested to propose more than one expert, the non-refundable amount accompanying the Request for Proposal and to be paid by the requesting Person is the amount specified in the preceding paragraph multiplied by the number of experts requested.

SECTION III
APPOINTMENT OF EXPERTS

Article 5
Recourse to the Centre

1

Any request for the appointment of an expert (the "Request for Appointment") shall be submitted to the Centre at the ICC International Secretariat in Paris. Any such request shall be processed by the Centre only when it is based upon an agreement between the parties for the appointment of an expert by the Centre or when the Centre is otherwise satisfied that there is a sufficient basis for appointing an expert.

2

The date on which the Request for Appointment is received by the Centre shall, for all purposes, be deemed to be the date of the commencement of the agreed or required expertise.

3

The Request for Appointment shall include:

a) the name, address, telephone and facsimile numbers and e-mail address of each Person filing the Request for Appointment and of any other persons involved in the expertise;

b) a statement that the requesting Person is seeking the appointment of an expert by the Centre;

c) a description of the field of activity of the expert to be appointed along with any desired qualifications of the expert, including but not limited to education, language skills and professional experience, and any undesired attributes of the expert;

d) a description of any matters which would disqualify a potential expert;

e) a description of the work to be carried out by the expert and the desired time frame for completing such work; and

f) a copy of any agreement for the appointment of an expert by the Centre and/or of any other elements which form the basis for the Request for Appointment.

4

The Centre shall promptly inform the other party or parties in writing of the Request for Appointment once the Centre has sufficient copies of the Request for Appointment and has received the non-refundable amount required under Article 8.

5

When the Request for Appointment is not made jointly by all of the parties, and/or when the parties do not agree on the qualifications of the expert, and/or when the parties do not agree on the expert's work, the Centre shall send a copy of the Request for Appointment to the other party or parties who may make observations within a time limit fixed by the Centre. Observations received shall be communicated by the Centre to the other party or parties for comments within a time limit fixed by the Centre.

6

The Centre shall proceed with the Request for Appointment as it sees fit and will inform the parties of how it will proceed.

Article 6
Written Notifications or Communications

1

All written communications submitted to the Centre by any party to the expertise, as well as all documents annexed thereto, shall be supplied in a number of copies sufficient to provide one copy for the Centre, one copy for each party and one copy for each expert.

2

All notifications or communications from the Centre shall be made to the last address of the party or its representative for whom the same are intended, as notified by the party in question or by the other party. Such notification may be made by delivery against receipt, registered post, courier, facsimile transmission, telex, telegram or any other means of telecommunication that provides a record of the sending thereof.

3

A notification or communication shall be deemed to have been made on the day it was received by the party itself or by its representative, or would have been received if made in accordance with the preceding paragraph.

Article 7
The Expert

1

Any appointment of an expert by the Centre shall be made by the Centre either through an ICC national committee or otherwise.

2

Prior to the appointment of an expert, the Centre shall consider in particular the prospective expert's qualifications relevant to the circumstances of the case, the expert's availability, place of residence, and relevant language skills, and any observations, comments or requests made by the parties. In appointing the expert the Centre shall apply any agreement of the parties related to the appointment.

3

Every expert must be independent of the parties involved in the expertise proceedings, unless otherwise agreed in writing by such parties.

4

Before an appointment, a prospective expert shall sign a statement of independence and disclose in writing to the Centre any facts or circumstances which might be of such a nature as to call into question the expert's independence in the eyes of the parties. The Centre shall provide such information to the parties in writing and fix a time limit for any comments from them.

Article 8
Costs for the Appointment of an Expert

1

Each Request for Appointment must be accompanied by the non-refundable amount specified in Article 2 of Appendix II. This amount represents the total cost for the appointment of one expert by the Centre. No Request for Appointment shall be processed unless accompanied by the requisite payment.

2

When the Centre is requested to appoint more than one expert, the non-refundable amount accompanying the Request for Appointment and to be paid by the requesting Person is the amount specified in the preceding paragraph multiplied by the number of experts requested.

3

When the Centre is requested to appoint an expert who has already been proposed by the Centre in connection with the same matter, the Centre shall charge half of the non-refundable amount specified in Article 2 of Appendix II in addition to the already paid amount specified in Article 1 of Appendix II.

SECTION IV
ADMINISTRATION OF EXPERTISE PROCEEDINGS

Article 9
Recourse to the Centre

1

Any request for the administration of expertise proceedings (the "Request for Administration") shall be submitted to the Centre at the ICC International Secretariat in Paris. Any such request shall be processed by the Centre only when it is based upon an agreement for the administration of expertise proceedings by the Centre or when the Centre is otherwise satisfied that there is a sufficient basis for administering expertise proceedings.

2

The date on which the Request for Administration is received by the Centre shall, for all purposes, be deemed to be the date of the commencement of the expertise proceedings.

3

The Request for Administration shall include:

a) the name, address, telephone and facsimile numbers and e-mail address of each Person filing the Request for Administration and of any other persons involved in the expertise proceedings;

b) a statement that the requesting Person is seeking the administration of expertise proceedings by the Centre;

c) a description of the field of activity of the expert along with any desired qualifications of the expert, including but not limited to education, language skills and professional experience, and any undesired attributes of the expert;

d) a description of any matters which would disqualify a potential expert;

e) a description of the work to be carried out by the expert and the desired time frame for completing such work; and

f) a copy of any agreement for the administration of expertise proceedings by the Centre and/or of any other elements which form the basis for the Request for Administration.

4

The Centre shall promptly inform the other party or parties in writing of the Request for Administration once the Centre has sufficient copies of the Request for Administration and has received the non-refundable amount required under Article 14.

5

The administration of the expertise proceedings by the Centre shall consist inter alia of:

a) coordination between the parties and the expert;

b) initiating the appropriate steps to encourage the expeditious completion of the expertise proceedings;

c) supervising the financial aspects of the proceedings;

d) appointment of an expert using the procedure referred to in Section III or confirmation of an expert agreed to by all of the parties;

e) review of the form of the expert's report;

f) notification of the expert's final report to the parties; and

g) notification of the termination of the expertise proceedings.

Article 10
Written Notifications or Communications

1

All written communications submitted to the Centre by any party to the expertise proceedings, as well as all documents annexed thereto, shall be supplied in a number of copies sufficient to provide one copy for the Centre, one copy for each party and one copy for each expert.

2

All notifications or communications from the Centre and the expert shall be made to the last address of the party or its representative for whom the same are intended, as notified either by the party in question or by the other party. Such notification may be made by delivery against receipt, registered post, courier, facsimile transmission, telex, telegram or any other means of telecommunication that provides a record of the sending thereof.

3

A notification or communication shall be deemed to have been made on the day it was received by the party itself or by its representative, or would have been received if made in accordance with the preceding paragraph.

Article 11
Independence of the Expert—Replacement of the Expert

1

Every expert must remain independent of the parties involved in the expertise proceedings, unless otherwise agreed in writing by such parties.

2

An expert appointed by the Centre, who has died or resigned or is unable to carry out the expert's functions, shall be replaced.

3

An expert appointed by the Centre shall be replaced upon the written request of all of the parties.

4

If any party objects that the expert does not have the necessary qualifications or is not fulfilling the expert's functions in accordance with these Rules or in a timely fashion, the Centre may replace the expert after having considered the observations of the expert and the other party or parties.

5

When an expert is to be replaced, the Centre has discretion to decide whether or not to follow the original appointing process.

Article 12
The Expert's Mission

1

The expert, after having consulted the parties, shall set out the expert's mission in a written document. That document shall not be inconsistent with anything in these Rules and shall be communicated to the parties and to the Centre. Such document shall include:

a) the names, addresses, telephone and facsimile numbers and e-mail addresses of the parties;

b) a list of issues to be treated in the expert's report;

c) the name(s), address(es), telephone and facsimile numbers and e-mail address(es) of the expert or experts;

d) the procedure to be followed by the expert and the place where the expertise should be conducted; and

e) a statement indicating the language in which the proceedings will be conducted. Modifications to the expert's mission may be made by the expert, in writing, only after full consultation with the parties. Any such written modifications shall be communicated to the parties and to the Centre.

2

Upon preparing the document setting out the expert's mission or as soon as possible thereafter, the expert, after having consulted the parties, shall prepare a provisional timetable for the conduct of the expertise proceedings. The timetable shall be communicated to the parties and to the Centre. Any subsequent modifications of the provisional timetable shall be promptly communicated to the parties and to the Centre.

3

The expert's main task is to make findings in a written expert's report within the limits set by the expert's mission after giving the parties the opportunity to be heard and/or to make written submissions. Unless otherwise agreed by all of the parties, the findings of the expert shall not be binding upon the parties.

4

Unless otherwise agreed by the parties, the expert's report shall be admissible in any judicial or arbitral proceeding in which all of the parties thereto were parties to the expertise proceedings in which such report was prepared.

5

Any information given to the expert by the Centre or any party during the course of the expertise shall be used by the expert only for the purposes of the expertise and shall be treated by the expert as confidential.

6

The expert's report shall be submitted in draft form to the Centre before it is signed. The Centre may lay down modifications only as to the form of the report. No report shall be communicated to the parties by the expert. No report shall be signed by the expert prior to the Centre's approval of such report.

7

The Centre may waive the requirements laid down in Article 12(6) if expressly requested to do so in writing by all the parties and if the Centre considers that such a waiver is appropriate under the circumstances of the case.

8

The expert's report, after it is signed by the expert, shall be sent to the Centre in as many copies as there are parties plus one for the Centre. Thereafter, the Centre shall notify the expert's report to the party or parties and declare in writing that the expertise proceedings have been terminated.

Article 13
Duties and Responsibilities of the Parties

1

The non-participation of a party in the expertise proceedings does not deprive the expert of the power to make findings and render the expert's report, provided that such party has been given the opportunity to participate.

2

In agreeing to the application of these Rules the parties undertake to provide the expert with all facilities in order to implement the expert's mission and, in particular, to make available all documents the expert may consider necessary and also to grant the expert free access to any place where the expert may be required to go for the proper completion of the expert's mission.

Article 14
Costs for the Administration of Expertise Proceedings

1

Each Request for Administration must be accompanied by the non-refundable amount specified in Article 3 of Appendix II. This amount will be credited to the requesting party's or parties' portion of the deposit pursuant to Article 14(3).

2

When the Centre is requested to administer expertise proceedings where the expert has already been proposed or appointed by the Centre in connection with the same matter, the non-refundable amount specified in Article 3 of Appendix II shall not be paid in addition to the non-refundable amounts paid for the proposal or the appointment of an expert and specified in Articles 1 and 2 of Appendix II.

3

Following the receipt of a Request for Administration the Centre shall request the parties to pay a deposit in an amount likely to cover the administrative expenses of the Centre and the fees and expenses of the expert for the expertise proceedings, as set out in Article 3, paragraphs (2) and (3), of Appendix II. The expertise proceedings shall not go forward until payment of such deposit has been received by the Centre.

4

In any case where the Centre considers that the deposit is not likely to cover the total costs of the expertise proceedings, the amount of such deposit may be subject to readjustment. When the request for the corresponding payments has not been complied with, the Centre may suspend the expertise proceedings and set a time limit, on the expiry of which the expertise proceedings may be considered withdrawn.

5

Upon termination of administered expertise proceedings, the Centre shall settle the total costs of the proceedings and shall, as the case may be, reimburse the party or parties for any excess payment or bill the party or parties for any balance required pursuant to these Rules. The balance, if any, shall be payable before the notification of the final expert's report to the party or parties.

6

All above deposits and costs shall be borne in equal shares by the parties, unless they agree otherwise in writing. However, any party shall be free to pay the unpaid balance of such deposits and costs should the other party or parties fail to pay its or their share.

SECTION V
MISCELLANEOUS

Article 15
Waiver

A party which proceeds with the expertise proceedings without raising an objection to a failure to comply with any provision of these Rules, any direction given by the Centre or by the expert, or any requirement of the expert's mission, or any requirement relating to the appointment of an expert or to the conduct of the expertise proceedings, shall be deemed to have waived its right to object.

Article 16
Exclusion of Liability

Neither the experts, nor the Centre, nor ICC and its employees, nor the ICC national committees shall be liable to any person for any act or omission in connection with the expertise procedure.

Article 17
General Rule

In all matters not expressly provided for in these Rules, the Centre and the experts shall act in the spirit of these Rules.

APPENDIX I
STATUTES OF THE STANDING COMMITTEE OF THE ICC INTERNATIONAL CENTRE FOR EXPERTISE

Article 1
Composition of the Standing Committee

The Standing Committee is composed of a maximum of eleven members (a chairman, two vice-chairmen and up to eight members) appointed by ICC for a three-year renewable term.

Article 2
Meetings

A meeting of the Standing Committee shall be convened by its chairman whenever necessary.

Article 3
Function and Duties of the Standing Committee

1

The function of the Standing Committee is to assist the Secretariat in reviewing the qualifications of the experts to be proposed and/or appointed by the ICC International Centre for expertise. The Standing Committee shall advise the Secretariat concerning all aspects of expertise to help to assure the quality of the Centre.

2

In the absence of the chairman, or otherwise at the chairman's request, one of the two vice-chairmen shall be appointed by the chairman or by the Secretariat in the absence of an appointment by the chairman to fulfil the tasks of the chairman, including taking decisions pursuant to these statutes.

3

The Secretariat shall inform the members of the Standing Committee about all Requests for Proposal and Requests for Appointment and ask the members for their advice. The chairman of the Standing Committee shall make the final decision on the proposal or appointment of the expert.

4

In the case of a Request for Administration pursuant to Section IV:

A) the Standing Committee shall be informed of the death or resignation of an expert as well as of any objection by the party or parties or the Centre concerning an expert, or of any other matter requiring the replacement of the expert. It shall advise the Secretariat whether the objection of the party or parties pursuant to Article 11(3) or of the Centre pursuant to Article 11(4) of the Rules for Expertise is justified and make recommendations to the chairman. The chairman shall decide on the justification of any objection and/or on the manner in which the replacement will be made;

B) the chairman shall fix the expert's or experts' fees and expenses in accordance with Article 3(3) of Appendix II to the Rules for Expertise; and

C) upon the premature termination of the expertise, the chairman shall fix the costs of the expertise pursuant to Article 3(4) of Appendix II to the Rules for Expertise.

Article 4
Confidentiality

The work of the Standing Committee and the Secretariat is of a confidential nature which must be respected by everyone who participates in that work in whatever capacity.

APPENDIX II
SCHEDULE OF EXPERTISE COSTS

Article 1
Costs for Proposal

The non-refundable amount for the proposal of an expert pursuant to the Rules for Expertise is US$2,500, provided, however, that the proposal of an expert made at the request of an arbitral tribunal acting pursuant to the ICC Rules of Arbitration shall be free of charge. The non-refundable amount is payable by the requesting Person(s). No request shall be processed unless accompanied by the requisite payment.

Article 2
Costs for Appointment

The non-refundable amount for the appointment of an expert pursuant to the Rules for Expertise is US$2,500. This amount is payable by the requesting Person(s). No request shall be processed unless accompanied by the requisite payment.

Article 3
Costs for Administration

1

The non-refundable amount for sole administration of the expertise proceedings pursuant to the Rules is US$2,500. This amount is payable by the requesting Person(s). No request shall be processed unless accompanied by the requisite payment.

2

The administrative expenses of the Centre for the expertise proceedings shall be fixed at the Centre's discretion depending on the tasks carried out by the Centre. They shall not exceed 15% of the total expert's fees and not be less than US$2,500.

3

The fees of the expert shall be calculated on the basis of the time reasonably spent by the expert in the expertise proceedings, at a daily rate fixed for such proceedings by the Centre in consultation with the expert and the party or parties. Such daily rate shall be reasonable in amount and shall be determined in light of the complexity of the dispute and any other relevant circumstances. The amount of reasonable expenses of the expert shall be fixed by the Centre.

4

If an expertise terminates before the notification of the final report, the Centre shall fix the costs of the expertise at its discretion, taking into account the stage attained by the expertise proceedings and any other relevant circumstances.

5

Amounts paid to the expert do not include any possible value added taxes (VAT) or other taxes or charges and imposts applicable to the expert's fees. Parties have a duty to pay any such taxes or charges; however, the recovery of any such charges or taxes is a matter solely between the expert and the party or parties.

C. VIENNA CONCILIATION RULES

RULES OF ARBITRATION AND CONCILIATION OF THE INTERNATIONAL ARBITRAL CENTRE OF THE FEDERAL ECONOMIC CHAMBER VIENNA*

Adopted by the Extended Board of the Austrian Federal Economic Chamber on 3 May 2006 with effect from 1 July 2006

* * *

Conciliation Rules

Article 1

At the request of a party, conciliation proceedings can be conducted where the Centre has jurisdiction as to the subject matter. They are not subject to the existence of a valid arbitration agreement.

Article 2

The request for the opening of conciliation proceedings shall be filed with the Secretariat of the Centre. The latter shall invite the opposing party or parties to reply within thirty days after service of the request. If a party refuses to participate in the conciliation proceedings or does not reply within that period, the attempted conciliation shall be considered as having failed.

* Reprinted with kind permission of the International Arbitral Centre of the Austrian Federal Economic Chamber.

Article 3

When the opposing party or parties accepts/accept recourse to conciliation, the Board shall nominate one of its members or another qualified person to act as conciliator. The latter shall study the documents submitted by the parties, shall convene them to a hearing and shall then submit proposals for the amicable settlement of the dispute.

Article 4

If agreement is reached, that shall be the subject of a record signed by the parties and the conciliator. If a valid arbitration agreement exists, the Board shall appoint the conciliator as sole arbitrator, provided that all parties so request. The sole arbitrator must authenticate the agreement in the form of a settlement or, if the parties so wish, make an award on the basis of the agreement.

Article 5

If no agreement is reached, the conciliation shall be considered as having failed. Declarations made by the parties in the course of conciliation proceedings shall not bind them in later arbitration proceedings. Except under the conditions set forth in Article 4 of these Rules, the conciliator may not be appointed as an arbitrator in subsequent arbitration proceedings.

Article 6

The costs of the conciliation proceedings and those of any activity of the conciliator under the conditions set forth in Article 4 shall be set by the Secretary General at an appropriate share of the charges applicable for arbitration proceedings on the basis of the corresponding amount in dispute (Article 36 paragraph 1 of the Rules of Arbitration). The same shall apply to the deposits against costs to be set by the Secretary General.

VI. Codes of Ethics

■ ■ ■

A. AAA/ABA CODE OF ETHICS FOR ARBITRATORS IN COMMERCIAL DISPUTES*

Effective March 1, 2004

The Code of Ethics for Arbitrators in Commercial Disputes was originally prepared in 1977 by a joint committee consisting of a special committee of the American Arbitration Association and a special committee of the American Bar Association. The Code was revised in 2003 by an ABA Task Force and special committee of the AAA.

PREAMBLE

The use of arbitration to resolve a wide variety of disputes has grown extensively and forms a significant part of the system of justice on which our society relies for a fair determination of legal rights. Persons who act as arbitrators therefore undertake serious responsibilities to the public, as well as to the parties. Those responsibilities include important ethical obligations.

Few cases of unethical behavior by commercial arbitrators have arisen. Nevertheless, this Code sets forth generally accepted standards of ethical conduct for the guidance of arbitrators and parties in commercial disputes, in the hope of contributing to the maintenance of high standards and continued confidence in the process of arbitration.

This Code provides ethical guidelines for many types of arbitration but does not apply to labor arbitration, which is generally conducted under the Code of Professional Responsibility for Arbitrators of Labor–Management Disputes.

There are many different types of commercial arbitration. Some proceedings are conducted under arbitration rules established by various organizations and trade associations, while others are conducted without such rules. Although most proceedings are arbitrated pursuant to voluntary agreement of the parties, certain types of disputes are submitted to arbitration by reason of particular laws. This Code is intended to apply to all such proceedings in which disputes or claims are submitted for decision

* The text can be found at http://www.adr.org/si.asp?id=4582. Reprinted by permission of the American Arbitration Association.

to one or more arbitrators appointed in a manner provided by an agreement of the parties, by applicable arbitration rules, or by law. In all such cases, the persons who have the power to decide should observe fundamental standards of ethical conduct. In this Code, all such persons are called "arbitrators," although in some types of proceeding they might be called "umpires," "referees," "neutrals," or have some other title.

Arbitrators, like judges, have the power to decide cases. However, unlike full-time judges, arbitrators are usually engaged in other occupations before, during, and after the time that they serve as arbitrators. Often, arbitrators are purposely chosen from the same trade or industry as the parties in order to bring special knowledge to the task of deciding. This Code recognizes these fundamental differences between arbitrators and judges.

In those instances where this Code has been approved and recommended by organizations that provide, coordinate, or administer services of arbitrators, it provides ethical standards for the members of their respective panels of arbitrators. However, this Code does not form a part of the arbitration rules of any such organization unless its rules so provide.

Note on Neutrality

In some types of commercial arbitration, the parties or the administering institution provide for three or more arbitrators. In some such proceedings, it is the practice for each party, acting alone, to appoint one arbitrator (a "party-appointed arbitrator") and for one additional arbitrator to be designated by the party-appointed arbitrators, or by the parties, or by an independent institution or individual. The sponsors of this Code believe that it is preferable for all arbitrators including any party-appointed arbitrators to be neutral, that is, independent and impartial, and to comply with the same ethical standards. This expectation generally is essential in arbitrations where the parties, the nature of the dispute, or the enforcement of any resulting award may have international aspects. However, parties in certain domestic arbitrations in the United States may prefer that party-appointed arbitrators be non-neutral and governed by special ethical considerations. These special ethical considerations appear in Canon X of this Code.

This Code establishes a presumption of neutrality for all arbitrators, including party-appointed arbitrators, which applies unless the parties' agreement, the arbitration rules agreed to by the parties or applicable laws provide otherwise. This Code requires all party-appointed arbitrators, whether neutral or not, to make pre-appointment disclosures of any facts which might affect their neutrality, independence, or impartiality. This Code also requires all party-appointed arbitrators to ascertain and disclose as soon as practicable whether the parties intended for them to serve as neutral or not. If any doubt or uncertainty exists, the party-appointed arbitrators should serve as neutrals unless and until such doubt or uncertainty is resolved in accordance with Canon IX. This Code expects all arbitrators, including those serving under Canon X, to preserve the integrity and fairness of the process.

Note on Construction

Various aspects of the conduct of arbitrators, including some matters covered by this Code, may also be governed by agreements of the parties, arbitration rules to which the parties have agreed, applicable law, or other applicable ethics rules, all of which should be consulted by the arbitrators. This Code does not take the place of or supersede such laws, agreements, or arbitration rules to which the parties have agreed and should be read in conjunction with other rules of ethics. It does not establish new or additional grounds for judicial review of arbitration awards.

All provisions of this Code should therefore be read as subject to contrary provisions of applicable law and arbitration rules. They should also be read as subject to contrary agreements of the parties. Nevertheless, this Code imposes no obligation on any arbitrator to act in a manner inconsistent with the arbitrator's fundamental duty to preserve the integrity and fairness of the arbitral process.

Canons I through VIII of this Code apply to all arbitrators. Canon IX applies to all party-appointed arbitrators, except that certain party-appointed arbitrators are exempted by Canon X from compliance with certain provisions of Canons I–IX related to impartiality and independence, as specified in Canon X.

CANON I.

AN ARBITRATOR SHOULD UPHOLD THE INTEGRITY AND FAIRNESS OF THE ARBITRATION PROCESS

A. An arbitrator has a responsibility not only to the parties but also to the process of arbitration itself, and must observe high standards of conduct so that the integrity and fairness of the process will be preserved. Accordingly, an arbitrator should recognize a responsibility to the public, to the parties whose rights will be decided, and to all other participants in the proceeding. This responsibility may include pro bono service as an arbitrator where appropriate.

B. One should accept appointment as an arbitrator only if fully satisfied:

(1) that he or she can serve impartially;

(2) that he or she can serve independently from the parties, potential witnesses, and the other arbitrators;

(3) that he or she is competent to serve; and

(4) that he or she can be available to commence the arbitration in accordance with the requirements of the proceeding and thereafter to devote the time and attention to its completion that the parties are reasonably entitled to expect.

C. After accepting appointment and while serving as an arbitrator, a person should avoid entering into any business, professional, or personal relationship, or acquiring any financial or personal interest, which is likely to affect impartiality or which might reasonably create the appearance of partiality. For a reasonable period of time after the decision of a case, persons who have served as arbitrators should avoid entering into any such relationship, or acquiring any such interest, in circumstances which might reasonably create the appearance that they had been influenced in the arbitration by the anticipation or expectation of the relationship or interest. Existence of any of the matters or circumstances described in this paragraph C does not render it unethical for one to serve as an arbitrator where the parties have consented to the arbitrator's appointment or continued services following full disclosure of the relevant facts in accordance with Canon II.

D. Arbitrators should conduct themselves in a way that is fair to all parties and should not be swayed by outside pressure, public clamor, and fear of criticism or self-interest. They should avoid conduct and statements that give the appearance of partiality toward or against any party.

E. When an arbitrator's authority is derived from the agreement of the parties, an arbitrator should neither exceed that authority nor do less than is required to exercise that authority completely. Where the agreement of the parties sets forth procedures to be followed in conducting the arbitration or refers to rules to be followed, it is the obligation of the arbitrator to comply with such procedures or rules. An arbitrator has no ethical obligation to comply with any agreement, procedures or rules that are unlawful or that, in the arbitrator's judgment, would be inconsistent with this Code.

F. An arbitrator should conduct the arbitration process so as to advance the fair and efficient resolution of the matters submitted for decision. An arbitrator should make all reasonable efforts to prevent delaying tactics, harassment of parties or other participants, or other abuse or disruption of the arbitration process.

G. The ethical obligations of an arbitrator begin upon acceptance of the appointment and continue throughout all stages of the proceeding. In addition, as set forth in this Code, certain ethical obligations begin as soon as a person is requested to serve as an arbitrator and certain ethical obligations continue after the decision in the proceeding has been given to the parties.

H. Once an arbitrator has accepted an appointment, the arbitrator should not withdraw or abandon the appointment unless compelled to do so by unanticipated circumstances that would render it impossible or impracticable to continue. When an arbitrator is to be compensated for his or her services, the arbitrator may withdraw if the parties fail or refuse to provide for payment of the compensation as agreed.

I. An arbitrator who withdraws prior to the completion of the arbitration, whether upon the arbitrator's initiative or upon the request of one or more of the parties, should take reasonable steps to protect the interests of the parties in the arbitration, including return of evidentiary materials and protection of confidentiality.

Comment to Canon I

A prospective arbitrator is not necessarily partial or prejudiced by having acquired knowledge of the parties, the applicable law or the customs and practices of the business involved. Arbitrators may also have special experience or expertise in the areas of business, commerce, or technology which are involved in the arbitration. Arbitrators do not contravene this Canon if, by virtue of such experience or expertise, they have views on certain general issues likely to arise in the arbitration, but an arbitrator may not have prejudged any of the specific factual or legal determinations to be addressed during the arbitration.

During an arbitration, the arbitrator may engage in discourse with the parties or their counsel, draw out arguments or contentions, comment on the law or evidence, make interim rulings, and otherwise control or direct the arbitration. These activities are integral parts of an arbitration. Paragraph D of Canon I is not intended to preclude or limit either full discussion of the issues during the course of the arbitration or the arbitrator's management of the proceeding.

CANON II.

AN ARBITRATOR SHOULD DISCLOSE ANY INTEREST OR RELATIONSHIP LIKELY TO AFFECT IMPARTIALITY OR WHICH MIGHT CREATE AN APPEARANCE OF PARTIALITY

A. Persons who are requested to serve as arbitrators should, before accepting, disclose:

(1) any known direct or indirect financial or personal interest in the outcome of the arbitration;

(2) any known existing or past financial, business, professional or personal relationships which might reasonably affect impartiality or lack of independence in the eyes of any of the parties. For example, prospective arbitrators should disclose any such relationships which they personally have with any party or its lawyer, with any co-arbitrator, or with any individual whom they have been told will be a witness. They should also disclose any such relationships involving their families or household members or their current employers, partners, or professional or business associates that can be ascertained by reasonable efforts;

(3) the nature and extent of any prior knowledge they may have of the dispute; and

(4) any other matters, relationships, or interests which they are obligated to disclose by the agreement of the parties, the rules or

practices of an institution, or applicable law regulating arbitrator disclosure.

B. Persons who are requested to accept appointment as arbitrators should make a reasonable effort to inform themselves of any interests or relationships described in paragraph A.

C. The obligation to disclose interests or relationships described in paragraph A is a continuing duty which requires a person who accepts appointment as an arbitrator to disclose, as soon as practicable, at any stage of the arbitration, any such interests or relationships which may arise, or which are recalled or discovered.

D. Any doubt as to whether or not disclosure is to be made should be resolved in favor of disclosure.

E. Disclosure should be made to all parties unless other procedures for disclosure are provided in the agreement of the parties, applicable rules or practices of an institution, or by law. Where more than one arbitrator has been appointed, each should inform the others of all matters disclosed.

F. When parties, with knowledge of a person's interests and relationships, nevertheless desire that person to serve as an arbitrator, that person may properly serve.

G. If an arbitrator is requested by all parties to withdraw, the arbitrator must do so. If an arbitrator is requested to withdraw by less than all of the parties because of alleged partiality, the arbitrator should withdraw unless either of the following circumstances exists:

(1) An agreement of the parties, or arbitration rules agreed to by the parties, or applicable law establishes procedures for determining challenges to arbitrators, in which case those procedures should be followed; or

(2) In the absence of applicable procedures, if the arbitrator, after carefully considering the matter, determines that the reason for the challenge is not substantial, and that he or she can nevertheless act and decide the case impartially and fairly.

H. If compliance by a prospective arbitrator with any provision of this Code would require disclosure of confidential or privileged information, the prospective arbitrator should either:

(1) Secure the consent to the disclosure from the person who furnished the information or the holder of the privilege; or

(2) Withdraw.

CANON III.

AN ARBITRATOR SHOULD AVOID IMPROPRIETY OR THE APPEARANCE OF IMPROPRIETY IN COMMUNICATING WITH PARTIES

A. If an agreement of the parties or applicable arbitration rules establishes the manner or content of communications between the arbitrator and the parties, the arbitrator should follow those procedures notwithstanding any contrary provision of paragraphs B and C.

B. An arbitrator or prospective arbitrator should not discuss a proceeding with any party in the absence of any other party, except in any of the following circumstances:

(1) When the appointment of a prospective arbitrator is being considered, the prospective arbitrator:

(a) may ask about the identities of the parties, counsel, or witnesses and the general nature of the case; and

(b) may respond to inquiries from a party or its counsel designed to determine his or her suitability and availability for the appointment. In any such dialogue, the prospective arbitrator may receive information from a party or its counsel disclosing the general nature of the dispute but should not permit them to discuss the merits of the case.

(2) In an arbitration in which the two party-appointed arbitrators are expected to appoint the third arbitrator, each party-appointed arbitrator may consult with the party who appointed the arbitrator concerning the choice of the third arbitrator;

(3) In an arbitration involving party-appointed arbitrators, each party-appointed arbitrator may consult with the party who appointed the arbitrator concerning arrangements for any compensation to be paid to the party-appointed arbitrator. Submission of routine written requests for payment of compensation and expenses in accordance with such arrangements and written communications pertaining solely to such requests need not be sent to the other party;

(4) In an arbitration involving party-appointed arbitrators, each party-appointed arbitrator may consult with the party who appointed the arbitrator concerning the status of the arbitrator (i.e., neutral or non-neutral), as contemplated by paragraph C of Canon IX;

(5) Discussions may be had with a party concerning such logistical matters as setting the time and place of hearings or making other arrangements for the conduct of the proceedings. However, the arbitrator should promptly inform each other party of the discussion and should not make any final determination concerning the matter discussed before giving each absent party an opportunity to express the party's views; or

(6) If a party fails to be present at a hearing after having been given due notice, or if all parties expressly consent, the arbitrator may discuss the case with any party who is present.

C. Unless otherwise provided in this Canon, in applicable arbitration rules or in an agreement of the parties, whenever an arbitrator communicates in writing with one party, the arbitrator should at the same time send a copy of the communication to every other party, and whenever the arbitrator receives any written communication concerning the case from one party which has not already been sent to every other party, the arbitrator should send or cause it to be sent to the other parties.

CANON IV.

AN ARBITRATOR SHOULD CONDUCT THE PROCEEDINGS FAIRLY AND DILIGENTLY

A. An arbitrator should conduct the proceedings in an even-handed manner. The arbitrator should be patient and courteous to the parties, their representatives, and the witnesses and should encourage similar conduct by all participants.

B. The arbitrator should afford to all parties the right to be heard and due notice of the time and place of any hearing. The arbitrator should allow each party a fair opportunity to present its evidence and arguments.

C. The arbitrator should not deny any party the opportunity to be represented by counsel or by any other person chosen by the party.

D. If a party fails to appear after due notice, the arbitrator should proceed with the arbitration when authorized to do so, but only after receiving assurance that appropriate notice has been given to the absent party.

E. When the arbitrator determines that more information than has been presented by the parties is required to decide the case, it is not improper for the arbitrator to ask questions, call witnesses, and request documents or other evidence, including expert testimony.

F. Although it is not improper for an arbitrator to suggest to the parties that they discuss the possibility of settlement or the use of mediation, or other dispute resolution processes, an arbitrator should not exert pressure on any party to settle or to utilize other dispute resolution processes. An arbitrator should not be present or otherwise participate in settlement discussions or act as a mediator unless requested to do so by all parties.

G. Co-arbitrators should afford each other full opportunity to participate in all aspects of the proceedings.

Comment to paragraph G

Paragraph G of Canon IV is not intended to preclude one arbitrator from acting in limited circumstances (e.g., ruling on discovery issues) where authorized by the agreement of the parties, applicable rules or law, nor does it preclude a majority of the arbitrators from proceeding with any aspect of the arbitration if an arbitrator is unable or unwilling to participate and such action is authorized by the agreement of the parties or applicable rules or law. It also does not preclude ex parte requests for interim relief.

CANON V.

AN ARBITRATOR SHOULD MAKE DECISIONS IN A JUST, INDEPENDENT AND DELIBERATE MANNER

A. The arbitrator should, after careful deliberation, decide all issues submitted for determination. An arbitrator should decide no other issues.

B. An arbitrator should decide all matters justly, exercising independent judgment, and should not permit outside pressure to affect the decision.

C. An arbitrator should not delegate the duty to decide to any other person.

D. In the event that all parties agree upon a settlement of issues in dispute and request the arbitrator to embody that agreement in an award, the arbitrator may do so, but is not required to do so unless satisfied with the propriety of the terms of settlement. Whenever an arbitrator embodies a settlement by the parties in an award, the arbitrator should state in the award that it is based on an agreement of the parties.

CANON VI.

AN ARBITRATOR SHOULD BE FAITHFUL TO THE RELATIONSHIP OF TRUST AND CONFIDENTIALITY INHERENT IN THAT OFFICE

A. An arbitrator is in a relationship of trust to the parties and should not, at any time, use confidential information acquired during the arbitration proceeding to gain personal advantage or advantage for others, or to affect adversely the interest of another.

B. The arbitrator should keep confidential all matters relating to the arbitration proceedings and decision. An arbitrator may obtain help from an associate, a research assistant or other persons in connection with reaching his or her decision if the arbitrator informs the parties of the use of such assistance and such persons agree to be bound by the provisions of this Canon.

C. It is not proper at any time for an arbitrator to inform anyone of any decision in advance of the time it is given to all parties. In a proceeding in which there is more than one arbitrator, it is not proper at any time for an arbitrator to inform anyone about the substance of the deliberations of the arbitrators. After an arbitration award has been made, it is not proper for an arbitrator to assist in proceedings to enforce or challenge the award.

D. Unless the parties so request, an arbitrator should not appoint himself or herself to a separate office related to the subject matter of the dispute, such as receiver or trustee, nor should a panel of arbitrators appoint one of their number to such an office.

CANON VII.

AN ARBITRATOR SHOULD ADHERE TO STANDARDS OF INTEGRITY AND FAIRNESS WHEN MAKING ARRANGEMENTS FOR COMPENSATION AND REIMBURSEMENT OF EXPENSES

A. Arbitrators who are to be compensated for their services or reimbursed for their expenses shall adhere to standards of integrity and fairness in making arrangements for such payments.

B. Certain practices relating to payments are generally recognized as tending to preserve the integrity and fairness of the arbitration process. These practices include:

(1) Before the arbitrator finally accepts appointment, the basis of payment, including any cancellation fee, compensation in the event of withdrawal and compensation for study and preparation time, and all other charges, should be established. Except for arrangements for the compensation of party-appointed arbitrators, all parties should be informed in writing of the terms established;

(2) In proceedings conducted under the rules or administration of an institution that is available to assist in making arrangements for payments, communication related to compensation should be made through the institution. In proceedings where no institution has been engaged by the parties to administer the arbitration, any communication with arbitrators (other than party appointed arbitrators) concerning payments should be in the presence of all parties; and

(3) Arbitrators should not, absent extraordinary circumstances, request increases in the basis of their compensation during the course of a proceeding.

CANON VIII.

AN ARBITRATOR MAY ENGAGE IN ADVERTISING OR PROMOTION OF ARBITRAL SERVICES WHICH IS TRUTHFUL AND ACCURATE

A. Advertising or promotion of an individual's willingness or availability to serve as an arbitrator must be accurate and unlikely to mislead. Any statements about the quality of the arbitrator's work or the success of the arbitrator's practice must be truthful.

B. Advertising and promotion must not imply any willingness to accept an appointment otherwise than in accordance with this Code.

Comment to Canon VIII

This Canon does not preclude an arbitrator from printing, publishing, or disseminating advertisements conforming to these standards in any electronic or print medium, from making personal presentations to prospective users of arbitral services conforming to such standards or from responding to inquiries concerning the arbitrator's availability, qualifications, experience, or fee arrangements.

CANON IX.

ARBITRATORS APPOINTED BY ONE PARTY HAVE A DUTY TO DETERMINE AND DISCLOSE THEIR STATUS AND TO COMPLY WITH THIS CODE, EXCEPT AS EXEMPTED BY CANON X

A. In some types of arbitration in which there are three arbitrators, it is customary for each party, acting alone, to appoint one arbitrator. The third arbitrator is then appointed by agreement either of the parties or of the two arbitrators, or failing such agreement, by an independent institution or individual. In tripartite arbitrations to which this Code applies, all three arbitrators are presumed to be neutral and are expected to observe the same standards as the third arbitrator.

B. Notwithstanding this presumption, there are certain types of tripartite arbitration in which it is expected by all parties that the two arbitrators appointed by the parties may be predisposed toward the party appointing them. Those arbitrators, referred to in this Code as "Canon X arbitrators," are not to be held to the standards of neutrality and independence applicable to other arbitrators. Canon X describes the special ethical obligations of party-appointed arbitrators who are not expected to meet the standard of neutrality.

C. A party-appointed arbitrator has an obligation to ascertain, as early as possible but not later than the first meeting of the arbitrators and parties, whether the parties have agreed that the party-appointed arbitrators will serve as neutrals or whether they shall be subject to Canon X, and to provide a timely report of their conclusions to the parties and other arbitrators:

(1) Party-appointed arbitrators should review the agreement of the parties, the applicable rules and any applicable law bearing upon arbitrator neutrality. In reviewing the agreement of the parties, party-appointed arbitrators should consult any relevant express terms of the written or oral arbitration agreement. It may also be appropriate for them to inquire into agreements that have not been expressly set forth, but which may be implied from an established course of dealings of the parties or well-recognized custom and usage in their trade or profession;

(2) Where party-appointed arbitrators conclude that the parties intended for the party-appointed arbitrators not to serve as neutrals, they should so inform the parties and the other arbitrators. The arbitrators may then act as provided in Canon X unless or until a different determination of their status is made by the parties, any administering institution or the arbitral panel; and

(3) Until party-appointed arbitrators conclude that the party-appointed arbitrators were not intended by the parties to serve as neutrals, or if the party-appointed arbitrators are unable to form a reasonable belief of their status from the foregoing sources and no decision in this regard has yet been made by the parties, any administering institution, or the arbitral panel, they should observe all of the obligations of neutral arbitrators set forth in this Code.

D. Party-appointed arbitrators not governed by Canon X shall observe all of the obligations of Canons I through VIII unless otherwise required by agreement of the parties, any applicable rules, or applicable law.

CANON X.

EXEMPTIONS FOR ARBITRATORS APPOINTED BY ONE PARTY WHO ARE NOT SUBJECT TO RULES OF NEUTRALITY

Canon X arbitrators are expected to observe all of the ethical obligations prescribed by this Code except those from which they are specifically excused by Canon X.

A. *Obligations under Canon I*

Canon X arbitrators should observe all of the obligations of Canon I subject only to the following provisions:

(1) Canon X arbitrators may be predisposed toward the party who appointed them but in all other respects are obligated to act in good faith and with integrity and fairness. For example, Canon X arbitrators should not engage in delaying tactics or harassment of any party or witness and should not knowingly make untrue or misleading statements to the other arbitrators; and

(2) The provisions of subparagraphs B(1), B(2), and paragraphs C and D of Canon I, insofar as they relate to partiality, relationships, and interests are not applicable to Canon X arbitrators.

B. *Obligations under Canon II*

(1) Canon X arbitrators should disclose to all parties, and to the other arbitrators, all interests and relationships which Canon II requires be disclosed. Disclosure as required by Canon II is for the benefit not only of the party who appointed the arbitrator, but also for the benefit of the other parties and arbitrators so that they may know of any partiality which may exist or appear to exist; and

(2) Canon X arbitrators are not obliged to withdraw under paragraph G of Canon II if requested to do so only by the party who did not appoint them.

C. *Obligations under Canon III*

Canon X arbitrators should observe all of the obligations of Canon III subject only to the following provisions:

(1) Like neutral party-appointed arbitrators, Canon X arbitrators may consult with the party who appointed them to the extent permitted in paragraph B of Canon III;

(2) Canon X arbitrators shall, at the earliest practicable time, disclose to the other arbitrators and to the parties whether or not they intend to communicate with their appointing parties. If they have disclosed the intention to engage in such communications, they may thereafter communicate with their appointing parties concerning any other aspect of the case, except as provided in paragraph (3);

(3) If such communication occurred prior to the time they were appointed as arbitrators, or prior to the first hearing or other meeting of the parties with the arbitrators, the Canon X arbitrator should, at

or before the first hearing or meeting of the arbitrators with the parties, disclose the fact that such communication has taken place. In complying with the provisions of this subparagraph, it is sufficient that there be disclosure of the fact that such communication has occurred without disclosing the content of the communication. A single timely disclosure of the Canon X arbitrator's intention to participate in such communications in the future is sufficient;

(4) Canon X arbitrators may not at any time during the arbitration:

(a) disclose any deliberations by the arbitrators on any matter or issue submitted to them for decision;

(b) communicate with the parties that appointed them concerning any matter or issue taken under consideration by the panel after the record is closed or such matter or issue has been submitted for decision; or

(c) disclose any final decision or interim decision in advance of the time that it is disclosed to all parties.

(5) Unless otherwise agreed by the arbitrators and the parties, a Canon X arbitrator may not communicate orally with the neutral arbitrator concerning any matter or issue arising or expected to arise in the arbitration in the absence of the other Canon X arbitrator. If a Canon X arbitrator communicates in writing with the neutral arbitrator, he or she shall simultaneously provide a copy of the written communication to the other Canon X arbitrator;

(6) When Canon X arbitrators communicate orally with the parties that appointed them concerning any matter on which communication is permitted under this Code, they are not obligated to disclose the contents of such oral communications to any other party or arbitrator; and

(7) When Canon X arbitrators communicate in writing with the party who appointed them concerning any matter on which communication is permitted under this Code, they are not required to send copies of any such written communication to any other party or arbitrator.

D. *Obligations under Canon IV*

Canon X arbitrators should observe all of the obligations of Canon IV.

E. *Obligations under Canon V*

Canon X arbitrators should observe all of the obligations of Canon V, except that they may be predisposed toward deciding in favor of the party who appointed them.

F. *Obligations under Canon VI*

Canon X arbitrators should observe all of the obligations of Canon VI.

G. *Obligations under Canon VII*

Canon X arbitrators should observe all of the obligations of Canon VII.

H. *Obligations under Canon VIII*

Canon X arbitrators should observe all of the obligations of Canon VIII.

I. *Obligations under Canon IX*

The provisions of paragraph D of Canon IX are inapplicable to Canon X arbitrators, except insofar as the obligations are also set forth in this Canon.

* * *

B. THE IBA RULES OF ETHICS FOR INTERNATIONAL ARBITRATORS*

Adopted by International Bar Association in 1986.

Introductory Note

International arbitrators should be impartial, independent, competent, diligent and discreet. These rules seek to establish the manner in which these abstract qualities may be assessed in practice. Rather than rigid rules, they reflect internationally acceptable guidelines developed by practicing lawyers from all continents. They will attain their objectives only if they are applied in good faith. The rules cannot be directly binding either on arbitrators, or on the parties themselves, unless they are adopted by agreement. Whilst the International Bar Association hopes that they will be taken into account in the context of challenges to arbitrators, it is emphasised that these guidelines are not intended to create grounds for the setting aside of awards by national courts.

If parties wish to adopt the rules they may add the following to their arbitration clause or arbitration agreement:

> "The parties agree that the rules of Ethics for International Arbitrators established by the International Bar Association, in force at the date of the commencement of any arbitration under this clause, shall be applicable to the arbitrators appointed in respect of such arbitration."

The International Bar Association takes the position that (whatever may be the case in domestic arbitration) international arbitrators should in principle be granted immunity from suit under national laws, except in extreme cases of wilful or reckless disregard of their legal obligations. Accordingly, the International Bar Association wishes to make it clear that it is not the intention of these rules to create opportunities for aggrieved parties to sue international arbitrators in national courts. The normal sanction for breach of an ethical duty is removal from office, with consequent loss of entitlement to remuneration. The International Bar Association also emphasises that these rules do not affect, and are intend-

* The IBA Rules of Ethics for International Arbitrators, reprinted with permission from the International Bar Association.

ed to be consistent with, the International Code of Ethics for lawyers, adopted at Oslo on 25th July 1956, and amended by the General Meeting of the International Bar Association at Mexico City on 24th July 1964.

1. Fundamental Rule

Arbitrators shall proceed diligently and efficiently to provide the parties with a just and effective resolution of their disputes, and shall be and shall remain free from bias.

2. Acceptance of Appointment

2.1 A prospective arbitrator shall accept an appointment only if he is fully satisfied that he is able to discharge his duties without bias.

2.2 A prospective arbitrator shall accept an appointment only if he is fully satisfied that he is competent to determine the issues in dispute, and has an adequate knowledge of the language of the arbitration.

2.3 A prospective arbitrator should accept an appointment only if he is able to give to the arbitration the time and attention which the parties are reasonably entitled to expect.

2.4 It is inappropriate to contact parties in order to solicit appointment as arbitrator.

3. Elements of Bias

3.1 The criteria for assessing questions relating to bias are impartiality and independence. Partiality arises where an arbitrator favours one of the parties, or where he is prejudiced in relation to the subject-matter of the dispute. Dependence arises from relationships between an arbitrator and one of the parties, or with someone closely connected with one of the parties.

3.2 Facts which might lead a reasonable person, not knowing the arbitrator's true state of mind, to consider that he is dependent on a party create an appearance of bias. The same is true if an arbitrator has a material interest in the outcome of the dispute, or if he has already taken a position in relation to it. The appearance of bias is best overcome by full disclosure as described in Article 4 below.

3.3 Any current direct or indirect business relationship between an arbitrator and a party, or with a person who is known to be a potentially important witness, will normally give rise to justifiable doubts as to a prospective arbitrator's impartiality or independence. He should decline to accept an appointment in such circumstances unless the parties agree in writing that he may proceed. Examples of indirect relationships are where a member of the prospective arbitrator's family, his firm, or any business partner has a business relationship with one of the parties.

3.4 Past business relationships will not operate as an absolute bar to acceptance of appointment, unless they are of such magnitude or nature as to be likely to affect a prospective arbitrator's judgment.

3.5 Continuous and substantial social or professional relationships between a prospective arbitrator and a party, or with a person who is known to be a potentially important witness in the arbitration, will normally give rise to justifiable doubts as to the impartiality or independence of a prospective arbitrator.

4. Duty of Disclosure

4.1 A prospective arbitrator should disclose all facts or circumstances that may give rise to justifiable doubts as to his impartiality or independence. Failure to make such disclosure creates an appearance of bias, and may of itself be a ground for disqualification even though the non-disclosed facts or circumstances would not of themselves justify disqualification.

4.2 A prospective arbitrator should disclose:

(a) any past or present business relationship, whether direct or indirect as illustrated in Article 3.3, including prior appointment as arbitrator, with any party to the dispute, or any representative of a party, or any person known to be a potentially important witness in the arbitration. With regard to present relationships, the duty of disclosure applies irrespective of their magnitude, but with regard to past relationships only if they were of more than a trivial nature in relation to the arbitrator's professional or business affairs. Non-disclosure of an indirect relationship unknown to a prospective arbitrator will not be a ground for disqualification unless it could have been ascertained by making reasonable enquiries;

(b) the nature and duration of any substantial social relationships with any party or any person known to be likely to be an important witness in the arbitration;

(c) the nature of any previous relationship with any fellow arbitrator (including prior joint service as an arbitrator);

(d) the extent of any prior knowledge he may have of the dispute;

(e) the extent of any commitments which may affect his availability to perform his duties as arbitrator as may be reasonably anticipated.

4.3 The duty of disclosure continues throughout the arbitral proceedings as regards new facts or circumstances.

4.4 Disclosure should be made in writing and communicated to all parties and arbitrators. When an arbitrator has been appointed, any previous disclosure made to the parties should be communicated to the other arbitrators.

5. Communications with Parties

5.1 When approached with a view to appointment, a prospective arbitrator should make sufficient enquiries in order to inform himself whether there may be any justifiable doubts regarding his impartiality or independence; whether he is competent to determine the issues in dispute;

and whether he is able to give the arbitration the time and attention required. He may also respond to enquiries from those approaching him, provided that such enquiries are designed to determine his suitability and availability for the appointment and provided that the merits of the case are not discussed. In the event that a prospective sole arbitrator or presiding arbitrator is approached by one party alone, or by one arbitrator chosen unilaterally by a party (a "party-nominated" arbitrator), he should ascertain that the other party or parties, or the other arbitrator, has consented to the manner in which he has been approached. In such circumstances he should, in writing or orally, inform the other party or parties, or the other arbitrator, of the substance of the initial conversation.

5.2 If a party-nominated arbitrator is required to participate in the selection of a third or presiding arbitrator, it is acceptable for him (although he is not so required) to obtain the views of the party who nominated him as to the acceptability of candidates being considered.

5.3 Throughout the arbitral proceedings, an arbitrator should avoid any unilateral communications regarding the case with any party, or its representatives. If such communication should occur, the arbitrator should inform the other party or parties and arbitrators of its substance.

5.4 If an arbitrator becomes aware that a fellow arbitrator has been in improper communication with a party, he may inform the remaining arbitrators and they should together determine what action should be taken. Normally, the appropriate initial course of action is for the offending arbitrator to be requested to refrain from making any further improper communications with the party. Where the offending arbitrator fails or refuses to refrain from improper communications, the remaining arbitrators may inform the innocent party in order that he may consider what action he should take. An arbitrator may act unilaterally to inform a party of the conduct of another arbitrator in order to allow the said party to consider a challenge of the offending arbitrator only in extreme circumstances, and after communicating his intention to his fellow arbitrators in writing.

5.5 No arbitrator should accept any gift or substantial hospitality, directly or indirectly, from any party to the arbitration. Sole arbitrators and presiding arbitrators should be particularly meticulous in avoiding significant social or professional contacts with any party to the arbitration other than in the presence of the other parties.

6. Fees

Unless the parties agree otherwise or a party defaults, an arbitrator shall make no unilateral arrangements for fees or expenses.

7. Duty of Diligence

All arbitrators should devote such time and attention as the parties may reasonably require having regard to all the circumstances of the case, and shall do their best to conduct the arbitration in such a manner that costs do not rise to an unreasonable proportion of the interests at stake.

8. Involvement in Settlement Proposals

Where the parties have so requested, or consented to a suggestion to this effect by the arbitral tribunal, the tribunal as a whole (or the presiding arbitrator where appropriate), may make proposals for settlement to both parties simultaneously, and preferably in the presence of each other. Although any procedure is possible with the agreement of the parties, the arbitral tribunal should point out to the parties that it is undesirable that any arbitrator should discuss settlement terms with a party in the absence of the other parties since this will normally have the result that any arbitrator involved in such discussions will become disqualified from any future participation in the arbitration.

9. Confidentiality of the Deliberations

The deliberations of the arbitral tribunal, and the contents of the award itself, remain confidential in perpetuity unless the parties release the arbitrators from this obligation. An arbitrator should not participate in, or give any information for the purpose of assistance in, any proceedings to consider the award unless, exceptionally, he considers it his duty to disclose any material misconduct or fraud on the part of his fellow arbitrators.

C. IBA GUIDELINES ON CONFLICTS OF INTEREST IN INTERNATIONAL ARBITRATION*

Approved on 22 May 2004 by the Council of the International Bar Association

Introduction

1. Problems of conflicts of interest increasingly challenge international arbitration. Arbitrators are often unsure about what facts need to be disclosed, and they may make different choices about disclosures than other arbitrators in the same situation. The growth of international business and the manner in which it is conducted, including interlocking corporate relationships and larger international law firms, have caused more disclosures and have created more difficult conflict of interest issues to determine. Reluctant parties have more opportunities to use challenges of arbitrators to delay arbitrations or to deny the opposing party the arbitrator of its choice. Disclosure of any relationship, no matter how minor or serious, has too often led to objections, challenge and withdrawal or removal of the arbitrator.

---

* The Guidelines can be found at http://www.ibanet.org/Publications/publications_IBA_guides_and_free_materials.aspx. Reprinted by permission of the International Bar Association.

2. Thus, parties, arbitrators, institutions and courts face complex decisions about what to disclose and what standards to apply. In addition, institutions and courts face difficult decisions if an objection or a challenge is made after a disclosure. There is a tension between, on the one hand, the parties' right to disclosure of situations that may reasonably call into question an arbitrator's impartiality or independence and their right to a fair hearing and, on the other hand, the parties' right to select arbitrators of their choosing. Even though laws and arbitration rules provide some standards, there is a lack of detail in their guidance and of uniformity in their application. As a result, quite often members of the international arbitration community apply different standards in making decisions concerning disclosure, objections and challenges.

3. It is in the interest of everyone in the international arbitration community that international arbitration proceedings not be hindered by these growing conflicts of interest issues. The Committee on Arbitration and ADR of the International Bar Association appointed a Working Group of 19 experts[1] in international arbitration from 14 countries to study, with the intent of helping this decision-making process, national laws, judicial decisions, arbitration rules and practical considerations and applications regarding impartiality and independence and disclosure in international arbitration. The Working Group has determined that existing standards lack sufficient clarity and uniformity in their application. It has therefore prepared these Guidelines, which set forth some General Standards and Explanatory Notes on the Standards. Moreover, the Working Group believes that greater consistency and fewer unnecessary challenges and arbitrator withdrawals and removals could be achieved by providing lists of specific situations that, in the view of the Working Group, do or do not warrant disclosure or disqualification of an arbitrator. Such lists—designated Red, Orange and Green (the 'Application Lists')—appear at the end of these Guidelines.[2]

4. The Guidelines reflect the Working Group's understanding of the best current international practice firmly rooted in the principles expressed in the General Standards. The Working Group has based the General Standards and the Application Lists upon statutes and case law in jurisdictions and upon the judgment and experience of members of the Working Group and others involved in international commercial arbitration. The Working Group has attempted to balance the various interests of parties, representatives, arbitrators and arbitration institutions, all of

1. The members of the Working Group are: (1) Henri Alvarez, Canada; (2) John Beechey, England; (3) Jim Carter, United States; (4) Emmanuel Gaillard, France, (5) Emilio Gonzales de Castilla, Mexico; (6) Bernard Hanotiau, Belgium; (7) Michael Hwang, Singapore; (8) Albert Jan van den Berg, Belgium; (9) Doug Jones, Australia; (10) Gabrielle Kaufmann-Kohler, Switzerland; (11) Arthur Marriott, England; (12) Tore Wiwen Nilsson, Sweden; (13) Hilmar Raeschke-Kessler, Germany; (14) David W. Rivkin, United States; (15) Klaus Sachs, Germany; (16) Nathalie Voser, Switzerland (Rapporteur); (17) David Williams, New Zealand; (18) Des Williams, South Africa; (19); Otto de Witt Wijnen, The Netherlands (Chair).

2. Detailed Background Information to the Guidelines has been published in *Business Law International* at BLI Vol. 5, No 3, September 2004, pp. 433–458 and is available at the IBA website www.ibanet.org.

whom have a responsibility for ensuring the integrity, reputation and efficiency of international commercial arbitration. In particular, the Working Group has sought and considered the views of many leading arbitration institutions, as well as corporate counsel and other persons involved in international arbitration. The Working Group also published drafts of the Guidelines and sought comments at two annual meetings of the International Bar Association and other meetings of arbitrators. While the comments received by the Working Group varied, and included some points of criticisms, the arbitration community generally supported and encouraged these efforts to help reduce the growing problems of conflicts of interests. The Working Group has studied all the comments received and has adopted many of the proposals that it has received. The Working Group is very grateful indeed for the serious considerations given to its proposals by so many institutions and individuals all over the globe and for the comments and proposals received.

5. Originally, the Working Group developed the Guidelines for international commercial arbitration. However, in the light of comments received, it realized that the Guidelines should equally apply to other types of arbitration, such as investment arbitrations (insofar as these may not be considered as commercial arbitrations).[3]

6. These Guidelines are not legal provisions and do not override any applicable national law or arbitral rules chosen by the parties. However, the Working Group hopes that these Guidelines will find general acceptance within the international arbitration community (as was the case with the IBA Rules on the Taking of Evidence in International Commercial Arbitration) and that they thus will help parties, practitioners, arbitrators, institutions and the courts in their decision-making process on these very important questions of impartiality, independence, disclosure, objections and challenges made in that connection. The Working Group trusts that the Guidelines will be applied with robust common sense and without pedantic and unduly formalistic interpretation. The Working Group is also publishing a Background and History, which describes the studies made by the Working Group and may be helpful in interpreting the Guidelines.

7. The IBA and the Working Group view these Guidelines as a beginning, rather than an end, of the process. The Application Lists cover many of the varied situations that commonly arise in practice, but they do not purport to be comprehensive, nor could they be. Nevertheless, the Working Group is confident that the Application Lists provide better concrete guidance than the General Standards (and certainly more than existing standards). The IBA and the Working Group seek comments on the actual use of the Guidelines, and they plan to supplement, revise and refine the Guidelines based on that practical experience.

---

3. Similarly, the Working Group is of the opinion that these Guidelines should apply by analogy to civil servants and government officers who are appointed as arbitrators by States or State entities that are parties to arbitration proceedings.

8. In 1987, the IBA published Rules of Ethics for International Arbitrators. Those Rules cover more topics than these Guidelines, and they remain in effect as to subjects that are not discussed in the Guidelines. The Guidelines supersede the Rules of Ethics as to the matters treated here.

Part I: General Standards Regarding Impartiality, Independence And Disclosure

(1) General Principle

Every arbitrator shall be impartial and independent of the parties at the time of accepting an appointment to serve and shall remain so during the entire arbitration proceeding until the final award has been rendered or the proceeding has otherwise finally terminated.

Explanation to General Standard 1:

The Working Group is guided by the fundamental principle in international arbitration that each arbitrator must be impartial and independent of the parties at the time he or she accepts an appointment to act as arbitrator and must remain so during the entire course of the arbitration proceedings. The Working Group considered whether this obligation should extend even during the period that the award may be challenged but has decided against this. The Working Group takes the view that the arbitrator's duty ends when the Arbitral Tribunal has rendered the final award or the proceedings have otherwise been finally terminated (e.g., because of a settlement). If, after setting aside or other proceedings, the dispute is referred back to the same arbitrator, a fresh round of disclosure may be necessary.

(2) Conflicts of Interest

(a) *An arbitrator shall decline to accept an appointment or, if the arbitration has already been commenced, refuse to continue to act as an arbitrator if he or she has any doubts as to his or her ability to be impartial or independent.*

(b) *The same principle applies if facts or circumstances exist, or have arisen since the appointment, that, from a reasonable third person's point of view having knowledge of the relevant facts, give rise to justifiable doubts as to the arbitrator's impartiality or independence, unless the parties have accepted the arbitrator in accordance with the requirements set out in General Standard (4).*

(c) *Doubts are justifiable if a reasonable and informed third party would reach the conclusion that there was a likelihood that the arbitrator may be influenced by factors other than the merits of the case as presented by the parties in reaching his or her decision.*

(d) *Justifiable doubts necessarily exist as to the arbitrator's impartiality or independence if there is an identity between a party and the arbitrator, if the arbitrator is a legal representative of a legal entity that is a party in the arbitration, or if the arbitrator has a significant financial or personal interest in the matter at stake.*

Explanation to General Standard 2:

(a) It is the main ethical guiding principle of every arbitrator that actual bias from the arbitrator's own point of view must lead to that arbitrator declining his or her appointment. This standard should apply regardless of the stage of the proceedings. This principle is so self-evident that many national laws do not explicitly say so. See e.g. Article 12, UNCITRAL Model Law. The Working Group, however, has included it in the General Standards because explicit expression in these Guidelines helps to avoid confusion and to create confidence in procedures before arbitral tribunals. In addition, the Working Group believes that the broad standard of 'any doubts as to an ability to be impartial and independent' should lead to the arbitrator declining the appointment.

(b) In order for standards to be applied as consistently as possible, the Working Group believes that the test for disqualification should be an objective one. The Working Group uses the wording 'impartiality or independence' derived from the broadly adopted Article 12 of the UNCITRAL Model Law, and the use of an appearance test, based on justifiable doubts as to the impartiality or independence of the arbitrator, as provided in Article 12(2) of the UNCITRAL Model Law, to be applied objectively (a 'reasonable third person test'). As described in the Explanation to General Standard 3(d), this standard should apply regardless of the stage of the proceedings.

(c) Most laws and rules that apply the standard of justifiable doubts do not further define that standard. The Working Group believes that this General Standard provides some context for making this determination.

(d) The Working Group supports the view that no one is allowed to be his or her own judge; i.e., there cannot be identity between an arbitrator and a party. The Working Group believes that this situation cannot be waived by the parties. The same principle should apply to persons who are legal representatives of a legal entity that is a party in the arbitration, like board members, or who have a significant economic interest in the matter at stake. Because of the importance of this principle, this nonwaivable situation is made a General Standard, and examples are provided in the non-waivable Red List.

The General Standard purposely uses the terms 'identity' and 'legal representatives.' In the light of comments received, the Working Group considered whether these terms should be extended or further defined, but decided against doing so. It realizes that there are situations in which an employee of a party or a civil servant can be in a position similar, if not identical, to the position of an official legal representative. The Working Group decided that it should suffice to state the principle.

(3) Disclosure by the Arbitrator

(a) *If facts or circumstances exist that may, in the eyes of the parties, give rise to doubts as to the arbitrator's impartiality or independence, the arbitrator shall disclose such facts or circumstances to the parties, the arbitration institution or other appointing authority (if any, and if so required by the applicable institutional rules) and to the co-arbitrators, if any, prior to accepting his or her appointment or, if thereafter, as soon as he or she learns about them.*

(b) *It follows from General Standards 1 and 2(a) that an arbitrator who has made a disclosure considers himself or herself to be impartial and independent of the parties despite the disclosed facts and therefore capable of performing his or her duties as arbitrator. Otherwise, he or she would have declined the nomination or appointment at the outset or resigned.*

(c) *Any doubt as to whether an arbitrator should disclose certain facts or circumstances should be resolved in favour of disclosure.*

(d) *When considering whether or not facts or circumstances exist that should be disclosed, the arbitrator shall not take into account whether the arbitration proceeding is at the beginning or at a later stage.*

Explanation to General Standard 3:

(a) General Standard 2(b) above sets out an objective test for disqualification of an arbitrator. However, because of varying considerations with respect to disclosure, the proper standard for disclosure may be different. A purely objective test for disclosure exists in the majority of the jurisdictions analyzed and in the UNCITRAL Model Law. Nevertheless, the Working Group recognizes that the parties have an interest in being fully informed about any circumstances that may be relevant in their view. Because of the strongly held views of many arbitration institutions (as reflected in their rules and as stated to the Working Group) that the disclosure test should reflect the perspectives of the parties, the Working Group in principle accepted, after much debate, a subjective approach for disclosure. The Working Group has adapted the language of Article 7(2) of the ICC Rules for this standard. However, the Working Group believes that this principle should not be applied without limitations. Because some situations should never lead to disqualification under the objective test, such situations need not be disclosed, regardless of the parties' perspective. These limitations to the subjective test are reflected in the Green List, which lists some situations in which disclosure is not required. Similarly, the Working Group emphasizes that the two tests (objective test for disqualification and subjective test for disclosure) are clearly distinct from each other, and that a disclosure shall not automatically lead to disqualification, as reflected in General Standard 3(b). In determining what facts should be disclosed, an arbitrator should take into account all circumstances known to him or her, including to the extent known the culture and the customs of the country of which the parties are domiciled or nationals.

(b) Disclosure is not an admission of a conflict of interest. An arbitrator who has made a disclosure to the parties considers himself or herself to be impartial and independent of the parties, despite the disclosed facts, or else he or she would have declined the nomination or resigned. An arbitrator making disclosure thus feels capable of performing his or her duties. It is the purpose of disclosure to allow the parties to judge whether or not they agree with the evaluation of the arbitrator and, if they so wish, to explore the situation further. The Working Group hopes that the promulgation of this General Standard will eliminate the misunderstanding that disclosure demonstrates doubts sufficient to disqualify the arbitrator. Instead, any challenge should be successful only if an objective test, as set forth above, is met.

(c) Unnecessary disclosure sometimes raises an incorrect implication in the minds of the parties that the disclosed circumstances would affect his or her impartiality or independence. Excessive disclosures thus unnecessarily undermine the parties' confidence in the process. Nevertheless, after some debate, the Working Group believes it important to provide expressly in the General Standards that in case of doubt the arbitrator should disclose. If the arbitrator feels that he or she should disclose but that professional secrecy rules or other rules of practice prevent such disclosure, he or she should not accept the appointment or should resign.

(d) The Working Group has concluded that disclosure or disqualification (as set out in General Standard 2) should not depend on the particular stage of the arbitration. In order to determine whether the arbitrator should disclose, decline the appointment or refuse to continue to act or whether a challenge by a party should be successful, the facts and circumstances alone are relevant and not the current stage of the procedure or the consequences of the withdrawal. As a practical matter, institutions make a distinction between the commencement of an arbitration proceeding and a later stage. Also, courts tend to apply different standards. Nevertheless, the Working Group believes it important to clarify that no distinction should be made regarding the stage of the arbitral procedure. While there are practical concerns if an arbitrator must withdraw after an arbitration has commenced, a distinction based on the stage of arbitration would be inconsistent with the General Standards.

(4) Waiver by the Parties

(a) *If, within 30 days after the receipt of any disclosure by the arbitrator or after a party learns of facts or circumstances that could constitute a potential conflict of interest for an arbitrator, a party does not raise an express objection with regard to that arbitrator, subject to paragraphs (b) and (c) of this General Standard, the party is deemed to have waived any potential conflict of interest by the arbitrator based on such facts or circumstances and may not raise any objection to such facts or circumstances at a later stage.*

(b) *However, if facts or circumstances exist as described in General Standard 2(d), any waiver by a party or any agreement by the parties to have such a person serve as arbitrator shall be regarded as invalid.*

(c) *A person should not serve as an arbitrator when a conflict of interest, such as those exemplified in the waivable Red List, exists. Nevertheless, such a person may accept appointment as arbitrator or continue to act as an arbitrator, if the following conditions are met:*

(i) *All parties, all arbitrators and the arbitration institution or other appointing authority (if any) must have full knowledge of the conflict of interest; and*

(ii) *All parties must expressly agree that such person may serve as arbitrator despite the conflict of interest.*

(d) *An arbitrator may assist the parties in reaching a settlement of the dispute at any stage of the proceedings. However, before doing so, the arbitrator should receive an express agreement by the parties that acting in such a manner shall not disqualify the arbitrator from continuing to serve as arbitrator. Such express agreement shall be considered to be an effective waiver of any potential conflict of interest that may arise from the arbitrator's participation in such process or from information that the arbitrator may learn in the process. If the assistance by the arbitrator does not lead to final settlement of the case, the parties remain bound by their waiver. However, consistent with General Standard 2(a) and notwithstanding such agreement, the arbitrator shall resign if, as a consequence of his or her involvement in the settlement process, the arbitrator develops doubts as to his or her ability to remain impartial or independent in the future course of the arbitration proceedings.*

Explanation to General Standard 4:

(a) The Working Group suggests a requirement of an explicit objection by the parties within a certain time limit. In the view of the Working Group, this time limit should also apply to a party who refuses to be involved.

(b) This General Standard is included to make General Standard 4(a) consistent with the non-waivable provisions of General Standard 2(d). Examples of such circumstances are described in the non-waivable Red List.

(c) In a serious conflict of interest, such as those that are described by way of example in the waivable Red List, the parties may nevertheless wish to use such a person as an arbitrator. Here, party autonomy and the desire to have only impartial and independent arbitrators must be balanced. The Working Group believes persons with such a serious conflict of interests may serve as arbitrators only if the parties make fully informed, explicit waivers.

(d) The concept of the Arbitral Tribunal assisting the parties in reaching a settlement of their dispute in the course of the arbitration proceedings is well established in some jurisdictions but not in others. Informed consent by the parties to such a process prior to its beginning should be regarded as effective waiver of a potential conflict of interest. Express consent is generally sufficient, as opposed to a consent made in writing which in certain jurisdictions requires signature. In practice, the requirement of an express waiver allows such consent to be made in the minutes or transcript of a hearing. In addition, in order to avoid parties using an arbitrator as mediator as a means of disqualifying the arbitrator, the General Standard makes clear that the waiver should remain effective if the mediation is unsuccessful. Thus, parties assume the risk of what the arbitrator may learn in the settlement process. In giving their express consent, the parties should realize the consequences of the arbitrator assisting the parties in a settlement process and agree on regulating this special position further where appropriate.

(5) Scope

These Guidelines apply equally to tribunal chairs, sole arbitrators and party-appointed arbitrators. These Guidelines do not apply to non-neutral arbitrators, who do not have an obligation to be independent and impartial, as may be permitted by some arbitration rules or national laws.

Explanation to General Standard 5:

Because each member of an Arbitral Tribunal has an obligation to be impartial and independent, the General Standards should not distinguish among sole arbitrators, party-appointed arbitrators and tribunal chairs. With regard to secretaries of Arbitral Tribunals, the Working Group takes the view that it is the responsibility of the arbitrator to ensure that the secretary is and remains impartial and independent.

Some arbitration rules and domestic laws permit party-appointed arbitrators to be non-neutral. When an arbitrator is serving in such a role, these Guidelines should not apply to him or her, since their purpose is to protect impartiality and independence.

(6) Relationships

(a) *When considering the relevance of facts or circumstances to determine whether a potential conflict of interest exists or whether disclosure should be made, the activities of an arbitrator's law firm, if any, should be reasonably considered in each individual case. Therefore, the fact that the activities of the arbitrator's firm involve one of the parties shall not automatically constitute a source of such conflict or a reason for disclosure.*

(b) *Similarly, if one of the parties is a legal entity which is a member of a group with which the arbitrator's firm has an involvement, such facts or circumstances should be reasonably considered in each individual case. Therefore, this fact alone shall not automatically constitute a source of a conflict of interest or a reason for disclosure.*

(c) *If one of the parties is a legal entity, the managers, directors and members of a supervisory board of such legal entity and any person having a similar controlling influence on the legal entity shall be considered to be the equivalent of the legal entity.*

Explanation to General Standard 6:

(a) The growing size of law firms should be taken into account as part of today's reality in international arbitration. There is a need to balance the interests of a party to use the arbitrator of its choice and the importance of maintaining confidence in the impartiality and independence of international arbitration. In the opinion of the Working Group, the arbitrator must in principle be considered as identical to his or her law firm, but nevertheless the activities of the arbitrator's firm should not automatically constitute a conflict of interest. The relevance of such activities, such as the nature, timing and scope of the work by the law firm, should be reasonably considered in each individual case. The Working Group uses the term 'involvement' rather than 'acting for' because a law firm's relevant connections with a party may include activities other than representation on a legal matter.

(b) When a party to an arbitration is a member of a group of companies, special questions regarding conflict of interest arise. As in the prior paragraph, the Working Group believes that because individual corporate structure arrangements vary so widely an automatic rule is not appropriate. Instead, the particular circumstances of an affiliation with another entity within the same group of companies should be reasonably considered in each individual case.

(c) The party in international arbitration is usually a legal entity. Therefore, this General Standard clarifies which individuals should be considered effectively to be that party.

(7) *Duty of Arbitrator and Parties*

(a) *A party shall inform an arbitrator, the Arbitral Tribunal, the other parties and the arbitration institution or other appointing authority (if any) about any direct or indirect relationship between it (or another company of the same group of companies) and the arbitrator. The party shall do so on its own initiative before the beginning of the proceeding or as soon as it becomes aware of such relationship.*

(b) *In order to comply with General Standard 7(a), a party shall provide any information already available to it and shall perform a reasonable search of publicly available information.*

(c) *An arbitrator is under a duty to make reasonable enquiries to investigate any potential conflict of interest, as well as any facts or circumstances that may cause his or her impartiality or independence to be questioned. Failure to disclose a potential conflict is not excused by lack of knowledge if the arbitrator makes no reasonable attempt to investigate.*

Explanation to General Standard 7:

To reduce the risk of abuse by unmeritorious challenge of an arbitrator's impartiality or independence, it is necessary that the parties disclose any relevant relationship with the arbitrator. In addition, any party or potential party to an arbitration is, at the outset, required to make a reasonable effort to ascertain and to disclose publicly available information that, applying the general standard, might affect the arbitrator's impartiality and independence. It is the arbitrator or putative arbitrator's obligation to make similar enquiries and to disclose any information that may cause his or her impartiality or independence to be called into question.

PART II: Practical Application of the General Standards

1. The Working Group believes that if the Guidelines are to have an important practical influence, they should reflect situations that are likely to occur in today's arbitration practice. The Guidelines should provide specific guidance to arbitrators, parties, institutions and courts as to what situations do or do not constitute conflicts of interest or should be disclosed. For this purpose, the members of the Working Group analyzed their respective case law and categorized situations that can occur in the following Application Lists. These lists obviously cannot contain every situation, but they provide guidance in many circumstances, and the Working Group has sought to make them as comprehensive as possible. In all cases, the General Standards should control.

2. The Red List consists of two parts: 'a non-waivable Red List' (see General Standards 2(c) and 4(b)) and 'a waivable Red List' (see General Standard 4(c)). These lists are a non-exhaustive enumeration of specific situations which, depending on the facts of a given case, give rise to justifiable doubts as to the arbitrator's impartiality and independence; i.e., in these circumstances an objective conflict of interest exists from the point of view of a reasonable third person having knowledge of the relevant facts (*see* General Standard 2(b)). The nonwaivable Red List includes situations deriving from the overriding principle that no person can be his or her own judge. Therefore, disclosure of such a situation cannot cure the conflict. The waivable Red List encompasses situations that are serious but not as severe. Because of their seriousness, unlike circumstances described in the Orange List, these situations should be considered waivable only if and when the parties, being aware of the conflict of interest situation, nevertheless expressly state their willingness to have such a person act as arbitrator, as set forth in General Standard 4(c).

3. The Orange List is a non-exhaustive enumeration of specific situations which (depending on the facts of a given case) in the eyes of the parties may give rise to justifiable doubts as to the arbitrator's impartiality or independence. The Orange List thus reflects situations that would fall under General Standard 3(a), so that the arbitrator has a duty to disclose such situations. In all these situations, the parties are deemed to have accepted the arbitrator if, after disclosure, no timely objection is made. (General Standard 4(a)).

4. It should be stressed that, as stated above, such disclosure should not automatically result in a disqualification of the arbitrator; no presumption regarding disqualification should arise from a disclosure. The purpose of the disclosure is to inform the parties of a situation that they may wish to explore further in order to determine whether objectively—i.e., from a reasonable third person's point of view having knowledge of the relevant facts—there is a justifiable doubt as to the arbitrator's impartiality or independence. If the conclusion is that there is no justifiable doubt, the arbitrator can act. He or she can also act if there is no timely objection by the parties or, in situations covered by the waivable Red List, a specific acceptance by the parties in accordance with General Standard 4(c). Of course, if a party challenges the appointment of the arbitrator, he or she can nevertheless act if the authority that has to rule on the challenge decides that the challenge does not meet the objective test for disqualification.

5. In addition, a later challenge based on the fact that an arbitrator did not disclose such facts or circumstances should not result automatically in either non-appointment, later disqualification or a successful challenge to any award. In the view of the Working Group, non-disclosure cannot make an arbitrator partial or lacking independence; only the facts or circumstances that he or she did not disclose can do so.

6. The Green List contains a non-exhaustive enumeration of specific situations where no appearance of, and no actual, conflict of interest exists from the relevant objective point of view. Thus, the arbitrator has no duty to disclose situations falling within the Green List. In the opinion of the Working Group, as already expressed in the Explanation to General Standard 3(a), there should be a limit to disclosure, based on reasonableness; in some situations, an objective test should prevail over the purely subjective test of 'the eyes of the parties.'

7. Situations falling outside the time limit used in some of the Orange List situations should generally be considered as falling in the Green List, even though they are not specifically stated. An arbitrator may nevertheless wish to make disclosure if, under the General Standards, he or she believes it to be appropriate. While there has been much debate with respect to the time limits used in the Lists, the Working Group has concluded that the limits indicated are appropriate and provide guidance where none exists now. For example, the three-year period in Orange List 3.1 may be too long in certain circumstances and too short in others, but the Working Group believes that the period is an appropriate general criterion, subject to the special circumstances of any case.

8. The borderline between the situations indicated is often thin. It can be debated whether a certain situation should be on one List of instead of another. Also, the Lists contain, for various situations, open norms like 'significant'. The Working Group has extensively and repeatedly discussed both of these issues, in the light of comments received. It believes that the decisions reflected in the Lists reflect international

principles to the best extent possible and that further definition of the norms, which should be interpreted reasonably in light of the facts and circumstances in each case, would be counter-productive.

9. There has been much debate as to whether there should be a Green List at all and also, with respect to the Red List, whether the situations on the Non–Waivable Red List should be waivable in light of party autonomy. With respect to the first question, the Working Group has maintained its decision that the subjective test for disclosure should not be the absolute criterion but that some objective thresholds should be added. With respect to the second question, the conclusion of the Working Group was that party autonomy, in this respect, has its limits.

1. Non–Waivable Red List

1.1. There is an identity between a party and the arbitrator, or the arbitrator is a legal representative of an entity that is a party in the arbitration.

1.2. The arbitrator is a manager, director or member of the supervisory board, or has a similar controlling influence in one of the parties.

1.3. The arbitrator has a significant financial interest in one of the parties or the outcome of the case.

The arbitrator regularly advises the appointing party or an affiliate of the appointing party, and the arbitrator or his or her firm derives a significant financial income therefrom.

2. Waivable Red List

2.1. Relationship of the arbitrator to the dispute

2.1.1 The arbitrator has given legal advice or provided an expert opinion on the dispute to a party or an affiliate of one of the parties.

2.1.2 The arbitrator has previous involvement in the case.

2.2. Arbitrator's direct or indirect interest in the dispute

2.2.1 The arbitrator holds shares, either directly or indirectly, in one of the parties or an affiliate of one of the parties that is privately held.

2.2.2 A close family member[4] of the arbitrator has a significant financial interest in the outcome of the dispute.

2.2.3 The arbitrator or a close family member of the arbitrator has a close relationship with a third party who may be liable to recourse on the part of the unsuccessful party in the dispute.

2.3. Arbitrator's relationship with the parties or counsel

2.3.1 The arbitrator currently represents or advises one of the parties or an affiliate of one of the parties.

4. Throughout the Application Lists, the term 'close family member' refers to a spouse, sibling, child, parent or life partner.

2.3.2 The arbitrator currently represents the lawyer or law firm acting as counsel for one of the parties.

2.3.3 The arbitrator is a lawyer in the same law firm as the counsel to one of the parties.

2.3.4 The arbitrator is a manager, director or member of the supervisory board, or has a similar controlling influence, in an affiliate[5] of one of the parties if the affiliate is directly involved in the matters in dispute in the arbitration.

2.3.5 The arbitrator's law firm had a previous but terminated involvement in the case without the arbitrator being involved himself or herself.

2.3.6 The arbitrator's law firm currently has a significant commercial relationship with one of the parties or an affiliate of one of the parties.

2.3.7 The arbitrator regularly advises the appointing party or an affiliate of the appointing party, but neither the arbitrator nor his or her firm derives a significant financial income therefrom.

2.3.8 The arbitrator has a close family relationship with one of the parties or with a manager, director or member of the supervisory board or any person having a similar controlling influence in one of the parties or an affiliate of one of the parties or with a counsel representing a party.

2.3.9 A close family member of the arbitrator has a significant financial interest in one of the parties or an affiliate of one of the parties.

3. Orange List

3.1. Previous services for one of the parties or other involvement in the case

3.1.1 The arbitrator has within the past three years served as counsel for one of the parties or an affiliate of one of the parties or has previously advised or been consulted by the party or an affiliate of the party making the appointment in an unrelated matter, but the arbitrator and the party or the affiliate of the party have no ongoing relationship.

3.1.2 The arbitrator has within the past three years served as counsel against one of the parties or an affiliate of one of the parties in an unrelated matter.

3.1.3 The arbitrator has within the past three years been appointed as arbitrator on two or more occasions by one of the parties or an affiliate of one of the parties.[6]

---

5. Throughout the Application Lists, the term 'affiliate' encompasses all companies in one group of companies including the parent company.

6. It may be the practice in certain specific kinds of arbitration, such as maritime or commodities arbitration, to draw arbitrators from a small, specialized pool. If in such fields it is the custom and practice for parties frequently to appoint the same arbitrator in different cases, no disclosure of this fact is required where all parties in the arbitration should be familiar with such custom and practice.

3.1.4 The arbitrator's law firm has within the past three years acted for one of the parties or an affiliate of one of the parties in an unrelated matter without the involvement of the arbitrator.

3.1.5 The arbitrator currently serves, or has served within the past three years, as arbitrator in another arbitration on a related issue involving one of the parties or an affiliate of one of the parties.

3.2. Current services for one of the parties

3.2.1 The arbitrator's law firm is currently rendering services to one of the parties or to an affiliate of one of the parties without creating a significant commercial relationship and without the involvement of the arbitrator.

3.2.2 A law firm that shares revenues or fees with the arbitrator's law firm renders services to one of the parties or an affiliate of one of the parties before the arbitral tribunal.

3.2.3 The arbitrator or his or her firm represents a party or an affiliate to the arbitration on a regular basis but is not involved in the current dispute.

3.3. Relationship between an arbitrator and another arbitrator or counsel.

3.3.1 The arbitrator and another arbitrator are lawyers in the same law firm.

3.3.2 The arbitrator and another arbitrator or the counsel for one of the parties are members of the same barristers' chambers.[7]

3.3.3 The arbitrator was within the past three years a partner of, or otherwise affiliated with, another arbitrator or any of the counsel in the same arbitration.

3.3.4 A lawyer in the arbitrator's law firm is an arbitrator in another dispute involving the same party or parties or an affiliate of one of the parties.

3.3.5 A close family member of the arbitrator is a partner or employee of the law firm representing one of the parties, but is not assisting with the dispute.

3.3.6 A close personal friendship exists between an arbitrator and a counsel of one party, as demonstrated by the fact that the arbitrator and the counsel regularly spend considerable time together unrelated to professional work commitments or the activities of professional associations or social organizations.

3.3.7 The arbitrator has within the past three years received more than three appointments by the same counsel or the same law firm.

3.4. Relationship between arbitrator and party and others involved in the arbitration

7. Issues concerning special considerations involving barristers in England are discussed in the Background Information issued by the Working Group.

3.4.1 The arbitrator's law firm is currently acting adverse to one of the parties or an affiliate of one of the parties.

3.4.2 The arbitrator had been associated within the past three years with a party or an affiliate of one of the parties in a professional capacity, such as a former employee or partner.

3.4.3 A close personal friendship exists between an arbitrator and a manager or director or a member of the supervisory board or any person having a similar controlling influence in one of the parties or an affiliate of one of the parties or a witness or expert, as demonstrated by the fact that the arbitrator and such director, manager, other person, witness or expert regularly spend considerable time together unrelated to professional work commitments or the activities of professional associations or social organizations.

3.4.4 If the arbitrator is a former judge, he or she has within the past three years heard a significant case involving one of the parties.

3.5. Other circumstances

3.5.1 The arbitrator holds shares, either directly or indirectly, which by reason of number or denomination constitute a material holding in one of the parties or an affiliate of one of the parties that is publicly listed.

3.5.2 The arbitrator has publicly advocated a specific position regarding the case that is being arbitrated, whether in a published paper or speech or otherwise.

3.5.3 The arbitrator holds one position in an arbitration institution with appointing authority over the dispute.

3.5.4 The arbitrator is a manager, director or member of the supervisory board, or has a similar controlling influence, in an affiliate of one of the parties, where the affiliate is not directly involved in the matters in dispute in the arbitration.

4. Green List

4.1. Previously expressed legal opinions

4.1.1 The arbitrator has previously published a general opinion (such as in a law review article or public lecture) concerning an issue which also arises in the arbitration (but this opinion is not focused on the case that is being arbitrated).

4.2. Previous services against one party

4.2.1 The arbitrator's law firm has acted against one of the parties or an affiliate of one of the parties in an unrelated matter without the involvement of the arbitrator.

4.3. Current services for one of the parties

4.3.1 A firm in association or in alliance with the arbitrator's law firm, but which does not share fees or other revenues with the arbitrator's law firm, renders services to one of the parties or an affiliate of one of the parties in an unrelated matter.

4.4. Contacts with another arbitrator or with counsel for one of the parties

4.4.1 The arbitrator has a relationship with another arbitrator or with the counsel for one of the parties through membership in the same professional association or social organization.

4.4.2 The arbitrator and counsel for one of the parties or another arbitrator have previously served together as arbitrators or as co-counsel.

4.5. Contacts between the arbitrator and one of the parties

4.5.1 The arbitrator has had an initial contact with the appointing party or an affiliate of the appointing party (or the respective counsels) prior to appointment, if this contact is limited to the arbitrator's availability and qualifications to serve or to the names of possible candidates for a chairperson and did not address the merits or procedural aspects of the dispute.

4.5.2 The arbitrator holds an insignificant amount of shares in one of the parties or an affiliate of one of the parties, which is publicly listed.

4.5.3 The arbitrator and a manager, director or member of the supervisory board, or any person having a similar controlling influence, in one of the parties or an affiliate of one of the parties, have worked together as joint experts or in another professional capacity, including as arbitrators in the same case.

* * *

D. EUROPEAN CODE OF CONDUCT FOR MEDIATORS (2004)

This code of conduct sets out a number of principles to which individual mediators can voluntarily decide to commit, under their own responsibility. It is intended to be applicable to all kinds of mediation in civil and commercial matters.

Organisations providing mediation services can also make such a commitment, by asking mediators acting under the auspices of their organisation to respect the code. Organisations have the opportunity to make available information on the measures they are taking to support the respect of the code by individual mediators through, for example, training, evaluation and monitoring.

For the purposes of the code mediation is defined as any process where two or more parties agree to the appointment of a third-party—hereinafter "the mediator"—to help the parties to solve a dispute by reaching an agreement without adjudication and regardless of how that process may be called or commonly referred to in each Member State.

Adherence to the code is without prejudice to national legislation or rules regulating individual professions.

Organisations providing mediation services may wish to develop more detailed codes adapted to their specific context or the types of mediation services they offer, as well as with regard to specific areas such as family mediation or consumer mediation.

1. COMPETENCE AND APPOINTMENT OF MEDIATORS

1.1 Competence

Mediators shall be competent and knowledgeable in the process of mediation. Relevant factors shall include proper training and continuous updating of their education and practice in mediation skills, having regard to any relevant standards or accreditation schemes.

1.2 Appointment

The mediator will confer with the parties regarding suitable dates on which the mediation may take place. The mediator shall satisfy him/herself as to his/her background and competence to conduct the mediation before accepting the appointment and, upon request, disclose information concerning his/her background and experience to the parties.

1.3 Advertising/promotion of the mediator services

Mediators may promote their practice, in a professional, truthful and dignified way.

2. INDEPENDENCE AND IMPARTIALITY

2.1 Independence and neutrality

The mediator must not act, or, having started to do so, continue to act, before having disclosed any circumstances that may, or may be seen to, affect his or her independence or conflict of interests. The duty to disclose is a continuing obligation throughout the process.

Such circumstances shall include

- any personal or business relationship with one of the parties,
- any financial or other interest, direct or indirect, in the outcome of the mediation, or
- the mediator, or a member of his or her firm, having acted in any capacity other than mediator for one of the parties.

In such cases the mediator may only accept or continue the mediation provided that he/she is certain of being able to carry out the mediation with full independence and neutrality in order to guarantee full impartiality and that the parties explicitly consent.

2.2 Impartiality

The mediator shall at all times act, and endeavour to be seen to act, with impartiality towards the parties and be committed to serve all parties equally with respect to the process of mediation.

3. THE MEDIATION AGREEMENT, PROCESS, SETTLEMENT AND FEES

3.1 Procedure

The mediator shall satisfy himself/herself that the parties to the mediation understand the characteristics of the mediation process and the role of the mediator and the parties in it.

The mediator shall in particular ensure that prior to commencement of the mediation the parties have understood and expressly agreed the terms and conditions of the mediation agreement including in particular any applicable provisions relating to obligations of confidentiality on the mediator and on the parties.

The mediation agreement shall, upon request of the parties, be drawn up in writing.

The mediator shall conduct the proceedings in an appropriate manner, taking into account the circumstances of the case, including possible power imbalances and the rule of law, any wishes the parties may express and the need for a prompt settlement of the dispute. The parties shall be free to agree with the mediator, by reference to a set of rules or otherwise, on the manner in which the mediation is to be conducted.

The mediator, if he/she deems it useful, may hear the parties separately.

3.2 Fairness of the process

The mediator shall ensure that all parties have adequate opportunities to be involved in the process.

The mediator if appropriate shall inform the parties, and may terminate the mediation, if:

— a settlement is being reached that for the mediator appears unenforceable or illegal, having regard to the circumstances of the case and the competence of the mediator for making such an assessment, or

— the mediator considers that continuing the mediation is unlikely to result in a settlement.

3.3 The end of the process

The mediator shall take all appropriate measures to ensure that any understanding is reached by all parties through knowing and informed consent, and that all parties understand the terms of the agreement.

The parties may withdraw from the mediation at any time without giving any justification.

The mediator may, upon request of the parties and within the limits of his or her competence, inform the parties as to how they may formalise the agreement and as to the possibilities for making the agreement enforceable.

3.4 Fees

Where not already provided, the mediator must always supply the parties with complete information on the mode of remuneration which he intends to apply. He/she shall not accept a mediation before the principles of his/her remuneration have been accepted by all parties concerned.

4. CONFIDENTIALITY

The mediator shall keep confidential all information, arising out of or in connection with the mediation, including the fact that the mediation is to take place or has taken place, unless compelled by law or public policy grounds. Any information disclosed in confidence to mediators by one of the parties shall not be disclosed to the other parties without permission or unless compelled by law.

†

